Literature
for
Children

SEVENTH EDITION

Literature
for
Children

A Short Introduction

David L. Russell

Ferris State University

Boston ▪ Columbus ▪ Indianapolis ▪ New York ▪ San Francisco ▪ Upper Saddle River
Amsterdam ▪ Cape Town ▪ Dubai ▪ London ▪ Madrid ▪ Milan ▪ Munich ▪ Paris ▪ Montreal ▪ Toronto
Delhi ▪ Mexico City ▪ Sao Paulo ▪ Sydney ▪ Hong Kong ▪ Seoul ▪ Singapore ▪ Taipei ▪ Tokyo

Vice President, Editor-in-Chief: Aurora Martínez Ramos
Editor: Erin K. L. Grelak
Editorial Assistant: Michelle Hochberg
Vice President, Director of Marketing: Margaret Waples
Executive Marketing Manager: Krista Clark
Production Editor: Annette Joseph
Editorial Production Service: TexTech International
Manufacturing Buyer: Megan Cochran
Electronic Composition: TexTech International
Art Director: Linda Knowles
Cover Designer: Susan Paradise

Library of Congress Cataloging-in-Publication Data
Russell, David L.
    Literature for children : a short introduction / David L. Russell. —7th ed.
        p. cm.
    ISBN-13: 978-0-13-217379-7
    ISBN-10: 0-13-217379-4
    1. Children's literature—History and criticism.   2. Children—Books and reading.   I. Title.
    PN1009.A1R87 2011
    028.5—dc22   2011000318

10 9 8 7 6 5 4   RRD-VA   15   14   13   12

www.pearsonhighered.com

ISBN-10: 0-13-217379-4
ISBN-13: 978-0-13-217379-7

This is for my grandchildren
Mason, Mariya, Emily, Sarah, Lily, and *Ella*

And to the memory of
Tookie Brian Woods (2008)
and
William Brian Woods, Jr. (1977–2009)

About the Author

David L. Russell is a professor of languages and literature in Michigan where he teaches children's literature and folk literature. He is the author of *Patricia MacLachlan* and *Scott O'Dell,* both published by Twayne, as well as *Stuart Academic Drama: An Edition of Three University Plays,* published by Garland. Additionally, he has published numerous scholarly articles on children's literature and was a contributor to *The Oxford Encyclopedia of Children's Literature, The Continuum Encyclopedia of Children's Literature,* and *The Cambridge Guide to Children's Books in English.* He is currently co-editor of *The Lion and the Unicorn.*

Contents

Chapter 3   The Elements of Story: The Building Blocks of Literature   34

Chapter 4   Exploring Books: Reading, Talking, Doing   52

Chapter 5   Reading the World: Cultural Diversity and Inclusion   69

Part II ● The Kinds of Children's Literature

Chapter 6 Beginning Books: Knowledge through Delight 91

Chapter 7 Picture Books: The Collaboration of Story and Art 118

Chapter 8   Poetry: For the Love of Language   147

Chapter 9   Folk Narratives: The Oldest Stories   170

Chapter 10   Fantasy: The World of Make-Believe   197

Chapter 11   Realistic Fiction: The Days
of Our Lives   222

Appendix Children's Book Awards   281

Glossary   307

Children's Literature Resources   311

Preface

Katherine Paterson famously said, "I love revision. Where else can spilled milk be turned into ice cream?" It is with this spirit that I have entered into this seventh edition. Certainly, being asked to do a revision is both an honor and an opportunity—and I have tried to make the most of that opportunity. In doing so, I hope to have preserved the features that faithful users have liked, and to have made changes that will improve the text for everyone.

This revision turned out to be more dramatic than I had originally envisioned. Large portions have been rewritten in the interest of clarity and economy. More examples have been included, which has often permitted a streamlining of the text. I have always believed one of the virtues of this book is its adaptability to a wide variety of course designs. Instructors may present the chapters in whatever order best suits the needs and goals of their specific courses. Consequently, I have not toyed with the arrangement of the chapters themselves. However, the chapters themselves contain some significant changes, and these are outlined below.

New to This Edition

- The writing style has been tightened up and more specific examples from the literature are given in the way of explanation, usually resulting in leaner but more productive chapters, recognizing the wisdom of Blaise Pascal, who apologized to a correspondent: "I didn't have the time to write a short letter, so I wrote a long one instead."

- The end-of-chapter questions, now retitled "For Reflection and Discussion," have been redesigned so that they will better accommodate alternative classroom delivery methods, including online courses.

- The focus of the history chapter (Chapter 1) is now a discussion of precursors only, leaving discussions of the modern works to the genre chapters.

- A time line showing the milestones in children's literature has been added to Chapter 1.

- The child development chapter (Chapter 2) has been reorganized by shifting the Vygotsky discussion to Chapter 4 (where it leads naturally to the discussion of using literature in the classroom) and, conversely, the discussions of bibliotherapy and censorship have shifted from Chapter 4 to Chapter 2, for which I believe there is sufficient rationale.

- The focus of the chapter on the study of literature (Chapter 3) has changed to a discussion of story elements—indeed, the chapter title has been altered to "The Elements of Story" to reflect that—resulting in the elimination of much of the material on literary criticism, which is perhaps more appropriate in graduate rather than undergraduate classes.

- A full-color insert in the picture book chapter (Chapter 7) has been added—not for mere decoration but to provide examples of the effective use of color in children's picture books.

- Chapter 8, "Poetry," has been rewritten to eliminate some of the more arcane terminology and to include more examples of the wide variety of children's poetry available.

- New topics not covered in previous editions, including "Sentimentalism" and "Irony" in Chapter 3 and "Graphic Novels" in Chapter 7, have been included.

- The reference lists and booklists at the end of each chapter, as well as the awards lists at the end of the book, have been updated.

- A glossary and a list of standard children's literature reference sources have been added.

Literature for Children: A Short Introduction was originally written as a supplement to primary texts used in the classroom. My own students spend most of their time reading the primary material—the picture books, the poetry, the folktales, the fantasies, the realistic fiction, the nonfiction. This book is but a guide—and I hope a friendly one. Finally, I offer no apology for my approach, which is decidedly literary, reflecting my own background as a teacher of English literature. My hope is that all who use this book come away with more than just ideas about how to make reading fun in the classroom (however important that is). Children's literature provides an excellent opportunity for us to develop an appreciation for the art of literature and an understanding of how literature reflects our world and ourselves.

As always, I close with a quotation from *Ecclesiasticus,* a question that goes to the heart of education:

If thou hast gathered nothing in thy youth, how canst thou find anything in thine age?

PEARSON
myeducationkit

Dynamic Resources Meeting Your Needs

MyEducationKit is a dynamic website that connects the concepts addressed in the text with effective teaching practice. Plus, it's easy to use and integrate into assignments and courses. Visit the website to access a variety of multimedia resources geared to meet the diverse teaching and learning needs of instructors and students.

Children's Literature Database

A searchable database of thousands of excellent children's literature titles comes with the MyEducationKit for the Russell text. This database allows users to find books in every genre, by hundreds of authors and illustrators, by awards won, by year published, by topic and description, as well as many other search options. In the Assignments and Activities section of the MyEducationKit site, users will learn how to use the database to

- Create text sets to accommodate lesson needs
- Develop an individualized reading list
- Pull together trade books to enrich a math, science, or social studies unit
- Prepare an author or illustrator study

Assignments and Activities

Designed to save instructors preparation time and enhance student understanding, these assignable exercises show concepts in action (through database use, video, cases, and/or student and teacher artifacts). They help students synthesize and apply concepts and strategies they read about in the book.

Multimedia Resources

The rich media resources you will encounter throughout MyEducationKit include

- *Videos.* The authentic classroom videos in MyEducationKit show how real teachers handle actual classroom situations. Discussing and analyzing these videos not only deepens understanding of concepts presented in the text, but also builds skills in observing children and classrooms.
- *Student and teacher artifacts.* Real K–12 student and teacher classroom artifacts— tied to the chapter topics in your text—offer practice in working with the different materials teachers encounter daily in their classrooms.
- *Web links.* On MyEducationKit you don't need to search for the sites that connect to the topics covered in your chapter. Here, you can explore websites that are important in the field and that give you perspective on the concepts covered in your text.
- *Extension activities.* These course assignments give teachers many options for valuable classroom activities.

General Resources on MyEducationKit

The Resources section on MyEducationKit is designed to help students pass their licensure exams, put together effective portfolios and lesson plans, prepare for and navigate the first year of their teaching careers, and understand key educational standards, policies, and laws.

This section includes:

- *Licensure Exams:* Contains guidelines for passing the Praxis exam. The *Practice Test Exam* includes practice multiple-choice questions, case study questions, and video case studies with sample questions.
- *Lesson Plan Builder:* Helps students create and share lesson plans.
- *Licensure and Standards:* Provides links to state licensure standards and national standards.
- *Beginning Your Career:* Offers tips, advice, and valuable information on:
  - *Resume Writing and Interviewing:* Expert advice on how to write impressive resumes and prepare for job interviews.
  - *Your First Year of Teaching:* Practical tips on setting up a classroom, managing student behavior, and planning for instruction and assessment.
  - *Law and Public Policies:* Includes specific directives and requirements educators need to understand under the No Child Left Behind Act and the Individuals with Disabilities Education Improvement Act of 2004.

Visit www.myeducationkit.com *for a demonstration of this exciting new online teaching resource.*

The History of Children's Literature

How We Got Here

Introduction

Children's literature is a phenomenon of the modern world. Throughout most of recorded time, children shared in the oral storytelling experiences of their elders, often gathered around a roaring fire and listening to tales, comic and tragic, sacred and profane, instructional and entertaining. Literature was a communal experience and it helped knit the society together. But some 300 years ago changes began to take place that resulted in a new attitude toward children and childhood, and eventually in a new literature for children. Today, children's literature is a thriving industry publishing thousands of works each year and reaching millions of young people. How did this transformation come about? Let's begin by looking at the roots of children's literature, which are, in fact, quite deep.

The Ancient World: Greece and Rome (C. 850 BCE TO 476 CE)

We have little evidence that much in the way of literature for children was written before about 1700. However, much was written for adults that children could enjoy. Although our chief subject is children's literature in English, it is necessary to look back more than 2,500 years to ancient Greece because modern children's stories have been so strongly influenced by this important culture as well as by ancient Rome. Many young Greeks and Romans were literate and read books written on papyrus or linen scrolls. Certainly teenagers in ancient Greece (about 500 to 250 BCE) enjoyed the tales from Homer's *Iliad*, that most exciting of war stories, or Homer's *Odyssey*, that most exciting of travel adventures. Surely they read Aesop's moral animal tales, the *Fables*, such as the stories of the fox and the sour grapes or the tortoise and the hare. Roman children of the first century CE undoubtedly were hooked on the fanciful tales of Ovid's *Metamorphoses*, retellings of the magical tales from Greek and Roman mythology, such as the story of Orpheus and Eurydice and of Pygmalion, and, of course, they knew well their own national epic, Virgil's *Aeneid*. Indeed, today the works of Homer, Aesop, and Ovid and other ancients are still being retold for children. (Padraic Colum's *The Children's Homer and The Golden Fleece*, Jeanne Steig's lively *A Gift from Zeus: Sixteen Favorite Myths*, and Marcia Williams's *Greek Myths* are examples.) Like the stories from the Bible, these tales are part of Western heritage and ought to be part of every child's education.

The Medieval World (C. 476–1450)

After the fall of Rome in 476 CE, European civilization was on the skids and much of the classical heritage would have been lost had it not been for a few tireless monks who labored to copy and preserve the old stories. Few people bothered to learn to read—most were too busy trying to eke out a living, for, after the collapse of Rome, the entire economy fell apart. So during this long period (from about 500 to 1500), Europe was largely an oral culture. Most people were poor peasant farmers, and the Roman Catholic Church dominated people's lives. Not surprisingly, the biblical stories were an important part of a young person's education, as were the so-called saints' lives, stories of Christian saints and martyrs that were used as examples of how to live one's life.

In addition to the Bible stories and saints' lives that people heard in church, there were the entertainments supplied by traveling minstrels, storytellers and performers who delighted their audiences with tales of fantasy and adventure. Very popular was the epic tale of *Beowulf*, the great Danish hero who slew the monster, Grendel, and Grendel's mother (who was even worse than Grendel). Other favorites were the tales of King Arthur and his Knights of the Round Table, including Sir Gawain, Sir Lancelot, and Sir Galahad, and of Tristan and Iseult, and so on. The most celebrated English version of these stories is Thomas Malory's *Le Morte d'Arthur (The Death of Arthur)*, first published in 1485. These stories remain popular with children today and many modern versions are available. Michael Morpurgo and illustrator Michael Foreman have teamed up to produce beautiful editions of *Beowulf* and *Sir Gawain and the Green Knight*, and Benedict Flynn has recently prepared an edition of *King Arthur and the Knights of the Round Table*, complete with a CD, which is one of many children's versions of Malory's work.

In the late fourteenth century, the great English poet, Geoffrey Chaucer, wrote his famous *Canterbury Tales*, a wonderful assortment of stories (moral tales, fantasies, adventure stories, comic tales) ostensibly told by pilgrims on their way to St. Thomas Becket's shrine in Canterbury Cathedral. Many of these stories have been enjoyed by children ever since. (Marcia Williams's *Chaucer's Canterbury Tales* is a recent illustrated version for young readers.) In the fifteenth century, we begin to see the tales of Robin Hood, the populist

English bandit who, with his band of merry men (and Maid Marian), stole from the rich and gave to the poor. One of the earliest versions was *A Gest of Robyn Hode* (ca. 1450). Robin Hood stories have reappeared throughout the centuries, including the American Howard Pyle's *The Merry Adventures of Robin Hood* (1883) and Robert Leeson's *The Story of Robin Hood* (1994).

The Renaissance (C. 1450–1700)

Renaissance, a term meaning "rebirth," refers to the period following Europe's emergence from the Middle Ages (which some have called the "Dark Ages" because of the widespread illiteracy, poverty, suffering, famine, and warfare). The people of the Renaissance greatly admired the societies of ancient Greece and Rome and wished to see the ancient ideals reborn; they copied their art, their architecture, and their literature. It was also about this time that something would happen to change the Western world forever. The oral culture of the Middle Ages was about to give way to a new literate society. Around 1450, a man, perhaps Johannes Gutenberg, perfected the movable-type printing press (originally a Chinese invention). Now, instead of each book having to be copied by hand (which could take years), a machine could print multiple copies in a fraction of the time. Books became more plentiful, cheaper, and readily available. This resulted in an explosion of ideas, and led to an increase in literacy—now it paid to learn how to read.

The printing press brought about radical changes in society—much like the computer has done in our age. For one thing, the printing press, because it helped spread ideas quickly, contributed to the religious upheaval of the sixteenth century—the Protestant Reformation, the Catholic Counter-Reformation, and the countless splinter groups, including the Pilgrims who landed at Plymouth Rock in 1620. It also inspired the publication of many religious works, at least one of which caught the imagination of children. John Foxe's *The Book of Martyrs* (1563) describes the lives and deaths of Christian martyrs, and was intended to be used as an example of upright, moral living. This enormous work (over 2,000 pages) details the persecution of Christian martyrs, especially Protestant martyrs. Foxe is often accused of sensationalism (some of the stories are actually quite grisly, which may have attracted some young readers!). One critic points out that "much of the *Book of Martyrs* reads like a good melodrama with vivid heroes . . . standing firm upon the faith against the threats and blandishments of . . . treacherous, potent, and godless villains" (Wooden 77). Here is an example of Foxe's style as he depicts the tormenting of a Protestant clergyman by some Catholic soldiers:

> They spit in his face, pulled his nose, and pinched him in most parts of his body. He was hunted like a wild beast, until ready to expire with fatigue. They made him run the gauntlet between two ranks of them, each striking him with a twig. He was beat with their fists. He was beat with ropes. They scourged him with wires. He was beat with cudgels. They tied him up by the heels with his

head downwards, until the blood started out of his nose, mouth, etc. They hung him by the right arm until it was dislocated, and then had it set again. The same was repeated with his left arm. Burning papers dipped in oil were placed between his fingers and toes. His flesh was torn with red-hot pincers. He was put to the rack. They pulled off the nails of his right hand. [And it gets worse!]

from "The Persecution of Zisca," *The Book of Martyrs*

Yes, children read this and continued to read it into the twentieth century. In the sixteenth century, English law decreed that a copy should be placed in every church, near the Bible. So long as a work was deemed to have a strong moral message, it was considered appropriate for children.

Beginning in the sixteenth and seventeenth centuries, we find a shift in adult attitudes toward children. When you think about it, childhood today is, in many ways, a privileged position. Little children are adored, coddled, waited on hand and foot, and completely without responsibilities—or so it seems (more about that in Chapter 2). But the widespread hardships of the Middle Ages meant that most children died in infancy or in the first years of life. Medieval life expectancy was about 35 years of age, and everyone had to grow up quickly. By the time they were 7 or 8 years old, most children were expected to contribute to the family's well-being. When they were teenagers, they married, raised families, and fought wars. Those lucky enough to live to be 30 had reached venerable middle age. If you were 50 years old, you were ancient. So you see, there was precious little time to dawdle in childhood.

However, this way of life gradually changed with the newfound prosperity of the Renaissance. More schools began to pop up as society saw the value of education. One interesting development in this period was the hornbook (see Figure 1.1), a wooden slab shaped as a paddle for easy handling to which might be attached the alphabet, perhaps a prayer, or some basic vocabulary. It was used by very young children as a study aid and first reader. Its name comes from the transparent cattle horn that was used to cover the parchment to improve the durability—an early form of lamination. The hornbook has become something of a symbol of education.

In 1658, John Comenius published what is considered the first picture book for children, *Orbis Sensualium Pictus* (see Figure 1.2), which was actually a textbook intended to teach Latin. Latin being the *lingua franca* of the period, all educated people were expected to know it. The Puritans were especially interested in education, for they thought everyone should know how to read the Bible (in English, not Latin). The Puritans, like all Protestants, believed each individual was responsible for his or her own salvation, so it was important to have firsthand knowledge of the Bible. Perhaps inadvertently, this new attitude resulted in a general expansion of education for everyone. The Puritans founded the first college in America, Harvard, originally for training clergy. They were also largely responsible for the famed *New England Primer*, a reading textbook for the American colonies that first appeared in the 1680s—and it taught American children to read for the next 140 years (see Figure 1.3).

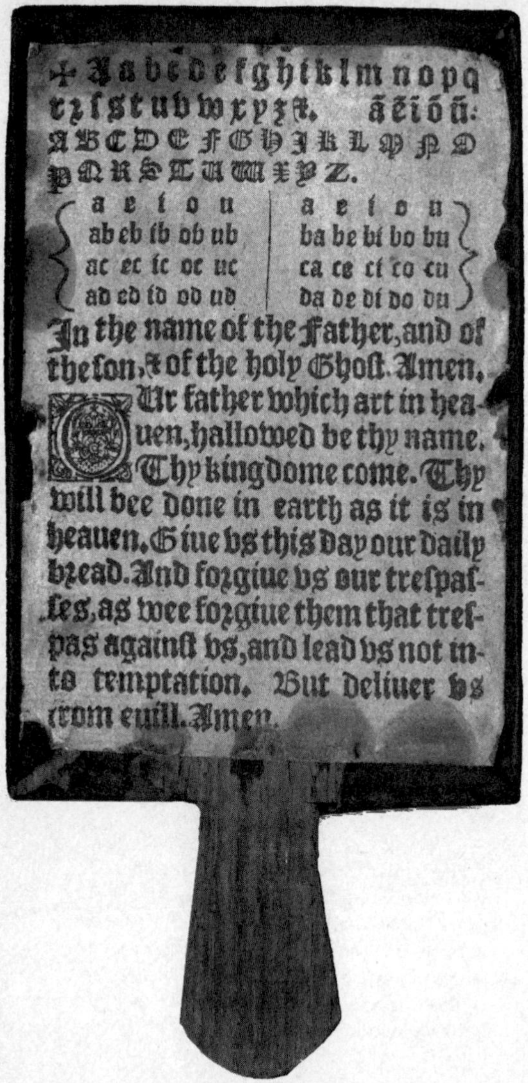

Figure 1.1 ● This typical hornbook from the time of Shakespeare illustrates the religious nature of education at that time. It is simply parchment fastened to a wooden paddle and laminated with animal horn for durability. Very young students in the sixteenth and seventeenth centuries would have learned to read using such a teaching device.

Source: By permission of the Folger Shakespeare Library.

For the most part, literate children of this era still had to find their reading enjoyment in adult books. Three books especially deserve mention. John Bunyan's *A Pilgrim's Progress* (1678) is a religious allegory about a man's journey toward salvation, but youthful readers probably found the exciting battles with horrific monsters more to their liking. It is a story that is often retold for children, most recently by Gary Schmidt (1994). In 1719, Daniel Defoe's *Robinson Crusoe* appeared. This is the granddaddy of all survival stories—about a man shipwrecked alone on a deserted island. This work engendered an entire subgenre of literature and it is still re-emerging in children's versions today. Youthful readers also were drawn to Jonathan Swift's *Gulliver's Travels* (1726), a biting satire, but also a wonderful

CXXXVI.

Ludi Pueriles.

Boyes-Sport

Boys used to play either with *Bowling-stones* 1. or throwing a *Bowl,* 2. at *Nine-pins,* 3. or striking a *Ball,* through a *Ring,* 5. with a *Bandy,* 4. or scourging a *Top,* 6. with a *Whip,* 7. or shooting with a *Trunk,* 8. and a *Bow,* 9. or going upon *Stilts,* 10. or tossing and swinging themselves upon a *Merry-totter,* 11.

Pueri solent ludere vel *Globis fictilibus,* 1. vel jactantes *Globum,* 2. ad *Conas,* 3. vel *mit-tentes* Sphærulam per *Annulum,* 5. *Clava,* 4. versantes *Turbinem,* 6. *Flagello,* 7. vel jacu-lantes *Sclopo,* 8. & *Arcu,* 9. vel incidentes *Grallis,* 10. vel super *Petaurum,* 11. se agi-tantes & oscillantes.

Figure 1.2 ● John Comenius's *Orbis Sensualium Pictus* is often considered the first children's picture book. It first appeared in 1658 as a German/Latin textbook and was an immediate success. It revolutionized Latin instruction, a necessity in a society in which Latin was still the language of scholarship. The English/Latin version, from which this illustration is taken, appeared in 1659. Although the woodcut illustrations may be crude, they provide a wealth of information about seventeenth-century European life.

fantasy whose protagonist travels, in turn, to a miniature land, a land of giants, a land of floating islands, and a land of talking horses. This, too, remains in today's repertoire of adult classics adapted for children, including both print and film versions.

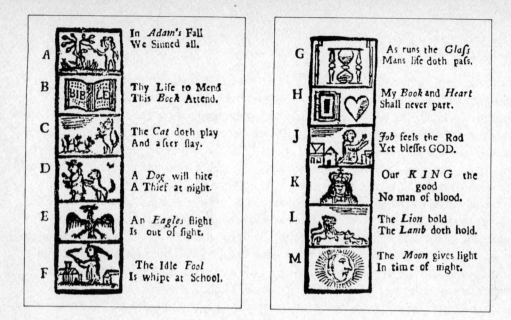

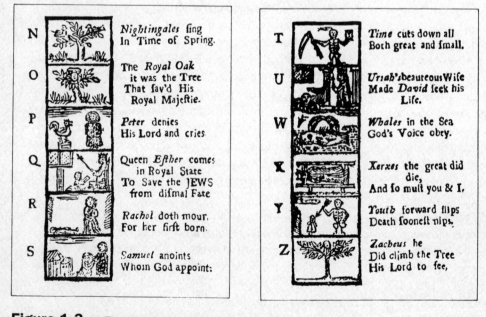

Figure 1.3 ● The *New England Primer* was one of the longest-lived school texts in American history, flourishing from approximately 1690 to 1830. The earliest surviving copy is from 1727, from which these illustrations are taken. Intended to teach the children of the early Puritans how to live a godly life, the book is unabashedly didactic, which is evident even in its rhyming alphabet, recalling a time when church and state were not so completely separate as they are now.

The Eighteenth Century

It was not until around the eighteenth century that children's literature as we know it—books written and published specifically for children's enjoyment as well as their edification—finally emerged. We owe this phenomenon, in part, to the philosophical contributions of two men who were to transform our ideas about education: John Locke (1632–1704) and Jean-Jacques Rousseau (1712–1778). Locke was an English philosopher who wrote, among other things, an essay titled *Thoughts Concerning Education.* In this work he explained his idea that a child's mind at birth was like a blank slate (in Latin, *tabula rasa*) ready to be written upon and thereby receiving knowledge. Looking at a drooling and cooing infant flailing those rubbery limbs, we can easily see how Locke came to that conclusion. He argued that everyone was born with equal abilities to learn and it was up to the adults to ensure that every child's blank slate was filled with the appropriate material. (Locke's ideas also had a profound influence on the authors of the Declaration of Independence, declaring that all "are created equal.") Locke's emphasis on the importance of our environment inspired generations of well-meaning children's writers whose goal was to ensure that young readers were surrounded by books with the proper moral messages. The intention may have been admirable, but it spawned an awful lot of mediocre literature.

Today, genetic studies have seriously challenged Locke's ideas and suggest that the environment is not necessarily the chief factor determining our development, and that, instead, we inherit much of who and what we are (see especially Steven Pinker's *The Blank Slate*). A newborn child's mind is not a "blank slate" at all, but, in fact, a fairly well-wired network—sort of like a newly purchased computer already filled with programs. And not everyone is alike; we all have different strengths and weaknesses that we can do little to change. Some of us are athletic, some are musical, some are skilled with their hands, and so on. The trick is for every one to discover what that gift is, and to work at that. It is interesting that our use of the term *gifted* is really an acknowledgment that hard work alone is not enough. I can practice singing 10 hours a day, but if a beautiful voice is not my gift, I'll never be performing at the Met or accepting that Grammy. And so the argument between nature and nurture continues.

Rousseau, a Frenchman, whose book *Emile* (1762) was written as a narrative describing the "ideal" education of a youth, had perhaps an even greater impact on children's literature than Locke. Rousseau advocated living a moral life through simplicity, and he preferred the peaceful countryside to the hectic city. (He actually rejected the reading of most books, but he liked Defoe's *Robinson Crusoe* because it demonstrated a man living an uncomplicated life away from the constraints of society.) Rousseau's ideas influenced the Romantic Movement at the end of the eighteenth century, especially in his celebration of the simple life and his desire to get "back to nature." Perhaps unfortunately, his ideas encouraged the writing of didactic books for children. The term *didactic* means educational or instructive, and there is nothing inherently wrong with that, in the right place. (The book you're reading is, technically, didactic.) However, a didactic storybook, as we will see, often results in heavy-handed moral messages, boring characters, and trite plots (more about this in Chapter 3).

Writing after Locke, but before Rousseau, was the English hymnist Isaac Watts (1674–1748) who composed one of the earliest poetry books exclusively for children, *Divine and Moral Songs for Children* (1720). Watts, most famous for writing the words to such hymns as "Joy to the World" and "O God Our Help in Ages Past," followed in the long tradition of providing sound moral lessons for young readers:

Against Idleness and Mischief

How doth the little busy bee
Improve each shining hour,
And gather honey all the day
From every opening flower!

How skillfully she builds her cell!
How neat she spreads the wax!
And labours hard to store it well
With the sweet food she makes.

In works of labour or of skill,
I would be busy too:
For Satan finds some mischief still
For idle hands to do.

In books, or work, or healthful play,
Let my first years be passed,
That I may give for every day
Some good account at last.

Watts's poems are certainly gentler than John Foxe's portraits in *The Book of Martyrs*, but the didactic, moral message is still unmistakable.

Watts's *Songs*, however, is exceptional, for children's books were still very scarce in the early 1700s. But that was about to change, which brings us to one of the great pioneers in children's literature: John Newbery (1713–1778). Newbery was a businessman—a publisher, in fact—who had a bookstore in London. At that time, about the only books published for children were schoolbooks, like the *New England Primer*. And then in the 1740s, Newbery hit on the idea of creating and selling books especially for children. In 1744, he published *A Pretty Little Pocket Book*, a collection of stories, poems, and some crude illustrations, much of it written by Newbery himself (who, sad to say, was rather a hack writer). It was an instant success. Parents were eager to grab up a book for their children to read. Newbery had tapped into a long-neglected market. Perhaps his most famous publication was *Little Goody Two-Shoes* (1765)—the title says it all (more about this in Chapter 3). Other writers soon followed his lead, and at last prospective children's authors had an outlet. In the next 50 years, scores of writers influenced by Locke and Rousseau and encouraged by publishers like Newbery, produced stories for children. That most of these early writers were women simply shows the bias that long existed—male writers regarded children's books as trivial and beneath them. Nathaniel Hawthorne unkindly described his female literary counterparts as that "damned mob of scribbling women." It was not until men became prominent in the field in the later nineteenth century that children's literature was accorded respectable literary status.

Sarah Trimmer (1741–1810), one of the most active of these writers, campaigned against fairy tales because she thought they were sacrilegious and without moral purpose, and she believed that all literature for children should preach Christian morality. Although most writers of the time condemned talking animal stories because they were illogical and unholy (everyone knows God's animals can't talk), Trimmer wrote *Fabulous Histories* (1786), also known as *The Story of the Robins,* about a talking robin family and a human family who learn to coexist. Even Trimmer was a little nervous about the book and she refused to allow it to be illustrated for fear children might take the talking robins too literally.

Another writer, Maria Edgeworth, was famous for *Simple Susan* (1796), in which a good country girl triumphs over an ill-intentioned city lawyer. Also deserving mention is Anna Laetitia Barbauld, whose *Hymns in Prose for Children* (1781) and *Lessons for Children* (1778) were suitably didactic if not particularly thrilling. And we cannot ignore Mary Martha Sherwood (1775–1851), whose father forced her to wear for several years an iron collar with a backboard to prevent her from slouching. Some critics have suggested that this would explain why, when she wrote *The History of the Fairchild Family* (1818), she insisted on including frighteningly vivid stories about the souls of impious children moldering in the cold grave or being consigned to the fires of hell.

It is impossible to miss the heavy-handed moral lessons in most of these stories, since their aim was to instruct young minds in the conduct of proper living. Unfortunately, this kind of writing results in flat, uninteresting characters (either incorruptibly good or thoroughly wicked), in corny and contrived plots, and in a condescending tone that seems to shout, "I told you so." These are typical flaws in moralistic, didactic writing.

The Nineteenth Century

The rigid didacticism in children's books was not to last. Of course, the moral tales continued to be published for young readers—and still are published today. But one of the first signs that something new was in the air came from Germany in the early nineteenth century when two brothers, Jacob and Wilhelm Grimm, published their *Children's and Household Tales* (1812). This was a collection of hundreds of folktales that had long been part of the oral culture of Europe, enjoyed by peasants and aristocrats alike. As we noted, the moral writers of the eighteenth century had objected to the traditional folktales on religious grounds—magic spells, witches, wizards, and talking animals were regarded as blasphemous. But children naturally loved the stories. The Grimms' collections proved to be the first of many folktale collections that were to delight children throughout the century. The Danish writer, Hans Christian Andersen, published his famous *Fairy Tales* in 1835. Alongside the folktales were the collections of nursery rhymes and folk poetry that appeared in many editions, some even illustrated (see Figure 1.4).

In 1865, Lewis Carroll (pseudonym for Charles Dodgson) published *Alice's Adventures in Wonderland*, usually considered the first English children's story written purely for entertainment, without attempting to teach any lessons. The sequel, *Through the Looking-Glass*, appeared in 1871–72. This wild fantasy continues to fascinate both children and moviegoers today, and its unforgettable characters (Alice, the Mad Hatter, the Cheshire Cat, the Jabberwock, Tweedledum and Tweedledee, the Red Queen, the White Knight, and many others) are indelibly inscribed on English-speaking culture.

Encouraged by increasing prosperity, a rising middle class, the extension of public education, and the development of technology, children's literature began to flourish in the nineteenth century. By the latter half of the century, high-quality books covering a broad literary spectrum were appearing, including:

- *adventure stories* (R. M. Ballantyne's *The Coral Island*, 1857, and Mark Twain's *The Adventures of Tom Sawyer*, 1876)
- *historical novels* (Robert Louis Stevenson's *Kidnapped*, 1886, and Howard Pyle's *Otto of the Silver Hand*, 1888)
- *domestic and family stories* (Charlotte Yonge's *The Daisy Chain*, 1856, and Louisa May Alcott's *Little Women*, 1868)
- *school stories* (Thomas Hughes's *Tom Brown's School Days*, 1857, and Edward Eggleston's *The Hoosier Schoolmaster*, 1871)
- *fantasies* (George MacDonald's *The Princess and the Goblin*, 1872, and L. Frank Baum's *The Wonderful Wizard of Oz*, 1900)
- *poetry* (Edward Lear's *A Book of Nonsense*, 1846, and Robert Louis Stevenson's *A Child's Garden of Verses*, 1885)
- *folktales* (Andrew Lang's *The Blue Fairy Book*, 1889, and Joseph Jacobs's *English Fairy Tales*, 1890)

In addition, by the mid-1800s, printing technology had perfected color printing and this attracted many fine illustrators to the field of children's books, including Walter Crane (see Figure 1.5), George Cruikshank, Randolph Caldecott (see Figure 1.6), Kate Greenaway, Beatrix Potter, and others. The latter half of the nineteenth century is widely regarded as the Golden Age of children's literature—and certainly it was the period during which children's literature came into its own. However, the twentieth century did pretty well for itself.

9

The man in the moon came down too soon
To inquire the way to Norridge;
The man in the south, he burnt his mouth
With eating cold plum-porridge.

Figure 1.4 ● Abel Bowen's woodcut illustration of "The Man in the Moon," from *Mother Goose's Melodies,* dramatically depicts the contrast between the ridiculous and the sublime that underlies much of children's literature. On the left side, with grace and elegance, a youth descends from the crescent moon; on the right side, a buffoonish character is engaged in a nonsensical act. Dating from 1833, this illustration is among the earliest American children's books designed purely for the pleasure of young readers.

Figure 1.5 ● Walter Crane's sophisticated use of line and composition can be seen in his portrayal of Jack and Jill carrying the bucket of water down the hill, from *The Baby's Opera* (1877).

The Twentieth Century and Beyond

Since we will be looking more closely at twentieth- and twenty-first-century children's literature in the chapters that follow, we have no need to review it in any detail here. The nineteenth-century flowering of children's literature continued into the twentieth century. This was accompanied by a general elevation in prestige most notably marked by the creation of numerous children's book awards, starting with the Newbery Medal in 1922 (named for that intrepid entrepreneur, John Newbery). This is an American award given annually by the American Library Association for excellence in children's literature. In 1938 the Caldecott Medal was added for excellence in illustration. Great Britain has its counterparts: the Carnegie Medal for literature and the Greenaway Medal for illustration. Lifetime achievement awards have been added, such as the Laura Ingalls Wilder Award, named for the beloved author of the "Little House" books, and the Hans Christian Andersen Award and the Astrid Lindgren Award. (The latter two are international awards open to children's writers everywhere—the Lindgren Award, named for the Swedish author of the "Pippi Longstocking" books, is the nirvana of book awards, valued at nearly a million dollars.)

Figure 1.6 ● Randolph Caldecott, the great nineteenth-century English illustrator, was one of the pioneers of children's book illustration. His art is characterized by an economy of line and playfulness of manner that make his work appealing today, more than a century after his death. The American Library Association annually awards the Caldecott Medal, named in his honor, to what it judges the most distinguished picture book published in the United States. This illustration from *The Frog He Would A-Wooing Go* (1883) depicts Caldecott's lively sense of humor.

One of the most satisfying developments of the last 50 years has been the increasing diversity—racial, ethnic, gender, social, and so on—in children's books and children's writers. Another important development is the broadening scope of children's books. We now see books for children on virtually every subject—including some very controversial ones, such as war, abuse, and sexuality. Children's illustrators continue to explore new artistic styles and media, and children's picture books have achieved a new depth and sophistication. This is not to say, though, that the field is still not crowded with the mediocre, the cheap, the tawdry. Such books are found in great abundance. But we do have choices. Treasures are out there, but we have to know what we are looking for. Finding these treasures will be one of the goals of this book.

Summary

It has been a long journey from the days when children's literature entailed stories told in the glow of a fire at the end of a long day. The march of civilization, for good or ill, has brought us exciting tales of gods and goddesses, heroes and heroines, love and war, and arduous journeys. For centuries, children enjoyed the largely oral literature available to their parents. It was, however, a rich heritage, from the fanciful adventures of ancient Greek and Roman mythology to the equally exciting tales of the medieval King Arthur and the Knights of the Round Table.

With the social and political movements of the Renaissance, the invention of the printing press by Gutenberg, the rise of the middle class, and the influence of the Puritans, reading became widespread by the seventeenth and eighteenth centuries. The growth of a true children's literature was nurtured by individuals such as John Locke and Jean-Jacques Rousseau, who focused public attention on childhood education, and John Newbery, who launched the children's book publishing business and provided an outlet for many children's authors.

By the mid-nineteenth century, a flowering of children's literature was underway, particularly in England and the United States. The era produced memorable fantasies, adventure stories, and family stories, and great artists turned to illustrating children's books. Thus began a tradition that continues today. The twentieth century saw a continued flourishing of books for children, the establishment of prestigious book awards for children's writers and illustrators, and the founding of children's libraries and publishing houses. By mid-century, in fact, an entirely new field of study focusing on children's literature was coming into being, and by the end of the century it was possible for college students to get graduate degrees in children's literature. As we move ahead into the twenty-first century, we are hopeful that the demand for excellence in children's literature continues, for without reading, our civilization would disintegrate in a single generation. The ideas of our past would be lost forever, forcing humanity once again naked into the world. As students of children's literature, our great purpose is to bring the joy of reading to the next generation, giving them the tools they will need to build a better world than their parents have known.

For Reflection and Discussion

1. Locate several versions of the same Greek, Roman, or Norse myth as retold for children. Which ones are most effective and why?

2. Locate some examples of eighteenth- and early nineteenth-century children's stories. (Some can be found online by using a Google search for specific authors mentioned in the chapter.) Do the examples you find exhibit didacticism? Are they "moral" tales, intended to form a child's character? How do you think these stories would be received by today's child?

3. Choose a prominent eighteenth-century author of children's books (use the chapter or explore on your own to find names). Research the author's background. Is there anything surprising? Read at least one work written by the author and try to determine how the author's life has influenced the work.

4. Create a chart or other graphic tool (see Figure 1.7, for example) that depicts the major trends in the development of children's literature from the eighteenth century to the present. What are some of the factors—social, cultural, political, economic, and so on—that you believe have influenced these trends? Do you have any predictions for the future?

Figure 1.7 ● Time line for the history of children's literature

Time Line for the History of Children's Literature
Europe and North America

THE ANCIENT WORLD—c. 2750 BCE to the fall of Rome, 476 CE

c. 850 BCE	Homer, *The Iliad* and *The Odyssey*
c. 620-560 BCE	Aesop, *Fables*
c. 20 BCE	Virgil, *The Aeneid*
c. 8 CE	Ovid, *Metamorphoses*

THE MIDDLE AGES—c. 476-1450

c. 500 and on	Saints' Lives
c. 800-1000 CE	*Beowulf* (poetic epic set in Scandinavia)
c. 1150-1350	Medieval Romances (e.g., "Sir Gawain and the Green Knight")
c. 1391	Geoffrey Chaucer, *A Treatise on the Astrolabe* (one of the first books written specifically for a child—Chaucer's son)
c. 1450	"A Gest of Robyn Hode" (one of the earliest Robin Hood adventures)

THE RENAISSANCE—c. 1450-1700

c. 1450	Johannes Gutenberg invents the movable type printing press
1483-84	*Aesop's Fables*, printed by John Caxton
1563	John Foxe's *Book of Martyrs*
1658	Jan Comenius, *Orbis Pictus* (first picture book printed for children)
1672	James Janeway, *A Token for Children: Being an Exact Account of the Conversion, Holy and Exemplary Lives, and Joyful Deaths of Several Young Children*
1678	John Bunyan, *A Pilgrim's Progress*
1693	John Locke, *Some Thoughts Concerning Education*
1695	Charles Perrault, *Les Contes de ma Mère l'Oie* (*Tales of Mother Goose*)

THE EIGHTEENTH CENTURY

1719	Daniel Defoe, *Robinson Crusoe*
1720	Isaac Watts, *Divine and Moral Songs for Children*
1726	Jonathan Swift, *Gulliver's Travels*
1744	John Newbery, *A Pretty Little Pocket Book*

1762	Jean-Jacques Rousseau, *Emile*
late 18th century	Moral tales for children, chiefly by women writers (including Maria Edgeworth, Sarah Trimmer, Anna Laetitia Barbauld, Hannah More, and Mary Martha Sherwood)
1791	*Tales from the Arabian Nights* (published by Elizabeth Newbery)

THE NINETEENTH CENTURY

1812	Wilhelm and Jacob Grimm, *Kinder- und Hausmärchen* (*Children's and Household Tales*)
1827	First publication of *The Youth's Companion,* one of many American magazines for young readers
1835	Hans Christian Andersen, *Fairy Tales*
mid-19th century	Invention and gradual improvement of color printing processes
1865	Lewis Carroll, *Alice's Adventures in Wonderland*
1872	George MacDonald, *The Princess and the Goblin*
1876	Mark Twain, *The Adventures of Tom Sawyer*
1870s-1880s	First great children's illustrators: Walter Crane, *The Baby's Opera* (1877); Randolph Caldecott, *John Gilpin's Ride* (1878); Kate Greenaway, *The Pied Piper of Hamelin* (1888)

THE EARLY TWENTIETH CENTURY

1900	L. Frank Baum, *The Wonderful Wizard of Oz*
1901	Beatrix Potter, *A Tale of Peter Rabbit*
1904	J. M. Barrie, *Peter Pan*
1908	Kenneth Grahame, *The Wind in the Willows*
1922	Creation of the Newbery Medal, American award for excellence in children's literature
1926	A. A. Milne, *Winnie-the-Pooh*
1932	Laura Ingalls Wilder, *Little House in the Big Woods*
1937	Dr. Seuss, *And to Think That I Saw It on Mulberry Street*
1938	Creation of the Caldecott Medal, American award for excellence in children's book illustration
1940s to the present	Continued expansion of the field, including the advent of numerous talented writers and illustrators, the increasing diversity of children's books, the growth of scholarly research, the development of college courses in children's literature, and the creation of numerous book and author/illustrator awards

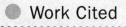 ## Work Cited

Wooden, Warren W. *Children's Literature of the English Renaissance.* Lexington: University of Kentucky Press, 1986.

● Recommended Readings

Aries, Philippe. *Centuries of Childhood: A Social History of Family Life.* New York: Knopf, 1962.

Carpenter, Humphrey. *Secret Gardens: A Study of the Golden Age of Children's Literature.* Boston: Houghton Mifflin, 1985.

Carpenter, Humphrey, and Mari Prichard. *The Oxford Companion to Children's Literature.* Oxford: Oxford University Press, 1984.

Cullinan, Bernice, and Diane G. Person, eds. *The Continuum Encyclopedia of Children's Literature.* New York: Continuum, 2001.

Darton, F. J. Harvey. *Children's Books in England, Five Centuries of Social Life.* Cambridge: Cambridge University Press, 1982.

Demers, Patricia. *Heaven Upon Earth: The Form of Moral and Religious Children's Literature, to 1850.* Knoxville: University of Tennessee Press, 1993.

Demers, Patricia, and Gordon Moyles, eds. *From Instruction to Delight.* Toronto: Oxford University Press, 1982.

"History of Children's Literature: A Pathfinder." Compiled by Ellen Decker and Ruffin Priest, www.ils.unc.edu (dated, but still with useful information)

Hunt, Peter, ed. *Children's Literature: An Illustrated History.* Oxford: Oxford University Press, 1995.

——. *An Introduction to Children's Literature.* Oxford: Oxford University Press, 1994.

Jackson, Mary V. *Engines of Instruction, Mischief, and Magic: Children's Literature in England from Its Beginnings to 1839.* Omaha: University of Nebraska, 1990.

Lerer, Seth. *Children's Literature: A Reader's History from Aesop to Harry Potter.* Chicago: University of Chicago Press, 2009.

Lystad, Mary. *From Dr. Mather to Dr. Seuss: 200 Years of American Books for Children.* Cambridge, MA: Harvard University Press, 1980.

MacDonald, Ruth. *Literature for Children in England and America from 1646 to 1774.* Troy, NY: Whitston, 1982.

MacLeod, Anne Scott. *A Moral Tale: Children's Fiction and American Culture, 1820–1860.* Hamden, CT: Archon, 1975.

Marcus, Leonard. *Minders of Make-Believe: Idealists, Entrepreneurs, and the Shaping of American Children's Literature.* New York: Houghton Mifflin Harcourt, 2008.

Meigs, Cornelia, Elizabeth Nesbitt, Anne Thaxter Eaton, and Ruth Hill. *A Critical History of Children's Literature: A Survey of Children's Books in English.* New York: Macmillan, 1969.

Nikolajeva, Maria, ed. *Aspects and Issues in the History of Children's Literature.* Contributions to the Study of World Literature, 60. Westport, CT: Greenwood, 1995.

Pickering, Samuel F., Jr. *John Locke and Children's Books in Eighteenth-Century England.* Knoxville: University of Tennessee Press, 1981.

——. *Moral Instruction and Fiction for Children, 1749–1820.* Athens: University of Georgia Press, 1993.

Pinker, Steven. *The Blank Slate: The Modern Denial of Human Nature.* New York: Viking, 2002.

Schorsch, Anita. *Images of Childhood: An Illustrated Social History.* New York: Mayflower, 1979.

"Social History of Children's Literature." Compiled by Kay Vandergrift, Rutgers University, www.comminfo.rutgers.edu/professional-development/childlit.

Summerfield, Geoffrey. *Fantasy and Reason: Children's Literature in the Eighteenth Century.* Athens: University of Georgia Press, 1983.

Thwaite, Mary F. *From Primer to Pleasure in Reading: An Introduction to the History of Children's Books in England.* Boston: The Horn Book, 1972.

Townsend, John Rowe. *Trade and Plum-Cake for Ever, Huzza! The Life and Work of John Newbery, 1713–1769.* Cambridge, UK: Colt, 1994.

——. *Written for Children: An Outline of English-Language Children's Literature,* 5th rev. ed. London: Kestrel, 1990.

Tucker, Nicholas. *The Child and the Book: A Psychological and Literary Exploration.* Cambridge: Cambridge University Press, 1981.

Watson, Victor, ed. *The Cambridge Guide to Children's Books in English.* Cambridge: Cambridge University Press, 2001.

Wooden, Warren W. *Children's Literature of the English Renaissance.* Lexington: University of Kentucky Press, 1986.

Zipes, Jack, ed. *The Oxford Encyclopedia of Children's Literature.* 4 vols. Oxford: Oxford University Press, 2006.

PEARSON
myeducationkit™

Go to the MyEducationKit for this text where you can:

- Search the Database of Children's Literature, housing more than 22,000 titles searchable in every genre by authors or illustrators, by awards won, by year published, and by topic and description.
- Explore genre-related Assignments and Activities, assignable exercises showing concepts in action through database use, video, cases, and student and teacher artifacts.

- Listen to podcasts and read interviews from some of the brightest and most enduring stars of children's literature in the Conversations.
- Discover Web Links that will lead you to sites representing the authors you learn about in these pages, classrooms with powerful children's literature connections, and literature awards.

Literature and Child Development

Growing through Reading

Introduction

The eminent psychologist Carl Gustav Jung wrote, "In studying the history of the human mind one is impressed again and again by the fact that the growth of the mind is the widening of the range of consciousness, and that each step forward has been a most painful and laborious achievement" (*Contributions to Analytical Psychology* 340). We noted in Chapter 1 that the state of childhood would appear to be a privileged one, with most children seeming to live carefree lives interrupted only occasionally by some minor distress (which adults are expected to relieve). But in many respects, as Jung suggests, childhood and adolescence are the most difficult, the most challenging, years of our lives. We are born completely helpless, unable to walk, talk, or feed ourselves. With each day, we are confronted with something new, something that causes us to re-evaluate our notions of the world around us, and we are forced continually to adapt to that world. All things considered, we might wonder how many adults could cope with the dramatic transformations that infants and toddlers experience on a daily basis. The child's ability to adapt and to absorb so much in so short a time is a marvel.

In this chapter, we will take a brief look at the various ways children develop, especially in the formative years between birth and the age of 6 or 7, and consider specifically how that development impacts their reading habits and tastes. As adults, we often underestimate children. It is good to remind ourselves how keen their perceptions are, how quickly they grasp concepts, and how sharply their imaginations work—for these are issues that directly influence the types of books they enjoy (or could be enjoying). Also in this chapter, we will consider two issues tangentially related to child development and reading: bibliotherapy and censorship. Bibliotherapy is a controversial and often misunderstood concept based on the belief that reading can be therapeutic and that certain emotional and psychological issues can be helped with the proper reading regimen. Censorship, a vitally important social issue and one that is even more controversial than bibliotherapy, is directly tied to our understanding of children's intellectual and emotional capabilities.

Language Acquisition

Before we look at the developmental theories, it might be helpful if we consider the one human ability that makes literature itself possible—the ability to use language to communicate. One area in which children seem to excel beyond the expectations of adults is language acquisition. It is amazing that in five short years, children can master the abstract concept of attaching meanings to certain sounds (words) and to organize those sounds into intelligible patterns (sentences) to convey those meanings.

Russian psychologist Lev Vygotsky, whom we will examine more closely in Chapter 3, was interested in how children learn language. He argued that language is, in fact, a way of thinking about something—that our ability to formulate words, to put ideas into words, actually helps us to think and to understand. (Anyone who has talked through personal problems with a friend or therapist or used a diary or journal to help sort out personal conflicts will understand Vygotsky's point.)

Steven Pinker, a psychologist who has studied human thought and language, is convinced that language acquisition is innate. He argues that we are born with the ability to memorize the meanings of words and irregular forms of words (such as verbs), and to assimilate the rules of grammar and syntax of the language that we hear on a daily basis. Very young children possess a linguistic plasticity or malleability that extends to their abilities to create sounds. Despite the popular notion that pronunciation is difficult for children, they actually have a much easier time of it than do adults. Indeed, the time for children to start learning a second language is when they're in preschool or early elementary—when it's easier to memorize, to make new sounds, and to adapt to new language patterns. It is a pity that the U.S. educational system has neglected this opportunity.

What all this research shows is that as adults—and as teachers—we should build on children's language abilities and their natural curiosity about sound, sense, and language. This means that we should not be talking to children in "baby talk" but in "grown-up" talk—allowing them to expand their vocabulary and practice pronunciation. It also means reading to them. Even the simplest Mother Goose rhymes offer exciting and challenging vocabulary, with their nonsense words and archaisms. Difficult vocabulary rarely discourages a child. Take, for example, Old Mother Hubbard who successively went to the joiner's, the fishmonger's, the cobbler's, and the hosier's; or the crooked man who went a crooked mile and "found a crooked six-pence against a crooked stile." In neither case do the obscure words spoil the child's pleasure in the rhyme.

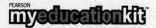

Visit the MyEducationKit for this course to enhance your understanding of chapter concepts with activities, web links, podcasts, and a searchable database of more than 22,000 children's literature titles.

Modern Theories of Child Development

As with everything else in their young lives—clothes, shoes, toys, and beds—children quickly outgrow their books. The books that fascinate

2-year-olds are likely to bore 5-year-olds. Before we know it, children outgrow their picture books and move into the more complex chapter books. If we want to help them choose good books, it is useful if we have an understanding of the developmental changes children are going through.

We will look at three of the most influential theories of child development, all of which complement each other. Jean Piaget was concerned with intellectual or cognitive development, Erik Erikson with social development, and Lawrence Kohlberg with the development of moral judgment. All three individuals viewed human development as occurring in a series of stages through which children pass on their way to maturity. Progressing through these stages is like climbing a mountain. If we don't have sure footing or a firm grasp, we will slip back down. Also, the movement through stages is gradual, almost imperceptible, and all individuals develop at different rates. Consequently, the age spans mentioned here are only approximations.

These theories have been criticized for ignoring female development, which, some argue, is not the same as male development. Males, for example, generally value competition, self-assertiveness, individual rights, and social rules. Females, on the other hand, value human relationships, responsibility to others, cooperation, community values, and tolerance for opposing viewpoints. Additionally, some argue that females reach these developmental stages more quickly than males do. Another criticism of these theories is that they neglect minority groups, whose values are often quite different from those of the majority. Nevertheless, these theories are helpful as a general guide—so long as we remember their limitations.

Jean Piaget and Cognitive Development

The Swiss psychologist Jean Piaget (1896–1980) is famous for his theory of cognitive development, which attempts to explain how we come to comprehend the world around us. Beginning in the 1920s and 1930s, Piaget outlined four major periods of intellectual development, some of which he subdivided into stages. What follows is a very broad overview.

SENSORIMOTOR PERIOD: BIRTH TO TWO YEARS ● During this earliest period, children are entirely egocentric (they are unaware of the needs of others), and they experience the world entirely through their senses (what they can see, hear, taste, touch, and smell). For them, books are objects to feel and manipulate with their hands—once they've learned that books are not objects to taste. For infants, durable cardboard and cloth books are great introductions to reading. Of course, babies respond visually to the pictures—no one sits down with a 1-year-old and opens up *Charlotte's Web*. It is chiefly through the pictures that these children identify their books and choose their favorites. Tactile books, such as Dorothy Kunhardt's classic, *Pat the Bunny*, allow them to touch and feel. Because they respond to sound, reading aloud to infants and toddlers is not only satisfying for them but a very important part of their development. Sounds fascinate them (even nonsense words), and they are always experimenting with their own voices. In time, they will respond to the sounds and rhythms of nursery rhymes ("Peter, Peter, Pumpkin Eater," "Hickory Dickory

Dock," and others). Most important is that they are getting acquainted with books, learning to hold books, to turn pages, and to connect language and books.

PREOPERATIONAL PERIOD: TWO TO SEVEN YEARS • The second of Piaget's periods is the time when children acquire and refine their motor skills. Their egocentrism gradually diminishes throughout this period (they start making friends). Although they still don't think logically, they can use symbols to represent ideas. And, although children can grasp certain concepts—colors, object shapes, opposites, the forms and sounds of letters of the alphabet, and counting objects—they still understand things only in concrete terms. In the early years of this period, children find alphabet, counting, and concept books fascinating. Most 3-year-olds can memorize letters of the alphabet or the numbers from 1 to 20, even if they do not truly grasp their meaning or function until much later in the preoperational period. Their excellent memories and their ability to recall often make preschoolers appear far more knowledgeable than they actually are. Also, they tend to give human qualities to everything (a concept known as animism), which helps explain their fondness for books about talking animals and animated toys and machines (such as the folktales or stories like Virginia Lee Burton's *Mike Mulligan and His Steam Shovel,* Margaret Wise Brown's *The Runaway Bunny,* and Dorothy Cronin's *Click, Clack, Moo: Cows That Type*). Eventually, they no longer require pictures to help tell the stories. By the final years of this developmental period, when they reach about second grade, children have learned to read and comprehend the fundamental ideas of plot, conflict, and character. Now they are ready to move onto a new level of understanding.

PERIOD OF CONCRETE OPERATIONS: SEVEN TO TWELVE YEARS • Although they still have difficulty with abstraction—they continue to see things in concrete terms—children in the third period are able to apply a kind of logic to their thinking. They are capable of understanding conservation (the fact that quantity is unaffected by appearance—for example, a tall thin glass may hold just as much water as a short chubby glass), reversibility (the notion that some things, like a knot in a shoestring, can be undone), assimilation (using past knowledge to explain new information), and accommodation (revising past knowledge in light of new information). Children begin to lay aside the picture books, which they now see as "babyish" (which doesn't mean they still don't enjoy some of them). These children start reading longer books and chapter books, which indicates that they are able to recall where they left off in their reading the day before. For example, that perennial favorite, E. B. White's *Charlotte's Web,* is typically read in second grade. The children are now able to grasp the concept of history and the passage of time (and can therefore enjoy Laura Ingalls Wilder's "Little House" books). Also, children at this stage are less egocentric; they begin to acquire friends, and they turn to books such as Judy Blume's *Blubber* and *Tales of a Fourth Grade Nothing* or Lois Lowry's "Anastasia" series, so they can read about children like themselves.

PERIOD OF FORMAL OPERATIONS: TWELVE TO FIFTEEN YEARS • Finally, the fourth period occurs between the ages of about 12 and 15 (when most children reach full cognitive maturity). In these early teen years, young people begin to use formal logic and engage in a true exchange of ideas, comprehending the viewpoints of others, and understanding what it means to live in a society. Having entered adolescence, most are ready for more mature topics, such as love, sexuality, social issues, and even politics.

Erik Erikson and Psychosocial Development

Whereas Piaget was interested how we develop intellectually, Erik Erikson (1902–1994) explored how we develop socially and psychologically. He classified the maturation process into a series of psychosocial conflicts, each of which must be resolved before one can move on to the next, in much the same way that Piaget saw successive levels in cognitive development. This is part of the "painful and laborious achievement" to which Jung was referring. Erikson's theory includes five principal stages of development throughout childhood, which complement, not compete with, Piaget's stages.

TRUST VERSUS MISTRUST: BIRTH TO EIGHTEEN MONTHS ● During this first stage, children have little option but to trust those who are their caregivers, but at the same time they must overcome such fears as abandonment when they are put to sleep in their own beds (which is why bedtime is often so difficult for some children). Books for this stage can provide both security and reassurance. Margaret Wise Brown's classic, *Goodnight Moon,* has long been popular with the very young. It exudes warmth and coziness as we observe a little bunny saying good night to all his favorite possessions in his womb-like bedroom. The repetitive patterns in both text and illustration are comfortably reassuring. Children in this stage also like hearing familiar books read night after night; these books become like old, reliable friends, providing stability and a sense of security.

AUTONOMY VERSUS DOUBT: EIGHTEEN MONTHS TO THREE YEARS ● This is when children begin to experiment with their independence—now that they can walk and talk. At the same time, however, they doubt their abilities. The independence is good, but it must be exercised with caution. Crockett Johnson's imaginative story *Harold and the Purple Crayon,* about a boy who creates his own world with a magical crayon, charmingly portrays an autonomous child who proves capable of handling his new-found independence—and extricating himself from some interesting dilemmas. The story might appeal nicely to 3-year-olds who are exploring their own imaginative world—often with crayons (and not always on paper).

INITIATIVE VERSUS GUILT: THREE TO SIX YEARS ● Now children begin to realize they have responsibilities (potty training springs to mind). Children want to take the initiative to do things on their own and to decide what to do and when to do it. However, they are also beginning to grasp the concept of right and wrong, and they struggle with guilt when they make the wrong choices. In Ezra Jack Keats's *Peter's Chair,* young Peter exhibits hostility when his parents decide to paint all his baby furniture pink for his new sister. Peter decides to run away, but soon comes to regret his selfishness. He finally offers his furniture to his sister of his own free will. Peter has arrived at a higher stage of psychosocial development, which is shown by his willingness to change his attitude and behavior. Such a book both validates a child's feelings and shows at least one method of coping with them.

INDUSTRY VERSUS INFERIORITY: SEVEN TO ELEVEN YEARS ● At this stage, children desire to achieve success, often working in concert with others. At the same time, however, they have a tendency to measure themselves against their peers and often feel inferior. Books such as Beverly Cleary's *Henry Huggins* and *Ramona the Pest* help young readers explore these desires for both personal achievement as well as acceptance and friendship.

IDENTITY VERSUS ROLE CONFUSION: ELEVEN YEARS AND BEYOND ● As they move toward adolescence, young people begin to discover who they are (not only their personal identities but cultural and social identities as well). Now they seek out books that show young people struggling with who they are, what is important, and how to deal with an increasingly complicated world—a world in a constant state of change. Teenagers continue to be conflicted about what their roles in life are to be, what society expects of them, and what they expect of themselves. They are torn between the familiar security of childhood and the natural, if uneasy, desire to become adults. Louise Fitzhugh's *Harriet the Spy* is a seriocomic story about a girl dealing with just these issues—and Fitzhugh sugarcoats nothing and provides no easy solutions. In other words, she tells the readers exactly what they need to hear. Most readers at this stage crave openness and honesty, preferring stories about others like themselves (realism), but many also find pleasure in escapist tales (fantasy, science fiction, and so on).

Lawrence Kohlberg and Moral Development

Lawrence Kohlberg (1927–1987) studied the development of moral reasoning and moral judgment—that is, how individuals determine what is right and wrong. Also, like Piaget, he saw development occurring in a series of stages through which an individual passes to moral maturity. Kohlberg identifies three different levels of development—Pre-Conventional, Conventional, and Post-Conventional—each subdivided into two parts, which he called "orientations." The first two levels are most important for our purposes.

PRE-CONVENTIONAL LEVEL ● This is the level at which children operate throughout most of elementary school. Kohlberg divided it into two parts.

Punishment/Obedience Orientation is when children obey rules because the rules come from some authority figure (whom few children ever question) or because the children wish to avoid punishment. In Beatrix Potter's *The Tale of Peter Rabbit*, we see Peter's sisters obeying their mother and enjoying delicious currant buns at the end of the story, whereas Peter, who disobeyed the rules, suffers in bed with a cold. Obedience to authority has some obvious advantages.

Self-Interest Orientation is when children believe that "right" behavior is any action that benefits them. In other words, the first question is "What's in it for me?" An excellent example of this in children's literature would be Templeton the rat in E. B. White's

Charlotte's Web. Templeton is a thoroughly self-centered creature who helps out only if he is promised food—that is, only if there is something in it for him. Of course, the whole point of White's portrayal is to show that this selfishness is unattractive and potentially destructive.

CONVENTIONAL LEVEL ● The second level is generally not reached until adolescence, and it is the stage in which most adults operate (which is why it was termed "conventional"). It also has two parts.

Interpersonal Concordance (or "*Good Boy/Good Girl*") *Orientation* is when behavior is governed by a desire to have the approval of others or to avoid rejection by peers. This usually occurs in the early teenage years, and the appearance of "cliques" and the need to conform are familiar aspects of adolescence. Many books for children in middle school and early high school focus on just these issues. Judy Blume's *Are You There, God? It's Me, Margaret,* the story of a girl facing her first menses along with a crisis in religious belief, is a popular example.

"*Law and Order" Orientation* is when individuals conform to group behavior in order to abide by the law and to live up to their obligations as members of society. People at this stage are aware of their place in the world and demonstrate concern for others—two important signs of maturity. On the other hand, criminal behavior reflects immaturity. This takes us beyond most children's literature, but Robert Cormier's *The Chocolate War,* about unscrupulous behavior in a private school, explores the issue of maintaining personal integrity when it comes up against peer pressure and social conformity.

POST-CONVENTIONAL LEVEL ● Kohlberg felt that most people never reached this final level, which is when individuals act in the interest of the welfare of others or of society as a whole—this is usually called the *Social Contract Orientation.* And the highest level, *Principled Conscience Orientation,* is when people act out of regard for ethical principles or their own conscience (those at this level are chiefly martyrs and saints).

The best children's literature is in touch with the intellectual, psychological, and sociological interests of its intended audience. As children develop, they put aside certain books and move on to others that are both more challenging and better suited to their developmental needs. In very young children, these transitions occur rapidly, and in the course of a very few years they outgrow the nursery rhymes and picture books, and require more complex stories, more compelling characters, and more probing themes.

To summarize, the reading tastes of children (and adults, for that matter) are determined not only by their intellectual development—including their vocabulary and syntactic understanding—but also by the psychological and emotional issues they are facing at any given time. That's why reading tastes can change—sometimes overnight. It is also why it is very unlikely that a teacher, for example, will find one book that will speak to all children in a classroom at the same time. Of course, this is an argument for making sure young readers are given a lot of books on a wide variety of subjects.

Bibliotherapy

Bibliotherapy is the practice of treating emotional or psychological issues by having people read books that might help them cope—usually by demonstrating that they are not alone, that their emotional responses are perfectly normal, that time heals all wounds, and so on. This is a popular notion. Indeed, one of the largest adult book markets today is that for self-help books. We see a similar trend in children's reading, with books such as Catherine Dee's *The Girls' Guide to Life* and Karen Gravelle and Nick and Chava Castro's *What's Going on Down There? Answers to Questions Boys Find Hard to Ask.* For very young children, the most famous examples of bibliotherapy are the *Berenstain Bears* books by Stan and Jan Berenstain. These popular picture books are unabashedly intended to be bibliotherapeutic. The characters are supposed to be a typical family—mother, father, daughter, son—except, of course, they are bears. (Bears aside, this family composition is scarcely typical—and never was!) Each book addresses a very specific childhood experience (*The Berenstain Bears and the Bad Dream* and *The Berenstain Bears Go to the Doctor* are two examples) and shows how both children and parents respond to these situations (and, presumably, the responses are "normal"). The Berenstains, who began writing in the 1950s and continued into the twenty-first century, evolved with society, eventually including stories about children who are physically challenged and children's encounters with drug dealers, among others. The "Berenstain Bears" books are undeniably didactic—the plots are predictable or contrived and the characters generally flat, since the important element is the lesson being taught.

However, it is important to remember that life lessons can be found in a book that is simply telling a good story. Margaret Wise Brown's classic picture-book story, *The Dead Bird,* is usually seen as an example of introducing very young children to the concept of death and how we might deal with it. In that story, several children find a dead bird, mourn for it, give it a funeral and burial, and then return to their play—a microcosm of the natural way of the universe. Ezra Jack Keats wrote and illustrated a series of books about Peter, a young African American boy growing up in the inner city and dealing with bullies (*The Snowy Day*), a new baby sister (*Peter's Chair*), and a first "crush" on a girl (*A Letter to Amy*). Lucille Clifton wrote a series of picture books in poetry describing the transitions in a young child's life, including the death of a parent (*Everett Anderson's Good-bye*), a mother's new boyfriend (*Everett Anderson's 1, 2, 3*), and, boldly, child abuse (*One of the Problems of Everett Anderson*)—all for children between the ages of about 4 and 6.

The problem with bibliotherapy is not whether it works—people have been assuaged and emboldened by books for centuries—but how it should be used. Do we wait until a grandparent dies to hunt down a children's book on death? And does the book have to be specifically about the death of a grandparent to do any good? Do we wait until a crisis occurs before sharing books about broken families? And does the book's crisis have to mirror our own? Just because we don't personally know a person in a wheelchair doesn't mean we shouldn't read a story about physical disabilities. One librarian, Maeve Visser

Knoth, has suggested that the best bibliotherapy is to encourage wide and deep reading that prepares children for life's eventualities—rather than to scramble for the perfect antidotal book when a difficult occasion arises. She writes:

> *I would rather inoculate children than treat the symptoms of the emotional trauma. We give children vaccinations against measles. We can't vaccinate against divorce, but we can give children some emotional knowledge to use when their families, or other families they know, do go through a divorce. I advocate that we read picture books about death and divorce and new babies when no one is dying, when a marriage is strong, before anyone is pregnant. (273–274)*

The simple point is that children learn a great deal from their reading—they learn about people, about their fears, their dreams, their failings, and their endurance; they learn how people cope with inevitable traumas of life. This is why it is vital that writers be honest in their writing, that the human feelings they describe be genuine, and that the characters they invent be emotionally real. It is also vital that children read books that tell of life's sorrows as well as of life's joys, and books that describe our human failings as well as our strengths. That is the best kind of bibliotherapy—the kind that prepares us for the curves life will surely throw us.

Censorium

In February 2007, a news item swept the nation when several librarians around the country announced that they were going to ban the winner of the Newbery Medal, Susan Patron's *The Higher Power of Lucky,* from their libraries because in the opening scene, on the very first page, we find the word *scrotum.* The book's female protagonist, 10-year-old Lucky Trimble, overhears the word when a boy describes a rattlesnake biting his dog—on the scrotum. Lucky, like so many children, is both curious and fascinated with language, and she wants to know what the word means. In other words, she is perfectly normal. So what is the big flap? Why would a book deemed worthy of the most prestigious American children's literary award be pulled from library shelves?

In fact, censorship, the action by some authority of determining what is and what is not appropriate reading for others, is commonplace in children's literature. It stems from society's desire to protect the "innocence" of childhood—an exaggerated and romantic notion. In their zeal to preserve that innocence, some adults actively try to keep children from reading certain kinds of material. What are the subjects of censorship in children's literature? Inappropriate language, as we have seen, references to sexuality, references to "unapproved" religious beliefs or philosophies, and undue violence are among the most common topics. However, examining lists of books banned from libraries and schools in the United States reveals some surprising results, including Mark Twain's *The Adventures of Huckleberry Finn,* Anne Frank's *Diary of a Young Girl,* Maurice Sendak's *In the Night Kitchen,* Shel Silverstein's *A Light in the Attic,* and all of J. K. Rowling's "Harry Potter" books, to name just a few. Indeed, a list of the most frequently banned books almost suggests that if a book has not been banned somewhere, it may not be any good at all.

Those who think that removing offensive books from the shelves will preserve their children's youthful innocence are kidding themselves. Children are going to grow up—with or without help from adults. Regulating children's reading through censorship will not protect them from the seamier side of life. In fact, censoring books almost always backfires. The quickest way to make a book popular is to ban it. Of course, I am not suggesting that as teachers it is our duty to expose young children to pornographic, violent, or seditious stories. Most intelligent people agree that some subjects and approaches require mental and emotional maturity. It would be foolish to share a story about a teenage girl's first menstrual cycle with a preschooler. On the other hand, many preschoolers have had to deal with deaths in the family, child abuse, divorce, and other traumas. So it is not unreasonable to think that many of them have some experience in these areas and they may benefit from well-written books on these subjects. Common sense is every educator's best asset.

Unfortunately, common sense is not always enough to avoid trouble. In 1998, a well-intentioned elementary teacher came under fire because she read to her students Carolivia Herron's *Nappy Hair,* a picture book containing the rollicking story of an African American girl with "the kinkiest, the nappiest, the fuzziest, the most screwed up, squeezed up, knotted up, tangled up, twisted up" hair (see both Clemetson and Martin in "Recommended Readings"). The teacher found herself besieged by irate parents who mistakenly thought the book was racially insensitive and made fun of African Americans. Of course, none of the complaining parents had actually read the book and none knew that the author herself was a distinguished African American professor. Nor did they know the book had been on recommended reading lists throughout the country. And few of the complaining parents actually had children in the teacher's classroom. Nor did it seem to matter that the children in the class—most of whom were African American or Latino—loved the book. As so often happens in such cases, the school administration buckled under public pressure and fired the teacher. When all the evidence finally came out, and everyone realized the book was actually a joyful celebration of African heritage, the school attempted to bring back the teacher, who had been very popular with the students, but she wisely declined the invitation.

In many ways, teachers are the guardians of our intellectual freedom, and this charge must be taken seriously and not tainted by poor judgment or foolhardiness. One place to turn for help is the National Coalition Against Censorship, an organization dedicated to protecting free speech, particularly in the classroom. The coalition's website is a good place to go to keep abreast of current censorship issues. (See Figure 2.1 for a guide to combating censorship and preserving intellectual freedom in our schools.)

As teachers or parents, we should never compromise our standards and surrender to fear and ignorance. Books can stimulate thinking, suggest new possibilities, and challenge old attitudes—and these are the very things that some people find threatening. Interestingly, most people who favor censorship do so on the premise that they are protecting established values. But it is the act of censorship that threatens the values of a free people and a democratic nation. Let us leave censorship to the dictators and despots. (Remember

Figure 2.1 ● A brief guide to preserving intellectual freedom in the classroom

1. **Know your rationale for using a book in the classroom. Answer these questions:**
   - Is the book appropriate for this age level?
   - Does the book meet your objectives in the class, and how?
   - Does the book appear on recommended lists, and what have been the reactions of critics?
   - What possible objections could be raised to the book—language, tone, theme, subject matter—and how can you best address these objections?
   - As a last resort, what alternative readings can you offer in place of this book?

2. **Have guidelines for handling community and parental objections. Carefully organized procedures can do much to stem the tide of emotionalism. Include the following:**
   - A complaint form on which specific objections are to be recorded
   - A clearly designated procedure for dealing with the complaint
   - A broad-based committee of teachers, administrators, and community representatives for hearing the complaints
   - A clear philosophical statement articulating the school's educational principles

3. **Join with other teachers and the administration to protect students' right to read (and the teachers' right to teach).**

4. **Actively support other teachers when they encounter censorship challenges.**

5. **Educate the community about the importance of intellectual freedom.**
   - Write letters or articles for the local newspaper.
   - Lobby the school board members and other community leaders.
   - Conduct or sponsor community workshops on censorship.

6. **Keep informed about censorship issues through professional journals, reports, association meetings, and new media.**

that one of the first acts of despots is to burn the books they don't agree with.) We should not fear challenges to our ideas and our way of life. If we never question our values, we risk losing sight of what is really important. The strength of our democracy is, and has always been, the free exchange of ideas.

Summary

Human development is a complex process that occurs on many different levels—physical, intellectual, and emotional. A child's developmental level directly impacts his or her response to reading. As adults, we often underestimate the abilities of small children—especially their linguistic abilities, such as imitating sounds, putting together sentences, and acquiring new vocabulary. In their first seven years, children go through developmental changes more rapidly than they will throughout the rest of their lives. Consequently, it is important to keep in mind the process of child development when we help them choose their books. The 1-year-old enjoys simple, cloth, wordless books, but by the age of 7 many children are ready for chapter books. Of course, children develop at differing rates, and we, as adults, are challenged to tune in to each child's needs and abilities. And fortunately, today we can find children's books to meet virtually every requirement and satisfy every desire.

The idea of bibliotherapy is nothing new; in fact, it is quite popular in our society. But we should realize that we don't always need a self-help book to get us through life's crises. Good stories—engaging characters and interesting plots—can be just as therapeutic. And reading widely on many topics from many points of view can be equally therapeutic, for it can help prepare us for the inevitable tough times we all have to face eventually.

Finally, censorship—or euphemistically, book selection—in children's reading is often misguided. The censor of children's books usually professes that censorship is necessary to protect children from the unsavory or from what they are too immature to understand. Unfortunately, adults are notorious for underestimating the intellectual capacities of children, and the attempt to shelter often backfires. A forbidden book becomes an object of desire. However, once we have an understanding of a child's intellectual, social, and moral development, we may come to realize the essential folly of censorship. Censorship implies that just a select few (and who selects them?) are capable of making decisions about what the rest of us read. Are we going to accept that? And not least important, we have to recognize that the very concept of censorship on moral, political, or religious grounds flies in the face of our democratic traditions.

For Reflection and Discussion

1. Select a modern picture book (such as one from the list at the end of Chapter 7) and analyze it from the standpoint of one or more of the development theories presented in this chapter. What age level does it seem to be addressing? What led you to that conclusion? What specific issues of that age level does the book seem to be concerned with?

2. Locate and read two modern picture books on a similar theme—new babies (such as Ezra Jack Keats' *Peter's Chair* and Martha Alexander's *Nobody Asked Me If I Wanted a Baby Sister*), parental relationships (perhaps Margaret Wise Brown's *Runaway Bunny* and Jane Yolen's *Owl Moon*), or death and dying (possibly Lucile Clifton's *Everett Anderson's Goodbye* and Tomie de Paola's *Nana Upstairs, Nana Downstairs*). What specific differences do you see in the way the writers and illustrators address the issue? Which, if either, is more effective? Why?

3. Locate a list of censored books. (There are many websites that provide such lists, including that of the American Library Association at www.ala.org. You may want to check out several websites and compare lists. You will be surprised. Please note: The ALA does *not* ban books—it publishes this list as part of its ongoing campaign for freedom of the press.) Which books surprise you the most? Why do you think they ended up on such a list? What specific organization is banning these books? What do you think the agenda of that organization is?

4. Prepare a written defense of a controversial book you might like to use in a classroom setting. Explain why you think the book is important, what its merits as literature are, and how you would handle objections from the school administration, parents, and the community at large. You may use the suggestions in Figure 2.1 as a general guide.

● Works Cited

Jung, Carl Gustav. *Contributions to Analytical Psychology*. London: Routledge & Kegan Paul, 1948.

Knoth, Maeve Visser. "What Ails Bibliotherapy?" *The Horn Book Magazine* (May/June 2006): 273–276.

● Recommended Readings

American Library Association. www.ala.org (a good place to look for a list of recently censored books)

Brainerd, Charles J. *Recent Advances in Cognitive Developmental Research*. New York: Springer-Verlag, 1983.

Brief, Jean-Claude. *Beyond Piaget: A Philosophical Psychology*. New York: Teachers College Press, 1983.

Celebration staff and Kenneth L. Donelson. *Literature for Today's Young Adults*, 6th ed. New York: Longman, 1997.

Clemetson, Lynette. "Caught in the Cross-Fire." *Newsweek 14* (December 1998): 38–39.

Erikson, Erik. *Childhood and Society*. New York: Norton, 1950.

Feldman, Robert S. *Child Development*, 5th ed. New York: Prentice-Hall, 2009.

Fields, M. V., K. Spangler, and D. M. Lee. *Let's Begin Reading Right*, 2nd ed. Columbus, OH: Merrill, 1991.

Gilligan, Carol. *In a Different Voice: Psychological Theory and Women's Development*. Cambridge, MA: Harvard University Press, 1982.

Greven, Philip. *Spare the Child: The Religious Roots of Punishment and the Psychological Impact of Physical Abuse*. New York: Knopf, 1990.

Griswold, Jerry. *Feeling Like a Kid: Childhood and Children's Literature*. Baltimore, MD: The Johns Hopkins University Press, 2006.

Hyde, Janet Shibley. *Half the Human Experience: The Psychology of Women*. Lexington, MA: D. C. Heath, 1985.

Kaestle, Carl F. *Literacy in the United States: Readers and Reading Since 1880*. New Haven, CT: Yale University Press, 1991.

Kohlberg, Lawrence. *The Philosophy of Moral Development*. San Francisco: Harper & Row, 1981.

——. *Essays on Moral Development. Vol. II: The Psychology of Moral Development, the Nature and*

Validity of Moral Stages. San Francisco: Harper & Row, 1985.

Kozulin, Alex, and others, eds. *Vygotsky's Educational Theory in Cultural Context.* Cambridge: Cambridge University Press, 2003.

Lane, Frederick S. *The Decency Wars: The Campaign to Cleanse American Culture.* Amherst, NY: Prometheus, 2006.

Lindfors, J. W. *Children's Language and Learning,* 2nd ed. Englewood Cliffs, NJ: Prentice-Hall, 1987.

Martin, Michelle H. "Never Too Nappy." *The Horn Book Magazine* (April/May 1999): 283–288.

National Coalition Against Censorship, 275 Seventh Avenue, New York, NY 10001. www.ncac.org.

Neubauer, John. *The Fin-De-Siecle Culture of Adolescence.* New Haven, CT: Yale University Press, 1992.

Piaget, Jean. *The Language and Thought of the Child.* New York: Harcourt, Brace, 1926.

——. "Piaget's Theory." In *Handbook of Child Psychology.* P. H. Mussen, ed. 4th ed. W. Kessen, ed. *Vol. 1: History, Theory, and Methods.* New York: John Wiley & Sons, 1983.

Pinker, Steven. *The Blank Slate: The Modern Denial of Human Nature.* New York: Viking, 2002.

——. *How the Mind Works.* New York: Norton, 1998.

——. *The Language Instinct.* New York: HarperCollins, 2000.

Ravitch, Diane. *The Language Police: How Pressure Groups Restrict What Students Learn.* New York: Knopf, 2003.

Santrock, John. *Child Development: An Introduction,* 12th ed. New York: McGraw-Hill, 2008.

Sugarman, Susan. *Piaget's Construction of the Child's Reality.* Cambridge: Cambridge University Press, 1987.

Vidal, Fernando. *Piaget before Piaget.* Cambridge, MA: Harvard University Press, 1994.

Vygotsky, L .S. *Mind in Society: Development of Higher Psychological Processes,* rev. ed. Cambridge, MA: Harvard University Press, 2006.

Walsh, Mary Roth, ed. *The Psychology of Women: Ongoing Debates.* New Haven, CT: Yale University Press, 1987.

Go to the MyEducationKit for this text where you can:

- Search the Database of Children's Literature, housing more than 22,000 titles searchable in every genre by authors or illustrators, by awards won, by year published, and by topic and description.

- Explore genre-related Assignments and Activities, assignable exercises showing concepts in action through database use, video, cases, and student and teacher artifacts.

- Listen to podcasts and read interviews from some of the brightest and most enduring stars of children's literature in the Conversations.

- Discover Web Links that will lead you to sites representing the authors you learn about in these pages, classrooms with powerful children's literature connections, and literature awards.

The Elements of Story
The Building Blocks of Literature

Introduction

Whether we are sharing Margaret Wise Brown's *Goodnight Moon* with a toddler, or "Cinderella" with a kindergartner, or E. B. White's *Charlotte's Web* with a second-grader, the books all have one thing in common—each describes the activities of one or more characters in a given time and place. But what is it about some stories that we can read them over and over and they stick with us forever, whereas other stories are forgotten almost as soon as we put down the book? Part of the answer, as we will see in Chapter 4, lies within each of us and what we bring to our reading. However, another part of the answer lies in the writer's skill as a storyteller—how the characters are drawn, plots constructed, setting detailed, language composed, and theme revealed. These are at the core of all stories, and in this chapter we will examine these elements to see what makes them work—or not work.

Characters

Central to every good story are believable and memorable characters. The creation of interesting characters is one of the most complicated parts of writing and involves several issues.

Character Type

The principal characters of a story include the protagonist (the central figure with whom we usually sympathize or identify) and the antagonist (the figure who opposes the protagonist and creates the conflict). We sometimes call these characters the hero and villain; however, protagonists are not always heroic, and antagonists are not always villainous. As a matter of fact, the most interesting and believable characters are the ones who are more complex. Heroes might be strong, compassionate, and fearless, but they may also be bull-headed and rash. Villains might be dastardly, but they might also have an unexpected streak of generosity.

Typically, several minor characters are included in the story as well. They include supporting characters—friends, family, or cohorts of the protagonist or antagonist. Supporting characters can be interesting in their own right—the Mad Hatter in *Alice's Adventures in Wonderland*, the Scarecrow and the Tin Woodsman in *The Wonderful Wizard of Oz*, for example. In addition to supporting characters, many stories include functionary characters, whose role is simply to perform certain essential plot functions (officials or servants, for example). These are typically stock characters who represent types rather than individuals—the flatterer, the show-off, the conceited, the tight-fisted, the addle-brained, the snob, and so on. When a character possesses the opposites of the main character, we call him or her a foil character—since the purpose is to make the main character look better ("foil" is a jeweler's term for a setting designed to make a jewel look bigger and brighter—the setting of a ring, for example). So, Templeton, the self-centered rat in *Charlotte's Web*, is a foil to Charlotte, further highlighting her kind and selfless nature.

Character Development

In a well-written story, the characters are real and believable. This is accomplished in several ways. First, characters ought to have good reasons for behaving as they do. This is called character motivation. We turn again to *Charlotte's Web*. In the beginning, Wilbur is insecure and lonely—after all, he has no family and has no idea what being a pig means. When he finds out, then he becomes frightened—for good reason, since most pigs end up as pork roast. His transformation into a caring, compassionate pig is the result of the example of his great friend and mentor, Charlotte (who also saves his life). Wilbur's actions are all motivated and we understand why he is the way he is.

Some characters are developed more fully than others, which brings us to two further ways of describing fictional characters. Characters are either flat or round, depending on how much we learn about them. Flat characters have no depth—we see but one side or aspect of them. Most characters are flat—in *Charlotte's Web*, Templeton, the stuttering goose, and the farm hand are all examples of one-sided characters. As readers, however, we are mainly interested in the round characters, for they are the most interesting characters and have more fully developed personalities. Charlotte, for example, is a round character—wise, compassionate, resourceful (and efficient in capturing her food!). And, of course, so is Wilbur, who is a complex figure with many sides. Naturally, in a story, most characters are going to be flat. And this is fine. After all, if every character were fully developed, the book would never end!

Most characters in a story are also what we call static characters—that is, they do not change. The selfish Templeton the rat is just the same at the end of the story as at the beginning. We can say the same for most of the farm animals and the humans (except for Fern). However, Wilbur is transformed in the course of the story. We have already seen that in the beginning he is self-absorbed, timid, and fearful, but he eventually becomes brave, forceful, and compassionate. In other words, he matures. A character who undergoes a change is called a dynamic character. However, we must not think that all round characters are dynamic. Charlotte, a round character, is wise, kind, and compassionate from the very beginning—and she remains that way. In fact, we don't want her to change. This makes her a round but static character. In fact, most stories have but one or two truly dynamic characters—there just isn't time for any more. (Incidentally, folktale characters are an exception to these rules and we will discuss them more fully in Chapter 9.)

Character Revelation

And finally, we should consider how we learn about characters—and whether what we learn is reliable. We learn about characters—or how they are revealed—in several ways:

1. *What the narrator says about the character.* This usually is the least memorable way of getting to know a character (it's like learning about someone from a lecture).

2. *What the other characters say about the character.* This evidence is only as reliable as the speaker; we must be wary of hidden motives or prejudices—do we trust what Templeton says about someone?

3. *What the character says about himself or herself.* This information is usually quite reliable, but we should remember that people do not always mean what they say, nor do they always understand themselves. At the beginning of *Charlotte's Web*, for instance, does Wilbur really understand why he is so timid and so self-absorbed?

4. *What the character actually does.* Actions, we all know, speak louder than words, and it is through actions that some of the most convincing evidence about character is revealed. The actions of Wilbur, Charlotte, and Templeton really tell us what the characters are like.

Setting

The setting refers to the time, the geographical location, and the social and political circumstances in a story. It can help establish the mood of a story. In Laura Ingalls Wilder's *Little House on the Prairie*, for example, the setting is on the Great Plains in the latter half of the nineteenth century. In addition to the time and place, the setting includes descriptions of the daily occupations of the Ingalls family—poor settlers eking out a living in an inhospitable environment, where wells have to be dug by hand, the nearest neighbor is miles away, and a family must huddle in a log cabin behind a door made from a blanket while wolves lurk perilously close outside. Writers of historical fiction, gothic romance, and fantasy often focus heavily on the setting, since it is likely to be unfamiliar to the reader, and it creates the appropriate mood or atmosphere.

Below is the opening paragraph of Natalie Babbitt's *Tuck Everlasting,* the story of a lonely girl's encounter with a strange family who accidentally stumbled on a magical spring that bestows immortality on all who drink from it. Notice the sensory imagery—both visual and tactile—that leaves us with a foreboding of things to come:

> *The first week of August hangs at the very top of summer, the top of the live-long year, like the highest seat of a Ferris wheel when it pauses in its turning. The weeks that come before are only a climb from a balmy spring, and those that follow a drop to the chill of autumn, but the first week of August is motionless, and hot. It is curiously silent, too, with blank white dawns and glaring noons, and sunsets smeared with too much color. Often at night there is lightning, but it quivers all alone. There is no thunder, no relieving rain. These are strange and breathless days, the dog days, when people are led to do things they are sure to be sorry for after. (3)*

The references to motionlessness, blank dawns, glaring noons, lightning quivering "all alone," and breathless days all suggest otherworldliness and loneliness. These two themes pervade the story of a family whose immortality has proven to be a lonesome burden.

Narrative Point of View

Every story has to have a storyteller. In fiction, we call the storyteller the narrator. (Incidentally, we should never assume that the author is the narrator. Instead, authors assume the mask—or *persona*—of the narrator.) Three common narrative approaches are found in most children's fiction.

First-Person Narrator

When the narrator is also a character in the story, he or she is called a first-person narrator (because the narrator refers to him- or herself as "I"). Richard Peck opens his Newbery Honor book, *A Long Way from Chicago,* this way: "It was always August when we spent a week with our grandma. I was Joey then, not Joe: Joey Dowdel, and my sister was Mary Alice. In our first visits we were still just kids, so we could hardly see her town because of Grandma. She was so big, and the town was so small" (1). Naturally, a first-person narrator can only tell us what he or she knows and feels (or what others tell the narrator). The first-person narrator is not necessarily the protagonist. In Richard Peck's book, Grandma is the protagonist; the narrator, her grandson Joey, just tells us her story.

Limited Narrator

The limited narrator is an outside storyteller (that is, not a character within the story) whose viewpoint is limited to that of a single character. In other words, the limited narrator tells us only what that one character knows and feels. In the first chapter of *Little House in the Big Woods*, Laura Ingalls Wilder introduces her characters like this:

> So far as the little girl could see, there was only the one little house where she lived with her Father and Mother, her sister Mary and baby sister Carrie. A wagon track ran before the house, turning and twisting out of sight in the woods where the wild animals lived, but the little girl did not know where it went, nor what might be at the end of it.
>
> The little girl was named Laura and she called her father, Pa, and her mother, Ma. In those days and in that place, children did not say Father and Mother, nor Mamma and Papa, as they do now. (2–3)

As the story continues, we realize that everything we are told by the narrator is filtered through Laura. Laura does not actually tell the story, but the reader can know no more than Laura knows. The narrator's viewpoint is limited to Laura's and we will not learn where the wagon track ends up until she does. The limited narrator is frequently used in children's stories because it allows for a more sophisticated vocabulary than if, for example, the 5-year-old Laura were telling the story herself.

Omniscient Narrator

The **omniscient narrator** is also an outside narrator, but one who knows the thoughts and feelings of all the characters in a story. Omniscient, in fact, means "all-knowing." Since both the omniscient narrator and the limited narrator are outside storytellers, it is not always obvious which is being used at first. E. B. White's *Charlotte's Web* opens with the exclamation of the young girl, Fern, "Where's Papa going with that axe?" We might suspect that this story is being told from Fern's point of view. But in the second chapter the focus shifts to the little pig, Wilbur. Later on, we see things through the eyes of the farmer and hired hand and then through Fern's parents' eyes. This is a good example of the use of the omniscient narrator. Only an omniscient narrator can give us multiple viewpoints in this way.

Plot

The novelist E. M. Forster once said, "The king died and then the queen died is a story. The king died, and then the queen died of grief is a plot." The point is that the plot is not just a series of events—it is a series of interrelated events. In life, a typical day might go like this: The phone rings while we're in the shower, a solicitor comes to the door, the mail carrier mistakenly gives us someone else's mail, a thunderstorm is brewing, and a roast burns in the oven. None of these events is related to the rest. This is not a plot—it's just a series of unfortunate events. In a plot, we expect every occurrence to have a specific purpose. The telephone call is from a long-lost relative, the solicitor turns out to be an old enemy, the mail is inadvertently opened and reveals a sinister scheme, the thunderstorm knocks out the electricity, and the burnt roast sets the house on fire. The point is that a plot makes connections between the various incidents. A plot comes in numerous patterns. Here are five patterns most prevalent in children's stories—the sequential and cumulative plots are found primarily in picture books.

Dramatic Plot

A dramatic plot is a narrative based on a single major conflict that must be resolved. Typically, it begins by introducing the characters, setting, and conflict, then follows a rising action that intensifies gradually until reaching a peak or turning point (called the climax) and then concludes with a denouement (the conclusion, including the wrapping up of loose ends). This structure, with its chronological arrangement, is probably the most familiar storyline; it is commonly found in mysteries, adventures, romances, folktales, and most picture-book stories. E. B. White's *Charlotte's Web* is a good example.

Episodic Plot

The episodic plot is a narrative comprised of a series of vignettes or shorter tales (usually organized into chapters or episodes) and all held together by a common theme or a common set of characters. Sometimes the episodes can stand alone as short stories. The episodic plot is used when the writer wants to convey the feeling of a period or to explore the relationships among a set of characters. Eleanor Estes's "Moffat" books (*The Moffats* and others), about a family living in Connecticut just after World War I, and Laura Ingalls Wilder's "Little House" books (*The Little House in the Big Woods* and its sequels) all use episodic plots. (Incidentally, episodic plots are found in most weekly television sitcoms and dramas, with each episode standing alone, although tied through theme or character to the series as a whole.)

Parallel Plot

When an author weaves two or more dramatic plots throughout a single book, we have a parallel plot structure. The plots are usually linked by a common character and/or a similar theme. Robert McCloskey's picture book, *Blueberries for Sal,* describes a mother and young daughter, Sal, going out to pick blueberries. At the same time, on the other side of the hill, a mother bear and her cub are out eating blueberries. Sal and the bear cub get lost and are accidentally paired up with the wrong mothers—to the surprise of both mothers. The pictures alternate between the adventures of Sal and of the bear cub. Eventually, each is restored to the proper mother and all ends happily. This is an unusual but good example of a parallel plot in a picture book.

Sequential Plot

Beatrice Schenk de Regniers' *May I Bring a Friend?*, about a little boy who is invited on six successive days to dine with the king and queen, is an example of a sequential plot. On each day, the little boy asks and is given permission to bring a friend, and each day he brings a different animal or group of animals. This same plot element occurs in a sequence of repetitions, each slightly varied and usually reaching a surprising conclusion. The folktale known as "The Mitten," a story frequently illustrated (by Jan Brett, among others), is another example. In this tale, a lost mitten becomes a shelter for a succession of forest animals, from a mole to a rabbit to a fox to a bear—the specific animals vary, but each is always larger than the last. The mitten expands to dangerous proportions until it finally explodes when a tiny animal (a grasshopper or a mouse) comes along and pokes one tiny leg inside—the proverbial straw breaking the camel's back. The repetition establishes familiarity with the storyline and creates expectancy in the child.

Cumulative Plot

A variation of the sequential plot is the cumulative plot, in which each successive addition to the plot is repeated as the story is told. An example is this famous nursery rhyme: "This is the house that Jack built. This is the malt that lay in the house that Jack built. / This is the rat that ate the malt that lay in the house that Jack built. . . ." Ed and Barbara Emberley's *Drummer Hoff*, about a company of Revolutionary War soldiers assembling a cannon, is based on an old folk rhyme, each sequence ending with the refrain: "But Drummer Hoff fired it off." The old folktale, "The Turnip," is about a succession of creatures trying to pull a huge turnip from the garden—here is a typical passage: "The dog took hold of the granddaughter, the granddaughter took hold of the old woman, the old woman took hold of the old man, the old man took hold of the turnip, they pulled and pulled, but couldn't pull it out. So the dog called the cat over." And thus the lines accumulate until eventually, with the aid of a mouse, the turnip comes up. Cumulative plots are almost always comical by their very nature, and their repetitive language invites children to memorize the pattern.

Other Plot Elements

Among the other aspects of plot structure we need to consider are the journey, foreshadowing, and flashbacks. The journey is a common plot device in which the main character or characters set out on a series of adventures. The journey, in fact, is probably the oldest plot device—it was used in *The Epic of Gilgamesh* some 4,000 years ago. The journey may be portrayed as real—as in Peter Rabbit's journey into Mr. McGregor's garden—or as imaginary—as in Max's dream adventure in *Where the Wild Things Are*. The journey may also be circular, with the hero finally returning home (as both Peter Rabbit and Max do); or it may be linear, with the hero making a new home (one example being the journey of Ged on his way to becoming a wizard in Ursula Le Guin's fantasy, *A Wizard of Earthsea*).

And remember Huck Finn's remark at the end of his adventurous journey: "But I reckon I got to light out for the Territory ahead of the rest, because Aunt Sally she's going to adopt me and sivilize me and I can't stand it. I been there before." Thus, Huck's journey, like that of all stories of growing up, is destined to become linear. Journeys allow for new experiences, new acquaintances, and new challenges. With each journey comes physical, mental, and spiritual growth, which makes the literary journey an ideal metaphor for life. It is little wonder that storytellers have so long been addicted to the journey.

Foreshadowing is the dropping of hints at what is to come in the future. An obvious example is in Mother's admonition to Little Red Riding Hood not to talk to strangers, which foreshadows the encounter in the woods. Foreshadowing is used to create suspense (horror films are addicted to foreshadowing) and to prepare the reader for possibilities, which makes the plot more believable. So when Peter Rabbit's mother reminds him of the catastrophe that befell his father in Mr. McGregor's garden (he was put into a pie), we become even more anxious for Peter when he foolishly ignores her warning.

The flashback is the device by which the narrator takes the reader back to a time and place before the story's present time. This is used in books for older readers, but is unusual in stories for preschoolers whose concept of time is not yet sophisticated enough to grasp the subtleties of the device. One very good example that children are familiar with is in Charles Dickens's *A Christmas Carol,* when the Ghost of Christmas Past takes Scrooge back to his youth. The flashback is a way of revealing necessary background information, such as explaining why a character behaves in a certain way.

Conflict

What makes a plot gripping is the conflict. Conflicts are sometimes depicted in terms of good versus evil or right versus wrong. For a story to hold our interest, something must be at stake. In most cases, a goal is to be accomplished and something achieved. It is to see the resolution of the conflict that most readers continue reading until the end of the story. Conflicts come in many varieties; we will look at the most common.

Protagonist against Another

This conflict occurs when two characters or two groups of characters (the protagonist and the antagonist) are pitted against each other. They may want the same thing— Cinderella and her wicked stepsisters all want to marry Prince Charming. Or perhaps what one character wants is contrary to what another wants—in *Charlotte's Web,* Wilbur wants to live and the humans want to eat him. Or perhaps one character is determined to prevent another from achieving a goal—in Natalie Babbitt's *Tuck Everlasting,* the heroine, Winnie, must stop the villain from finding the spring of immortality and selling its water for profit.

Protagonist against Society

This conflict occurs when the protagonist is pitted against mainstream society and its values and mores. This struggle is evident in many stories of racial prejudice, such as Mildred Taylor's *Roll of Thunder, Hear My Cry,* depicting the struggle of an African American family against a community of white racists.

Protagonist against Nature

This type of conflict occurs when the protagonist is engaged in a struggle for survival, usually alone in some natural wilderness or forbidding landscape. For example, Scott O'Dell's *Island of the Blue Dolphins* is the story of a young woman who is abandoned alone on a deserted island and how she manages to live for 18 years. In Jean Craighead George's *Julie of the Wolves,* a young girl must survive the harsh climate of the Alaskan wilderness. Interestingly, in most modern treatments of this conflict, the protagonists usually survive because they learn how to live with nature—not fight against it.

Protagonist against Self

Here, the conflict is an emotional or intellectual struggle within the protagonist himself or herself. Sendak's *Where the Wild Things Are* is an example of a picture book that deals with this sort of conflict. Max is torn between the conflicting desires to be a monster (doing exactly as he pleases) or to obey his mother (doing what he probably knows is right). Max's real enemy is not his mother. It is himself. This sort of conflict is perhaps more frequently found in books for adolescents, such as Judy Blume's *Are You There God? It's Me, Margaret,* depicting the various emotional conflicts arising in the early teen years.

A single story may contain more than one conflict, although one often predominates. *Are You There God? It's Me, Margaret* includes the protagonist's struggles with religious faith and coming to terms with her sexual maturity, for example. Without the conflict in a story, there would be little excitement, nor would there be the means for the growth and development of the main character.

Theme

The plot is what happens in a story, but the theme is what the story is really about. The theme is the controlling idea, the essential message that the writer wants to convey. In the eighteenth century, the messages were usually stated outright, such as this example from *The History of Little Goody Two-Shoes* (which will be discussed later in this chapter):

> *Remember this Story, and take Care whom you trust; but don't be covetous, sordid and miserable; for the Gold we have is but lent us to do Good with. We received all from the Hand of God, and every Person in Distress hath a just Title to a Portion of it.*

Today, most readers prefer that the theme not be hammered into them. Rather, they prefer the theme to emerge organically from the events of the story itself. Beatrix Potter knew this well. In *The Tale of Peter Rabbit*, Peter openly disobeys his mother and ventures into Mr. McGregor's garden where he is nearly captured. He makes a harrowing escape, losing his clothes and catching a cold in the process. At home, Peter's mother does not scold him—instead, she puts him to bed and gives him medicine for his cold while his sisters (who were obedient) are enjoying currant buns. Is there a theme here? Perhaps it is that we have to pay for our transgressions one way or another—and that our parents will love us anyway. Potter, however, does not feel the need to make these statements. She trusts her story to get those points across.

All fiction writers have specific ideas they wish to share about people, society, and life in general—that's why they began writing in the first place. But the best writers also know that readers—including children—do not like to be preached at or lectured to. They want the themes woven into the fabric of the story, revealed through the actions and words of the characters. The good writer does not sacrifice story to message. After all, if the story is not interesting, it will not be read and the message will be lost.

Some of the common themes we find in children's literature are these:

"A parent's love is unconditional."

"We must all pay for our mistakes."

"Growing up means taking on personal responsibilities."

"True friendship requires personal sacrifice."

"Family relationships require tolerance and understanding."

"Success comes out of determination and hard work."

"Death is a natural and necessary part of life."

Notice that the theme is stated in a complete sentence—that is the only way to express an idea. ("Love," "family," "friendship," and "death" are subjects, but they are not themes.)

Style

It is not enough that a writer has a good story to tell; the story should be told well. When we read a book such as Margaret Wise Brown's *The Runaway Bunny* to a child, we find it enjoyable not only because of the comforting story but also because of the lovely language—every word is important and in exactly the right place. This is what we mean by style. The best writers know what power words hold and they know how to arrange those words to the greatest effect.

Words

Words indeed have power. For example, the Declaration of Independence would likely have had less impact had it been written by a hack. In children's literature, we should look for that power as well. Naturally, in children's stories, the author's word choice is constrained by the child's limited vocabulary—abstract terminology doesn't work very well with preschoolers. It is, however, a mistake to think that children cannot handle sophisticated words. Beatrix Potter, for example, does not hesitate to use such terms as *exert, fortnight,* and *chamomile tea.* They are not everyday words, but they are words that are easily explained ("work hard," "two weeks," and "a warm drink made from a weed"). Potter also knows that young children will either pick up the meanings from the context or they will ask someone if it seems important. Even as adults, we are constantly running into words we do not know—that doesn't mean the books we're reading are too hard for us or that we shouldn't be reading them. After all, reading is meant to challenge us, to get us thinking. That's just as true for children as for adults.

As we already discussed in Chapter 2, children are rarely confounded by a difficult pronunciation—not having learned to be embarrassed, they will try anything. In fact, they seem to enjoy pronouncing language. And they recognize it when certain words sound good together—they love the musicality of nursery rhymes (see Chapter 6) and jump-rope jingles. Rhyme and rhythm are not lost on them (as we will see in Chapter 8).

Sentences

Sentences, both by their length and their construction, can increase or diminish our enjoyment of a work. Short sentences best convey suspense, tension, and swift action. Longer sentences work best when complicated explanations and descriptions are needed. But don't imagine that a long sentence is necessarily difficult to understand. A well-written long sentence can be just as simple as a short sentence. Notice how E. B. White, in the following paragraph from *Charlotte's Web,* effectively combines short and long sentences as he moves from describing action to thought and back to action:

> *Wilbur looked everywhere. He searched his pen thoroughly. He examined the window ledge, stared up at the ceiling. But he saw nothing new. Finally he decided he would have to speak up. He hated to break the lovely stillness of dawn by using his voice, but he couldn't think of any other way to locate the mysterious new friend who was nowhere to be seen. So Wilbur cleared his throat. (34)*

Prose has rhythm just as poetry does. The best writers can make a prose paragraph read as beautifully as a well-crafted poem. The juxtaposition of sounds, the use of repetition with a slight variation, the nature images so well suited to a story of pioneer life, all work together to create a lyrical passage in the conclusion to Patricia MacLachlan's *Sarah, Plain and Tall:*

> *Autumn will come, then winter, cold with a wind that blows like a wind off the sea in Maine. There will be nests of curls to look for, and dried flowers all winter long. When there are storms,*

Papa will stretch a rope from the door to the barn so we will not be lost when we feed the sheep and the cows and Jack and Old Bess. And Sarah's chickens, if they aren't living in the house. There will be Sarah's sea, blue and gray and green, hanging on the wall. And songs, old ones and new. And Seal with yellow eyes. And there will be Sarah, plain and tall. (58)

Exposition and Dialogue

Exposition refers to the narrator's explanations and descriptions—exposition gives us necessary background material. It may be used to set the scene, introduce a character, and move the action along, as in this example from Laura Ingalls Wilder's *Little House in the Big Woods*:

When Laura and Mary had said their prayers and were tucked snugly under the trundle bed's covers, Pa was sitting in the firelight with the fiddle. Ma had blown out the lamp because she did not need its light. On the other side of the hearth she was swaying gently in her rocking chair and her knitting needles flashed in and out above the sock she was knitting. (236)

Dialogue refers to the words spoken by the characters in the story to each other. (If one character is talking by himself or herself and addressing the reader, it is called a monologue.) Young readers especially enjoy dialogue as a realistic and convincing way of defining character. Dialogue allows the author to convey individual peculiarities, such as the goose's quirky speech in *Charlotte's Web* when she replies to Wilbur's inquiry about the time: "Probably-obably-obably about half-past eleven. . . . Why aren't you asleep, Wilbur?" (33). Charlotte's intellectual superiority over the other barnyard animals is clearly demonstrated by her greeting to Wilbur: "'Salutations!' said [Charlotte]. Wilbur jumped to his feet. 'Salu-*what?*' he cried" (35).

Tone

The **tone** of a story refers to the writer's attitude toward the subject. For example, the tone may be serious, humorous, satirical, passionate, sensitive, zealous, caustic, indifferent, poignant, warm, agitated, and so on. The story's tone is revealed through the author's words—and sometimes through what the author does not say. (For example, Beatrix Potter avoids a didactic tone in *The Tale of Peter Rabbit* by *not* having Mrs. Rabbit scold her wayward son or telling him "I told you so.")

Tone is closely related to style. Here is Mark Twain's opening to *The Adventures of Huckleberry Finn*, which is narrated by Huckleberry himself. The word choice and sentence structure establish the humorous, folksy tone:

You don't know about me without you have read a book by the name of The Adventures of Tom Sawyer; *but that ain't no matter. That book was made by Mr. Mark Twain, and he told the truth, mainly. There was things which he stretched, but mainly he told the truth.*

If we did not understand the concept of tone, we would be tempted to criticize Mark Twain for his bad grammar.

Humor

Rare is the child who does not like a funny story. Most scholars agree that incongruity is the foundation of humor—we laugh at the tension resulting from something out of the ordinary. But humor is also elusive; a joke told by one person can be a hoot, but told by someone else can be a complete dud. And humor tends to be age specific; what is funny when we are 3 years old is seldom funny when we are 21. Katharine Kappas identifies various types of humor most commonly found in books for children up through early adolescence. They include exaggeration, incongruity, surprise, slapstick, absurdity, uncomfortable situations, ridicule, defiance, violence, and verbal humor (see Kappas in the "Recommended Readings"). Some of these will seem surprising (or disturbing). But it is the child's penchant for physical humor that makes Roald Dahl's controversial works popular. In Dahl's *Charlie and the Chocolate Factory,* for example, several disagreeable children meet their ends in bizarre ways while touring a candy factory. Books such as these do not invite children to find humor in cruelty or the misfortunes of others. Rather, they allow children to release social and psychological tensions and give them a way of coping with uncomfortable, out-of-the-ordinary situations.

Humor is how all human beings express latent hostility. Take, for example, a familiar comic situation: A man steps on a banana peel, his heels go straight up in the air, and he lands on his behind. People laugh at this for several reasons. The movement is incongruous and unexpected, and it contains a touch of slapstick. It also makes the observers feel superior (they weren't the ones who fell), and they are relieved the man was not hurt. One of the important prerequisites for laughter provoked by someone else's misfortune is that the victim must seem to deserve the fate or the harm must not be critical. (The banana peel mishap is funnier if the victim is a pompous bore, but it is not funny if the victim is a sweet, old lady—or if the victim dies.)

It is through laughter that we learn to survive. Because it puts everyone on the same human level, laughter becomes the salve of the oppressed and the balm of the weak and vulnerable. And who in our society feels weaker and more vulnerable than the child? It is little wonder children find humor so indispensable to their well-being.

Didacticism

To be didactic simply means to teach, to be instructive. We expect didacticism in a textbook—like this one. But we often find it annoying in a story we are reading for pleasure. Didacticism was the predominant tone of eighteenth-century children's literature (see Chapter 1), which was obsessed with instilling the proper moral values in young people. The problem is that when an author sets out to teach a moral lesson through a story, the literary elements of the story suffer. The setting, plot, character development, and language become subverted to the instructional purpose—the book becomes a sermon rather than a story. Characters are stereotyped and undeveloped, plots are silly and contrived, and the language is phony.

We see this most obviously in eighteenth-century stories. Take, for example, *The History of Little Goody Two-Shoes* (1765)—published by Newbery and written by an unknown author—in which the moral is unmistakable, but the characters are cardboard and the plot is outworn. This is the story of an orphan girl who has but one shoe. When a sympathetic rich man gives her a new pair, she goes about rejoicing that she now has "two shoes." The girl's name is Margery Meanwell, whose father is ruined by two men, Timothy Gripe and Farmer Graspall. Margery meets a nasty girl at school named Polly Sullen—well, you get the picture. Margery becomes a popular teacher "who had the Art of moralizing and drawing Instructions from every Accident," and when her students lose a favorite pet, she reads "them a Lecture on the Uncertainty of Life, and the Necessity of being always prepared for Death." Eventually, her goodness brings her to the attention of a widowed lord who is happy to marry her, proving that virtue does, indeed, pay off. There is nothing subtle about a didactic story. Not only is the tale didactic, reminding us that we should be more like Goody Two-Shoes, but it is sentimental as well, which brings us to another subject.

Sentimentalism

Sentimentalism is the outward show of excessive emotion—or of emotion that is inappropriate to the circumstances. In other words, it is the expression of feeling without substance. Many tears are shed in *The History of Little Goody Two-Shoes,* and we are told that her death was "the greatest Calamity that ever was felt in the Neighbourhood" and that a monument "was erected to her Memory in the Church-yard, over which the Poor as they pass weep continually, so that the Stone is ever bathed in Tears." A later example of sentimentalism in children's books is found in the "Elsie Dinsmore" series, written by Martha Finley, beginning in 1867. The young Elsie Dinsmore faces many tribulations throughout the series and she triumphs because of her religious piety and sweetness. But one critic complained, as far back as 1896, that "nothing can be more dreary than the recital of Elsie's sorrows and persecutions. Every page is drenched with tears." "Even," the critic continues, "on comparatively cheerful nights [Elsie] is content to shed 'a few quiet tears upon her pillow'" (Repplier, n.p.). This is a sure sign of a sentimental work.

Eleanor Porter's *Pollyanna,* made famous by a 1950s Disney film, is another good example of sentimentalism. The young heroine, through her incessant cheerfulness, transforms a perennially gloomy town into a place of "gladness." The problem with sentimentalism, as with most excesses, is that it smacks of phoniness and lack of sincerity.

Parody

Parody is a literary imitation of another piece of literature, usually for comic effect. Parody is to literature what cartoon caricature is to art—both exaggerate in order to ridicule. For a good antidote to sentimentalism we can turn to Mark Twain's *The Adventures of Huckleberry Finn,* which contains a parody of nineteenth-century sentimentalism described above. Huck describes the character of Emmeline Grangerford, a young girl, obsessed with death, who "kept a scrap-book . . . and used to paste obituaries and accidents and cases of patient suffering in it . . . and write poetry after them out of her own head" (Twain 100). When Huck learns that Emmeline has died, he utters the classically unsentimental remark: "I reckoned that with her disposition she was having a better time in the graveyard." Twain's comic satire foreshadows the decline of sentimentalism in modern children's stories.

Parody implies a degree of sophistication; after all, if we are not familiar with the original work, we will not get the joke. Once rare in children's literature, parodies are becoming especially popular in children's picture books. Jon Scieszka's *The True Story of the Three Little Pigs* is a popular retelling of the familiar tale from the wolf's point of view (he was framed!). Another reversal is found in Eugene Trivizas's *The Three Little Wolves and the Big Bad Pig,* which has a heavy-handed but very funny message of nonviolence. And David Wiesner's *The Three Little Pigs* is a sophisticated tale that cleverly deconstructs the story and depicts the characters forming alliances with characters from other nursery stories. Parodies demonstrate the vitality of literature and can suggest to children new ways of interpreting old tales.

Irony

You may recall in *The Wonderful Wizard of Oz* that Dorothy undertakes a journey to seek the help of a wizard so she can get back home. On the way, she meets three new friends—a Scarecrow who wishes for brains, a Tin Woodsman who wishes for a heart, and a Cowardly Lion who wishes for courage. On the journey, each friend learns that he already possesses what he longed for—the Scarecrow is wise, the Tin Woodsman is kind and tender, and the Cowardly Lion is brave and fearless. On the other hand, the Wizard of Oz is revealed to be a phony, an eccentric humbug. In the end, Dorothy finds that she had the ability to get home on her own all along (through the magic of her ruby slippers). These are all examples of irony. Irony is the use of language to express something very different—indeed, often quite the opposite—of what the language literally means. We might think of it as literary deception, where things turn out to be different from what they appear. It can be intentional—as with the wizard—or circumstantial—as with Dorothy and her friends. Irony adds layers to a story's meaning. It can be humorous. It can be tragic. It reminds us that the world is not always what it seems.

Sometimes irony can devolve into cynicism, which is the opposite of sentimentalism. The cynic believes that human nature is fundamentally corrupt and the world is a rotten place to be. Obviously, this is not a tone that is normally found in children's literature. However, it is a feature of many of the works for adolescents written by Robert Cormier— *The Chocolate War, I Am the Cheese,* and others. Cormier deals with dark topics: government corruption, greed and depravity in individuals, a generally debased society, and personal crises such as teen suicide. Frankly realistic, Cormier offers no happy endings or even signs of hopefulness, which, as you might imagine, has caused considerable controversy over his writings.

Summary

Storytelling is an art, and like all art, it contains certain conventions that we must be acquainted with in order to enjoy fully a story's impact. Children need not memorize endless lists of technical terms to enjoy literature, but if they are introduced to the general literary concepts, their reading experiences might be richer, and it certainly makes literature easier to talk about if we have a common vocabulary. Most stories focus on characters—a protagonist who is the main sympathetic character and an antagonist who opposes the main character. Character development can be very complex, with some characters being fully developed, round characters, and others being one-dimensional, flat characters. Likewise, the protagonist is usually a dynamic character who undergoes a change, whereas most other characters are static characters who remain essentially the same throughout the story.

The setting consists of both the time and location of the story's action. All stories need a storyteller or narrator, of which there are several types. The most common are the first-person narrator (a character within the story), a limited narrator (an outside narrator telling the story from one character's point of view), and an omniscient narrator (an outside storyteller with a pervasive viewpoint). The plot may be dramatic (a chronological tale with the action moving toward a climax and conclusion), episodic (a series of independent vignettes tied together by theme, setting, and/or character), or parallel (two or more dramatic plots told side by side). Stories require a conflict in which something is at stake—an essential element if the story is to retain our interest. And all stories are based on a theme—an idea that the author wants to get across.

Finally are the matters of style (the way in which the author uses language) and tone (the author's attitude toward the theme). Some stories are humorous; others are serious. Didactic and sentimental tones, popular in the eighteenth century, have fallen out of favor today, but they still persist. In more sophisticated stories for older children we find irony, where things are not always as they seem. Parody, the comic imitation of a literary work, can also be found in children's stories.

All these elements are key to children's stories as they are to adult literature. The best writers know how to use these elements to greatest advantage, to create memorable characters, to tell a gripping tale, and to leave us with an indelible impression. There is no reason we should not judge a children's book with the same rigorous literary standards we would use for an adult's book. Children deserve no less.

For Reflection and Discussion

1. Select any children's picture storybook, and try to analyze it by its narrative point of view, setting, character types, plot, conflict, and theme. As you consider each element, determine how effectively you believe the writer has succeeded in producing a literary work. Do you have suggestions for improving it?

2. Repeat the exercise above but this time using a folktale. See how your responses differ from the picture-book analysis.

3. Locate some parodies of children's stories—children's picture books include many examples of folktale parodies. There are even parodies of children's books written for adults. See *Goodnight Bush* by Gan Golen and Erich Origen (Boston: Little, Brown, 2008), a political parody of Margaret Wise Brown's classic *Goodnight Moon*. Consider what makes an effective parody. Try writing some guidelines.

4. Try to recall books from your own childhood that you now recognize as moralizing or sentimental. If you can locate them, reread them to see if they leave the same effect on you.

● Works Cited

Babbitt, Natalie. *Tuck Everlasting.* New York: Farrar, Straus & Giroux, 1975.

Baum, L. Frank. *The Wizard of Oz.* 1900. Ed. Michael Patrick Hearn. Illus. W. W. Denslow. New York: Schocken, 1983.

History of Little Goody Two-Shoes, The, 5th ed. London: Newbery and Carnan, 1768.

MacLachlan, Patricia. *Sarah, Plain and Tall.* New York: Harper & Row, 1985.

Peck, Richard. *A Long Way from Chicago.* New York: Dial, 1998.

Repplier, Agnes. "Little Pharisees in Fiction." *Scribner's Magazine* (December 1896). www.readseries.com.

White, E. B. *Charlotte's Web.* New York: Harper, 1952.

Wilder, Laura Ingalls. *Little House in the Big Woods.* Illus. Garth Williams. New York: Harper & Row, 1953.

● Recommended Readings

Cameron, Eleanor. *The Green and Burning Tree.* Boston: Little, Brown, 1969.

Cart, Michael. *What's So Funny?: Wit and Humor in American Children's Literature.* New York: HarperCollins, 1995.

Hearne, Betsy, and Roger Sutton, eds. *Evaluating Children's Books: A Critical Look.* Urbana: University of Illinois Press, 1993.

Hilkick, Wallace. *Children and Fiction.* Cleveland: World, 1971.

Horning, Kathleen T. *From Cover to Cover: Evaluating and Reviewing Children's Books,* rev. ed. New York: Collins, 2010.

Hunt, Peter. *An Introduction to Children's Literature.* Oxford: Oxford University Press, 1994.

Kappas, Katharine H. "A Developmental Analysis of Children's Response to Humor." *The Library Quarterly* 37 (January 1967): 67–77.

May, Jill P. *Children's Literature and Critical Theory.* New York: Oxford University Press, 1995.

McGillis, Roderick. *The Nimble Reader: Literary Theory and Children's Literature.* New York: Twayne, 1996.

Nodelman, Perry. *The Hidden Adult: Defining Children's Literature.* Baltimore: The Johns Hopkins University Press, 2008.

——. *The Pleasures of Children's Literature,* 3rd ed. Boston: Allyn & Bacon, 2002.

Purves, Alan C., and Dianne L. Monson. *Experiencing Children's Literature.* Glenview, IL: Scott, Foresman, 1984.

Rudd, David, ed. *The Routledge Companion to Children's Literature.* New York: Routledge, 2010.

Tatar, Maria. *Enchanted Hunters: The Power of Stories in Childhood.* New York: Norton, 2009.

PEARSON
myeducationkit™

Go to the topic "Evaluating Children's Literature" on the MyEducationKit for this text, where you can:

- Search the Database of Children's Literature, housing more than 22,000 titles searchable in every genre by authors or illustrators, by awards won, by year published, and by topic and description.

- Explore genre-related Assignments and Activities, assignable exercises showing concepts in action through database use, video, cases, and student and teacher artifacts.

- Listen to podcasts and read interviews from some of the brightest and most enduring stars of children's literature in the Conversations.

- Discover Web Links that will lead you to sites representing the authors you learn about in these pages, classrooms with powerful children's literature connections, and literature awards.

Exploring Books

Reading, Talking, Doing

Introduction

The great Greek philosopher Socrates said, "Education is the kindling of a flame, not the filling of a vessel." This is especially true of reading, for it is an attitude or habit, rather than a block of knowledge or set of facts. This chapter suggests ways that we—as caregivers and educators—can help kindle that flame so that it will continue to burn throughout a lifetime.

One of the greatest gifts we can give to a child is a love for reading. This love is usually developed early in life. However, a college student of mine spent the summer of his eighteenth year alone in a cabin in the wilderness, far from civilization and without electricity or running water. He had never been much of a reader, but lacking television or video games to entertain him, he turned to books. A window opened for him. "Now," he told me, "I can't get enough to read." So it's never too late to acquire a love for reading, but we cannot count on young people isolating themselves in the north woods to accomplish this. As adults, we have a responsibility to do whatever we can to encourage reading and instill a passion for books.

As with most lessons of life, example is the best teacher. Children are more likely to read if they see the adults around them reading and if books are readily available. Also, there are many exciting ways to promote good reading experiences for children, both at home and in the classroom. This chapter is directed primarily to educators and most of the ideas are for use in the classroom.

Lev Vygotsky and Education

Lev Vygotsky (1896–1934) was a Russian psychologist whose ideas on child development sharply parted with the ideas of Piaget and his followers (see Chapter 3). Vygotsky discarded the stage theory of development and instead believed that human development was a continuing and never-ending process, and that we have no developmental "goals" to reach, only a series of lifelong transformations to experience. He also believed that human beings are essentially social creatures and that it is through our social interaction that we learn about ourselves and the world.

One of Vygotsky's most important concepts is called the zone of proximal development (ZPD), which is simply the difference between what we can learn on our own and what we can learn by interacting with others. Vygotsky's argument was that humans are able to achieve more if we have the help of other people. This may seem like a "no-brainer" to us today, but it revolutionized education, suggesting that it is a reciprocal process and a communal venture in which both the teacher and the students have responsibility for instruction—students learn from teachers, teachers learn from students, and students learn from each other. In other words, we should strive to operate in our zone of proximal development.

Consequently, the traditional classroom, in which the teacher delivers information and the students absorb it, is tossed out the window. In its place is a room of clustered desks, workspaces for small groups, and specialized learning stations. It is now a place where everyone is responsible for teaching as well as learning—education becomes a matter of mutual give and take. Small group discussions replace lectures and team projects replace individual examinations. Students assume responsibility for helping each other. The teacher relinquishes the authoritarian grip over the classroom in exchange for a cooperative community of learning.

It is with Vygotsky's ideas in mind that we should approach the remainder of this chapter. What follows are suggestions for incorporating children's literature into the classroom on a variety of levels. These are only suggestions and I would encourage you to experiment with your own variations or devise your own entirely new approaches.

The Reader-Centered Approach to Literature

One of the most popular approaches to using books in the classroom emphasizes the individual as a reader-responder. This approach is based on reader-response theory which argues that reading a literary text is part of a complex process that includes a collaboration between the writer (who has a message), the text (the symbols the writer uses to convey the message), and the reader (who receives the message and embellishes it with his or her own experiences, thoughts, and beliefs).

The text is no longer an object with secret meanings (presumably planted cleverly by the author) that we as readers are supposed to uncover. Rather, the text is a stimulus that elicits responses from us based on our past experiences, our previous reading, our thoughts, and our feelings. Furthermore, each time we reread a text we may feel differently about it than we did before, since the circumstances surrounding the reading are different each time. So the text acts on the reader and the reader interacts with the text. (Some call this process transaction, and hence this method is often referred to as transactional analysis.) Consequently, a text is re-created every time it is read, and it becomes, in the process, increasingly richer.

The familiar folktale "Rumpelstiltskin" provides an interesting opportunity for a response activity. "Rumpelstiltskin," you will remember, is the story of a miller who lies to the king about his daughter's ability to spin straw into gold. The greedy king promises to marry the daughter if she spins a roomful of straw into gold each night for a year. Naturally, she cannot do that, but a mysterious dwarfish stranger, Rumpelstiltskin, comes to her rescue, but demands the girl's first-born child in return for his help. Students can examine their own ethical attitudes by rank-ordering the characters—Rumpelstiltskin, the miller, the daughter, the king—according to the level of their ethical behavior (who acts most ethically, who acts least ethically, and so on). Surprisingly, a comparison of student responses often reveals a wide range of attitudes and little general agreement. Each of the characters is likely to be ranked first by some of the respondents and last by others. Often, no agreement can be reached on just who is the hero and who the villain. What explains this confusion?

The answer lies in the varying attitudes and value systems the readers bring to the text—attitudes and value systems formulated over a lifetime of experiences, reading, and thinking. For some readers, the miller's daughter is the innocent victim, a pawn in the hands of greedy men. But for others, the thought of the daughter bargaining with the life of her own child is abhorrent. For still other readers, Rumpelstiltskin is villainous and opportunistic, but some believe him to be acting fairly in accordance with the agreement with the miller's daughter. Some react negatively toward the miller for his basic dishonesty and the careless way in which he puts his daughter's life in jeopardy, whereas others believe he was simply trying to give his daughter a break in life by arranging for her marriage to the king. Many people regard the king as merely greedy, but some see him as a victim, deceived by the miller and his daughter, and the only character who remains true to his bargain. This exercise causes readers to evaluate their own ethical beliefs and to prioritize their own values. And as readers share their ideas, they soon discover how difficult it is to establish absolutes—and reader-response theory teaches us that there are no absolutes. Such an exercise points out the complexity of human behavior and motivation, the difficulty in ascertaining right and wrong, and the interdependencies involved in any social construct.

Reader-response approaches have proved very popular in the elementary classroom (and they are enormously successful with older readers as well). In *How Porcupines Make Love: Teaching a Response-Centered Literature Curriculum*, Purves, Rogers, and Soter (47) identify four objectives of the reader-centered approach:

1. To encourage individual readers to feel comfortable with their own responses to a literary work,
2. To encourage readers to seek out the reasons for their responses and thereby come to understand themselves better,

3. To encourage readers to recognize, in the responses of others, the differences among people and to respect those differences, and

4. To encourage readers to recognize, in the responses of others, the similarities among people.

Such an approach is not so much an attempt to "teach" literature as it is an effort to bring children and literature together.

In a response-centered approach, we, as adults who are interested in the interaction of children with books, need to do a variety of things. Again, Purves, Rogers, and Soter (56) have suggested specific actions that define the role of adults in creating a successful reading experience for young people. The adults' responsibilities are

1. To bring children and books together,

2. To give them as many different types of literature as possible,

3. To encourage honest and open responses,

4. To challenge them to explore those responses and learn something about themselves,

5. To provide them with the critical language to clearly express their responses,

6. To encourage tolerance, and

7. To encourage mutual understanding.

Reading Experiences

Following are some ideas for bringing about a connection between children and the books they read. This list of suggestions is certainly not exhaustive.

Reading Aloud

From a parent's gentle singing of a lullaby while rocking an infant to sleep to the reading of such childhood classics as *Alice's Adventures in Wonderland* or *Pinocchio,* sharing literature orally with children can be one of the most fulfilling human experiences. The relaxing moments of story-time with young children are among the most cherished memories of parenthood. And the times are equally magical when young children want to read the stories to us. However, we should not think that only small children like to be read to. Even college students enjoy it. Effective reading aloud can be modeled by observing a few guidelines.

1. Read stories you enjoy (unless you are a very good actor and can pretend to like the story). Your own enthusiasm will be contagious.

2. Choose stories that are suitable to the children's intellectual, emotional, and social developmental levels (see Chapter 2). Don't be afraid if the text includes a few challenging words—that never bothers children—just make sure you know how to pronounce the words and what they mean. (Young children don't let you get away with much.)

3. If the book is a picture book, make sure the illustrations can be seen easily by everyone. This is easy when you're reading to a single child, but trickier when reading to a class of 25. Breaking a large class into smaller groups can help. Remember, however, it is most effective if your audience can see the pictures as you are reading—not before or afterward.

4. Keep the reading experience an interactive one. Depart from the text when it seems necessary. Allow for questions and comments as you read—and you should feel free to ask questions as well.

5. Rehearse your reading and be sure to use the proper inflections, the appropriate cadence, and the right tone (some books call for a soothing voice, others require a livelier delivery). If there is dialogue, assume different voices. Children love this.

The reward for you is a grateful and delighted audience—and that is well worth the effort you put into this exercise.

Storytelling

Storytelling, the art of narrating a tale from memory rather than reading it, is one of the oldest of all art forms, reaching back to prehistoric times. Through storytellers, virtually all the traditional folktales were preserved for centuries, most having been committed to paper only in the past two or three centuries. Storytelling involves two elements; selection and delivery. First, a successful storyteller chooses good stories. Pick your favorites and prepare a repertoire of stories to draw on. Make sure you understand the story and its message. Second, a successful storyteller is also a performer. Practice your delivery. Assume voices for the various characters. Remember that timing is everything—speeding up, slowing down, and pausing at the right time. And most important—rehearse, rehearse, rehearse.

Folktales are natural sources for storytellers. They include easily memorized patterns and ample dialogue to enliven the story, and they are brief enough to be relayed in a single sitting. Also, they lend themselves well to adaptation, so the storyteller can adjust the tale to the audience. Some storytellers like to create their own tales, sometimes from their own experiences, or from their imaginations. All stories work best when they gradually build to a climax and quickly end while the audience's interest is still at a peak.

Of course, a rich and beautiful voice is an asset to any would-be storyteller. However, if you don't have such a voice, don't worry. Develop some other assets—effective body movement, facial expressions, eye contact, clear enunciation, meaningful inflection, and appropriate pauses (maybe even fancy dress). And, with practice, you can develop a greater vocal range and a voice that will project. Much of the storyteller's skill derives from knowing how to pace the telling, when to slow down, when to speed up, when to talk in near whispers, when to shout, and so on. For the storyteller, movement on a staging area can be significant. Natural body gestures (and at times even exaggerated ones, depending on the nature of the story) and direct eye contact will help engage the audience totally. Finally, don't be afraid to ham it up. This is no time to be shy.

Book Discussions

One of the most common classroom approaches to literature is the book discussion, which, if successful, will go beyond a simple series of questions from the teacher and the expected "correct" answers from the students. In fact, children in the middle elementary grades, with some encouragement, should be able to conduct book discussions on their own with some specific direction and good modeling.

A good book discussion (which, by the way, can be prepared for virtually any age level from 8 to 98) requires serious preparation. Also, a good book discussion evolves and metamorphoses as it proceeds. Be sure that you are well prepared before beginning the book discussion. This means not only reading the book carefully but also finding out what other readers (including critics) have said about it. Although they are not always necessary, you might consider preparing visual stimulants, such as photographs of the author, a story map of the plot (see the section on Webbing and Mapping later in this chapter), a time line (if it seems appropriate), charts, posters, PowerPoint presentations, and anything else that might give readers some useful insight. Integral to most book discussions are the questions asked by the leader. The questions can be posed to elicit varying levels of responses—for example, the following levels of questions progress from least to most sophisticated.

MEMORY QUESTIONS • Memory questions are the simplest type of questions. The readers are asked to recall facts from a story: plot incidents, character identifications, details of the setting, and so on. It is good to begin a discussion with memory questions because they are easy to answer (for those who read the book) and they make good "icebreakers." It also lets teachers know how much the readers understand and what needs to be filled in. However, memory questions that dwell on insignificant details are a waste of time. Questions like "What was Wilbur's favorite food?" or "What was Charlotte's oldest child's name?" serve no useful purpose. Instead, you might ask, "In Beatrix Potter's *The Tale of Peter Rabbit*, what happened to Peter's father?" The answer to this question has a direct bearing on the theme of the story since it shows that Peter was aware of the dangers of entering Mr. McGregor's garden. In a discussion of E. B. White's *Charlotte's Web*, for example, we might begin with memory questions such as "Why was Wilbur's life in danger?" and "How did Fern save Wilbur?" These questions can be answered from reading the book, and they have some thematic significance.

INTERPRETATION QUESTIONS • Interpretation questions ask the readers to go beyond reciting details from the story and ask for conclusions drawn from the facts. These questions are popular because many readers are anxious to offer their own opinions. However, the only useful opinion is the one based on facts and it should rely on the evidence found in the work itself—don't let this part of the discussion devolve into a free-for-all. For example, "Why does Peter's mother not punish him for his disobedience?" might be a good interpretation question for *The Tale of Peter Rabbit,* for it leads into a discussion of one of the major ideas of the story. For *Charlotte's Web,* we might ask such questions as "How does the relationship between Fern and Wilbur change over the course of the book?" and "How does Wilbur's character change from the beginning to the end of the book?"

APPLICATION QUESTIONS ● Application questions ask the readers to apply knowledge received from a book (perhaps to their own lives or to another literary work). These questions help readers see the relationships between literature and life. Again, these are also favorite questions, since they invite the readers to talk about themselves—something we wanted to avoid with the interpretation questions, but now it's fine. After hearing the story of *The Tale of Peter Rabbit,* children might be asked to discuss a time when they were in a situation similar to Peter's (that is, when they were disobedient). While discussing *Charlotte's Web,* students might be asked, "In what ways do Templeton, Charlotte, and Wilbur remind you of people you know?"

EVALUATION QUESTIONS ● Older, more experienced, readers (perhaps upper elementary or middle school) may be ready for the fourth level of questioning, which involves critical evaluation—that is, determining what makes a good book. Examples of an evaluation question might be, "Compare *Charlotte's Web* with Kenneth Grahame's *Wind in the Willows* or with Robert Lawson's *Rabbit Hill.*" "How are they alike?" "How are they different?" "Which is most believable and why?" "Compare *Charlotte's Web* with another of E. B. White's fantasies—*Stuart Little* or *Trumpet of the Swan.*" "What similarities do you see?" "What differences?" "If you prefer one over another, why?" The same kinds of questions might be asked of movies, artworks, and other matters that require an aesthetic judgment.

All these questions are attempting to help readers understand why they feel the way they do about a piece of literature.

Writing Experiences

As early as second grade, most children are capable of responding to literature through writing. Certainly by the time they reach the middle elementary grades, children should be writing as a regular part of their total curriculum. Several possibilities are available at all grade levels.

Webbing and Mapping

Webbing is a visual means of demonstrating relationships between story elements or concepts. A web consists of a figure (the simplest resembles a spider's web, which is where the term comes from) on which labels are placed showing the connections between aspects of a literary work. For example, the web in Figure 4.1 illustrates the ways in which the principal characters in the folktale "Cinderella" are opposites. Almost any image can be a potential tool for webbing or mapping a story. The petals of a flower, the steps of a stairway, the points of a star, or the branches of a tree are just some of the images that can be used to demonstrate the connections in a work of literature. For example, we might label the petals of a flower with a character's personality traits to show how the individual grows (or "blossoms") throughout the course of a story. Since many people are visual learners and grasp ideas more quickly if they can see them illustrated, webbing is an effective tool for examining relationships in a poem, story, or play.

Very similar to a web, a story map charts the progress of the plot in a visual manner. Figure 4.2 is a very simple story map illustrating the circular journey of Hansel and Gretel from their home to the witch's cottage and back. The labels suggest possible character development that might occur in the children along the way. In addition to being educational, a webbing exercise can be fun for children to create.

Response Journals

When we have to commit our ideas to writing, we are compelled to think them through thoroughly. A response journal, in which young readers can freely record their feelings, is an easy way to add this written dimension to their reading experience. One approach to a useful response journal is to have students write a paragraph after completing each chapter of a book. In that paragraph they may express whatever they wish about the characters, the plot, the setting, the theme, and so on. A more directed approach is to give students a set of

Figure 4.1 ● Web for "Cinderella"

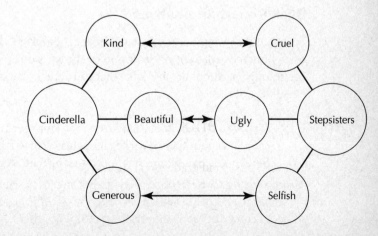

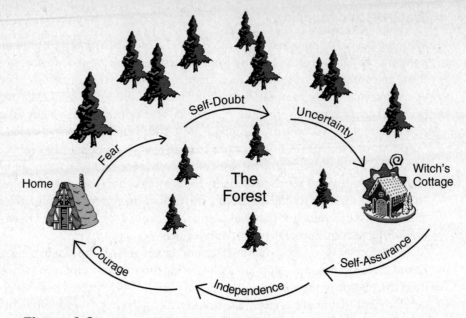

Figure 4.2 ● Story map for "Hansel and Gretel"

questions to respond to in their journals (review the various types of questions discussed above). Sharing journals (with other students, with teachers, with parents) can also be a rewarding experience, but if this is to happen, make sure the students know it from the beginning, for journal writing can be a very private affair. Under no circumstances should a private journal (even if the writer knows the teacher will be reading it) be shared with others. Journal writing is most effective when it is habitual and when the individual entries are long enough to explore ideas and feelings—two sentences do not make a journal entry.

Book Report Alternatives

For many, book reports conjure up dreary memories of dull and rambling plot summaries often inflicted on an entire classroom of students on an appointed day. However, many interesting variations are available that can actually be stimulating (see Figure 4.3). Here are a few suggestions:

- *Writing a New Episode.* Children may enjoy writing new, original episodes or book chapters about their favorite characters: Peggy Parrish's "Amelia Bedelia" series or Beverly Cleary's "Ramona" books can provide starting points for younger readers.
- *Writing a News Article.* Newspaper stories based on events in books can also be fun to write: Roald Dahl's *James and the Giant Peach* and *Charlie and the Chocolate Factory* offer some interesting possibilities here.

Figure 4.3 • Twenty-five things to do with a book

1. Create a story map for the book.
2. Prepare a two-minute radio spot promoting the book.
3. Write a biographical sketch of the author.
4. Turn one chapter into a child's picture book.
5. Create a collage or montage emphasizing the plot or theme.
6. Write a three- or four-paragraph book review for the local newspaper.
7. Create a dust jacket for the book.
8. Make a list of your 10 favorite things about the book.
9. Create a poster advertising the book.
10. Write a defense for the villain's actions.
11. Pick a favorite scene or chapter and prepare a dramatic reading.
12. Create a diorama of your favorite scene.
13. Create a mobile or stabile representing the theme or a character.
14. Make a cast list of well-known actors for a film of the book.
15. Create a geographical map of the setting based on evidence from the book.
16. Prepare a time line for events in the story.
17. Write a news article reporting on an event in the story, as if it just happened.
18. Write a new episode for the book using the same characters.
19. Create a bulletin board display to entice others to read the book.
20. Rewrite an episode from a different point of view.
21. Write a poem about the book.
22. Create a web illustrating the interactions of the main characters.
23. Rewrite a scene to include yourself as a new character.
24. Write a fictional biographical sketch of your favorite character.
25. Rewrite one chapter as a one-act play.

- *Writing about (or to) an Author.* Some children may enjoy reading and writing about the life of a favorite author. Perhaps some would like to write open letters to authors, living or dead, to share their own attitudes and opinions about a book. The letters do not need to be mailed—and many authors would prefer that they not be!
- *Writing an Imaginary Diary.* Writing the imaginary diary of a fictional character can help children understand the concept of point of view. It can also be fun to pretend to be someone else.

- *Writing a Script.* Scriptwriting, in which children must devise dialogue for characters, can enrich their understanding of language differences and characterization. They may, for instance, want to write a script for a television sit-com or a dramatic episode that they can then share with the class.

- *Plugging a Book.* Sometimes it is very useful to give children the opportunity to be book reviewers for the class—some may be familiar with film reviews on television. The opinions of their peers tend to carry far more weight with children than the opinions of adults. The success of the "Harry Potter" books had as much to do with the enthusiastic word of mouth from child to child as it did with clever marketing by adults.

Dramatic Experiences

Dramatic responses to literature offer opportunities for individual creativity and cooperative achievement. Most of the following dramatic exercises can be adapted to folktales or to chapters from favorite books.

Story Circle

Outside a little town in northern Michigan, poet-performer Terry Wooten has created an outdoor storytelling theater called the Stone Circle, where all are invited to share their stories, poems, and songs during the cool northern summer evenings. The atmosphere is magically charged with its dancing campfire and the primeval boulders forming the perimeter of the theater. It is reminiscent of an African community storytelling performance—a celebration of the oral culture. A similarly magical time can be had in less awesome circumstances, even in a classroom. The informality of the circular arrangement—where everyone is equal and there is no possibility of failure—makes this a potentially rewarding experience. Although at the Stone Circle performers must recite from memory or extemporize (no reading, in other words), it certainly would be permissible to allow young children to bring a favorite story or poem to read. Encouraging memorization might be a good goal, though. Requirements should be few—no one is called on and no one is required to speak. If the story circle concept is nurtured properly, in time, most will want to speak. It is a terrific way to remind children of the power of the spoken word.

Story Theater

Story theater is a pantomime accompanied by a narrator who reads or tells the story while others act out the plot. Since even inanimate objects (such as a tree) might be portrayed by an actor, story theater allows for a very flexible number of performers (some children may enjoy portraying objects like the moon, for example). The performance can be as simple or elaborate as the means dictate. Pantomime, because it does not require memorization, is one of the simpler dramatic forms for children. It does require one good reader, however, and some uninhibited actors. Since the youngest children tend to be the least inhibited, story theater is a good exercise to begin in the early elementary years. The best tales for a story theater presentation are those with plenty of action; otherwise the performers would be little more than furniture. Many folktales are good sources for story theater, particularly the farcical tales, such as "Clever Gretel," where action rather than dialogue dominates.

Reader's Theater

True reader's theater is traditionally performed without any action whatsoever. Instead, the readers are usually seated and each takes on one of the speaking parts in a script. The old-time radio dramas were, in essence, a form of reader's theater. All the audience's attention is directed to the language, so the readers must be expressive and read with clarity and precision. To avoid distraction from the reading, performers might want to wear uniform clothing—usually in black or black and white. But a reader's theater performance does not have to be a formal affair. It can be readily adapted to the classroom—even on an impromptu basis. It requires no memorization, physical movement, scenery, or properties—just a lively script. The best reader's theater stories are those with several speaking parts, ample dialogue, a fairly easy vocabulary but with expressive language, and, finally, a good conflict. "Hansel and Gretel," for example, would involve at least five characters (Hansel, Gretel, father, wicked stepmother, and witch) and a narrator (to read the exposition). To increase the number of parts so more readers can participate, it is easy to divide the narrator's part among several readers. The real fun in reader's theater happens when the readers themselves become engaged in their roles and begin to read with feeling and conviction. (See Recommended Readings at the end of this chapter for a good website for reader's theater resources.)

Puppet Theater

Combining both dramatic and artistic responses to literature, puppet theater is a favorite medium of young (and sometimes old) children. Puppet making is an elaborate and time-honored art form, but it is one that can be easily adapted for children of most ages. Puppets can be made from old socks, paper bags, construction paper and sticks, cardboard cylinders, vegetables (they make wonderful puppets, but don't wait too long to do the show), or, for the truly creative, string-operated marionettes with movable hands, feet, eyes, and mouths. The puppet theater itself can be as simple as a table draped with a sheet to hide the puppeteers. Large appliance boxes open up many possibilities. Once the puppet is made, the dramatic part of the experience begins. Stories with ample dialogue and action work best. And, since lines need not be memorized and the puppeteers are hidden from the audience's view, puppet theater can be an ideal form for beginning thespians. It is also perfect for shy children who, behind the mask of the puppet, may find an exhilarating outlet for their deepest feelings.

Creative Dramatics

Creative dramatics involves the dramatization of a story with improvised dialogue. This allows children to perform their own versions of stories without strict adherence to a script—although in creative dramatics, the actors are expected to remain faithful to the story line. This activity requires some preparation and may be as elaborate in setting, properties, and theatrical accoutrements as the director desires. Creative dramatics can be less intimidating than a more traditional play, since no one has to memorize lines. It also allows for improvisation. One of the great advantages of creative dramatics is that many folktales and other short stories or even chapters from favorite books (e.g., *Winnie-the-Pooh* or *The Wind in the Willows*) can be readily adapted to its form.

Artistic Experiences

Another popular means of exploring literature is through art. As soon as they can handle a crayon or pencil, even the youngest children can be asked to draw pictures in response to a story. And for older children, the possibilities are limitless.

Graphic Art

Children love working with paints, watercolors, crayons, and pencils. Drawings and paintings require the simplest of art supplies and minimal initial instruction, yet they allow for a great deal of originality. Having children draw pictures suggested by picture storybooks can be a means of getting them to explore different artistic styles, such as the Art Nouveau style of Kay Nielsen's illustrations for *East of the Sun, West of the Moon,* Beatrix Potter's delicate representational style in *The Tale of Peter Rabbit,* and Ludwig Bemelmans's expressionism in *Madeline.* (Illustrations from these works are shown in Chapter 7.) Encouraging children to draw pictures after hearing stories read to them can result in some of the most highly individualistic creations, for they do not have another artist's work to imitate.

For those who have limited graphic skills, a collage or montage is a viable alternative. A collage is a picture created from various materials (cloth, wood, cotton, leaves, rocks, and so on), that can be fixed to a posterboard or other surface to make a unified work. Quite similar is the montage, which is composed entirely of pictures (cut from magazines, newspapers, and so on). Creating a collage or a montage about a favorite story can be both enjoyable and enlightening, since it requires a certain amount of synthesis and analysis. Posters can be made to represent a theme, a character, plot details, or even mood, using the collage or montage method.

Plastic Art

The plastic arts include the three-dimensional works (unlike graphic works that generally are two-dimensional). Although sculpture and pottery can be unwieldy to create in the typical classroom, figures can be made from clay, paper, or wood to represent story characters or objects. Another artwork that can be accomplished in the classroom is the mobile, a free form usually cut from paper or cardboard and interconnected and suspended by string or wire so that when hung, the parts turn freely in the breeze. A mobile can demonstrate the relationships between plot elements or characters of a story. The diorama is a three-dimensional scene often created from a shoebox or other carton (an unused fish aquarium, with its glass sides, provides some interesting opportunities as well) and decorated with cardboard cutouts, plastic figures, or other suitable objects.

Creating Books

Making their own books is a rewarding activity for children of all ages, and it is an activity that combines a variety of literary experiences. Very young children can create alphabet, counting, or concept books, or do take-offs on favorite nursery rhymes or poems. Older children may want to experiment with ghost stories, adventure stories, family stories, or poetry. Books can be illustrated with a variety of media—crayon, watercolor, collage, montage, pencil, and so on. Binding the books can be as simple as fastening them in a loose-leaf folder or as elaborate as sewing the pages together and making cloth-covered cardboard covers. Not only does this project give children firsthand experiences in designing books and laying out pages, but it can also result in an attractive finished product suitable for a gift or a keepsake. Such a project is a rewarding way of bringing a writing exercise to a satisfying climax.

Regardless of the art project, it is important to remember that the art is an extension of the literature and not an end in itself. In other words, we are not reading *Pinocchio* for the purpose of making our own puppet when we are finished. And the art should not be simply gratuitous ("Now that we have read *Pinocchio,* let's all draw a picture of his nose"). The art project should become a meaningful part of the study of the literature, helping children to understand and appreciate the literature.

Summary

As adults we understand that we must attend to the physical and emotional well-being of children, but just as important is attending to their intellectual well-being. Today we live in a world beset by media—mostly visual, from computers to movies to television—all competing to see which can produce the wildest stimulation. This makes our encouragement of reading and of the love of books all the more important. Marshall McLuhan, a famous educator, categorized the various media—from lectures to seminars to photographs to radio to television to books (he lived before the widespread use of computers)—according to how much participation was required from the user. A hot medium requires very little participation (television was considered a hot medium, since it is possible to watch it without doing much thinking at all). A cool medium requires considerable participation and therefore encourages thought (a book was considered a very cool medium, since it requires constant effort on the reader—admittedly, some books require more effort than others). In other words, the cooler the medium, the more we have to think. That's why reading is so vital to one's mental development.

Reading should be at the center of the learning experience. But we also should look for ways to keep children engaged in their reading. The reader-response approach to literature is a method that encourages children to go beyond merely reading the words in a book, but invites them to bring their own personal responses to the reading, to find in the reading what is meaningful to them, and to explore the responses of others.

A variety of activities can help in achieving these goals. Some suggestions include reading aloud, storytelling, book discussions, writing experiences (including webbing, mapping, journal writing, and various written responses to books), dramatic experiences (including story circles, reader's theater, puppetry, and creative dramatics), artistic responses in both the graphic and plastic arts, and even creating original books. All these can broaden children's understanding, stimulate their imagination, and embolden their passion. A sign in one my favorite local bookstores advises—Eat, Sleep, Read. It really is that important.

For Reflection and Discussion

1. Read a children's story or a folktale and then write a personal response to it. Take into account what we have said about a reader's response to literature. What are the influences in your life that you think may have had an effect on your reading and interpretation?

2. Choose a favorite children's book and prepare a set of discussion questions that might be asked of elementary or middle school students, making sure to include all four levels of questioning.

3. Choose a favorite children's story—a folktale or any other story—and prepare a web or a story map that might be useful in illustrating some important aspect of the work.

4. Choose one of your favorite folktales and prepare an oral reading—or, better yet, an oral storytelling in your own words. Practice your storytelling technique until you feel completely comfortable and then seek an audience, preferably of young children. Enjoy your celebrity!

Work Cited

Purves, Alan, et al. *How Porcupines Make Love: Teaching a Response-Centered Literature Curriculum.* White Plains, NY: Longman, 1990.

Recommended Readings

This list barely scratches the surface, but it is intended only to provide examples of some of the methods discussed in the chapter. There is no shortage of ideas. Hundreds and hundreds of education books are in print with more coming out each year, and thousands of websites provide instructional materials as well.

Barton, Bob, and David Booth. *Stories in the Classroom.* Portsmouth, NH: Heinemann, 1991.

Blatt, Gloria T., ed. *Once Upon a Folktale: Capturing the Folklore Process with Children.* New York: Teachers College Press, 1993.

Bosma, Betty. *Fairy Tales, Fables, Legends, and Myths: Using Folk Literature in Your Classroom,* 2nd ed. New York: Teachers College Press, 1996.

Bromley, Karen D'Angelo. *Webbing with Literature: Creating Story Maps with Children's Books,* 2nd ed. New York: Simon & Schuster, 1995.

"Carol Hurst's Children's Literature Website" by Carol Otis Hurst and Rebecca Otis (a compendium of booklists and classroom ideas on a wide range of subjects), www.carolhurst.com.

Chambers, Aidan. *Introducing Books to Children,* 2nd ed. Boston: Horn Book, 1983.

Engler, Larry, and Carol Fijan. *Making Puppets Come Alive: How to Learn and Teach Hand Puppetry.* New York: Dover, 1997.

Hanford, Robert Ten Eyck. *Puppets and Puppeteering.* New York: Sterling, 1981.

Kennedy, John. *Puppet Planet: The Most Amazing Puppet-Making Book in the Universe.* Cincinnati, OH: North Light Books, 2006.

MacDonald, M. R. *The Storyteller's Sourcebook: A Subject, Title and Motif Index to Folklore Collections for Children.* Detroit, MI: Heal-Schuman, 1982.

McCaslin, Nellie. *Creative Drama in the Classroom and Beyond,* 8th ed. Boston: Allyn and Bacon, 2006.

Mikkelsen, Nina. *Powerful Magic: Learning from Children's Responses to Literature.* New York: Teachers College Press, 2005.

Norfolk, Sherry, Jane Stenson, and Diane Williams. *The Storytelling Classroom: Applications Across the Curriculum.* Westport, CT: Libraries Unlimited, 2006.

Pellowski, Ann. *The Storytelling Handbook: A Young People's Collection of Unusual Tales and Helpful Hints on How to Tell Them.* New York: Simon & Schuster, 1995.

Raines, Shirley, and Rebecca Isbell. *Tell It Again: Easy-to-Tell Stories with Activities for Young Children.* Beltsville, MD: Gryphon House, 2000.

"Reader's Theater Editions" by Aaron Shepherd (a fine source for free Reader's Theater scripts for elementary and middle school use), www.aaronshep.com.

Rothlein, Liz, and Anita Meyer Menibach. *Legacies: Using Children's Literature in the Classroom.* Boston: Allyn and Bacon, 1996.

Routman, Regie. *Transitions: From Literature to Literacy.* Portsmouth, NH: Heinemann, 1990.

Salem, Linda C. *Children's Literature Studies: Cases and Discussions.* Westport, CT: Libraries Unlimited, 2005.

Sawyer, Ruth. *The Way of the Storyteller.* New York: Penguin, 1942.

Schickedanz, J. A., and Renee Casberque. *Writing in Preschool: Learning to Orchestrate Meaning and Marks,* 2nd ed. Newark, DE: International Reading Association, 2009.

Shedlock, Marie. *The Art of the Storyteller*. 1915. New York: Dover, 1951.

Sloan, Glenna Davis. *The Child as Critic: Developing Literacy through Literature, K–8*, 4th ed. New York: Teachers College Press, 2003.

Trelease, Jim. *The Read-Aloud Handbook*, 6th ed. New York: Penguin, 2006.

Yopp, Ruth Helen, and Hallie Kay Yopp. *Literature-Based Reading Activities*, 5th ed. Boston: Allyn and Bacon, 2009.

PEARSON
myeducationkit

Go to the topic "Evaluating Children's Literature" on the MyEducationKit for this text, where you can:

- Search the Database of Children's Literature, housing more than 22,000 titles searchable in every genre by authors or illustrators, by awards won, by year published, and by topic and description.

- Explore genre-related Assignments and Activities, assignable exercises showing concepts in action through database use, video, cases, and student and teacher artifacts.

- Discover Web Links that will lead you to sites representing the authors you learn about in these pages, classrooms with powerful children's literature connections, and literature awards.

Reading the World
Cultural Diversity and Inclusion

Introduction

Dr. Martin Luther King Jr. dreamed of a time when we would all be judged not by the color of our skin but by the content of our character. He would have also added, I am sure, that we should not be judged by our religious beliefs, our gender, our sexual orientation, our disabilities, or anything else that makes us "different." Throughout history, these differences among us have resulted in a great deal of senseless strife, when, in fact, we should have been celebrating them. The famed socio-biologist Edward O. Wilson wrote that "diversity is the way a parent hedges its bets against an unpredictably changing environment" (122). In other words, if we were all exactly alike, our chances for survival would be diminished if some catastrophic event, such as an epidemic, occurred. Sameness is not only dull, it also leads to a general weakening of the species. So, it is in our differences, our diversity, that we often find our greatest strength.

Where, then, does our fear of differences come from? Ironically, the impulse to fear and mistrust those who are different from us is also part of our survival mechanism. We are wary of the unknown, the unfamiliar—and that makes us wisely cautious. If we're trudging through the jungle in the dark, we had better be fearful of the unknown. But if these fears are allowed to consume us and to overtake our rationality, they lead to bigotry and prejudice, which are ultimately destructive, both for the individual and for society.

How do we overcome bigotry and prejudice? How do we come to understand and accept human differences? Perhaps the best answer is education. We fear and mistrust what we don't understand. Usually, the greater our knowledge, the less our fear. Here is where books can help—especially children's books. One of the great benefits of children's literature is that it can broaden young minds and show children the fundamental humanity in all people regardless of their color, religious beliefs, language, and customs. Literature can expand our horizons, deepen our understanding, and show us ultimately that we are all in this world together, sharing the same fears, hopes, and dreams. Books tend to focus on individuals—not types. And when we begin to see people as individuals, it is not so easy to harbor bigotry and prejudice.

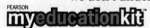

In this chapter we will be looking at books that can help raise our consciousness about other cultures and about people who face challenges different from our own. Reading their stories heightens our awareness and deepens our sensitivity.

Definition of Culturally Diverse Literature

Culturally diverse literature in the United States consists of stories about people outside the Anglo American ethnic group. Unfortunately, the appearance of heroes from minority cultural groups has been a belated one in children's literature. Only in the latter half of the twentieth century, beginning with the social movements of the 1960s, do we begin to see significant numbers of books about people outside the European American culture (or, for that matter, outside the Anglo American culture). The United States is one of the most culturally diverse nations on earth, and rather than let our diversity destroy us, we should embrace it. So it is vitally important that children's reading reflects the influence of African Americans, Native Americans, Latinos, Asian Americans, and the myriad other ethnic groups that make up our rich culture. But we should not forget that the true goal of recognizing cultural diversity is to bring about the inclusion of those diverse cultures into the wider circle of humanity.

Rudine Sims Bishop has very clearly identified the necessity for culturally diverse literature, as well as the detriment in not having it:

> If literature is a mirror that reflects human life, then all children who read or are read to need to see themselves reflected as part of humanity. If they are not, or if their reflections are distorted and ridiculous, there is the danger that they will absorb negative messages about themselves and people like them. Those who see only themselves or who are exposed to errors and misrepresentations are miseducated into a false sense of superiority, and the harm is doubly done. (quoted in Harris 43)

In other words, culturally diverse literature enriches everyone. First, it provides the minority cultures with positive role models and bolsters cultural pride and individual dignity. Second, it provides the majority culture with exposure to the various minority cultures and thus helps break down old prejudices and dispel misunderstandings.

Some critics insist that only members of an ethnic group can honestly write about that group. August Wilson, an African American playwright, argues that "someone who does not share the specifics of a culture remains outside, no matter how astute a student or well meaning the intentions" (quoted in Harris 42). Thus, Wilson insists that only African Americans should write about African Americans, only Native Americans about Native Americans, and so on. However, another African American, the critic Henry Louis Gates Jr. disagrees: "No human culture is so inaccessible to someone who makes the effort to understand, to learn, to inhabit another world" (Gates 30). In other words, Gates believes that a writer does not have to be African American to write about African Americans, but that writer does have to know a lot about them and has to be able to empathize with them, to walk in their shoes. Let us hope that Gates is correct, for that offers us the promise of a better world.

How can we tell if a writer is being culturally sensitive? To begin with, we can look for these qualities in a literary work about ethnic, racial, religious, or other groups:

1. The characters are portrayed as individuals, with genuine feelings, thoughts, and beliefs, and not as types representing a specific cultural group.

2. The characters' habits, language, and personality traits are individualized and not presented as habits or traits of an ethnic group.

3. The work is free from suggestions that all members of a specific cultural group share the same socioeconomic status and similar occupations, tastes, and so on.

4. The culture is portrayed respectfully and accurately, neither distorted nor romanticized.

5. The work is good on its own literary merits, and not simply because it happens to be about a certain ethnic group.

These statements should apply to all works that include specific cultural groups. What follows is a brief discussion of some of the major cultural groups in the United States and their treatment in modern children's literature.

Types of American Cultural Diversity

African Americans

Because of widespread racism, African Americans were seldom portrayed in children's books prior to the 1940s, and then usually as servants or other menials and almost always as comical characters that were easy targets for derision. Indeed, it is virtually impossible to find a picture book about an African American child published before the 1960s.

One of the first picture books featuring an African American protagonist was *The Snowy Day*, appearing in 1962. Written and illustrated by Ezra Jack Keats (who was, in fact, a white Jewish American), this Caldecott-Medal winning book describes a young, inner-city African American boy, Peter, enjoying the simple pleasures of the fresh snowfall one wintry day. Although the book lacks "cultural specificity"—that is, nothing except Peter's skin color identifies him as an African American—it remains an important groundbreaker and is still being enjoyed by children. The book has several sequels in which we see Peter gradually growing up. The importance of books like Keats's is that they dispel the stereotypes. Ever since the Civil War, racist whites had subjected African Americans to demeaning racial stereotypes, humiliating caricatures, and vicious epithets—all calculated to dehumanize them and thus make it easier to be cruel to them (for that is the purpose of stereotyping). In Peter, we see a boy with the same joys, hopes, worries, and fears shared by all children. He is just like us. Once African Americans begin to appear in literature as humanized characters with sensitively drawn human traits, then it is more difficult to maintain the cruel stereotypes.

Soon, other African American protagonists entered children's picture books, including Lucille Clifton's Everett Anderson (about whom we will learn more later on). Carolivia Herron's *Nappy Hair*, appearing in 1997, celebrates a young black girl's unruly, nappy hair—a feature that was once a source of ridicule from racist whites. In Herron's story, the hair becomes a proud symbol of the girl's black heritage. And Herron deftly recreates the joyous black dialect with its pattern of call and response, adding both flavor and authenticity to the story. White readers initially misinterpreted the book as racist, but black readers immediately recognized its positive message. (See the discussion on Censorship in Chapter 2.)

Books for older readers featuring African American protagonists can be traced back to 1945 when Jesse Jackson (not the minister/politician/activist) wrote what was considered a groundbreaking book, *Call Me Charley*. It is the story of a young African American boy attempting to assimilate into a white, middle-class neighborhood. Jackson deals frankly with racial conflict, and his main character, Charley, sets the tone when he retorts to a boy who refers to him as "Sambo": "My name is Charles . . . . Sometimes I'm called Charley. Nobody calls me Sambo and gets away with it" (8). The story seems dated now. Charley is finally accepted by the white community, but only because he abandons his black identity and his cultural roots. The book reflects the American attitudes in the 1940s, when everyone believed in the idea of the melting pot. Cultural minorities, if they wanted to fit in, were expected to give up their distinctive habits, language, dress, and so on and adopt the ways of the dominant white culture.

The Civil Rights Movement would change that, and by the 1970s, many books began to appear that extolled African American values and cultural identity. Award-winning writers such as Virginia Hamilton (*The Planet of Junior Brown*), Rosa Guy (*Ruby*), Walter Dean Myers (*Scorpion*), and Jacqueline Woodson (*Locomotion*) have captured the vitality of the African American culture, dispelling stereotypes and portraying genuine, flesh-and-blood characters engaged in the business of living. In books like Mildred Taylor's *Roll of Thunder, Hear My Cry* and Christopher Paul Curtis's *The Watsons Go to Birmingham—1963* and *Bud, Not Buddy*, we are given vivid portrayals of America's deep-seated racism. As with all good literature, these stories compel us to re-examine our own lives and attitudes.

The establishment of the Coretta Scott King Award in 1970, honoring African American contributions to children's literature, has helped to encourage continued high quality in the field of African American literature.

Native Americans

Native Americans have been the subject of a mythology that continues to cloud the general public's perception. Too often we lump together all Native Americans (some Native Americans prefer the term *American Indian* and still others prefer *Amerind*) into one vision of a beaded, feathered, and moccasined warrior. For a long time, children's picture books either ignored the Native American altogether or fell back on the stereotypes. Perhaps too many still do. Native Americans argue that even today's picture books rely on the old images and fail to portray the modern American Indian realistically. Indeed, by and large, picture books on Native Americans continue to focus on the traditional images and ignore the fact that currently about two million Native Americans live in the United States without teepees, headdresses, or bows and arrows. They have homes, cars, careers, hobbies—but they also enjoy a rich and ancient heritage.

Some of the finest examples of Native American literature are found in the ample store of folktales that have been collected, many in handsomely illustrated books (including those by Joseph Bruchac, Craig Kee Strete, and others). The best of these children's versions of the folktales identify the specific Native American tribal affiliations (e.g., Iroquois, Sioux, Ojibway, etc.) and the Native tellers themselves.

Two important and popular types of Native American literature are historical fiction and nonfiction. Since about 1970, the predominant theme of this literature is the correcting of misconceptions (about the relationships between whites and American Indians, for example). Scott O'Dell, although not Native American himself, was one of the earliest children's writers to attempt to set the record straight. His *Sing Down the Moon* is a fictionalized account of the brutal, forced relocation of the Navajo in the nineteenth century. Margaret Craven's *I Heard the Owl Call My Name* is the story of a priest sent to work in a First Nations parish on the coast of British Columbia (in Canada, the native populations are referred to as First Nations). This moving and beautiful story describes the priest's coming to terms with the traditional native culture, as well the difficulties facing that culture and its survival in the modern world.

True stories are every bit as compelling as fiction. Ignatia Broker's *Night Flying Woman: An Ojibway Narrative* describes the life of the author's great-great-grandmother and the uprooting of her people by nineteenth-century whites. For works with a modern setting, we have the compelling stories of Alexie Sherman, including *The Absolutely True Story of a Part-Time Indian,* describing life on a reservation, and *War Dances,* a collection of writings expressing the writer's keen observations on modern Native American life. Sherman's works are acutely realistic, with a healthy dose of humor.

The themes of most of the books on contemporary Native Americans include the need to preserve cultural identity and the importance of the extended family. Culturally conscious books include portraits of Native Americans as individuals, sensitive descriptions of Native American cultural traditions, and an awareness that each Native American society is a distinctive cultural entity—that there are Ojibway, Iroquois, Sioux, and so on. These books reject demeaning vocabulary, artificial dialogue, and cruel and insensitive Indian stereotypes. Donnarae MacCann suggests that we ask ourselves: "[I]s there anything in the book that would make a Native American child feel embarrassed or hurt to be what he or she is? Can the child look at the book and recognize and feel good about what he or she sees?" (quoted in Harris 161).

Latinos/Latinas

The term "Hispanic American" refers to those whose heritage is derived from the Spanish-speaking nations south of the U. S. border; whereas "Latino" ("Latina" is the feminine form) is a broader term, including those of Portuguese-speaking Brazilian heritage. Latino is gradually becoming the more popular term, especially among the younger generations. Latinos are the largest minority group in the United States. Their culture has been characterized by the Spanish language, the Roman Catholic Church, and by the folk traditions of Central and Latin America. They are a group still vastly underrepresented in children's books and their portrayal has been controversial. Unfortunately, we still find in the modern media the unfair and negative stereotypes of the criminal alien or the helpless victim, the volatile Latin temperament, the male machismo, and so on. Although children's books usually avoid these stereotypes, they do often portray an overabundance of poor migrant workers or other rural laborers. This image is quite contrary to the reality. Today, most Latinos are city dwellers, and they can be found in all walks of life.

We are now seeing more and more writers of Latino heritage producing some very fine works for young readers. One popular Latino American author, Gary Soto, has distinguished himself as both a poet and a storyteller, with prose works like *Baseball in April* and *Buried Onions*, and the poetry collections including *A Fire in My Hands* and *Canto Familia*. His subjects are modern-day Latino children pursuing their hopes and dreams like all other children. Pat Mora has published several poetry collections, including *Borders, Chants,* and *Communion,* in addition to several family stories for young children, such as *A Birthday Basket for Tia.* Mora's poems for young children are filled with images of the Southwest and Latino culture, and throughout she scatters Spanish expressions, reminders that the Latino culture is a culture of two languages. Latina writer Sandra Cisneros gained fame for her book for older children, *The House on Mango Street.* All these writers focus on the importance of the family—especially the extended family—in the Latino community, which is key to their personal identity. The characters also tend to be bilingual, which allows them to cling to their traditional heritage as well as function successfully in the English-speaking culture. The prevalence of the Spanish language in the United States has inspired a new trend in modern picture books—the dual-language book, such as Carmen Lomas Garza's *Family Picture/Cuadros de Familia.*

It is a demographic reality that in the coming years Latinos will assume increasing social and political influence in American society. There has never been a greater need for sensitive, honest, and intelligent children's books representing Latino culture.

Asian Americans

Asian Americans, too, have been subjected to unkind stereotypes—misogynistic males, submissive females, all speaking English very poorly and being reticent and docile. Claire Huchet Bishop's *Five Chinese Brothers*, published first in 1938, is an example of what was thought to be an innocent folktale that took on racial overtones. The text tells us, for example, that the five brothers "all look alike," and Kurt Wiese's illustrations have been criticized for caricaturing Chinese stereotypes. (This story has also been criticized because of violent references in the text—an issue we will discuss in Chapter 9.) To be sure, we have to take into consideration the book's age and that it reflects the attitudes of an earlier era. But that argument will mean little to 5- and 6-year-old children (the presumed audience of *The Five Chinese Brothers*). When using a book portraying another culture, our first concerns should be whether it would offend any member of the audience and whether it would create inaccurate or unfavorable views about the culture being represented.

Naturally, the most responsible modern writers and illustrators try to undo the deplorable stereotypes of Asian Americans, and this often begins with distinguishing between the multitude of Asian cultures—many of whom have little in common with each other. To lump people of Chinese, Japanese, Korean, Thai, and Vietnamese descent all together as if they were a single national/ethnic group is both inaccurate and insensitive. Literature can and should reflect these differences and celebrate their distinctions.

Today, several writers and illustrators are producing beautiful picture books that accurately evoke Asian and Asian American cultures. Ed Young has both written and illustrated children's books reflecting his passion for his native China and his art reflects the influence of traditional Chinese painting. His *Lon Po Po: A Red-Riding Hood Story from China* won the 1990 Caldecott Medal. Allen Say's beautifully illustrated books, such as *Grandfather's Journey* (the 1994 Caldecott medalist), which tells the story of Japanese American immigrants, are fine examples of culturally sensitive narratives.

Laurence Yep's *Dragonwings*, a work for older children, describes life as it was lived in San Francisco's Chinatown in the early 1900s. In *Coolies*, Rosanna Yin describes the experiences of the earliest Chinese immigrants, the workers who helped lay the transcontinental railroad in the nineteenth century. *A Step from Heaven*, by An Na, describes the difficult experiences of a young Korean girl growing up in America. The harrowing story of the Japanese American internment during World War II has given rise to several moving books, both fictional and historical. Perhaps the most famous is the autobiographical *Farewell to Manzanar* by Jeanne Wakatsuki and James D. Houston.

Jewish Americans

Judaism as a culture transcends national boundaries. Jewish Americans have long played crucial roles in American culture, including the arts, business, education, and politics. On the other hand, anti-Semitism has been a blot on Western civilization, and the United States has its own history of discrimination against Jews. Of course, when we think of anti-Semitism, most of us see visions of the Holocaust and the slaughter of six million innocent victims of the Nazi regime. Indeed, when it comes to children's literature about Judaism, stories of the Holocaust dominate the list. Anne Frank's *The Diary of a Young Girl*, a teenager's firsthand account of the horrors of the Nazi occupation of the Netherlands, is the most famous. Other memoirs include Aranka Siegal's *Upon the Head of a Goat: A Childhood in Hungary, 1939–1944*, describing the atrocities perpetrated in eastern Europe. Lois Lowry's

Number the Stars is a fictional account of events in war-torn Denmark during the Nazi occupation. Lowry writes for readers in upper elementary grades, and although her story is far more hopeful than most (she tells how the vast majority of Danish Jews were saved through the brave efforts of their Danish friends), she does not sugarcoat her message.

Aside from books about the Holocaust, books about Jewish culture tend to fall into three categories: folktales, informational books, and contemporary novels. Isaac Bashevis Singer, the Nobel laureate, recorded many tales of Jewish life, including *Shlemiel Went Warsaw and Other Stories, Zlateh the Goat and Other Stories,* and *Mazel and Shlimazel.* These are partly his own original stories and partly retellings of traditional Jewish folktales that he heard as a child. They are filled with a rich sense of humanity and the warm humor often associated with Jewish culture. The informational books generally describe Jewish customs and religious rituals. Michele Lee Meyer's *My Daddy Is Jewish and My Mommy Is Christian* is a picture book that describes circumstances becoming increasingly familiar in U.S. society. Among the novelists, one of the most celebrated is Chaim Potok, whose *My Name Is Asher Lev* is the story of a young Hasidic Jew, an artist engaged in the conflict between his faith and his art as well as tradition and modernity. Teenage readers, both Jewish and non-Jewish, will recognize the coming-of-age struggles, the familial strife, and the personal doubts that face the protagonist. As we have already noted, one of the benefits from reading books about people from other cultures is that we discover how much alike we all are.

Other Cultures

Not surprisingly, one culture that has attracted tremendous interest in the past few years is the Muslim culture (or Islam). We should perhaps say "cultures" since, like Christianity and Judiasm, the Muslim faith consists of many variations. Recent books about the Muslim culture reveal several tendencies. Demi's *Muhammad* is a picture book describing the life of the prophet who founded the faith in the seventh century. Joelle Stoltz's *The Shadows of Ghadames* is a novel set in Libya in the nineteenth century, providing some historical perspective on Islam. And Elizabeth Fama's *Overboard* is set in Indonesia (the world's most populous Muslim country) and is a contemporary story that brings together Muslims and Western Christians. It is impossible to cover all cultures and ethnic groups, and any omission here is not intended as a slight. Any good book about a culture or a place or a people we do not know can only make us better world citizens—tolerant, understanding, and empathetic.

Rosa Guy, a distinguished writer of books for young adults (*The Friends, Ruby,* and others) and a native of the former British colony of Trinidad, has issued this call to arms for all cultural groups:

> *I reject the young of each succeeding generation who dare to say: "I don't understand you people . . ." "I can't stand those people . . ." or, "Do you see the way they act . . .?" They are us! Created by us for a society which suits our ignorance.*

I insist that Everychild understand this. I insist that Everychild go out into the world with this knowledge: there are no good guys. There are no bad guys. We are all good guys. We are all bad guys. And we are all responsible for each other. (34)

Gender Awareness

Another part of cultural awareness is gender awareness—specifically, the fair treatment of the sexes. For thousands of years, most of human society has been male dominated, effectively relegating the woman's position to one of subservience. Society has come to value the so-called masculine traits of physical strength, assertiveness, independence, power, aggressiveness, and ambition, and to devalue the so-called feminine traits of passivity, docility, emotionalism, physical weakness, dependence, and accommodation. These stereotypes are both inaccurate and unfair—to both men and women. We see this bias in three distinct areas.

1. Gender-based language refers to the labels we use in speaking and writing, such as using "he" to mean both men and women, or using words such as "chairman," "mailman," "policeman," and "businessman"—all of which remind us of the historical dominance of the male. We use "sissy" as a disparaging term, but it's seen as good for someone to "stand up and take it like a man."

2. Gender roles still plague our society, which often assigns dominating roles to men and subservient roles to women. Earlier children's books show us doctors, bankers, pilots, and school principals as males; whereas nurses, secretaries, flight attendants, and teachers are females. Books that persist in these stereotypes only reinforce old gender biases in our society.

3. Gender behavior casts men and women in predetermined roles. Our society has traditionally differentiated between what it perceives to be male and female behavior or standards of conduct. Women have been cast as the fairer sex, but also the weaker sex—weaker physically, emotionally, and intellectually. Males, conversely, have been seen as physically strong, emotionally stable, and intellectually superior, but also insensitive, self-important, and, in some cases, inept. Hence, the male child is expected to be physically active, even mischievous. The female child who shows such traits may be labeled a "tomboy," another disparaging term. Tears are expected of a female and condemned in a male, and so on. Of course, all this is nonsense and we should learn to reject such stereotypes.

Children need books that portray positive images of women and men, without the stereotyping of roles and behavior. We can find books with clever and independent heroines such as Louise Fitzhugh's *Harriet the Spy* or Mildred Taylor's *Roll of Thunder, Hear*

My Cry, and there are books with sensitive males, such as Beverly Cleary's *Dear Mr. Henshaw.*

However, we do have to give a pass to exceptional books from earlier eras even though they possess gender and cultural stereotypes. We can't fault a nineteenth-century writer such as Mark Twain because his language seems gender biased or he stereotypes female and male roles. That doesn't mean his books aren't insightful, wise, and entertaining. If we rejected books from the past because they do not live up to our standards of gender decorum, we would have to eliminate virtually everything written before about 1970. That would be ridiculous. To use a well-worn saw, let's not toss the baby out with the bathwater. But, as stated earlier, young readers may not always appreciate the fact that an attitude or viewpoint found in a book from an earlier era is no longer acceptable. So, we ultimately have to fall back on our own better judgment, and I would suggest erring on the side of honesty and openness.

Alternative Families

I grew up watching the sitcoms of the 1950s—*Father Knows Best, Leave It to Beaver, The Donna Reed Show,* and so on. Perhaps I enjoyed them, but I certainly did not identify with them. How different those families were from my own blended family of stepparents and step- and half-siblings, which, I concluded, made us outsiders. I now know that few children grow up in homes in the suburbs with two parents, a sibling, and a dog. No longer do most mothers don their aprons in the morning and spend their days cleaning and cooking for their families, while the fathers head off to the office and bring home the bacon. Single-parent homes are commonplace, and the vast majority of women now work outside the home. Modern children's books are at last coming to reflect this reality. Children who have stepparents, step-siblings, and half-siblings may find comfort in books depicting other families like theirs. Books that were once controversial, such as Norma Klein's *Mom, the Wolfman, and Me,* which deals with an unmarried mother, her boyfriend, and her daughter, are now commonplace. Katherine Paterson's *The Great Gilly Hopkins,* about an unruly child in foster care, and Cynthia Voigt's *Homecoming,* about four children abandoned by their mother in a parking lot, are tragically realistic in their portrayal of modern dysfunctional families.

Another family-related issue, child abuse—physical, emotional, and sexual—has come late to children's books, despite the fact that it is one that concerns children deeply. Among the recent offerings on the subject are Chris Crutcher's *Staying Fat for Sarah Byrnes,* James Howe's *The Watcher,* and Mirjam Pressler's *Halinka.* This subject, like so many delicate issues, has been swept under society's carpet of respectability for too long. We do no service to young people by ignoring the problem, and, in the hands of a capable writer, much good can come of sharing both facts and feelings.

The Physically, Emotionally, and Intellectually Challenged

Another change taking place in our society is a more receptive attitude toward individuals with special needs. These individuals were once virtually ignored in children's books, undoubtedly a holdover from the time when people with physical, emotional, or intellectual differences were largely hidden away from society—either institutionalized or secluded at home. Society is now more sensitive to the needs of this group. Our laws now recognize the existence of physically challenged individuals, and our schools seek to include and accommodate all children. Among the children's books dealing with these issues are Taro Yashima's *Crow Boy*, about a Japanese boy suffering from shyness; Lucille Clifton's *My Friend Jacob*, describing the relationship between a young black boy and his older white friend who is intellectually challenged; and Virginia Hamilton's *Sweet Whispers, Brother Rush*, about a family coping with an inherited mental disorder. Physical disabilities are featured in such books as Carolyn Meyer's *Killing the Kudu*, which tackles stereotypes about people in wheelchairs.

The Challenges of Life—The Hard Issues

Life, under the best of circumstances, is not easy, and children discover that all too soon, despite the concerted efforts of well-meaning adults to protect them from its harsh realities. Marriages end in divorce, loved ones die, violence disrupts the city, war disrupts the society. Oftentimes, the very books that children need to be reading are the ones that adults want to keep from them—books about death, about divorce, about violence and war. Although, as adults, our first instinct is to protect and shelter our children from the hard facts of life, we should, instead, be preparing them. Now, this doesn't mean that we should go around bursting their bubbles of optimism and idealism. Preparing them for the hard facts of life is something we can accomplish with sensitivity and gentleness.

Death is often the first of life's difficult hurdles that children must confront—the deaths of pets, grandparents, even, sadly, parents, siblings, and friends. Books addressing the issue of death need not sugarcoat or sentimentalize the fact. The loss is painful. The sorrow is profound and necessary, but not permanent. Margaret Wise Brown's *The Dead Bird* is a simple picture book about a group of children who find a dead bird and proceed to give it a proper burial. After the obsequies, which are solemn and touching, the children soon find themselves engaged once again in play—the business of their lives, as it should be. Death is presented as part of the natural cycle of life, as *The Book of Common Prayer* correctly tells us, "In the midst of life, we are in death." Sometimes, death is approached metaphorically, as in *The Heart and the Bottle* by Oliver Jeffers, in which a young girl's grief over the death of her father—which is only implied, never obliquely stated—causes her to "bottle up" her heart. Only when she has accepted the loss and recognized that beauty and joy still exist in the world is she able to let her heart out of the bottle and move on—keeping the good memories. The best children's books about death are probably those that deal in metaphor and that resist the temptation to offer simple platitudes. We need to remember that not everyone shares our own spiritual outlook, not everyone is assuaged by a promise of an afterlife. Laura and Marc Brown's *When Dinosaurs Die,* like *The Dead Bird,* a story for young children, presents an honest description of death and sorrow, funeral and burial customs, and various interpretations of what happens after death. It is a fine representative of a book that respects all beliefs and honors all cultures.

Another issue that confronts many children in today's society is divorce. Although many manuals exist that explain how children can cope through this difficult time, for younger children a story is often the best way. Lucille Clifton's *Everett Anderson's 1-2-3* is one of a series of picture books about a young African American boy as he moves through a series of family adjustments—in this book, it is his parents' divorce. Other books show him coping with his mother's remarriage, a new sibling, and, eventually, his father's death. Unlike the how-to manuals, which can be dull and preachy (although the best are very helpful), Clifton's stories are told in lovely poetic lines and they show children surviving in a world that is not always kind, not always joyful, not always fair—in other words, they give us real life.

Surprisingly, we can find books for very young children on such unlikely subjects as war and its grim effects and even street violence. Why introduce such elements into a child's book? Quite simply because children are not immune from the effects of these dreadful experiences. Today in the United States there are far too many children who know the tragedy of losing a parent to war. We would not expect children to understand the politics of war, or its history, or its purpose (do we understand that ourselves?). Instead, children's books on war deal with the effects it has on society, on families, on individuals. One profoundly moving book is Roberto Innocenti and Christophe Gallaz's *Rose Blanche,* a story of a little German girl who discovers a Nazi concentration camp during World War II and secretly brings food to the prisoners. The uncompromising ending is sensitively handled and, although very sad, it is not without hope for the future.

One other subject that always stirs up controversy is that of homosexuality. Today, few subjects for children at puberty are so delicate as homosexuality. Virtually ignored—even taboo—in children's literature until the 1980s, sexual preference is now being recognized by many writers as an important social issue about which children need sensitive education. Pioneering works in this field include John Donovan's *I'll Get There. It Better Be Worth the Trip* and Isabelle Holland's *The Man Without a Face.* Other treatments of the subject include Marion Dane Bauer's *Am I Blue?: Coming Out from the Silence* (a selection of short stories by various writers), M. E. Kerr's *Deliver Us from Evie* (about a teenage lesbian), and Paula Fox's *The Eagle Kite.*

But books on homosexuality are not restricted to those for older children. Michael Willhoite's *Daddy's Roommate,* first published in 1991, is a picture book for preschoolers describing the weekends a young boy spends with his father and his father's male companion. You may wonder about the appropriateness of this subject for so young an audience. But today more and more children are raised by gay couples and small children are naturally curious. *Daddy's Roommate* is an example of an honest, yet sensitive, treatment of a subject many people find difficult to discuss. The simple illustrations and straightforward story told by a child narrator provide just the right amount of information for very young readers—the book concludes with the statement that being gay is just "one more kind of love." It is never too early to begin the campaign to stamp out bigotry and prejudice.

No one is suggesting that teachers should use these books in their classrooms—few of them were ever intended for that. But it is important for us to realize that these issues are not isolated, and that they affect a broad spectrum of our population. Knowing about some of these titles, being aware that these subjects are dealt with in good children's books, will come in handy at some point. Learning about the difficult issues of life through reputable books, sensitively written, and under the guidance of a caring and knowledgeable adult is surely preferable to picking up rumor and misinformation from the streets and playgrounds.

Summary

As human beings, our ability to flourish in the world has depended greatly on our diversity and our ability to adapt to ever new environments. Reading can help us in our efforts to adapt, for books enrich our personal experiences, enlarge our horizons, and nurture tolerance and understanding. And today's children's books present a wealth of possibilities for helping children toward those goals. Books about cultures different from ours and about people who worship different gods, practice different customs, hold different beliefs, and enjoy different lifestyles are now readily available. Reading a book is like throwing open a window. Perhaps such books will help society along toward one of its most important goals—to acknowledge the great proclamation in the *Universal Declaration of Human Rights* that "All human beings are born free and equal in dignity and rights."

In our effort to find children's books that treat all people with fairness and sensitivity, we can observe a few general guidelines:

- The author treats the subject with intelligence—no sloppy or incorrect facts.
- The author treats the subject with sensitivity—no prejudice or callousness.
- The characters are portrayed without sentimentality—pity is not the answer.
- The characters are portrayed with realism—pain, doubt, fear, even death are all a part of this realism (otherwise it's a fantasy).
- The solutions, when solutions are offered, seem to grow naturally from the characters and situations—no magic pills, no silver bullets, no fairy godmothers.

- The author does not let a didactic message get in the way of a good story—for then it would be a sermon. Most readers will forgive an author anything but boredom.

Finally, and most importantly, we should remember that the goal of celebrating diversity is really inclusion. It was perhaps best said by the popular American poet, Edwin Markham (1852–1940), when he wrote the following poem, titled "Outwitted":

He drew a circle that shut me out —
Heretic, rebel, a thing to flout.
But Love and I had the wit to win:
We drew a circle that took him in.

For Reflection and Discussion

1. Locate and read a book intended for young people (up through middle school) that deals with your personal cultural heritage or with a special issue with which you have some personal experience (gender, alternative family lifestyle, physical or emotional challenges, sexual preference, and so on). How do you feel the book deals with the issue? Is it fair, accurate, honest, complete? Is it interestingly written?

2. Locate and read a book intended for young people that deals with an ethnic or religious culture that you would like to learn more about. What did you learn about the culture? Does it seem to be represented accurately and sensitively? Do you see any evidence of stereotyping? When was the book published? How does that make a difference in your evaluation of the book?

3. Locate three or four picture books that all focus on one social or personal issue (such as three or four books on human sexuality or on alternate lifestyles or on emotional or physical challenges, and so on). Determine the intended audience— and note the publication date—for each book. Now read the books carefully and evaluate them on their content and approach. Is the subject represented accurately and sensitively? What differences do you see in the treatment of the subject? Does one book stand out from the rest? Why?

4. Locate a children's picture book on a controversial issue (death, sex, war, violence, and other such topics) and read it carefully yourself. Then share it with several different people—children would be ideal, but you may also want to share it with some friends both male and female to get as many points of view as possible. What have you learned through this experience? Did your response to the book change over the course of the various readings? Explain.

Works Cited

Gates, Henry Louis, Jr. "'Authenticity,' or The Lesson of Little Tree." *The New York Times* 24 (November 1991): 1, 26–30.

Guy, Rosa. "Innocence, Betrayal, and History." *School Library Journal* (November 1985): 33–34.

Harris, Violet, ed. *Teaching Multicultural Literature in Grades K–8*. Norwood, MA: Christopher-Gordon, 1993.

Wilson, Edward O. *On Human Nature*. Cambridge, MA: Harvard University Press, 1978.

Recommended Readings

Belensky, Mary Field, and others. *Women's Ways of Knowing*. New York: Harper, 1986.

Benes, Rebecca C. *Native American Picture Books of Change: The Art of Historic Children's Editions*. Santa Fe: Museum of New Mexico Press, 2004.

Botello, Maria José, and Marsha Kabakow Rudman. *Critical Multicultural Analysis of Children's Literature: Mirrors, Windows, and Doors*. (Language, Culture, and Teaching Series). New York: Routledge, 2009.

Day, Frances A. *Lesbian and Gay Voices: An Annotated Bibliography and Guide to Literature for Children and Young Adults*. Westport, CT: Greenwood, 2000.

Dowd, F. S. "Evaluating Children's Books Portraying Native American and Asian Cultures." *Childhood Education* 68, 4(1992): 219–224.

Fox, Dana L., and Kathy G. Short, eds. *Stories Matter: The Complexity of Cultural Authenticity in Children's Literature*. Urbana, IL: NCTE, 2003.

Frye, Northrop. *The Educated Imagination*. Bloomington: Indiana University Press, 1969.

Gebel, Doris. *Crossing Boundaries with Children's Books*. Lanham, MD: Scarecrow, 2006.

Gilligan, Carol. *In a Different Voice*. Cambridge, MA: Harvard University Press, 1982.

Gilliland, Hap. *Indian Children's Books*. Billings: Montana Council for Indian Education, 1980.

Giorgis, Cyndi, and Janelle Mathis. "Visions and Voices of American Indians in Children's Literature." *The New Advocate* 8, 2 (Spring 1995): 125–142.

Harada, V. H. "Issues of Ethnicity, Authenticity, and Quality in Asian-American Picture Books, 1983-93." *Journal of Youth Services in Libraries* 8, 2(1995): 135–149.

Harris, Violet J. "Continuing Dilemmas, Debates, and Delights in Multicultural Literature." *The New Advocate* 9, 2 (Spring 1996): 107–122.

Lindgren, Merri V. *The Multicultural Mirror: Cultural Substance in Literature for Children and Young Adults*. Fort Atkinson, WI: Highsmith Press, 1991.

Lo, Suzanne, and Ginny Lee. "Asian Images in Children's Books: What Stories Do We Tell Our Children?" *Emergency Librarian* 20, 5 (May–June 1993): 14–18.

Manna, Anthony L., and Carolyn S. Brodie, eds. *Many Faces, Many Voices: Multicultural Literary Experiences for Youth*. Fort Atkinson, WI: Highsmith, 1992.

McCann, Donnarae, and Gloria Woodard. *The Black American in Books for Children: Readings in Racism*. Metuchen, NJ: Scarecrow, 1985.

McIntosh, Peggy. "White Privilege: Unpacking the Invisible Knapsack." *Peace and Freedom* (July/August 1989): 10–12.

Miller-Lachman, L., ed. *Our Family, Our Friends, Our World: An Annotated Guide to Significant Multicultural Books for Children and Teenagers*. New Providence, NJ: R. R. Bowker, 1992.

Pang, V. O., C. Colvin, M. Tran, and R. H. Barba. "Beyond Chopsticks and Dragons: Selecting Asian-American Literature for Children." *The Reading Teacher* 46, 3 (1992): 216–224.

Pratt, Linda, and Janice J. Beaty. *Transcultural Children's Literature*. Upper Saddle River, NJ: Merrill/Prentice Hall, 1999.

Rochman, Hazel. *Against Borders: Promoting Books for a Multicultural World*. Chicago: American Library Association, 1993.

Rudman, Masha K. *Children's Literature: An Issues Approach*, 3rd ed. New York: Longman, 1995.

Sims, Rudine. *Shadow & Substance: Afro-American Experience in Contemporary Children's Fiction.* Urbana, IL: NCTE, 1982.

———. "Walk Tall in the World: African-American for Today's Children." *Journal of Negro Education* 58 (1990): 556–565.

Smith, Katherine Capshaw. *Children's Literature of the Harlem Renaissance.* Bloomington IN: Indiana University Press, 2004.

Selected Bibliography of Culturally Diverse and Inclusive Children's Books

The following list contains a sampling of fictional works focusing on diverse cultural groups. Also look for other books by these authors.

African American

Brooks, Bruce. *Everywhere.* New York: Harper, 1990.

Brooks, Gwendolyn. *Bronzeville Boys and Girls.* 1967. Illus. Faith Ringgold. New York: Amistad, 2006.

Bryan, Ashley. *All Night, All Day: A Child's First Book of African-American Spirituals.* New York: Atheneum, 1991.

Childress, Alice. *A Hero Ain't Nothin' But a Sandwich.* New York: Coward, 1973.

Clifton, Lucille. *All Us Come Cross the Water.* New York: Holt, 1973.

Crews, Nina, illus. *The Neighborhood Mother Goose.* New York: Amistad, 2003.

Curry, Barbara K., and James Michael Brodie. *Sweet Words So Brave: The Story of African American Literature.* Middleton, WI: Zino, 1996.

Curtis, Christopher Paul. *Bud, Not Buddy.* New York: Scholastic, 2000.

Dawes, Kwame. *I Saw Your Face.* Illus. Tom Feelings. New York: Dial, 2005.

Diakité, Penda. *I Lost My Tooth in Africa.* Illus. Baba Wagué Diakité. New York: Scholastic, 2006.

Dunbar, Paul. *Little Brown Baby.* 1895. New York: Dodd, Mead, 1968.

Duncan, Alice Faye. *Honey Baby Sugar Child.* Illus. Susan Keeter. New York: Simon & Schuster, 2005.

Feelings, Tom. *The Middle Passage: White Ships/Black Cargo.* New York: Dial, 1995.

———. *Soul Looks Back in Wonder.* New York: Dial, 1993. (A collection of poems for all ages)

Fox, Paula. *The Slave Dancer.* New York: Bradbury, 1973.

Giovanni, Nikki. *Shimmy Shimmy Shimmy Like My Sister Kate: Looking at the Harlem Renaissance Through Poems.* New York: Holt, 1996.

Greenfield, Eloise. *Big Friend, Little Friend.* New York: Black Butterfly Children's Books, 1991.

Grimes, Nikki. *The Road to Paris.* New York: Putnam, 2006.

Guy, Rosa. *Ruby.* New York: Viking, 1976.

Hamilton, Virginia. *M. C. Higgins, the Great.* New York: Macmillan, 1974.

Herron, Carolivia. *Nappy Hair.* Illus. Joe Cepeda. New York: Knopf, 1997.

Hoffman, Mary. *Amazing Grace.* Illus. Caroline Binch. New York: Dial, 1991.

Hunter, Kristin. *Guests in the Promised Land.* New York: Schribner's, 1973.

Johnson, Angela. *Wind Flyer.* Illus. Loren Long. New York: Simon & Schuster, 2007.

Jordan, June. *His Own Where.* New York: Crowell, 1971.

Langstaff, J. *What a Morning! The Christmas Story in Black Spirituals.* New York: Margaret K. McElderry, 1987.

Mathis, Sharon Bell. *Teacup Full of Roses.* New York: Viking, 1972.

McKissack, Patricia. *Mirandy and Brother Wind*. New York: Knopf, 1988.

McKissack, Patricia, and Frederick McKissack. *The Long Hard Journey*. New York: Knopf, 1989.

McKissack, Patricia, and Jean Moss Onawumi. *Precious and the Boo Hag*. Illus. Kyrsten Brooker. New York: Atheneum, 2005.

Myers, Walter Dean. *Dream Bearer*. New York: HarperCollins, 2003.

Nolen, Jerdine. *Big Jabe*. Illus. Kadir Nelson. New York: Lothrop, 2000.

Raven, Margot Theis. *Circle Unbroken*. Illus. E. B. Lewis. New York: Farrar, Straus & Giroux, 2004.

Ringgold, Faith. *Tar Beach*. New York: Crown, 1991.

Robinet, Harriette. *Twelve Travelers, Twenty Horses*. New York: Atheneum, 2003.

Steptoe, John. *Mufaro's Beautiful Daughters*. New York: Lothrop, 1947.

Stuve-Bodeen, Stephanie. *Mama Elizabeti*. Illus. Christy Hale. New York: Lee & Low, 2000.

Tate, Eleanora E. *Blessing in Disguise*. New York: Dell, 1996.

Taylor, Mildred. *Roll of Thunder, Hear My Cry*. New York: Dial, 1976.

Whittenberg, Allison. *Sweet Thang*. New York: Delacorte, 2006.

Wiles, Deborah. *Freedom Summer*. Illus. Jerome Laguerrique. New York: Aladdin, 2005.

Woodson, Jacqueline. *If You Come Softly*. New York: Speak, 2010.

Wyeth, Sharon Dennis. *Message in the Sky: Corey's Underground Railroad Diary*. New York: Scholastic, 2003.

Native American

Andrews, Jan. *Very Last First Time*. Illus. Ian Wallace. Vancouver, BC: Douglas & McIntyre, 2002.

Armer, Laura Adams. *Waterless Mountain*. New York: McKay, 1931.

Broker, Ignatia, *Night Flying Woman: An Ojibwa Narrative*. St. Paul: Minnesota Historical Society Press, 1983.

Brooke, Lauren. *Every New Day*. New York: Scholastic, 2002.

Brown, D. *Creek Mary's Blood*. New York: Franklin Library, 1980.

Bruchac, Joseph. *Crazy Horse's Vision*. Illus. S. D. Nelson. New York: Lee & Low, 2000.

———. *Wabi*. New York: Dial, 2006.

Cannon, A. E. *The Shadow Brothers*. New York: Delacorte, 1990.

The Children of La Loche and Friends. *Byron through the Seasons: A Dene-English Story Book*. Calgary, AB: Fifth House, 1990.

Clark, Ann Nolan. *Medicine Man's Daughter*. New York: Farrar, 1963.

Craven, Margaret. *I Heard the Owl Call My Name*. New York: Bantam, 1973.

Dorris, Michael. *Guests*. New York: Hyperion/Disney, 1994.

Erdrich, Louise. *The Game of Silence*. New York: HarperCollins, 2005.

George, Jean Craighead. *Julie of the Wolves*. New York: Harper, 1972.

Highwater, Jamake. *Anpao: An American Indian Odyssey*. New York: Harper, 1977.

Hill, Kirkpatrick. *Minuk: Ashes in the Pathway*. Middleton, WI: Pleasant Company, 2002.

Hirschfelder, Arlene. *Rising Voices: Writings of Young Native Americans*. New York: Random House, 1993.

Houston, John. *Ghost Fox*. New York: Harcourt, 1977.

Hudson, Jan. *Sweetgrass*. New York: Philomel, 1989. (Tree Frog, 1984)

Kadohata, Cynthis. *Weedflower*. New York: Atheneum, 2006.

Katz, Jane B. *This Song Remembers: Self-Portraits of Native Americans in the Arts*. Boston: Houghton Mifflin, 1980.

Katz, William Loren. *Black Indians: A Hidden Heritage*. New York: Atheneum, 1986.

Keeshig-Tobias, Lenore. *Emma and the Trees*. Illus. Polly Keeshig-Tobias. Ojibway tr. Rose Nadjiwon. Toronto: Sister Vision: Black Women and Women of Color Press, 1996.

Lacapa, Kathleen, and Michael Lacapa. *Less than Half, More than Whole*. Illus. Michael Lacapa. Menomonie, WI: Northland, 1994.

Lacapa, Michael. *The Flute Player*. Menomonie, WI: Northland, 1990.

Manitonquat (Medicine Story), reteller. *The Children of the Morning Light: Wampanoag Tales*. New York: Macmillan, 1994.

McDonald, Megan. *Tundra Mouse: A Storyknife Tale*. Illus. S. D. Schindler. New York: Orchard, 1997.

Means, Florence Crannell. *Our Cup Is Broken*. Boston: Houghton Mifflin, 1969.

Mikaelsen, Ben. *Touching Spirit Bear*. New York: HarperCollins, 2002.

O'Dell, Scott. *Sing Down the Moon*. Boston: Houghton Mifflin, 1970.

Pearsall, Shelley. *Crooked River*. New York: Knopf, 2005.

Richter, Conrad. *Light in the Forest*. New York: Knopf, 1953.

Sanderson, Esther. *Two Pairs of Shoes*. Illus. David Beyer. Saint Paul, MN: Pemmican Publications, 1990.

Savageau, Cheryl. *Muskrat Will Be Swimming*. Illus. Robert Hynes. Menomonie, WI: Northland, 1996.

Shaw, Janet Beeler. *Kaya: An American Girl*. Middleton, WI: Pleasant Company, 2002.

Sherman, Alexie. *The Absolutely True Diary of a Part-Time Indian*. New York: Little Brown, 2007.

———. *War Dances*. New York: Grove, 2009.

Sneve, Virginia Driving Hawk. *Dancing Teepees: Poems of American Indian Youth*. Illus. Stephen Gammell. New York: Holiday House, 1989.

Spalding, Andrea, and Alfred Scow. *Secret of the Dance*. Illus. Darlene Gait. Victoria, British Columbia: Orca, 2006.

Speare, Elizabeth George. *The Sign of the Beaver*. Boston: Houghton Mifflin, 1983.

Strete, Craig Kee. *Big Thunder Magic*. Illus. Craig Brown. New York: Greenwillow, 1990.

Tingle, Tom. *Crossing Bok Chitto: A Choctaw Tale of Friendship and Freedom*. El Paso, TX: Cinco Puntos Press, 2006.

Waboose, Jan Bourdeau. *Morning on the Lake*. Illus. Karen Reczuch. Toronto: Kids Can Press, 1998.

Wheeler, Bernelda. *Where Did You Get Your Moccasins?* Illus. Herman Bekkering. Grand Forks, ND: Peguis Publications, 1992.

Wyss, Thelma Hatch. *Bear Dancer: The Story of a Ute Girl*. New York: Margaret K. McElderry, 2005.

Yellow Robe, Rosebud. *Tonweya and the Eagles and Other Lakota Stories*. Illus. Jerry Pinkney. New York: Dial, 1979.

Latinos/Latinas

Anaya, Rodolfo. *The Farolitos of Christmas: A New Mexico Christmas Story*. Santa Fe: New Mexico Magazine, 1987.

———. *Maya's Children: The Story of La Llorona*. Illus. Maria Baca. New York: Hyperion, 1997.

Buss, Fran Leeper, and Daisy Cubias. *Journey of the Sparrows*. New York: Lodestar, 1991.

Chavez, Denise. *The Last of the Menu Girls*. Houston, TX: Arte Público Press, 1988.

Cisneros, Sandra. *Hairs/Pelitos*. Illus. Terry Ybánez. New York: Knopf, 1994.

———. *The House on Mango Street*. New York: Random House, 1984.

Dorros, Arthur. *Abuela*. New York: Dutton, 1991.

Foresman, Bettie. *From Lupita's Hill*. New York: Atheneum, 1973.

Galarza, Ernesto. *Barrio Boy*. Notre Dame, IN: University of Notre Dame Press, 1971.

Garcia, Maria. *The Adventures of Connie and Diego/ Las adventuras de Connie y Diego*. San Francisco: Children's Book Press, 1978.

Garza, Carmen Lomas. *Family Picture/Cuadros de Familia*. San Francisco: Children's Book Press, 1990.

Griego, M. C., and others. *Tortillitas para Mama and Other Nursery Rhymes, Spanish and English*. New York: Holt, n.d.

Herrera, Juan Felipe. *Calling the Doves/El Canto de las Palomas*. Illus. Elly Simmons. 1990. San Francisco: Children's Book Press, 2001.

Hewett, Joan. *Hector Lives in the United States Now: The Story of a Mexican-American Child*. New York: Lippincott, 1990.

Krumgold, Joseph. *. . . and now Miguel*. New York: Crowell, 1953.

Martinez, Victor. *Parrot in the Oven: Mi Valda*. New York: HarperCollins, 1996.

Means, Florence Crannell. *Us Malthbys*. Boston: Houghton Mifflin, 1966.

Meltzer, Milton. *The Hispanic Americans*. New York: Crowell, 1982.

Mohr, Nicholasa. *El Bronx Remembered: A Novella and Stories*. New York: Harper, 1975.

Mora, Pat. *Borders*. Houston, TX: Arte Público Press, 1985.

———. *Confetti: Poems for Children*. Illus. Enrique O. Sanchez. New York: Lee and Low, 1996.

O'Dell, Scott. *The Black Pearl*. Boston: Houghton Mifflin, 1967.

Pérez, Amada Irma. *My Very Own Room/Mi Propio Cuartito*. Illus. Maya Christina Gonzalez. San Francisco: Children's Book Press, 2000.

Pinchot, Jane. *The Mexicans in America*. Minneapolis, MN: Lerner, 1989.

Rice, David. *Crazy Loco*. New York: Dial, 2001.

Soto, Gary. *A Fire in My Hands: A Book of Poems*. New York: Scholastic, 1990.

———. *Snapshots from the Wedding*. Illus. Stephanie Garcia. New York: Putnam, 1997.

Tafolla, Carmen. *Patchwork Colcha: A Children's Collection*. Flagstaff, AZ: Creative Educational Enterprises, 1987.

Taylor, Theodore. *The Maldonado Miracle*. New York: Avon, 1986.

Torres, Leyla. *Subway Sparrow/Gorrión del Metro*. New York: Farrar, Straus & Giroux, 1993.

Ulibarrí, Sabine. *Pupurupú: Cuentos de Ninos/ Children's Stories*. Mexico, D. F.: Sainz Luiselli Editores, 1987.

Viramontes, Helena Maria. *The Moths and Other Stories*. Houston, TX: Arte Público Press, 1985.

Zubizarreta, Rosalma. *The Woman Who Outshone the Sun: The Legend of Lucia Zenten.*,1992. San Francisco: Children's Book Press, 1994.

Asian American (Including Asian Heritage)

Bang, Molly. *The Paper Crane*. New York: Greenwillow, 1985. (Japanese)

Coutant, Helen, and Vo-Dinh Coutant. *First Snow*. New York: Knopf, 1974. (Vietnamese)

Crew, Linda. *Children of the River*. New York: Bantam, 1989. (Cambodian)

Degens, T. *On the Third Ward*. New York: Harper, 1990. (Chinese)

Fritz, Jean. *Homesick:* My Own Story. New York: Putnam, 1982. (Chinese)

Ho, Minfong. *Rice without Rain*. New York: Lothrop, 1990. (Thai)

Houston, Jeanne Wakatsuki, and James D. Houston. *Farewell to Manzanar*. New York: Bantam, 1973. (Japanese)

Kim, Helen. *The Long Season of Rain*. New York: Holt, 1996. (Korean)

Lin, Grace. *The Year of the Dog*. New York: Little Brown, 2006. (Chinese)

Liu, Cynthea. *The Great Call of China (S.A.S.S.)*. New York: Speak, 2009.

Lord, Bette Bao. *In the Year of the Boar and Jackie Robinson*. New York: Harper, 1984. (Chinese)

Louie, Ai-Ling. *Yeh-Shen: A Cinderella Story from China*. Illus. Ed Young. New York: Philomel, 1982. (Chinese)

Mahy, Margaret. *The Seven Chinese Brothers*. Illus. Jean and Mou-Sein Tseng. New York: Scholastic, 1990. (Chinese)

Na, An. *A Step from Heaven*. Asheville, NC: Front Street, 2001. (Korean)

Oeschlager, Vanita. *Made in China: A Story of Adoption*. Illus. Kristin Blackwood. Akron, OH: Vanita Books, 2008. (Chinese)

Say, Allen. *Grandfather's Journey*. Boston: Houghton Mifflin, 1994. (Japanese)

Uchida, Yoshiko. *A Jar of Dreams*. New York: Atheneum, 1991. (Japanese)

Wang, Rosalind C. *The Fourth Question*. Illus. Ju-Hong Chen. New York: Holiday House, 1991. (Chinese)

Wong, Janet S. *Buzz*. Illus. Margaret Chodos-Irvine. San Diego: Harcourt, 2000. (Chinese)

Yacowitz, Caryn. *The Jade Stone*. Illus. Ju-Hong Chen. New York: Holiday House, 1992. (Chinese)

Yagawa, Sumiko. *The Crane Wife*. Tr. Katherine Paterson. Illus. Suekichi Akaba. New York: Mulberry, 1987. (Japanese)

Yashima, Taro, and Mitsu Yashima. *Umbrella*. New York: Viking, 1958. (Japanese)

Yep, Laurence. *Angelfish*. New York: Putnam, 2001. (Chinese)

———. *Dragon Prince: A Chinese Beauty and the Beast Tale*. Illus. Kam Mak. New York: HarperCollins, 1997. (Chinese)

———. *Tales from Gold Mountain: Stories of the Chinese in the New World*. New York: Macmillan, 1990. (Chinese)

Yin, Rosanna Yin Lau. *Coolies*. New York: Penguin, 2001. (Chinese)

Young, Ed. *Lon Po Po: A Red-Riding Hood Story from China*. New York: Philomel, 1990. (Chinese)

———. *My Mei Mei*. New York: Philomel, 2006. (Chinese)

Jewish American

Blanc, Esther Silverstein. *Berchick*. Illus. Tennessee Dixon. Volcano, CA: Volcano, 1989.

Bresnick-Perry, Roslyn. *Leaving for America*. Illus. Mira Reisberg. Danbury, CT: Children's, 1992.

Chaikin, Miriam. *I Should Worry, I Should Care*. Illus. by Richard Egielski. New York: Harper, 1979.

Cohen, Barbara. *Molly's Pilgrim*. Illus. by M. J. Deraney. New York: Lothrop, Lee, and Shepard, 1983.

Frank, Anne. *The Diary of a Young Girl: The Definitive Edition*. New York: Doubleday, 1995. (Dutch)

Geras, Adele. *My Grandmother's Stories*. New York: Knopf, 1990.

Gottfried, Ted. *Children of the Slaughter: Young People of the Holocaust*. Brookfield, CT: Twenty-First Century Books, 2001.

Heyman, Anna. *Exit from Home*. New York: Crown, 1977. (Russian)

Hurwitz, Johanna. *Once I Was a Plum Tree*. New York: Morrow, 1980.

Innocenti, Roberto, and Christophe Gallaz. *Rose Blanche*. New York: Creative Education, 1985.

Kerr, Judith. *When Hitler Stole Pink Rabbit*. New York: Coward McCann & Geoghegan, 1971.

Lasky, Kathryn. *The Night Journey*. New York: Warne, 1981. (Russian)

Meyer, Michele Lee. *My Daddy Is Jewish and My Mommy Is Christian*. Charleston, SC: BookSurge, 2006.

Muggamin, Howard. *The Jewish Americans*. New York: Chelsea House, 1988.

Oriev, Uri. *The Man from the Other Side*. Boston: Houghton Mifflin, 1991. (Eastern European)

Potok, Chaim. *My Name Is Asher Lev*. New York: Knopf, 1972.

Polacco, Patricia. *The Keeping Quilt*. New York: Simon and Schuster, 1988.

Schmidt, Gary. *Mara's Stories: Glimmers in the Darkness*. New York: Holt, 2001.

Singer, Isaac Bashevis. *The Death of Methuselah and Other Stories*. New York: Farrar, Straus & Giroux, 1971.

Suhl, Yuri. *The Merrymaker*. New York: Four Winds, 1975.

Sussman, Susan. *Hanukkah: Eight Lights Around the World*. Illus. Judith Friedman. Chicago: Whitman, 1988.

Taylor, Sydney. *All-of-a-Kind Family*. Chicago: Follett, 1951. (Includes several sequels)

Other Cultures

Case, Dianne. *Love, David*. New York: Dutton, 1991. (South African)

Clark, Ann Nolan. *Secret of the Andes*. New York: Viking, 1952. (Peruvian Indian)

Cunnane, Kelly. *For You Are a Kenyan Child.* Illus. Ana Juan. New York: Atheneum, 2006.

Demi. *Muhammad.* New York: Margaret K. McElderry, 2003. (Muslim)

Ellis, Deborah. *The Heaven Shop.* Markham, Ontario: Fitzhenry and Whiteside, 2004. (Sub-Saharan Africa and AIDS)

Fama, Elizabeth. *Overboard.* Peru, IL: Cricket, 2002. (Muslim)

Hall, Lynn. *Danza!* New York: Scribner's, 1981. (Puerto Rican)

Joseph, Lynn. *The Color of My Words.* New York: HarperCollins, 2000. (Dominican Republic)

Kherdian, David. *The Road from Home: The Story of an Armenian Girlhood.* New York: Greenwillow, 1979. (Armenian)

Lingard, Joan. *Tug of War.* New York: Lodestar, 1990. (Latvian)

McCormick, Patricia. *Sold.* New York: Hyperion, 2006. (Life in modern-day India—verse novel)

Moeri, Louise. *The Forty-third War.* Boston: Houghton Mifflin, 1989. (Central American)

Naidoo, Beverley. *The Other Side of Truth.* New York: HarperCollins, 2001. (Nigeria)

O'Dell, Scott. *My Name Is Not Angelica.* Boston: Houghton Mifflin, 1989. (African, Caribbean Islanders)

Ryan, Pam Muñoz. *Esperanza Rising.* New York: Scholastic, 2000. (Mexico)

Say, Allen. *Kamishibai Man.* New York: Houghton Mifflin, 2005. (Japan)

Staples, Suzanne Fisher. *Shabanu: Daughter of the Wind.* New York: Knopf, 1989. (Pakistani)

Stoltz, Joelle. *The Shadows of Ghardames.* New York: Delacorte, 2004. (Muslim)

Books about the Hard Issues—Sexuality, Divorce, Death, War, Conflict, and Violence

(See also the booklists in Chapter 11, which includes books for older readers, and Chapter 12, which includes nonfiction books on these subjects.)

Sexuality

Bauer, Marion Dane. *Am I Blue? Coming Out from the Silence.* New York: HarperCollins, 1995.

Brannon, Sarah. *Uncle Bobby's Wedding.* New York: Putnam, 2008.

Bryan, Jennifer. *The Different Dragon.* Illus. Danamarie Hosler. Ridley Park, PA: Two Lives, 2006.

Donovan, John. *I'll Get There. It Better Be Worth the Trip.* New York: Harper & Row, 1969.

Fox, Paula. *The Eagle Kite.* New York, Orchard Books, 1995.

Holland, Isabelle. *The Man Without a Face.* New York: Harper, 1987.

Kerr, M. E. *Deliver Us from Evie.* New York: Harper, 1994.

Newman, Lesléa. *Daddy, Papa, and Me.* Berkeley, CA: Tricycle Press, 2009.

———. *Heather Has Two Mommies.* Illus. Diana Souza. Northampton, MA: In Other Words Publishing, 1989.

———. *Mommy, Mama, and Me.* Berkeley, CA: Tricycle Press, 2009.

Parnell, Peter. *And Tango Makes Three.* Illus. Justin Richardson. New York: Simon and Schuster, 2005.

Willhoite, Michael. *Daddy's Roommate.* Boston: Alyson, 1990.

Divorce

Brown, Laurie Krasny, and Marc Brown. *Dinosaurs Divorce.* New York: Little Brown, 1988.

Clifton, Lucille. *Everett Anderson's 1-2-3.* Illus. Ann Grifalconi. New York: Holt, 1977.

Ekster, Carol Gordon. *Where Am I Sleeping Tonight?* Illus. Sue Rama. Weaverville, CA: Boulden, 2008.

Levins, Sandra. *Was It the Chocolate Pudding? A Story for Little Kids about Divorce.* Illus. Bryan Langdo. Washington, DC: American Psychological Association, 2005.

Masurel, Claire. *Two Homes.* Illus. Kady McDonald Denton. New York: Candlewick, 2005.

Death

Brown, Laurie Krasny, and Marc Brown. *When Dinosaurs Die: A Guide to Understanding Death.* New York: Little Brown, 1996.

Brown, Margaret Wise. *The Dead Bird.* Illus. Remy Charlip. New York: HarperCollins, 2005.

Clifton, Lucille. *Everett Anderson's Goodbye.* Illus. Ann Grifalconi. New York: Holt, 1983.

Demas, Corinne. *Saying Goodbye to Lulu.* Illus. Ard Hoyt. New York: Little, Brown, 2009.

De Paolo, Tomie. *Nana Upstairs, Nana Downstairs.* New York: Putnam, 1973.

Jeffers, Oliver. *The Heart and the Bottle.* New York: Philomel, 2010.

Ryland, Cynthia. *Dog Heaven.* New York: Blue Sky Press, 1995.

Viorst, Judith. *The Tenth Good Thing about Barney.* Illus. Erik Blegvad. New York: Aladdin, 1987.

War, Conflict, and Violence

Bunting, Eve. *Smoky Night.* Illus. David Diaz. New York: Harcourt, 1994.

———. *The Wall.* Illus. Ronald Himler. Port Orchard, WA: Sandpiper, 1992.

Fitzhugh, Louise, and Sandra Scoppettone. *Bang, Bang, You're Dead.* New York: Harper, 1969.

Holliday, Laurel. *Why Do They Hate Me?: Young Lives Caught in War and Conflict.* New York: Simon Pulse, 1999.

Innocenti, Roberto, and Christophe Gallaz. *Rose Blanche.* New York: Creative Education, 1985.

Maruki, Toshi. *Hiroshima No Pika.* Boston: Lothrop, Lee, & Shepard, 1982.

Yolen, Jane. *The Devil's Arithmetic.* Logan, IA: Perfection Learning, 1990.

PEARSON
myeducationkit

Go to the topic "Multicultural Literature" on the MyEducationKit for this text, where you can:

- Search the Database of Children's Literature, housing more than 22,000 titles searchable in every genre by authors or illustrators, by awards won, by year published, and by topic and description.

- Explore genre-related Assignments and Activities, assignable exercises showing concepts in action through database use, video, cases, and student and teacher artifacts.

- Listen to podcasts and read interviews from some of the brightest and most enduring stars of children's literature in the Conversations.

- Discover Web Links that will lead you to sites representing the authors you learn about in these pages, classrooms with powerful children's literature connections, and literature awards.

Beginning Books

Knowledge through Delight

Introduction

From the lullabies of the nursery (e.g., "Rock-a-Bye Baby") to the alphabet song set to Mozart's familiar melody to the tuneful counting rhymes (e.g., "One, Two, Buckle My Shoe"), there is no shortage of memorable songs, poems, and literary entertainments to share with small children. And how early should we begin introducing children to the miracle of language? Some parents begin reading to the unborn child still in the womb. It's not a bad idea, even if it is only good practice for the parents. Few things in life are more rewarding than sharing a good picture book with a young child who, curled up in your lap, eagerly awaits to see what happens on the next page.

In this chapter we will look at Mother Goose books; alphabet, counting, and concept books; as well as the popular tactile and movable books designed for the very young. There is certainly no shortage of books for preschoolers; however, not all of these books are worthwhile. The trick is finding the good ones. And, since little children have to rely on us for their book selection, it's important that we do what we can to find the very best. Childhood is so very brief and children grow so very quickly that it would be a shame to waste that time on inferior books when so many fascinating, beautiful, and challenging books are readily available. This chapter will provide some guidance in that book selection process.

Mother Goose Rhymes

Definition and Origin

No one knows who Mother Goose was, or even where the name came from. In the seventeenth century, a Frenchman, Charles Perrault, named his collection of folktales *Tales from Mother Goose,* but he included no nursery rhymes. Some speculate the name may have been given to the woman who, in earlier times, kept the village geese and who was the traditional community storyteller. Whatever her origins, by the end of the eighteenth century, books of nursery rhymes were being published in New England with the name Mother Goose on them, and since then she has been inextricably tied to the songs of the nursery.

These familiar rhymes—"This little pig went to market," "London Bridge is falling down," "Lady bird, lady bird, fly away home," and others—are not only a child's first introduction to literature but many are also an indelible part of our cultural heritage. They find their way into a multitude of references in our daily lives. Their lilting rhythms, their comical rhymes, their unusual sounds ("Doctor Foster went to Gloucester," "Ride a cock horse to Banbury Cross," "As I was going to St. Ives, I met a man with seven wives," and so on) endear them to young children. These are often the first words they memorize. And these rhymes are often a child's first introduction to memorable fictional characters—Little Miss Muffet, Jack Sprat, Humpty Dumpty, Little Jack Horner, Little Bo Peep, Old King Cole, the Queen of Hearts, Georgy Porgy, Little Boy Blue, Wee Willie Winkie, Simple Simon, Peter Piper, Old Mother Hubbard, Peter the Pumpkin Eater, and the Old Woman Who Lived in a Shoe (to name but a few).

Curiously, many of the nursery rhymes themselves were not originally meant for children. Instead, they are derived from war songs, romantic lyrics, proverbs, riddles, political jingles, lampoons, and the cries of street vendors (an early version of the television commercial). Most of the best-known rhymes can be traced back to the sixteenth, seventeenth, and eighteenth centuries. "Three Blind Mice" was set to music as early as 1609, "Jack Sprat" may have ridiculed a certain Archdeacon Spratt in the mid-seventeenth century, and "Little Jack Horner" may have referred to a Thomas Horner of Mells whose "plum" was the land he acquired from the monasteries dissolved by Henry VIII in 1536. The heroes of nursery rhymes typically come from the lower walks of life: Simple Simon, Tom the Piper's Son, Mother Hubbard, the Old Woman in the Shoe, and so on. Those that do mention kings and queens ("Sing a Song of Six Pence" and "Old King Cole," for example) are often comical and irreverent. Scarcely hidden beneath the surface of these rhymes and jingles are the jibe and the barb. Nursery rhymes—even before they entered the nursery—were meant for fun.

Mother Goose and Child Development

In addition to their sheer joy, nursery rhymes can help infants and toddlers in some unexpected ways. They can assist in cognitive development, such as counting—"One potato, two potato, three potato, four" and "One, two, three, four, five/Once I caught a fish alive." Nursery rhymes broaden vocabularies. "Mary, Mary, quite contrary," "Jack be nimble," and "Pease porridge hot," all include words not normally used by children. This is a great way to expand a child's language skills.

Along similar lines, Mother Goose rhymes can help with a child's aesthetic development, or the appreciation for beauty, particularly for the lovely sounds of language. Nursery rhymes, with their lively meter, appeal to a child's natural sense of rhythm, perhaps hearkening back to the womb and the rhythmical beat of the mother's heart. The repeated refrains and insistent rhymes provide children with the pleasures of balance and structure in language. The playful sounds of nonsense words ("Hickory dickory dock," "Diddle, diddle dumpling, my son John," "Higgledy, piggledy, my black hen," "Eeny, meeny, miny, mo") appeal to the sheer joy in the sounds of words.

Many nursery rhymes are interactive and can contribute to a child's physical development. "Pat-a-Cake, Pat-a-Cake" calls for physical coordination and interpersonal contact; "Ring Around the Rosey" and "London Bridge Is Falling Down" call for the exercise of large-motor skills as well as social interaction. Jump-rope rhymes are simply nursery rhymes gone to the playground, and they appear to be an almost worldwide childhood pastime (see Butler, *Skipping Around the World*). By extension we could also argue that some of these jingles help children release aggression and hostility in acceptable ways. Take, for example, this popular jump-rope jingle:

> Fudge, fudge, tell the judge
> Mother has a newborn baby;
> It isn't a girl and it isn't a boy;
> It's just a fair young lady.
> Wrap it up in tissue paper
> And send it up the elevator:
> First floor, miss;
> Second floor, miss;
> Third floor, miss;
> Fourth floor,
> Kick it out the elevator door.

This brings us to one of the controversies surrounding many nursery rhymes—their often violent content. We find babies dropping from treetops, cradle and all; a farmer's wife chopping off the tails (or heads) of three blind mice; a beleaguered old woman living in a shoe with unruly children whom she whips soundly; a ladybug whose children (save for one) are apparently lost in a fire; a man who keeps his wife in a pumpkin shell; and more. Indeed, one assiduous critic, Geoffrey Handley-Taylor, discovered, in a collection of some 200 familiar nursery rhymes, at least 100 rhymes with "unsavory elements," including eight allusions to murder, two cases of choking to death, one case of decapitation, seven cases of severing of limbs, and the list goes on (Baring-Gould and Baring-Gould 20). Sylvia Long has produced a beautifully illustrated modern collection of nursery rhymes, titled *Sylvia Long's Mother Goose*, that eliminates some of the more indelicate aspects of the verses. The baby who rocks in the tree top is a little bird who flies to safety when the bough breaks; the old woman who lives in shoe is a spider who doesn't spank her children, but kisses them before putting them to bed. These adaptations of the old rhymes are harmless—but probably unnecessary. Children are wise enough to realize that what occurs in a nonsense rhyme is not what ought to occur in real life. Reading provides vicarious pleasure—this is no different for children as for adults. Even very young children know when something is "just a story."

Illustrators of Mother Goose

Mother Goose books are among the most frequently illustrated texts in children's literature. On the following pages are comparative examples of illustrations by several famous artists of two popular rhymes with wildly different the interpretations.

"Jack Sprat" has been loved by children probably because of the delightful nonsense of the action—two grown people engaged in the ridiculous act of licking the platter clean. Yet it is curious how many noted illustrators fail to appreciate that fact, and focus instead on the rhyme's two distinctive characters, each with a clearly defined personality trait.

Figure 6.1 ● This rather crude wood engraving from one of the earliest American editions of Mother Goose depicts the Sprats licking the platter clean. The illustration lacks the comic touch of Raymond Briggs (see Figure 6.2) and the result is nearly grotesque.

Source: From *Mother Goose's Melodies*, Munroe & Francis, Boston, 1833.

Figure 6.2 ● Raymond Briggs captures the Sprats in their most bizarre behavior—that of licking the platter clean. Appropriate to the subject, Briggs's style is cartoon, which heightens the effect of the absurd.

Source: Illustration from *The Mother Goose Treasury* by Raymond Briggs (Hamish Hamilton 1969). Copyright © Raymond Briggs 1969. Reproduced by permission of Penguin Books Ltd.

JACK SPRAT could eat no fat,
His wife could eat no lean:

And so, betwixt them both, you see,
They lick'd the platter clean.

Figure 6.3 ● L. Leslie Brooke depicts a decidedly older couple and from an earlier time—the costumes are Renaissance. As always with Brooke, a close examination of his illustration reveals his wry humor: notice the bovine fattened for market prominently displayed on the Sprats' coat of arms. Like many Victorian children's artists, Brooke imbued his representational drawings with rich, subtle details.

Source: The Nursery Rhyme Book by Andrew Lang. Illustrated by L. Leslie Brooke. Copyright © 1972 by Dover Publications, Inc. Reprinted by permission.

Figure 6.4 ● Blanche Fisher Wright depicts an eighteenth-century husband and his solicitous mate. Typical of her illustrations for the popular collection, *The Real Mother Goose*, the lines are clean and sharp and her characters are well defined.

Source: From *The Real Mother Goose* illustrated by Blanche Fisher Wright. Copyright © 1916, 1944 Checkerboard Press, a division of Macmillan, Inc.

"Little Miss Muffet" is a wonderfully constructed rhyme, a complete story with setting, characters, conflict, climax, and resolution. It has been among the most popular of all Mother Goose verses, and most illustrators choose to depict the moment just prior to or at the point of the climax since it provides the most drama and the greatest possibilities for interpretation. Notice how each illustrator adds his or her own sense to that drama and how each Miss Muffet acquires a slightly different personality at the hands of the artist.

Little Miss Muffet,
Sat on a tuffet,
Eating some curds and whey ;
There came a great spider,
And sat down beside her,
And frightened Miss Muffet away.

Figure 6.5 ● Kate Greenaway could not bring herself to include unsavory elements in her illustrations; consequently she detracts from the drama by focusing all attention on the prim and proper Miss Muffet. The spider is barely noticeable off to the left. The colors are subdued and contribute to the air of quietness belying the circumstances.

Source: Kate Greenaway, *Mother Goose Nursery Rhymes,* London: Frederick Warne & Co., Ltd.

Figure 6.6 ● Arthur Rackham, in contrast to Greenaway, portrays a truly monstrous-looking, but not ungentlemanly, spider. The spider's appearance completely overwhelms the picture, and there is a wonderful contrast between the sedate Miss Muffet (somewhat more mature than Greenaway's), her lip daintily pursed, and the grotesque creature about to interrupt her. Rackham's surrealistic, frequently nightmarish quality is tempered here by a bit of wry humor as the spider gallantly doffs his hat.

Source: Little Miss Muffet by Arthur Rackham.

LITTLE MISS MUFFET

Little Miss Muffet
Sat on a tuffet,
Eating her curds and whey;
There came a big spider,
Who sat down beside her
And frightened Miss Muffet away.

Figure 6.7 ● Raymond Briggs portrays a looming creature, but his Miss Muffet looks more like a nineteenth-century school marm. The fact that Briggs's spider does not have the anatomically correct number of legs need not bother us, since the illustration is in a cartoon style, and exaggerations and distortions are to be expected.

Source: Illustration from *The Mother Goose Treasury* by Raymond Briggs (Hamish Hamilton 1969). Copyright © Raymond Briggs 1969. Reproduced by permission of Penguin Books Ltd.

Choosing Mother Goose Books

A good Mother Goose book should be a staple in every child's home. But there are so many to choose from, it is often difficult to tell which ones are the good ones. Below are some points to consider when choosing from the many collections available:

1. Is the book attractive and well made? These books get a lot of use and most Mother Goose books are intended to be read to (rather than by) children. A flimsy paperback may be, ultimately, a waste of money. And, since it is a shared book, you might as well get one you enjoy looking at as well.

2. Is there a balance between the familiar rhymes and those that are less often anthologized? You want the old standbys, but it's good to have some fresh verses as well.

3. Are the illustrations examples of good art, both imaginative and well executed? (For more about this, see Chapter 7.) It is usually best for each rhyme to have its own illustration, although if the collection is very large some illustrations are often sacrificed.

4. Are the pages uncluttered in appearance and are the rhymes juxtaposed with the proper pictures? The format should be clear enough for the child to follow.

5. Are rhymes from other cultures included—African, Asian, Native American, for example? Since multiculturalism is a relatively recent development in children's literature, we may find this diversity only in newer anthologies. It would be a mistake to reject such classic collections as Blanche Fisher Wright's *The Real Mother Goose* or Marguerite de Angeli's *Book of Nursery and Mother Goose Rhymes* or Raymond Briggs's *The Mother Goose Treasury* because they are not sufficiently multicultural. But you might wish to supplement them with nursery rhyme collections from other lands and cultures.

6. Are there enough rhymes to justify the cost of the book? Of course, if you have unlimited resources, this is not a concern. But if you can afford only one Mother Goose book, look for a generous collection.

7. Is there an index so that specific rhymes can be easily located? This is more for the adult reader than for the child, but an index is very helpful when you're trying to fill special requests.

Mother Goose rhymes hold tremendous possibilities for young children—and the children quickly figure that out. These rhymes need no defense—they are pure fun. Their delightful nonsense and eccentric characters remain with us long beyond childhood.

Alphabet and Counting Books

Also among the first books we share with small children are the those introducing the alphabet and the concept of counting. Books about letters and numbers provide authors and illustrators limitless creative possibilities, which is probably why there are so many of these books. Some of the best selections go beyond simply supplying a picture next to a letter or number. Rather, they function as works of art unified by a subject (such as animals in *Bert Kitchen's Animal Alphabet*) or a specific design pattern (for example, the intricate drawings surrounded by a detailed border in *Anno's Alphabet*) or an idea or theme (such as the alphabet drama in Chris Van Allsburg's *Z Was Zapped*). As with Mother Goose books, alphabet and counting books are far more complicated than we might first imagine—and they can also be very rewarding. We will first consider alphabet books, and then briefly look at counting books.

Alphabet Books

Most alphabet books operate on the premise that children learn the sounds of the alphabet through words that begin with those letters. This is, in many ways, a false premise. For example, the letter "A" might be represented by "Apple," even though we could just as well use "Aardvark," "Ape," or "Automobile"—all of which have very different "A" sounds. Of course, the consonants are usually much easier. The sounds of "B," "D," and "F," for example, are quite consistent, and Dr. Seuss's lively alphabet book, *Dr. Seuss's ABC,* can effectively demonstrate the sound of "F" with a nonsense word, the mythical creature called the "Fiffer Feffer Feff." However, the consonant "C" is another matter. Does it sound like the "C" in "Ceiling" or in "Cat" or in "Church" or in "Czar" or in "Chute"? It can even be silent as in "Chthonic" (meaning something related to the underworld) or in "Ctenoid" (meaning having teethlike structures, like a comb). And what about that troublesome "X"? It is interesting to see how many alphabet books resort to using "Xylophone," which really starts with the sound for "Z." We turn again to Dr. Seuss who had a better idea, showing us that we can learn the sound of "X" by listening to such words as "ax" and "extra fox."

The point is that, at their best, alphabet books can offer only approximate associations of sounds and letters. The use of phonics in English may be a good place to start, but children learn early on that the associative sounds of letters frequently don't help them pronounce or spell words. (I still recall, as a child, mispronouncing the name Stephen as Step-hen whenever I saw it in print.) In the end, we have to accept that the erratic spelling of English requires that we memorize the spellings and sounds of hundreds and hundreds of words.

So, in light of all these difficulties with the quirkiness of the English language, the alphabet book is an imperfect tool. As such, if it is designed to introduce letters and their sounds and shapes to children, its first goal should be clarity and simplicity. The design and the illustrations of an alphabet book require attention to detail. Most alphabet books juxtapose the letters and the pictures that represent them; that is, they are side by side on the same page or facing pages. (There are exceptions to this. In Chris Van Allsburg's *Z Was Zapped,* dramatic full-page illustrations depict some mysterious thing happening to each letter—the name of the action corresponding to the letter itself. So, for example, "B" is "badly bitten" and "K" is "kidnapped." We, as readers, are invited to guess the calamity that befalls each letter, with the answer found by turning the page.) It is helpful if the letters are set in a clear and easily recognizable typeface. Some books include both upper- and lower-case letters. The distinctions between upper-case letters are usually easier for very young children to spot; whereas certain lower-case letters (for example, "b," "d," "p," and "q") have more subtle variations and are more easily confused. But that doesn't mean they shouldn't appear in alphabet books—children have to learn lower-case letters, regardless.

Also, if the goal is to teach preschoolers the sounds and shapes of letters, the objects associated with the letters should be concrete items. Remember, we are still talking about children at the preoperational period. However, this doesn't mean the objects need always be familiar. Bert Kitchen's dramatic alphabet book, *Animal Alphabet,* includes stunning paintings of such creatures as an "ibex," a "dodo," and a "jerboa"—unfamiliar animals to most of us, to be sure, but children (and adults) can quickly learn what they are by looking at the pictures. After all, one of the important objectives of any book should be to expand our understanding of the world. How else do we learn new things? On the other hand, Joan Walsh Anglund's *A Is for Always,* a book intended for very young children, uses abstract concepts far beyond their cognitive skills. For example, "D" is for "Determined," "E" is for "Efficient," and "Y" is for "Young-in-heart." Try explaining those terms to a 3-year-old!

Finally, we come to those alphabet books that really have no intention of teaching the alphabet—the alphabet book for the advanced reader. Many of these books are really exercises in artistic creativity. Margaret Musgrove's *Ashanti to Zulu: African Traditions* is a rather sophisticated alphabet book for much older children (children in the period of concrete operations). It presents the alphabet through descriptions of traditional African cultures. Chris Van Allsburg's *Z Was Zapped,* mentioned previously, describes a series of alphabetical disasters befalling each letter in turn, and is clearly meant for readers who already know the alphabet. Judith Viorst's *The Alphabet from Z to A (With Much Confusion on the Way)* even casts aside the traditional order of the letters. Graeme Base's *Animalia* is a lavishly illustrated book, using, as the title suggests, animals to introduce the letters of the alphabet. The full-color pictures abound with objects that help to reinforce the letter sounds, and throughout are hidden pictures of the artist as a child. The result is a visual feast that accompanies an imaginative, tongue-twisting text—a treat for adults as well as for children. And, in a classic alphabet book filled with dark humor for much older readers, Edward Gorey's *The Gashlycrumb Tinies,* 26 children are done in by a series of preposterous catastrophes ("H is for Hector done in by a thug," and "Z is for Zillah who drank too much gin"). So, an alphabet book is not always an educational tool; it may just be an aesthetic treat for everyone to enjoy.

Counting Books

Counting books or number books (both names are used) may be even less successful than alphabet books in achieving their goal. The concept of counting is something that children do not fully grasp until they reach Piaget's period of concrete operations, for they need to understand the concepts of conservation (some things remain the same even if their shape changes), reversibility (some things can be undone), and so on. Nevertheless, many artists have created fascinating counting books for children—even if the result is that the children can simply recite the numbers without knowing exactly how to count.

Some of the best counting books are actually for readers who already understand the concept of numbers. Molly Bang's award-winning *Ten, Nine, Eight* is an example of a counting book that counts backwards. Children can benefit from this kind of number play only after they have mastered the fundamental elements of enumeration. Pat Hutchins's *The Doorbell Rang* includes the concepts of division and addition. Tom and Muriel Feelings's very beautiful counting book, *Moja Means One: A Swahili Counting Book,* introduces cultural information along with counting concepts. The familiar counting rhymes, such as "Over in the Meadow," have inspired books by such noted illustrators as Feodor Rojankovsky and Ezra Jack Keats. The beautiful counting rhyme by S. T. Garne, *One White Sail,* takes the reader to the magic of the Caribbean with such evocative lines as "Five blue doors / in the baking hot sun / Six wooden windows / let the cool wind run."

As with alphabet books, the simplest design in a counting book is best for beginners, especially if the object is to teach the numbers. The juxtaposition of text and pictures is an important feature in the design of counting books. Naturally, we expect to see the Arabic numerals depicted (1, 2, 3), but even some very simple counting books include the spelling of the number words (one, two, three). Since most counting books go only up to 10, they are often shorter than other books and make use of full-page spreads. Or, they may depict the number on one page with the illustration on the facing page. When many items appear on a single page, the artist can avoid a cluttered appearance by grouping the objects. Today, counting books have joined the ranks of the many very handsome picture books being produced for young children, and we no longer have to settle for the ordinary and the humdrum.

Perceptual Concept Books

In addition to alphabet and counting books, we can find many other types of concept books for toddlers and preschoolers on such subjects as colors, shapes, sizes, and sounds. Most concept books focus on the perception of colors (E. L. Konigsburg's *Samuel Todd's Book of Great Colors*) or shapes (Leonard Everett Fisher's *Look Around! A Book about Shapes*) or sizes (Tana Hoban's *Is It Larger? Is It Smaller?*) or opposites (Laura Vacaro Seeger's *Black? White! Day? Night!* and *Eric Carle's Opposites*) or sounds (Rebecca Emberley's *City Sounds*).

Obviously, not all concepts can be translated into a picture book—we would not, for instance, try to explain the concepts of "treason" or "loyalty" to a 3-year-old. The concepts must be those that can be easily classified, differentiated, and visually depicted—that is, the concepts of square, round, and triangular objects can be explained to children of a certain age, but distinguishing an equilateral triangle from an isosceles triangle is another matter; likewise, red, blue, and purple can be easily identified, but persimmon, vermilion, and mauve require a more sophisticated discernment. Also, the concepts must be easily explained through graphic illustrations. Some critics believe that books describing sounds (such as sounds of bells, horns, drums, and so on) are pointless—unless they contain, as many do now, actual recordings of the sounds being presented. Perhaps the most effective are those describing the sounds of animals. Some concepts are best taught in life experience rather than through the pages of a book.

A good concept book is straightforward and clearly organized, with a logical and easy progression throughout. Some are tactile or movable books (discussed later in this chapter), which invite the child's participation, such as Chuck Murphy's *Opposites (Slide 'n' Sleek)*, with tabs small children can pull to reveal the "opposite."

Concept books are didactic books—that is, they are meant to teach—but the best ones are also entertaining and attractive to look at. And even if children do not fully comprehend the concepts presented in their books, it doesn't mean they won't enjoy looking at them or listening to parents, grandparents, siblings, and others read them. Probably the most important thing is that the books are attractive, enjoyable, and stimulating—books that children will want read to them again and again. And happily, many talented artists have produced some very fine books with beautiful art, including Mitsumasa Anno's challenging paintings (*Anno's Sundial),* John Burningham's charming cartoonish figures (*John Burningham's Opposites*), Shelley Rotner's striking photography (*Close, Closer, Closest,* with Richard Olivo), and Nancy Tafuri's gentle illustrations (*All Year Long*).

Tactile Books and Movable Books

Beyond the alphabet, counting, and concept books, preschoolers can enjoy some extraordinary inventive books, including a variety of board books, cloth books, and movable or pop-up books. Board books, which are printed on very thick and glossy paperboard, and cloth books, made of fabric, are good choices for infants and toddlers for very practical reasons. Their tactile quality appeals to the sensorimotor period of development of children in these early years. The books are durable, can be easily washed, and will withstand rough treatment. They also work well for helping children learn how to properly handle books. Some are more successful than others. Scratch-and-sniff books, for example, are temporary objects indeed, seldom serving more than a few readings. Cloth books, despite their resilience, lack the feel of books, and they do not store very easily— unless we put them in sock or underwear drawers. Board books have become very plentiful and are the closest to feeling like a typical book. However, the very thick pages mean that the book itself has to be fairly short (otherwise it would become cumbersome to carry about). These are probably best thought of as preliminary books to be used until little hands can effectively turn the paper pages of a normal book.

Also popular with very young children (probably from about 1 to 3 years of age) are the tactile books—books that contain something for the children to touch and feel. Some of these have become classics. Dorothy Kunhardt's *Pat the Bunny* contains textured surfaces (cotton to suggest the bunny's fur and sandpaper to represent Daddy's scratchy beard) and movable parts (drawers that pull out). These make for great interactive books, since the child is asked to perform certain tasks during the reading of the story.

Movable books are those that incorporate movable parts within the pages—anything from lift-the-flap or pull-the-tab devices to pop-up mechanisms of extraordinary refinement. There are examples of movable books from the Middle Ages and the Renaissance, although those were not for children. For example, in the Renaissance, the pages with movable parts were used especially in anatomy books. The earliest movable books for children, dating from the eighteenth century, were of the lift-the-flap variety, inviting children to lift flaps to reveal a picture beneath—perhaps opening the shutter to a window or a door to a cabinet. Another early device, still widely used, is the pull-tab, which can be used to reveal a hidden picture or to operate several moving parts at once. Dorothy Kunhardt's *Pat the Bunny* uses both the lift-the-flap and pull-the-tab devices.

By Victorian times (the late nineteenth century), the movable book had approached high art. The Victorians produced elaborate pop-up books that opened up to reveal dramatic three-dimensional scenes with several moving parts, included rotating paper discs called *volvelles*. They also used a technique we call scanimation, in which sliding paper gives the illusion of motion, which is wonderfully used in Rufus Butler Seder's 2007 book, *Gallop!*

Two accomplished artists working in this medium today are Robert Sabuda and Matthew Reinhart. Sabuda is celebrated for his lavish movable books, almost always quite bulky because of the elaborate apparatus they require. His works, such as L. Frank Baum's *Winter's Tale* and *The Wonderful Wizard of Oz*, contain multiple moving parts on each page as magnificent scenes unfold before the viewer. Sabuda and Reinhart collaborated on *Encyclopedia Prehistorica: Dinosaurs*, a masterful work appealing to the fascination so many young children have with those awesome creatures. On his own, Reinhart has created works such as the intriguing concept books, *Animal Poposites: A Pop-up Book for Opposites*, and *Cinderella: A Pop-up Fairy Tale*. All of these books have raised the bar for future pop-up and movable books.

Almost always in a movable book, however, the text is relegated to second place as the visual medium takes over. Like cardboard books, movable books must necessarily contain fewer pages, so the story is usually simplified. When a folktale is transformed into a movable book, plot details and interesting language are usually replaced by moving figures and three-dimensional castles and forests. We shouldn't think of the pop-up "Cinderella" as a substitute for the story itself. Movable books are, after all, more visual art than literature.

Wordless Picture Books

Wordless picture books are, as the name implies, books without words. These are usually for the very young—but not always. The absence of language presents interesting challenges for both the illustrator and the reader. Because these books contain no language (some contain a few words or phrases, but rely chiefly on the pictures to tell the story), they have been the subject of much controversy over whether they actually constitute "literature." On the other hand, many wordless picture books contain all the familiar literary elements, including plot, point of view, theme, character, setting, and tone (see Chapter 3). In this manner they help children develop linguistic and storytelling skills. Also, because wordless picture books seem to demand an oral response from the reader, they play an important role in the development of positive reading habits and attitudes among children. (See the essays by Cianciolo [1984] and Groff [1984] for two different viewpoints on the value of wordless picture books.)

The key to a successful wordless picture book is the storytelling quality of its illustrations. Art in children's picture books is chiefly narrative art—that is, it tells a story. As suggested above, we cannot assume that just because a book has no words, it is for very young children. In fact, some are quite sophisticated, indeed, and only a much older reader will fully appreciate them. In Mitsumasa Anno's *Anno's Journey,* a lone traveler makes his way through Europe on horseback; moving from countryside to village to city, he travels across time as well. If we look closely we will see, among other things, Little Red Riding Hood and the Big Bad Wolf, Don Quixote tilting at a windmill, Big Bird and Kermit the Frog from *Sesame Street,* a developing romance, an escaping prisoner, and so on. It is also a seek-and-find book in which we are invited to locate the traveler in each picture. (The most famous seek-and-find books are probably the "Where's Wally" books, created by the British illustrator Martin Handford. First appearing in the 1980s, the series became an international phenomenon, with the character's name being adapted to different geographic regions—he is "Hetty" in India, "Hugo" in Sweden, and, of course, in the United States, he is "Waldo.")

David Wiesner, a three-time Caldecott medalist, is a modern master of the wordless picture book whose works delight all ages. His *Tuesday* (see Chapter 7, Color Plate D) is a fanciful tale of what might happen if, for one night only, frogs could fly. The stunning full-color illustrations, with an unsettling surrealistic mood, depict a series of vignettes—a record of the occurrences on this magical night. The story is simple enough for very young children to grasp and clever enough and amusing enough to captivate adults.

However, most wordless picture books are for preschoolers. Nancy Tafuro's *Have You Seen My Duckling?* is a beautifully illustrated wordless book intended for the youngest children. The bold, colorful illustrations depict a mother duck searching for her lost duckling, except that the duckling is not lost, but only hiding from its mother. In each double-page spread, we catch glimpses of the sly duckling, sometimes just a wing or tail, just outside the mother's vision, but not ours. Children delight in finding the duckling on each page. In this way, the book is not only entertaining but also helps young readers use their cognitive skills. (It is a sort of literary version of "Peek-a-boo.")

Pat Hutchins's *Rosie's Walk* contains one sentence—a string of prepositional phrases—describing an afternoon excursion of Rosie the hen. On her walk she goes across the yard, over the haystack, around the pond, and so on. What the text does not tell us is that Rosie, unbeknownst to her, is being stalked by a fox, whose attempts to capture Rosie are met with one comical disaster after another until he is finally besieged by hoards of bees and hightails it out of the story. The blissfully ignorant Rosie arrives back home in time for dinner. Lacking the illustrations, we would miss the whole plot—and all the enjoyment.

Eric Rohmann's charming Caldecott-winning *My Friend Rabbit* (see Figure 6.8) incorporates just enough text to let us know that well-meaning Rabbit is always getting into trouble, and following that is a delightful story in pictures showing Rabbit's wild scheme for retrieving Mouse's toy airplane from a treetop. The book's appeal is in the bold and comical illustrations of the assortment of animals enlisted by Rabbit to help. Words would be superfluous—the body language and facial expressions say it all.

"Not to worry, Mouse,
I've got an idea."

Figure 6.8 ● Eric Rohmann's Caldecott Award–winning *My Friend Rabbit* is virtually a wordless picture book, with only minimal text at the very beginning, in the middle, and at the end of the story. This illustration is the final one in the book and it suggests that the errant escapades of Rabbit will continue—he has flown the toy airplane of his friend, Mouse, into the treetops—again! Notice how space is used in the illustration—the figures all crowded in the upper right-hand corner, suggesting that they are high up in the tree. The broken line coming in from the upper left is an artistic convention indicating the path of motion, and the movement of the leaves and branches is also suggested by very short dashes. All these elements combine to present us with a precarious—albeit comical—situation.

Source: Image from *My Friend Rabbit* by Eric Rohmann. Copyright © 2002 by Eric Rohmann. Reprinted by arrangement with Henry Holt and Company, LLC.

Easy Readers

In 1957, Dr. Seuss, acting on a wager with his publisher, brought out *The Cat in the Hat* (see Figure 6.9), a book written with a vocabulary of just 236 words—and the easy reader book was born. In the same year, Else Holmelund Minarik came out with the first of her "Little Bear" series, illustrated by Maurice Sendak, and in 1970, Arnold Lobel's "Frog and Toad" series was launched. All of these books have in common a controlled vocabulary aimed at giving children in the early elementary grades practice in reading. The texts of

Figure 6.9 ● Dr. Seuss's simple cartoon drawings (here is his *The Cat in the Hat*) have delighted children for half a century. As is typical of cartoon illustration, the colors are bold and simple—in this case just red and white against a background of blue. No attempt is made to suggest reality. The comical exaggerations and disproportion are perfectly suited to the fanciful tale with its rollicking rhyme and rhythm.

Source: From *The Cat in the Hat* by Dr. Seuss, Trademark ™ and copyright © by Dr. Seuss Enterprises, L.P. 1957, renewed 1985. Used by permission of Random House Children's Books, a division of Random House, Inc.

some of these books are highly acclaimed. Two of Lobel's books, *Frog and Toad Are Friends* and *Frog and Toad Together,* received Newbery Honor citations. And the popular "Henry and Mudge" series is written by Newbery Award–winning author Cynthia Rylant and illustrated by Suçie Stevenson. Henry is a little boy, Mudge is his dog, and they engage in a series of often ingenious adventures that now runs to some 25 books and moves through various reading levels. Other series include Peggy Parish's much-loved "Amelia Bedelia" books for beginning readers, about the hapless maid who takes everything too literally. Syd Hoff wrote dozens of easy readers, typically with clever children and charming animals, including *Danny and the Dinosaur,* which some credit with starting the dinosaur craze among children.

Lest anyone should think these books are easy to write, we should note that many children's picture books contain somewhat sophisticated vocabularies, since the assumption is that adults will be reading them to the children. (Remember the example of Beatrix Potter?) In the easy readers, the vocabulary contains words that children can readily recognize or sound out. And words and phrases are frequently repeated for pedagogical purposes. Given these restrictions, the author then has to devise an interesting story with engaging characters—it is quite a challenge. Today's children are lucky to have literate and enjoyable stories to learn to read by—these books far surpass the dull fare of the basal readers widely used in the last century.

Summary

It is never too early to begin sharing books with children. Even tiny infants can learn the enjoyment of holding a cardboard or cloth book. By the time they are age 2, they will be asking for their favorite stories to be read to them. The time we have to share books with children is short indeed, for they grow up all too quickly. So it is very important that we don't waste that time on lackluster and mediocre books. Books for the very young are wonderfully varied. Alphabet and counting books can go far beyond instruction and can provide magical journeys into the imagination. Many books for the very young are designed to introduce such perceptual concepts as discerning shapes, colors, sizes, and opposites. Even though many of these books may be dealing with concepts that they may not be intellectually ready to grasp, the books that are well executed, interesting to look at, and stimulating to the imagination can still fascinate them.

For the very young audience—infants and toddlers—board books, cloth books, and tactile books are durable and can be very entertaining. Books with moving parts go beyond being books; they are visually stimulating artworks, and not for children only. And when children have mastered the alphabet and move on to word recognition and reading, they will find waiting for them a wide selection of easy readers, books combining interesting stories with controlled vocabularies that they can enjoy on their own. These first experiences with books should be happy ones for children. Their encounters with books should be frequent and varied, for a good book is food for both the child's mind and spirit.

For Reflection and Discussion

1. Locate and compare several alphabet and several counting books. Identify the purpose of each book and its intended audience. Then evaluate it according to the criteria described in this chapter. Be sure to consider the illustrations, the specific content, any thematic thread running through the book, its appropriateness to the intended audience, and so on.

2. Locate and compare several concept books on related topics—such as books on color, books on the seasons, books on animals, and so on. Identify the specific purpose of each book and its intended audience. Then evaluate each book according to the criteria described in this chapter.

3. Locate and read three or four tactile and/or movable books. How would you evaluate the story? How would you evaluate the tactile or movable quality of the book?

4. Locate and examine a movable book that retells a familiar folktale. Now read a standard of the tale itself. How has the tale been altered to accommodate the movable book format? Do you think it was successfully done or were crucial elements sacrificed?

5. Locate and read three or four easy readers, but choose each one from a different level (the levels are always numbered—0, 1, 2, 3, and so on—on the front cover). How would you describe the differences between the various levels? Are they only in vocabulary? Or do you find differences in the types of stories and their complexity?

Works Cited

Baring-Gould, William S., and Ceil Baring-Gould. *The Annotated Mother Goose*. New York: Potter, 1962.

Butler, Francelia. *Skipping Around the World: The Ritual Nature of Folk Rhymes*. New York: Ballantine, 1989.

Cianciolo, Patricia. "Visual Literacy, and to Study Literature." *Jump Over the Moon*. Ed. Pamela Barron and Jennifer Q. Burley. New York: Holt, 1984, 139–144.

Groff, Patrick. "Children's Literature Versus Wordless Books?" *Jump over the Moon*. Ed. Pamela Barron and Jennifer Q. Burley. New York: Holt, 1984, 145–154.

● Recommended Readings

Haining, Peter. *Movable Books: An Illustrated History.* London: New English Library, 1979.

Hopkins, Lee Bennett. "Pop Go the Books." *CLA Bulletin* 16 (Fall 1990): 10–12.

Kiefer, Barbara. "Critically Speaking: Literature for Children." *The Reading Teacher* (January 1985): 458–463.

Lindauer, Shelley L. Knudson. "Wordless Books: An Approach to Visual Literacy." *Children's Literature in Education* 19, 3 (1988): 136–142.

MacCann, Donnarae, and Olga Richard. *The Child's First Books.* New York: Wilson, 1973.

Pritchard, David. "'Daddy, Talk!' Thoughts on Reading Early Picture Books." *The Lion and the Unicorn* 7/8 (1983/84): 64–69.

Schoenfield, Madalynne. "Alphabet and Counting Books." *Day Care and Early Education* 10 (Winter 1982): 44.

Stewig, John Warren. "Alphabet Books: A Neglected Genre." In *Jump Over the Moon.* Ed. Pamela Barron and Jennifer Q. Burley. New York: Holt, 1984, 115–120.

Thomas, Della. "Count Down on the 1–2–3's." *School Library Journal* 15 (March 1971): 95–102.

Selected Bibliography of Mother Goose Books

Alderson, Brian, comp. *The Helen Oxenbury Nursery Rhyme Book.* Illus. Helen Oxenbury. New York: Morrow, 1986.

Briggs, Raymond, illus. *The Mother Goose Treasury.* New York: Coward, McCann & Geoghegan, 1966.

de Angeli, Marguerite, illus. *Book of Nursery and Mother Goose Rhymes.* Garden City, NY: Doubleday, 1953.

de Paola, Tomie, illus. *My First Mother Goose.* New York: Grosset and Dunlap, 2009.

Esposito, Pamela, designer. *Mother Goose: A Classic Collection of Nursery Rhymes.* Illus. Frederick Richardson. Atlanta, GA: Intervisual Books, 2008.

Glazer, Tom. *The Mother Goose Songbook.* Illus. David McPhail. New York: Doubleday, 1990.

Goldstein, Bobbie, ed. *Mother Goose on the Loose.* New York: Abrams, 2003.

Gustafson, Scott. *Favorite Nursery Rhymes from Mother Goose.* New York: Greenwich Workshop P, 2007.

Hader, Berta, and Elmer Hader. *Picture Book of Mother Goose.* 1930. New York: Crown, 1987.

Hague, Michael, illus. *Mother Goose: A Collection of Classic Nursery Rhymes.* New York: Holt, 1984.

Jerrold, Walter. *Mother Goose's Nursery Rhyme.* Illus. Charles Robinson. New York: Everyman, 1993.

Lang, Andrew, ed. *The Nursery Rhyme Book.* Illus. L. Leslie Brooke. New York: Dover, 1972.

Lines, Kathleen, ed. *Lavender's Blue.* Illus. Harold Jones. New York: Watts, 1973.

Lobel, Arnold, illus. *The Random House Book of Mother Goose.* New York: Random House, 1986.

Long, Sylvia, illus. *Sylvia Long's Mother Goose.* San Francisco: Chronicle Books, 1999.

Marcus, Leonard S., and Amy Schwartz, selectors. *Mother Goose's Little Misfortunes.* Illus. Amy Schwartz. New York: Bradbury, 1990.

Marshall, James. *James Marshall's Mother Goose.* 1986. New York: Square Fish (Macmillan), 2009.

Merriam, Eve. *The Inner City Mother Goose.* 1969. Illus. David Diaz. New York: Simon & Schuster, 1996.

Opie, Iona. *My Very First Mother Goose.* Illus. Rosemary Wells. New York: Candlewick, 1996.

Petersham, Maud, and Miska Petersham, illus. *The Rooster Crows: A Book of American Rhymes and Jingles.* New York: Macmillan, 1945.

Polacco, Patricia. *Babushka's Mother Goose.* New York: Philomel, 1995.

Provensen, Alice, and Martin Provensen, illus. *The Mother Goose Book.* New York: Random House, 1976.

Rackham, Arthur, illus. *Mother Goose.* 1913. New York: Marathon, 1978.

Reed, Philip, illus. *Mother Goose and Nursery Rhymes.* New York: Atheneum, 1963.

Sanderson, Ruth, illus. *Mother Goose and Friends.* Boston: Little, Brown, 2008.

Scarry, Richard, illus. *Richard Scarry's Best Mother Goose Ever.* New York: Golden Books, 1999.

Smith, Jessie Willcox, illus. *The Jessie Willcox Smith Mother Goose.* New York: Derrydale, 1986.

Sutherland, Zena, comp. *The Orchard Book of Nursery Rhymes.* Illus. Faith Jaques. New York: Orchard, 1990.

Tripp, Wallace, illus. *Granfa' Grig Had a Pig and Other Rhymes Without Reason from Mother Goose.* Boston: Little, Brown, 1976.

Tudor, Tasha, illus. *Mother Goose: Seventy-Seven Verses with Pictures by Tasha Tudor.* New York: Oxford University Press, 1944.

Watson, Clyde. *Father Fox's Pennyrhymes.* Illus. Wendy Watson. New York: HarperCollins, 2001.

Wildsmith, Brian, illus. *Brian Wildsmith's Mother Goose.* New York: Watts, 1965.

Withers, Carl, collector. *A Rocket in My Pocket: The Rhymes and Chants of Young America.* Illus. Susanne Suba. New York: Holt, 1946.

Wright, Blanche Fisher, illus. *The Real Mother Goose.* New York: Rand McNally, 1916.

Selected Bibliography of Alphabet, Counting, and Concept Books

The following books are organized according to types described in this chapter. This is only a representative selection of the many fine picture books available to young readers, and an effort has been made to balance the enduring classics with the more recent fare. Unless otherwise indicated, the author is also the illustrator.

Alphabet Books

Anno, Mitsumasa. *Anno's Alphabet.* New York: Harper, 1975.

Base, Graeme. *Animalia.* New York: Abrams, 1987.

Bourke, Linda. *Eye Spy: A Mysterious Alphabet.* New York: Chronicle, 1991.

Brown, Marcia. *Peter Piper's Alphabet.* New York: Scribner's, 1959.

Bruel, Nick. *Naughty Kitty.* New Milford, CT: Roaring Brook Press, 2005.

Burningham, John. *John Burningham's ABC's.* New York: Crown, 1985.

Chandra, Deborah. *A Is for Amos.* Illus. Keiko Narahashi. New York: Farrar, Straus & Giroux, 1999.

Feelings, Muriel. *Jambo Means Hello: A Swahili Alphabet Book.* Illus. Tom Feelings. New York: Dial, 1974.

Fujikawa, Gyo. *A to Z Picture Book.* New York: Grosset & Dunlap, 1974.

Gag, Wanda. *The ABC Bunny.* New York: Coward-McCann, 1933.

Garten, Jan. *The Alphabet Tale.* New York: Random House, 1964.

Gerstein, Mordecai. *The Absolutely Awful Alphabet.* New York: Harcourt, 1999.

Green, Dan. *Wild Alphabet: An A to Zoo Pop-up Book.* London: Kingfisher, 2010.

Grover, Max. *The Accidental Zucchini: An Unexpected Alphabet.* New York: Harcourt, 1993.

Hoban, Tana. *A, B, See.* New York: Greenwillow, 1982.

Isadora, Rachel. *City Seen from A to Z.* New York: Greenwillow, 1983.

Johnson, Stephen T. *Alphabet City.* New York: Viking Penguin, 1995.

Kitamura, Satoshi. *From Acorn to Zoo: And Everything in Between in Alphabetical Order.* New York: Farrar, 1992.

Kitchen, Bert. *Animal Alphabet.* New York: Dial, 1984.

Kowalski, Gary. *Earth Day: An Alphabet Book.* Illus. Rocco Baviera. Boston: Skinner House, 2009.

Lester, Alison. *Alice and Aldo.* Boston: Houghton Mifflin, 1998.

MacDonald, Suse. *Alphabatics.* New York: Bradbury, 1986.

Martin, Bill, Jr., and John Archambault. *Chicka Chicka Boom Boom.* Illus. Lois Ehlert. New York: Simon & Schuster, 1989.

McLimans, David. *Gone Wild: An Endangered Animal Alphabet.* New York: Walker, 2006.

McMullan, Kate. *I Stink!* Illus. Jim McMullan. New York: Joanna Cotler, 2002.

Merriam, Eve. *Where Is Everybody? An Animal Alphabet.* New York: Simon & Schuster, 1989.

Mullins, Patricia. *V for Vanishing: An Alphabet of Endangered Animals.* New York: HarperCollins, 1994.

Musgrove, Margaret. *Ashanti to Zulu: African Traditions.* Illus. Leo and Diane Dillon. New York: Dial, 1976.

Oxenbury, Helen. *Helen Oxenbury's ABC.* New York: Delacorte, 1983.

Poulin, Stephane. *Ah! Belle Cité!/A Beautiful City ABC.* Montreal: Tundra, 1985.

Rankin, Laura. *The Handmade Alphabet.* New York: Dial, 1991.

Seuss, Dr. (pseud. of Theodore Geisel). *Dr. Seuss's ABC.* New York: Random, 1988.

Sierra, Judy. *The Sleepy Little Alphabet: A Bedtime Story from Alphabet Town.* Illus. Melissa Sweet. New York: Knopf, 2009.

Van Allsburg, Chris. *Z Was Zapped.* Boston: Houghton Mifflin, 1987.

Viorst, Judith. *The Alphabet from Z to A (With Much Confusion on the Way).* New York: Atheneum, 1994.

Wilbur, Richard. *The Disappearing Alphabet.* Illus. David Diaz. Orlando: Harcourt, 1998.

Wildsmith, Brian. *Brian Wildsmith's ABC.* New York: Watts, 1962.

Counting Books

Anno, Mitsumasa. *Anno's Counting Book.* New York: Crowell, 1977.

——. *Anno's Magic Seeds.* New York: Philomel, 1995.

Bang, Molly. *Ten, Nine, Eight.* New York: Greenwillow, 1983.

Berkes, Marianne. *Over in the Ocean: In a Coral Reef.* Illus. Jeanette Canyon. Nevada City, CA: Dawn Publications, 2004.

Blackstone, Stella. *My Granny Went to Market: A Round-the-World Counting Rhyme.* Santa Rosa, CA: Barefoot Books, 2005.

Burningham, John. *John Burningham's 1,2,3's.* New York: Crown, 1985.

Carle, Eric. *My Very First Book of Numbers.* New York: Crowell, 1985.

——. *The Very Hungry Caterpillar.* Cleveland: World, 1970.

Cousins, Lucy. *Count with Maisy.* New York: Candlewick, 1997.

Falconer, Ian. *Olivia Counts.* New York: Atheneum, 2002.

Feelings, Muriel. *Moja Means One: A Swahili Counting Book.* Illus. Tom Feelings. New York: Dutton, 1971.

Garne, S. T. *One White Sail.* San Marcos, CA: Green Tiger, 1992.

Geisert, Arthur. *Pigs from 1 to 10.* Boston: Houghton Mifflin, 1992.

Hoban, Russell. *Ten What? A Mystery Counting Book.* New York: Scribner's, 1974.

Hoban, Tana. *Count and See.* New York: Macmillan, 1972.

——. *26 Letters and 99 Cents.* New York: Greenwillow, 1987.

Hutchins, Pat. *The Doorbell Rang.* New York: Greenwillow, 1986.

Keats, Ezra Jack. *Over in the Meadow.* New York: Scholastic, 1971.

Kitchen, Bert. *Animal Numbers.* New York: Dial, 1987.

Langstaff, John. *Over in the Meadow.* Illus. Feodor Rojankovsky. New York: Harbrace, 1973.

Marino, Gianna. *One Too Many: A Seek and Find Counting Book.* San Francisco, CA: Chronicle, 2010.

McMillan, Bruce. *Eating Fractions.* New York: Scholastic, 1991.

——. *Here a Chick, There a Chick.* New York: Lothrop, 1983.

Merriam, Eve. *Twelve Ways to Get to Eleven.* Illus. Bernie Karlin. New York: Simon & Schuster, 1993.

O'Keefe, Susan Heyboer. *One Hungry Monster: A Counting Book in Rhyme.* Boston: Little, Brown, 1989.

Oxenbury, Helen. *Numbers of Things.* New York: Watts, 1968.

Rankin, Laura. *The Handmade Counting Book.* New York: Dial, 1998.

Reasoner, Charles. *One Blue Fish: A Colorful Counting Book.* New York: Little Simon, 2010.

Reiss, John. *Numbers.* New York: Bradbury, 1971.

Scott, Ann Herbert. *One Good Horse: A Cowpuncher's Counting Book.* Illus. Lynn Sweat. New York: Greenwillow, 1990.

Sis, Peter. *Waving.* New York: Greenwillow, 1989.

Tafuri, Nancy. *The Big Storm: A Very Soggy Counting Book.* New York: Simon & Schuster, 2009.

Wadsworth, Olivia. *Over in the Meadow.* Illus. Anna Vojtech. New York: North South Books, 2002.

Wildsmith, Brian. *Brian Wildsmith's 1,2,3's.* New York: Watts, 1965.

Books about Colors, Shapes, and Sounds

Anno, Mitsumasa. *Anno's Sundial.* New York: Philomel, 1987.

Brown, Marcia. *Listen to a Shape.* New York: Watts, 1979.

Charles, N. N. *What Am I? Looking Through Shapes at Apples and Grapes.* New York: Scholastic, 1994.

Cottin, Menena. *The Black Book of Colors.* Trans. Elisa Amado. Illus. Rosana Faria. Toronto, CA: Groundwood, 2008.

Dodd, Emma. *Dog's Colorful Day: A Messy Story about Colors and Counting.* New York: Dutton, 2001.

Ehlert, Lois. *Color Farm.* New York: Lippincott, 1990.

——. *Color Zoo.* New York: Lippincott, 1989.

Emberley, Rebecca. *City Sounds.* Boston: Little, Brown, 1989.

——. *Jungle Sounds.* Boston: Little, Brown, 1989.

Fisher, Leonard Everett. *Look Around! A Book about Shapes.* New York: Viking, 1987.

Grifalconi, Ann. *The Village of Round and Square Houses.* Boston: Little, Brown, 1986.

Hoban, Tana. *Circles, Triangles and Squares.* New York: Macmillan, 1974.

Hughes, Shirley. *All Shapes and Sizes.* New York: Lothrop, 1986.

Konigsburg, E. L. *Samuel Todd's Book of Great Colors.* New York: Atheneum, 1990.

Lionni, Leo. *Colors, Numbers, Letters.* New York: Knopf, 2010.

MacKinnon, Debbie. *What Shape?* New York: Dial, 1992.

Pienkowski, Jan. *Shapes.* New York: Simon & Schuster, 1981.

Pledger, Maurice. *Sounds of the Wild: Safari.* San Diego, CA: Silver Dolphin Books, 2009.

Reiss, John. *Colors.* New York: Macmillan, 1987.

——. *Shapes.* New York: Macmillian, 1987.

Shannon, George. *White Is for Blueberry.* Illus. Laura Dronzek. New York: Greenwillow, 2005.

Sidman, Joyce. *Red Sings from the Tree Tops: A Year in Colors.* Illus. Pamela Zagarenski. New York: Houghton Mifflin, 2009.

Van Fleet, Matthew. *Monday the Bullfrog.* New York: Simon & Schuster, 2006.

Walsh, Ellen Stoll. *Mouse Paint.* New York: Harcourt, 1989.

Wood, Audrey. *The Deep Blue Sea: A Book of Colors.* Illus. Bruce Wood. New York: Blue Sky Press, 2005.

Books about Opposites (and Other Puzzles)

Burningham, John. *John Burningham's Opposites.* New York: Crown, 1986.

Carle, Eric. *Eric Carle's Opposites.* New York: Grosset and Dunlap, 2007.

Crowther, Robert. *Opposites.* New York: Candlewick, 2005.

Falconer, Ian. *Olivia's Opposites.* New York: Atheneum, 2002.

Gillham, Bill, and Susan Hulme. *Let's Look for Opposites*. Photographs by Jan Siegieda. New York: Coward, 1984.

Hoban, Tana. *Is It Larger, Is It Smaller?* New York: Greenwillow, 1985.

———. *Push-Pull, Empty-Full*. New York: Macmillan, 1972.

Kohn, Bernice. *How High Is Up?* Illus. Jan Pyk. New York: Putnam, 1971.

Macmillan, Bruce. *Dry or Wet?* New York: Lothrop, 1988.

Maestro, Betsy, and Guilio Maestro. *Traffic: A Book of Opposites*. New York: Crown, 1981.

Murphy, Chuck. *Opposites (Slide 'n' Seek)*. New York: Little Simon, 2001.

———. *Shapes (Slide 'n' Seek)*. New York: Little Simon, 2001.

Oakes, Bill, and Suse MacDonald. *Puzzlers*. New York: Dial, 1989.

Portis, Antoinette. *Not a Box*. New York: Harper-Collins, 2006.

Rotner, Shelley, and Richard Olivo. *Close, Closer, Closest*. Photographs by Shelley Rotner. New York: Simon & Schuster, 1997.

Ruben, Patricia. *True or False?* New York: Harper, 1978.

Seeger, Laura Vaccaro. *Black? White! Day? Night!: A Book of Opposites*. New York: Roaring Brook Press, 2006.

Spier, Peter. *Fast-Slow, High-Low: A Book of Opposites*. New York: Doubleday, 1972.

Tactile and Movable Books

Bataille, Marion. *ABC3D*. New York: Roaring Brook Press, 2008.

Baum, L. Frank. *The Wonderful Wizard of Oz*. Illus. Robert Sabuda. New York: Little Simon, 2000.

Brown, Margaret Wise. *The Goodnight Moon Room: A Pop-Up Book*. Illus. Clement Hurd. New York: Harper & Row, 1984. (A variation on the 1947 classic)

Carle, Eric. *The Very Hungry Caterpillar*. Cleveland: World, 1968.

Carter, David. *School Bugs: An Elementary Pop-up Book*. New York: Little Simon, 2009.

Hoban, Tana. *Look! Look! Look!* New York: Greenwillow, 1988.

Kunhardt, Dorothy. *Pat the Bunny*. Racine, WI: Golden, 1962.

Pienkowaki, Jan. *Haunted House*. New York: Dutton, 1979.

Reinhart, Matthew. *Cinderella: A Pop-up Fairy Tale*. New York: Little Simon, 2002.

———. *Animal Poposites: A Pop-up Book of Opposites*. New York: Little Simon, 2002.

Sabuda, Robert. *Winter's Tale: An Original Pop-up Journey*. New York: Little Simon, 2005.

Sabuda, Robert, and Matthew Reinhart. *Encyclopedia Prehistorica Dinosaurs*. 2005.

Santoro, Lucio, and Meera Santoro. *Predators: A Pop-up Book with Revolutionary Technology*. New York: Little Simon, 2008.

Sendak, Maurice, Matthew Reinhart, and Arthur Yorinks. *Mommy?* New York: Michael di Capua Books/Scholastic, 2006.

Scarry, Richard. *Is This the House of Mistress Mouse?* New York: Golden, 1968.

Sports Illustrated Kids, WOW! The Pop-up Book of Sports. New York: Sports Illustrated, 2009.

Selected Bibliography of Wordless Picture Books

Alexander, Martha. *Bobo's Dream*. New York: Dial, 1970.

Aliki. *Tabby*. New York: HarperCollins, 1995.

Anno, Mitsumasa. *Anno's Britain*. New York: Philomel, 1982.

———. *Anno's Journey*. New York: Philomel, 1978.

———. *Anno's U.S.A.* New York: Philomel, 1983.

Banyai, Istvan. *Zoom*. New York: Viking, 1995.

Briggs, Raymond. *Father Christmas*. New York: Puffin, 1973.

——. *The Snowman*. New York: Random House, 1978.

Carle, Eric. *Do You Want to Be My Friend?* New York: Crowell, 1971.

de Paola, Tomie. *The Hunter and the Animals: A Wordless Picture Book*. New York: Holiday House, 1981.

Drescher, Henrik. *The Yellow Umbrella*. New York: Bradbury, 1987.

Faller, Régis. *Polo: The Runaway Bunny*. New Milford, CT: Roaring Brook, 2007.

Geisert, Arthur. *Oink*. Boston: Houghton Mifflin, 1991.

Goodall, John S. *The Adventures of Paddy Pork*. New York: Harcourt, 1968.

——. *An Edwardian Summer*. New York: Atheneum, 1976.

——. *The Story of an English Village*. New York: Atheneum, 1979.

——. *The Story of Main Street*. New York: Macmillan, 1987.

Handford, Martin. *Where's Wally?* London: Little Brown, 1987. (Titled *Where's Waldo?* in the United States)

Hutchins, Pat. *Changes, Changes*. New York: Macmillan, 1971.

——. *Good-Night Owl*. New York: Macmillan, 1972.

——. *Rosie's Walk*. New York: Macmillan, 1968.

Jenkins, Steve. *Looking Down*. Boston: Houghton Mifflin, 2003.

Louchard, Antonin. *Little Star*. New York: Hyperion, 2003.

Mayer, Mercer. *Oops!* New York: Dial, 1977.

McCully, Emily Arnold. *New Baby*. New York: Harper, 1988.

——. *School*. New York: Harper, 1987.

Rohmann, Eric. *My Friend Rabbit*. New Milford, CT: Roaring Brook, 2002.

——. *Time Flies*. New York: Crown, 1994.

Spier, Peter. *Noah's Ark*. New York: Doubleday, 1977.

——. *Peter Spier's Rain*. New York: Doubleday, 1982.

Tafuri, Nancy. *Have You Seen My Duckling?* New York: Greenwillow, 1984.

——. *Junglewalk*. New York: Greenwillow, 1988.

Thomson, Bill. *Chalk*. Tarrytown, NY: Marshall Cavendish, 2010.

Vincent, Gabrielle. *Ernest and Celestine's Patchwork Quilt*. New York: Greenwillow, 1985.

Ward, Lynn. *The Silver Pony*. Boston: Houghton Mifflin, 1973.

Weisner, David. *Free Fall*. New York: Lothrop, 1988.

——. *Sector 7*. New York: Clarion, 1999.

——. *Tuesday*. New York: Clarion, 1991.

Winter, Paula. *Sir Andrew*. New York: Crown, 1980.

Young, Ed. *The Other Bone*. New York: Harper, 1984.

Easy Readers

These are all series books, and only the first book of each series is listed—most are still in print. Many are part of the I Can Read series and are categorized by reading level.

Hoff, Syd. *Danny and the Dinosaur*. New York: Harper, 1958.

Lobel, Arnold. *Frog and Toad Are Friends*. New York: Harper, 1970.

Minarik, Else Holmelund. *Little Bear*. Illus. Maurice Sendak. New York: Harper, 1957.

Parish, Peggy. *Amelia Bedelia*. Illus. Fritz Seibel. New York: Harper, 1963.

Seuss, Dr. (pseud. of Theodore Geisel). *The Cat and the Hat*. New York: Random House, 1958.

PEARSON
myeducationkit

Go to the topics "Picture Books" and "Traditional Literature" on the MyEducationKit for this text, where you can:

- Search the Database of Children's Literature, housing more than 22,000 titles searchable in every genre by authors or illustrators, by awards won, by year published, and by topic and description.
- Explore genre-related Assignments and Activities, assignable exercises showing concepts in action

through database use, video, cases, and student and teacher artifacts.

- Listen to podcasts and read interviews from some of the brightest and most enduring stars of children's literature in the Conversations.
- Discover Web Links that will lead you to sites representing the authors you learn about in these pages, classrooms with powerful children's literature connections, and literature awards.

Picture Books

The Collaboration of Story and Art

Introduction

In *Alice's Adventures in Wonderland*, Alice asks, "What is the use of a book . . . without pictures or conversations in it?" Alice's sentiments are shared by all young children who are, after all, first drawn into books by the illustrations. Some of our most lasting memories are of the picture books we read as children—Ludwig Bemelmans's *Madeline*, Maurice Sendak's *Where the Wild Things Are*, and Chris Van Allsburg's *The Polar Express* are just a few of the perennially popular ones. These are the works that combine the art of storytelling with the art of illustration. The picture storybook is, in fact, a complex work of art requiring thoughtful conception and skillful execution.

A true picture book is one in which the pictures and the words are equally important. The illustrations not only help to tell the story but they also establish the mood and add layers of meaning to the text. With a good picture book, a child is often able, after but a few readings, to tell the story from the pictures alone. This turns out to be a fairly reliable way to judge a picture book's effectiveness.

This chapter will focus on how the text and the illustrations work together to form a satisfying picture book. Specifically, we will consider the key elements of the picture book, including storytelling techniques, artistic styles and media, and the overall book design.

History of the Picture Book

It is important that we distinguish the picture book from the illustrated book, in which the pictures do not tell the story, but serve as decoration or instruction. *Alice's Adventures in Wonderland* is itself an illustrated book, and so is this textbook—as are most books for grown-ups. The first children's picture book is often taken to be Jan Comenius's *Orbis Pictus* (see Chapter 1 and Figure 1.2), a seventeenth-century textbook designed to teach Latin vocabulary through pictures. However, true picture storybooks do not appear until the latter half of the nineteenth century. The English artist Walter Crane began illustrating children's nursery rhymes in the 1860s (see Chapter 1, Figure 1.5). And in the late 1870s, Randolph Caldecott, another talented English artist, began illustrating books for children. He is credited with first juxtaposing pictures and text (that is, placing them side by side) to tell a story. He was a talented draftsman, and his pictures exhibit grace, liveliness, and humor. He often took simple nursery rhymes, such as "Hey, Diddle, Diddle, the Cat and the Fiddle," and turned them into full-length picture books (see Chapter 1, Figure 1. 6). His name was given to the Caldecott Medal, an annual award from the American Library Association for the most distinguished American picture book.

PEARSON
myeducationkit

Visit the MyEducationKit for this course to enhance your understanding of chapter concepts with activities, web links, podcasts, and a searchable database of more than 22,000 children's literature titles.

English artist Kate Greenaway, a contemporary of Crane and Caldecott, was famous for her delicate illustrations, especially of children. She too illustrated nursery rhymes as well as children's poems (see Chapter 6, Figure 6.5). Her name has been given to the British counterpart of the Caldecott Medal. The Greenaway Medal goes annually to the most distinguished contribution to British children's illustration.

In 1902, Beatrix Potter published *The Tale of Peter Rabbit,* her own original story with her lovely watercolor illustrations (Color Plate A). This was followed by L. Leslie Brook's *Johnnie Crow's Garden* (1903), an original animal tale with warmly humorous illustrations. All of these artists benefited from the new printing technology of the late nineteenth century, which permitted more detailed and full-color reproductions. Following these pioneers would be a splendid procession of children's picture books up to the present, ever more inventive, ever more challenging, exploring the rich possibilities of the marriage between illustrations and text.

In the United States, it is not until Wanda Gág's *Millions of Cats* appears in 1928 that we find true American picture books (although American illustrated books were common from the nineteenth century). Gág's undulating black ink illustrations are ideally suited to the comical and lilting tale of an old man on a journey to find a cat. Receiving a Newbery Honor Book citation for its rhythmic text, it has never been out of print. Another landmark came in 1937, when Theodor Geisel (better known as Dr. Seuss) published *And to Think That I Saw It on Mulberry Street*. This was followed by some 60 books with their rollicking rhymes and comical cartoon drawings (see Chapter 6, Figure 6.9). Dr. Seuss himself was the first to admit he had few drawing skills—but his pictures perfectly suited his texts. Throughout the 1930s, we find more and more talented artists venturing into the picture book field, and in 1938, the first Caldecott Medal was awarded (for Dorothy Lathrop's *Animals of the Bible*).

In 1942, in the midst of World War II, came the *The Poky Little Puppy,* written by Janette Sebring Lowrey and illustrated by Gustaf Tenggren, meeting the war-time need for inexpensive children's books. This was the first of the Golden Books, which quickly became a staple item in homes across America. Early contributors to this series, which is still being published, included authors Margaret Wise Brown and Ruth Krauss, and illustrators Feodor Rojanskovsky, Garth Williams, and Richard Scarry. Both Brown and Krauss were writers with an innate understanding of childhood psychology; many of their books remain in print still after 70 years. (See especially Brown's *Goodnight Moon* and *The Runaway Bunny* and Krauss's *The Carrot Seed* and *The Backward Day*.)

Many prominent writers and illustrators began their careers in the 1950s, but it was not until the 1960s that we see the next significant milestones in picture-book publishing. In 1962, Ezra Jack Keats's *The Snowy Day* appeared—the first major picture book to include an African American protagonist. And in 1963, Maurice Sendak's *Where the Wild Things Are* introduced a new psychology to children's picture books, exploring anger and rebellion in a young child. Skeptics worried that Sendak's monsters would frighten children or that Max's deplorable behavior would set a bad example. But the book rapidly became a hit. General prosperity and further advances in printing processes soon resulted in the pricey, oversized, glitzy books with glossy covers that we know today.

A perusal of a good children's bookstore or library will quickly reveal a dazzling array of picture-book formats and artistic styles. Stylish artists such as Chris Van Allsburg (Figure 7.1), Kay (pronounced "Kigh") Nielsen (Color Plate C), David Wiesner (Color Plate D), and Paul O. Zelinsky (Color Plate E)—to name but a few—have made unforgettable contributions to picture books. However, these developments should not suggest that these lavish books are better than the simpler, more conventional books of the past. Art may change over the years, but that doesn't mean it is better. Try reading Margaret Wise Brown's *The Runaway Bunny* to a child and you will quickly discover that the best art is, indeed, timeless. The new should supplement—not replace—the old. We can enjoy the exciting and innovative pictures of today alongside the exquisite charm and beauty of books of the past.

Picture Book Texts

The term picture book describes a format—a book design—not a genre, which refers to a book's subject matter. In fact, picture books may deal with almost any subject. The picture-book text may be a folktale ("The Twelve Dancing Princesses" or "Rapunzel"—Color Plates C and E), a talking animal story (Beatrix Potter's *The Tale of Peter Rabbit*—Color Plate A), a realistic story (Robert McCloskey's *One Morning in Maine*), magical realism (David Wiesner's *Tuesday*—Color Plate D), a dream fantasy (Maurice Sendak's *Where the Wild Things Are),* nursery rhymes and concept books (see Chapter 6), or poetry (see Chapter 8). Our chief concern in this chapter will be the picture storybook enjoyed by children from about the ages of 4 through 8. Of course, some picture books are intended for much older audiences, even adults, but by the third grade most children have moved into chapter books and begin to see picture books as "babyish." (Many will learn to enjoy them again when they get to be adults.)

Color Plate A ● This watercolor from Beatrix Potter's *The Tale of Peter Rabbit* shows Peter brazenly eating radishes from Mr. McGregor's garden—defying his mother's warning. The style is quite realistic (aside from the fact that the animals are treated as people, but if rabbits could walk upright and wore clothes, they would look like this). Potter's light hand and delicate watercolors give her illustrations a warmth and charm that are uniquely hers.

Source: Beatrix Potter, *The Tale of Peter Rabbit.* London: Warne, 1901.

Color Plate B ● John Burningham is noted for his striking use of color as seen in this portrait of a cat from *Mr. Gumpy's Outing,* a comical tale for very young readers. The style of the illustration is akin to naïve art, but there is an expressionistic quality in the unusual coloring and the cat that is entirely made of circles and rectangles, with two triangles for ears.

Source: "Illustration" from *Mr. Gumpy's Outing* by John Burningham. Copyright © 1971 John Burningham. Reprinted by arrangement with Henry Holt and Company, LLC. *Mr. Grumpy's Outing* published by Jonathan Cape. Reprinted by permission of The Random House Group Ltd.

Color Plate C ● Kay Nielsen, a Danish artist whose children's illustrations date from the first two decades of the twentieth century, was strongly influenced by the Art Nouveau Movement, characterized by highly stylized figures, graceful curving lines, decorative organic motifs (usual floral). This illustration from "The Twelve Dancing Princesses" does not attempt a realistic portrayal. Instead, the figures and the setting (which reminds us of a theatrical backdrop) are the epitome of refinement. This is just how a prince and princess should look—elegant, ethereal creatures belonging to an enchanted world. And indeed, this tale is about twelve princesses who each night journey to a magical castle underground where they dance until dawn.

Source: "The Twelve Dancing Princesses" in *Powder and Crinoline,* illustrated by Kay Nielsen, London: Hodder & Stoughton, 1913.

Color Plate D ● David Wiesner's *Tuesday,* a delightfully surreal story about frogs taking flight on the lily pads one evening, is superbly illustrated by these surrealistic images. Surrealism is all about startling juxtapositions—very realistic frogs engaged in very unreal behavior. Wiesner uses a color palate of blues and lavenders, appropriate to the evening, and his details are exquisitely realistic—notice the patterns on the rotting log and delicate water lily in bloom. But he does not take himself too seriously; he thoroughly enjoys giving human expressions to the fishes gaping up from the pond and the dumbfounded turtle as they watch the smug frogs lift off on their fanciful night journey.

Color Plate E ● Paul O. Zelinsky's dramatic illustration for *Rapunzel* is a deliberate attempt to create the feeling of Renaissance Italy. Everything from the evocative landscape to the carefully detailed architecture to the glorious clothing suggests the fifteenth-century Italian. Renaissance art was strongly influenced by the realism of the art of classical Greece and Rome. Here, the figure of Rapunzel, with the prince and their twins at the story's happy ending, is reminiscent of a Madonna by Raphael. Zelinsky uses Raphael's rich colors, and the entire effect reminds us of a Renaissance portrayal of the Holy Family.

Figure 7.1 ● We, the viewers, are at a child's eye level looking over the table and up at the menacing monkeys (made even more disturbing from this point of view) in this surrealistic pencil drawing from Chris Van Allsburg's *Jumanji*. The figures seem to crowd us, adding an almost claustrophobic feeling, and the whole scene appears to be a moment uncomfortably frozen in time—an appropriate mood for this story of a mysterious board game that comes to life.

Source: Illustration from *Jumanji* by Chris Van Allsburg. Copyright © 1981 by Chris Van Allsburg. Reprinted by permission of Houghton Mifflin Harcourt Publishing Company. All rights reserved.

Plot

The plot of a good picture book must necessarily be straightforward, since there is little space in which to develop entanglements—the typical picture book is 32 pages long. Simplicity is a hallmark in books for very young children. One of the most famous picture books is Margaret Wise Brown's *Goodnight Moon*, the story of a little bunny who, in a thinly disguised attempt to avoid bedtime, insists on saying "goodnight" to virtually everything in his room. The text has a subtle rhythm, rhyming words, and a repetitive pattern. The illustrations, by Clement Hurd, are in bold primary colors—reds, greens, yellows—and suggest a childlike naïveté. As the story progresses, the colors in the room darken until finally the little bunny goes to sleep. The illustrations capture the gentle mood of the text, resulting in one of the best bedtime stories ever created.

We find sequential plots (Bill Martin's *Brown Bear, Brown Bear, What Do You See?*) and cumulative plots (Janina Domanska's *The Turnip*) in picture books for very young children. More sophisticated plots, such as the parallel structure in Robert McCloskey's *Blueberries for Sal*, are found in books for older readers. (See the discussion on plot in Chapter 3.)

Character

Characterization in picture books is necessarily simple, and characters tend to be identified by one or two dominant traits—for example, Peter Rabbit is curious and impishly rebellious. Maurice Sendak's Max (of whom we will hear more later) is a typical, self-centered child (like most his age). Children tend to identify with characters like themselves, and protagonists in picture books are most often young children or animals (who exhibit childlike qualities). In fact, we can usually determine the age of the intended reader by establishing the age of the protagonist. Sendak's Max appears to be 4 or 5 years old—hence, the intended reader can be assumed to be around age 4 or 5. (This is admittedly a little harder when the protagonist is a talking animal or a machine, like Mary Ann, the steam shovel in Virginia Lee Burton's *Mike Mulligan's Steam Shovel*, in which case we have to rely on the treatment of the subject and the language.)

Language

Since picture books average only about 2,000 words, the words must be very carefully chosen. Many books rely heavily on dialogue, which can be great fun to read aloud, as most picture books are intended. Children have a love for language and are fascinated with repetitive patterns. Notice how many stories include refrains, such as the classic "hundreds of cats, thousands of cats, millions and billions and trillions of cats" in Wanda Gág's *Millions of Cats*. Children even like made-up words, such as in the jolly tale *Master of All Masters*, retold by Joseph Jacobs, where the maid must learn odd new names for everyday items (a bed becomes a "barnacle," a cat a "white-faced simminy," and a fire a "hot cockalorum"—it is hilarious wordplay).

Some of the best picture books have minimalist texts, since the illustrations are expected to carry at least half the storytelling load. So Pat Hutchins, in her imaginative *Rosie the Hen* (discussed in Chapter 6) tells the entire story of Rosie's walk around the farmyard in one sentence of just 32 words.

Subject and Tone

Because of their brevity, picture books tend to be sharply focused; that is, a single subject and tone clearly dominate. However, the range of subjects is virtually unlimited. Today few topics are taboo in picture books. For instance, we can find provocative picture books on the Holocaust (Roberto Innocenti and Christophe Gallaz's *Rose Blanche*), the Hiroshima atomic bomb (Toshi Maruki's *Hiroshima No Pika*), social violence (Eve Bunting's *Smoky Night,* about the Los Angeles race riots), and homosexuality (Michael Willhoite's *Daddy's Roommate*). Many of these delicate issues are deftly handled through sensitive illustrations, and usually (but not always) the harsher themes are tempered by a hopeful tone.

As we noted in Chapter 3, the tone of a book refers to the author's attitude toward the subject. Many picture books are comic in tone, such as the joyful slapstick of Dr. Seuss, or the gentle humor we find in the works of Margaret Wise Brown (*The Runaway Bunny*), Robert McCloskey (*Blueberries for Sal*), and Mo Willem (*Knuffle Bunny*). Romantic enchantment is the feeling appropriately captured by Kay Nielsen's illustrations for the folktale, "The Twelve Dancing Princesses" (Color Plate C). Picture books also give us suspense, as found in Potter's *The Tale of Peter Rabbit* (Color Plate A) or Sendak's *Outside Over There*. More serious, reflective books include Lucille Clifton's poetic series about an inner-city African American boy, Everett Anderson, or Allen Say's *Grandfather's Journey,* a family memoir about Japanese immigrants beginning their lives anew in a strange land. An even more sobering tone is found in the books about the Holocaust, city street violence, and death and dying, as mentioned above. Picture books with these emotionally charged subjects are often designed to prompt meaningful discussion with children—and what better place to have those discussions than at home with a caring adult?

Elements of Picture-Book Art

Certainly we should hold picture books to the same high literary standards as we do books for older readers. But picture books are only "literature" in part. They are also examples of visual art, and we have to consider how the pictures and the text complement each other to produce the whole. Above all, picture-book art is narrative art; that is, it tells a story. But an artist—by applying lines, shapes, textures, and colors to a flat surface, and effectively using space and arrangement—can create the illusion of three dimensions or evoke specific emotional responses in us, such as joy or sadness, serenity or agitation. Let's briefly examine the principal elements of graphic art to see how they are used in children's picture books.

Line

Lines convey meaning; they indicate the shapes of objects—that is, an artist uses a line to draw the shape of a dog—but lines can also suggest texture, depth, and motion. Horizontal lines suggest calm and stability (recalling firm, solid ground), whereas vertical lines suggest height and distance. Sharp and zigzagging lines suggest excitement and rapid movement (think of a lightning bolt). In Ludwig Bemelmans's illustration for *Madeline* (Figure 7.2) the lines direct our eyes from the bottom of the page to the top; because the walkway

Figure 7.2 ● Ludwig Bemelmans's popular picture storybook *Madeline* is a delightful comedy about a spunky little girl in a Parisian convent school. The illustrations are interesting examples of expressionistic art. Notice the angularity of the figures and the exaggerated height of the nun, Miss Clavel, accompanying the 12 little girls who walk, as we are told, in "two straight lines" (surely a commentary on convent school discipline). The trees are more like ideas of trees; there is no attempt at realistic depiction. There is a carefree jocularity in these pictures that aptly characterizes the mood of the story.

Source: From *Madeline* by Ludwig Bemelmans. Copyright © 1939 by Ludwig Bemelmans, renewed © 1996 by Madeline Bemelmans and Barbara Bemelmans Marciano. Reprinted by permission of the publisher, Viking Penguin, a division of Penguin Books USA Inc.

narrows at the top, we understand that the girls "in two straight lines" are moving away from us. The lines also suggest the orderliness of the convent school, overseen by the dominating figure of Miss Clavel at the bottom. In Nielsen's portrayal of the ball from "The Twelve Dancing Princesses" (Color Plate C) the sweeping curve of the lines suggests grace and elegance at once beautiful and otherworldly.

Shape

Circles, ovals, squares, rectangles, and triangles, like lines, can define objects, but they can also elicit emotional reactions. Rounded shapes tend to suggest comfort, security, and stability, as seen in Zelinsky's portrait of Rapunzel's family (Color Plate E). They can also suggest spontaneity and a natural quality (as in Lawson's comical illustration for *The Story of Ferdinand,* Figure 7.5). Geometric shapes—squares, rectangles, triangles, perfect circles, ovals—often appear more static even if the subject matter is unsettling. *Jumanji* (Figure 7.1) and *Anansi the Spider* (see Figure 7.3) both employ geometric shapes, the first eliciting an eerie sense of drama, the second depicting what might be rather unpleasant if drawn realistically—a fish swallowing a spider—instead, the abstract style suitably suggests African folk art and culture.

Space

We often do not think of space—literally the empty parts of the page—as an artistic element, but it is, in fact, very powerful. There is an old story about a Japanese artist who, when asked what was the most important part of a painting, replied, "The part that is left out." Space is actually what draws our attention to objects on the page. If a page contains very little empty space, but is instead crowded with images, our attention is necessarily divided—we do not know exactly where to look. The lack of open space on a page may contribute to a claustrophobic or uneasy feeling (see *The Story of Ferdinand,* Figure 7.4) or perhaps confusion or chaos (see *Jumanji,* Figure 7.1). However, if a page contains a great deal of space surrounding a single object, all our attention goes to that object. In Rohmann's illustration from *My Friend Rabbit* (see Chapter 6, Figure 6.8), nearly half of which is empty space, and our eyes move upward and to the right where Rabbit and Mouse are stuck in a tree.

Texture

One of the illusions the artist creates is to give a flat surface (the paper) the characteristics of three dimensions and texture—the suggestion of fur, wood grain, smooth silk, and so on. We refer to this artistic quality as texture. An artist who wants to emphasize the realistic quality of a picture may pay great attention to texture. Notice the furry texture achieved in *Jumanji* (Figure 7.1) and *The Story of Ferdinand* (Figure 7.4). Texture is achieved through the skillful use of the medium—paint layers, brush strokes, pencil marks, and so on.

Figure 7.3 ● Gerald McDermott's illustrations for the African folktale *Anansi the Spider* were inspired by African folk art. The stylized figures are decorated with geometric shapes and colored boldly in primary colors. Despite the abstract quality of the pictures, children have no difficulty in identifying the scene as that of a fish swallowing a spider.

Source: Image from *Anansi the Spider* by Gerald McDermott. Copyright © 1972 by Gerald McDermott. Reprinted by arrangement with Henry Holt and Company, LLC.

Composition

The composition refers to the arrangement of the objects in a picture. Composition is important to the narrative quality of the picture as well as to its emotional impact. For example, grouping many large shapes together may suggest stability (see *Rapunzel*, Color Plate E) or discomfort (see *Jumanji*, Figure 7.1). Beatrix Potter depicts Peter Rabbit defying his mother's warning and devouring radishes from Mr. McGregor's garden (see Color Plate A). But notice how she creates a further interest by adding the robin, perched on the shovel handle. Peter's eyes are directed to the robin and the robin looks skyward, leaving us to ponder what each is thinking. Notice also how the composition is effectively intersected by an imaginary diagonal line from the lower left to upper right—there is order among the potential chaos.

Perspective

In addition to the organization of objects, the artist must also consider where best to place the focal point, from what angle the picture is to be viewed, and what mood is to be conveyed. The point of view, or the perspective, refers to the vantage point from which we see the objects on the page. The closer we appear to be to the action, the more engaged we are likely to be (see *The Story of Ferdinand*, Figure 7.4). The farther away we seem to be, the more detached we are (see *Madeline*, Figure 7.2). We may view events from a worm's-eye

He didn't look where he was sitting and instead of sitting on the nice cool grass in the shade he sat on a bumble bee.

Figure 7.4 ● This illustration by Robert Lawson for *The Story of Ferdinand* by Munro Leaf is a good example of the correlation of picture and text (without the text, we might not understand what is about to happen to the bee). Notice also how the various textures are depicted—the bull's hair, the bee's body, the clover. We should not overlook the comically expressive eye of the bee as it realizes it is about to be sat upon.

Source: From *The Story of Ferdinand* by Munro Leaf, illustrated by Robert Lawson, copyright 1936 by Munro Leaf and Robert Lawson, renewed © 1964 by Munro Leaf and John W. Boyd. Used by permission of Viking Penguin, A Division of Penguin Young Readers Group, A Member of Penguin Group (USA) Inc., 345 Hudson Street, New York, NY 10014. All rights reserved.

view or a small child's perspective or a bird's-eye view. For example, Van Allsburg uses perspective to heighten the disturbing qualities of his surrealistic tale, *Jumanji*. It is the story of a board game that comes to life with frightening consequences. By using unusual perspectives (as in Figure 7.1), the artist makes us feel uncomfortable—we are viewing the scene from an unsettling angle, as if we were hiding behind the table. Films use the same technique to suggest that an unseen person (such as an intruder) is watching a character. Perspective can create drama, as in the surrealistic images of floating frogs in David Wiesner's *Tuesday* (Color Plate D).

The artist may wish to change points of view from illustration to illustration—perhaps to avoid monotony, but more probably to make us see and think about things in specific ways. Perry Nodelman points out that most picture books give us the "middle shot." We see few close-ups and few panoramic views. This is probably because each picture book has only a limited number of "shots" (recall that the typical picture book has approximately 32 pages), so the artist must compromise on the variety of perspectives. We view Peter Rabbit (Color Plate A) and Burningham's cat (Color Plate B) almost head on and from a short distance, but Nielsen gives us the middle shot and we view the royal ball from a comfortable distance (Color Plate C). Bemelmans gives us a bird's-eye view in Figure 7.2, and this contrasts interestingly with the viewpoint provided by Wiesner (Color Plate D) where the viewer is looking upward. Even in a brief picture book, an artist is able to provide a variety of perspectives—from extreme close-ups to long-distance shots.

Color/Black and White

Children are especially responsive to color, and very early on they choose "favorite" colors, which we like to imagine reflect their personalities. Color is one of the most emotionally evocative of artistic elements. Psychologists tell us that reds and yellows are warm or hot colors and suggest excitement, whereas blues and greens are cool or cold colors and suggest calm or quiet. These reactions may be embedded in our responses to the natural world—red and yellow are suggestive of warmth and happiness, and they are also the colors of sunlight and fire; blue we find to be soothing and melancholy perhaps because we associate it with calm waters or the broad expanse of the sky and the lonely universe beyond. Colors take on associative values—purple signifies royalty; green denotes envy or illness, but also life and renewal; red indicates danger, but also boldness; blue signals depression, but also loyalty and serenity; yellow suggests cowardice, but also cheerfulness; and so on. However, these responses are often cultural. In imperial China, for example, the color yellow was reserved for the emperor, and throughout Asia white is a traditional color of mourning and brides often wear red.

Artists use color to establish the tone of a work. Beatrix Potter uses soft earthy colors in her pastoral story, *The Tale of Peter Rabbit* (Color Plate A); whereas John Burningham, in his light-hearted story, *Mr. Gumpy's Outing* (Color Plate B), experiments with a wilder, less conventional, palette. Kay Nielsen uses sharp contrasts that focus our attention on the dancing couple in "The Twelve Dancing Princesses" (Color Plate C), and the colors inside the palace suggest an artificial almost otherworldly elegance. David Wiesner turns to deep blues and greens to suggest mystery in his magical tale, *Tuesday* (Color Plate D). And Paul Zelinsky uses rich, primary colors in his pleasant family portrait for *Rapunzel* (Color Plate E), in which he deliberately imitates the art of the Italian Renaissance—indeed, this takes on the feeling a portrait of the Holy Family by Raphael.

Some of the most-loved picture books, however, have no color at all. Wanda Gág uses simple black and white in *Millions of Cats,* as does Robert Lawson in *The Story of Ferdinand* (Figure 7.4) and Chris Van Allsburg in several books, including *Jumanji* (Figure 7.1). Robert McCloskey liked to use monochrome—that is, just a single color. His *Blueberries for Sal* is appropriately illustrated in blue. Professional photographers have long preferred black and white or monochrome for its evocative subtleties. Without color as a distraction, the viewers pay closer attention to the lines, shapes, composition, perspective, and texture. It is certainly a mistake to think that children require garish colors in their books or that they will reject books with black and white illustrations. Never dismiss a book because it is in black and white. It is unlikely that either *The Story of Ferdinand* or *Jumanji* would be improved by color.

Design and Meaning in Picture Books

Crucial to the success of picture-book illustration is the design of the entire book and how that design contributes to the meaning of both the text and pictures, for it is here that the picture book is truly a unique art form. Among the features important to the design and meaning of picture books are rhythm and movement, tension, and page layout.

Rhythm and Movement

John Warren Stewig defines rhythm as "controlled repetition in art" (76). Good picture-book design creates a sense of rhythm as we move from page to page—a rhythm that is suited to the nature of the narrative. Design is governed in large part by the simple fact that we read our books, and therefore our pictures, from left to right. Consequently, it is argued that we tend to identify most closely with objects on the left—protagonists often appear on the left and antagonists on the right. For example, Nielson's illustration from "The Twelve Dancing Princesses" depicts the princess on the left (Color Plate C). In the illustration from McDermott's *Anansi the Spider* (Figure 7.3) the spider Anansi, the hero, is on the left. And in Steptoe's illustration (see Figure 7.5), the protagonist, the little girl narrator, appears on the left. In Paul Zelinsky's *Rumpelstiltskin,* the fiendish title character appears on the right side in 9 of the 11 illustrations in which he appears. But in Van Allsburg's illustration from *Jumanji* (Figure 7.1), the presumed protagonist, the girl in the doorway, is on the right with the unsettling figures of the monkeys on the left. This reversal of the normal order of things may contribute to the apprehensive, eerie feeling that this illustration evokes—quite suited to the

Figure 7.5 ● A child of expressionism, Les Fauves art includes distinctive strong, black lines separating parts of the picture—much like the lines made by the lead framing in stained-glass windows. Also characteristic of this artistic style is a certain vibrance of line that suggests motion—and emotion—as in this illustration from John Steptoe's *Daddy Is a Monster . . . Sometimes,* a story of parent/child relationships.

Source: Daddy Is a Monster . . . Sometimes, Copyright © 1980 by John Steptoe. Use licensed by the John Steptoe Literary Trust.

surrealistic story of an innocent game board mysteriously coming to life. Burningham's cat stares out at us from the left (Color Plate B), causing us to look first at its face and then to the rest of its body. Zelinsky's children (Color Plate E) have a similar orientation; they are turned with their backs to the left and they are looking up to the right. Of course, these are not hard-and-fast rules, but, in general, story movement is from left to right. (We should note that the left-to-right orientation is purely conventional. Israeli picture books are designed to be read from right to left, since Hebrew texts are written in reverse of Western texts—right to left, back to front—and as a result the movement in the pictures is also from right to left.)

This movement also suggests another anomaly in the picture book—the interrupted rhythm that occurs when we read it. The movement is not continually forward; rather, we look at the pictures, then we read, then we look at the pictures again. The pictures create a starting and stopping pattern for which the text must accommodate. This is why some picture book texts sound fairly inane when read without the pictures. (By the same token, the pictures often make little sense without the text; a problem, as we have seen, that the successful wordless picture book must overcome.) Effective picture books are usually designed so that a natural pause occurs between the turning of pages. At the same time, the book should make us want to turn the page (either to be surprised or to have our expectations confirmed).

Tension

Good picture books also create what Nodelman refers to as "directed tension"—a tension between what the words say and what the illustrations depict, resulting in our heightened interest and excitement. A book without such tension, where, for example, the pictures do no more than mimic the words or vice versa, can quickly become boring.

A good example of tension is found in Leaf and Lawson's *The Story of Ferdinand* (Figure 7.4). Without the text, the picture would make little sense. The words explain the bee's wary expression (it is about to be sat upon), they explain what the looming figure at the top of the page is, and, although they are not mentioned in the text, the building in the background and the clover in the foreground both provide perspective. Without the words, as a matter of fact, we might suppose that the bee is the protagonist requiring our sympathy, when, in reality, it is Ferdinand, the gentle bull. Finally, the words and pictures together set up a dramatic tension that makes us want to turn the page to see what happens next. (For other good examples of tension, see *Jumanji*, Figure 7.1, and *Tuesday*, Color Plate D; notice how each picture invites speculation and urges us on to see what will happen next.)

The illustration from *The Story of Ferdinand* is also a good example of how the narrative nature of the picture book often prevents the individual pictures from functioning as artistically complete units in themselves. The picture of the bee in Figure 7.4 is only complete when we see it in sequence with the rest of the illustrations in the book, not unlike a cartoon strip, with which picture books have a great deal in common.

Page Layout

Another element of book design is the placement of the pictures and the text on the page. Here are some things to consider:

- What size and shape are the pages?
- Are all the pictures on the same side of the page or is the placement varied?

- Are they all the same size or are there large and small pictures?
- Is there a good reason for the placement and size?
- Where is the text in relation to the pictures?
- What style of typography is used and does it seem effective and appropriate?

For example, most picture books are wider than they are high, and this makes them especially suited to narrative illustration—landscapes are usually depicted this way. On the other hand, books that are tall and narrow usually focus on character and diminish the setting (see *Madeline,* Figure 7.2 and *Rapunzel,* Color Plate E). The size of a book also affects us. We often associate very small books and very large books with the youngest readers—small books are easy for little hands to handle and large books are eye-catching. Medium-sized books, on the other hand, are frequently more complex. These are all issues to be considered by the writer, artist, and editor before a book is produced. And how these issues are handled will affect our response to a book.

The picture-book layout may also include the use of borders, vignettes, and panels. Borders frame the page and can enclose either text or illustrations. Sometimes they are decorative, as in *Anno's Alphabet,* where the elaborate borders contain hidden pictures of objects whose names begin with the letter of the alphabet being presented. As we will see later, in the discussion of *Where the Wild Things Are,* borders can contribute to the meaning of a book.

The artist creates a panel by framing two or more illustrations on the same page or double-page spread, usually to allow for various perspectives or to add to the storyline. David Wiesner uses panels in *Tuesday* (Color Plate D) to illustrate a variety of activities occurring simultaneously or sequentially in the same magical evening when frogs mysteriously take to flight on their lily pads.

The vignette is a small, incidental picture that is integrated into to the principal illustration. It is often used to supply additional information and sometimes for humor. David Macaulay uses vignettes in his elaborate book *The New Way Things Work.* This large, nonfiction picture book visually describes how hundreds of machines and devices work— from toasters to computers. And on each page, Macaulay places tiny figures of wooly mammoths who wisecrack their way through the book. They add comic relief to a book that might overwhelm some readers.

The gutter of a book should not be neglected. This is simply the crease made by the binding of the book. The good book designer accommodates for this space and does not allow illustrations to get lost in the gutter between the pages. This is especially important when the illustrations are double-page spreads.

Finally, we should not forget the typography—the style and size of the lettering and the placement of the words on the page. First and foremost, readers like a typeface that is easy to read—nothing too **elegant** or too **ornate** or too **stylized** or too funky. On the other hand, with so many typefaces to choose from these days, it is often possible to find one that suits the mood of the story. In some books, we find more than one typeface being used to good effect. In Carolivia Herron's *Nappy Hair,* different typefaces are used to represent the various speakers in the story, including a general chorus. Sometimes we even find hand lettering (used by Wanda Gág in *Millions of Cats* and Jean de Brunhoff in *The Story of Babar*). Hand lettering can appear charming, but it can also be difficult to read. The first concern for young readers is that the text be legible. The placement of the text can range from the very formal—the text appearing in the same place on every page—to the very informal—the text moving about from page to page. We also see text forming patterns on the page, as in Lloyd Moss's *Zin! Zin! Zin! A Violin,* illustrated by Marjorie Priceman, where the words undulate as with the sounds of the music produced by various instruments. So the choice of typeface and placement of the text can have an important effect on our response to a picture book.

Artistic Media

The artistic medium is simply the material (or materials—*media*) an artist chooses to produce an illustration. Shall it be drawn with pencil or ink? Shall it be painted in oils or watercolors or tempera? Shall it be cut from a block of wood or linoleum? We can classify media generally into four broad categories: painterly techniques, graphic techniques, photography, and composite techniques.

Painterly Techniques

Painterly techniques are those by which an artist creates an image by applying a medium (paint, chalk, ink, and so on) to a surface (usually paper) with an instrument (such as a brush, pen, or pencil). Paint itself consists of pigment (usually powdered) mixed with some liquid or paste to make it spreadable. Many variations are possible depending on the medium used to mix with the pigment. Among the most common are the following:

- *Watercolors,* as their name implies, use water as the medium, resulting in transparent, typically soft, delicate pictures, as in Potter's *The Tale of Peter Rabbit* (Color Plate A).
- *Tempera* is made by mixing pigments with egg yolk or some other albuminous substance. Tempera is not as transparent as watercolor and can produce some brilliant hues. It was used by Maurice Sendak in his classic *Where the Wild Things Are.*
- *Gouache* (say "gwash") is a powdered paint similar to tempera, but mixed with a white base, resulting in a delicate hue. Gouache was the favorite medium of Margot Zemach in such works as *Duffy and the Devil.*

- *Oil paint* typically uses linseed oil as a base and is among the most opaque of media. One of the best examples is found in Paul O. Zelinsky's illustrations for *Rapunzel* (Color Plate E).

- *Acrylics* use a plastic base, a product of twentieth-century technology, and they produce very brilliant colors; Barbara Cooney's illustrations for Donald Hall's *Ox-Cart Man* are excellent examples.

- *Pastels* differ from the rest in that they are typically applied in powdered form (often with the fingers). Chris Van Allsburg used pastels in his *The Wreck of the Zephyr*.

- *Chalk, pencil, and ink* drawings, although technically not painting, follow the same general principles as painterly techniques. Chris Van Allsburg's *Jumanji* (Figure 7.1) is illustrated with pencil drawings.

- *Crayons* were used by John Burningham in his fanciful story *Come Away from the Water, Shirley*.

Each of these media produces differing effects, and two or more may be used in combination as well. Leo and Diane Dillon's illustrations for Margaret Musgrove's *From Ashanti to Zulu* combine watercolors, pastels, and acrylics.

Graphic Techniques

Graphic techniques refer to those methods by which the artist creates an image by cutting blocks or etching plates, inking them, and impressing them on a surface such as paper. As with painterly techniques, there are several varieties:

- *Woodblocks* were the very earliest form of reproducible art. The first printed book illustrations—dating from the late Middle Ages—were made from blocks of wood on which the artist carved away all the areas that were not to be printed. The blocks were inked and paper was pressed onto them, resulting in the transfer of the image from block to paper (see Chapter 1, Figures 1.2 and 1.3). Ed Emberley used woodblocks in his Caldecott Award–winning *Drummer Hoff* (retold by Barbara Emberley).

- *Linocuts* are similar to woodblocks in principle, but the artist uses blocks of linoleum rather than wood. Barbara Cooney's *Dick Whittington and His Cat* is an example.

- *Stone lithography* is a complex process that involves first drawing a design on a smooth, flat stone with a waxy mixture similar to a crayon. As in woodblocks, the image must be done in reverse. The stone is then treated with a chemical fixative, wetted with water, and finally inked. The ink sticks only to the waxed areas, and when paper is pressed onto the stone, an impression is made. Robert McCloskey's *One Morning in Maine* is an example of stone lithography.

Photography and Digital Art

Photography may be considered an artistic style as much as a technique, but it is neverthe-less an art. Photography is the art of composition—of arranging objects within a frame so that the result is intellectually stimulating. In picture books, we normally expect something more creative than cell phone shots, and when photographs are used to tell stories, it is principally for realistic stories. Photographs can also be especially effective in informational books. When imaginatively used in black and white or in color, photography can be dramatic, beautiful, and highly expressive.

Since the 1990s, digital art—that is, art generated by a computer—has become more prevalent in children's picture books. One of the first artists to make a name in this field was J. otto Seibold (yes, the lowercase *o* is how he signs his work). *Mr. Lunch Takes a Plane Ride* (1993) and its sequels, written by Vivian Walsh and illustrated by Seibold, are good examples of his work, which bears a resemblance to cubist abstraction, with its emphasis on geometric shapes. Yet it is not without detail and the illustrations fit beautifully with the convoluted and comical storyline.

Composite Techniques

Composite techniques involve cutting, pasting, and/or assembling of materials to create an artistic whole. Montage is the collection and assembling of a variety of different pictures or designs to create a single picture. Collage is similar to montage but uses materials other than or in addition to paper—string, cotton, weeds, anything is game. Both have been used effectively in children's picture books, notably in the work of Ezra Jack Keats (*The Snowy Day* and its sequels) and Leo Lionni (*Frederick, Fish Is Fish,* and others). Artistic media are limited only the artist's ingenuity. Fabric art, such as the batik used by Patricia MacCarthy in Margaret Mahy's *The Horrendous Hullabaloo,* is becoming popular. Rufus Butler Seder's *Gallop!* employs a technique described as scanimation, which is cleverly designed sliding paper that creates the sensation of motion when the pages are opened. It is an old-fashioned technique that has been described, justly, as mesmerizing.

Artistic Styles

Artistic style refers to the visual characteristics of the illustration, rather than the medium or the technique for getting it on the paper. Most picture-book illustrators are often trained professionals and consummate artists. So it is not surprising that we should find a wide variety of sophisticated artistic styles represented in children's picture books. In the best examples, the artistic style evokes the mood established by the text.

Realism

Realism, or realistic or representational art, portrays the world with faithful attention to lifelike detail. A few artists aim at photographic realism (see Stephen T. Johnson's remarkable *Alphabet City,* for example), but many artists, like Robert McCloskey in *One Morning in Maine,* prefer to approximate reality. Thus, the best representational art carries the individual stamp of the artist. Realistic art can be done in full color or in monochromes (i.e., one color, as in many of McCloskey's works), and it is particularly suited to illustrating realistic stories with serious content or themes. Zelinsky's exquisite illustrations for *Rapunzel* (Color Plate E) are inspired by the art of the Italian Renaissance, which was, in turn, influenced by the realistic art of classical Greece and Rome. The rich colors, the architectural and landscape detail, the elaborate clothing—all attest to the care with which Zelinsky is attempting to re-create the world of fifteenth- and sixteenth-century Italy.

Cartoon Art

Cartoon art is very popular in children's books, probably because of its playful humor. Cartoons consist of exaggerated caricatures that emphasize emotion and movement. They possess no subtlety; they are simple and straightforward, and are a frequent choice for illustrating humorous stories, nonsense, and comical satire. Dr. Seuss's drawings are cartoons at their most outrageous—the colors are bold and the lines are distinct. Eric Rohman's illustrations for *My Friend Rabbit* (see Chapter 6, Figure 6.8) and Dr. Seuss's *Cat in the Hat* (see Chapter 6, Figure 6.9) are two examples of cartoon art.

Folk Art

Folk art is associated with a specific cultural or social group and is usually decorative in nature, providing ornamentation for everyday utilitarian objects, such as dishes, pottery, furniture, jewelry, fabric, and so on. Because of its cultural associations, it is often favored for illustrating folktales. Gerald McDermott's *Anansi the Spider* (Figure 7.3), with its geometric designs and bold colors, suggests western African influences. Alice and Martin Provensen's primitive illustrations for *A Peaceable Kingdom: The Shaker Abecedarius* suggest the simple ways of the Shaker community. Barbara Cooney used a style of folk art to illustrate Donald Hall's *Ox-Cart Man,* giving it the feeling of the early nineteenth-century New England countryside. As you can see, folk art is as varied as the folk cultures from around the world that inspired it.

Naïve Art

Naïve art is made deliberately to resemble a child's drawings. The figures appear two-dimensional and usually disproportionate (for example, the head might be too big, the arms and legs do not bend, and so on). John Burningham's *Mr. Gumpy's Outing,* a charming story for preschoolers about farm animals who want to accompany Mr. Gumpy on a boat ride, is appropriately illustrated in this style—although his imaginative use of color suggests the influence of expressionism as well (Color Plate B). We should never assume that naïve art is practiced by unskilled artists. Mo Willems's charming books (*Knuffle Bunny,* for example) are all examples of naïve art, which in this case has a cartoonish quality. As we have noted, many artists simply refuse to be categorized!

Art Nouveau

Although now rare in children's books, this style was a late nineteenth-century reaction to the more formal academic art. It is characterized by organic motifs (especially floral motifs), fluid lines, and highly stylized forms. There was no attempt at creating realism. Art Nouveau, whose most famous representative was Aubrey Beardsley, was heavily influenced by oriental art, particularly Japanese watercolors. The result was a decorative and sophisticated style, exquisitely realized in the work of the Danish illustrator Kay Nielsen. Contrast Nielsen's work (Color Plate C) with the more realistic style of Paul Zelinsky (Color Plate E).

Expressionism

Also a development of the early twentieth century, particularly in Germany, Russia, and neighboring lands, Marc Chagall, Wassily Kandinsky, and Paul Klee are among the more famous expressionists. These artists emphasize emotional response rather than pictorial accuracy. They use distorted, misshapen figures, unusual perspectives, and colors that establish mood rather than depict reality. Again, true expressionism is rare in children's picture books, but in Bemelmans's illustrations for *Madeline* (Figure 7.2) we can see that the trees are playfully exaggerated shapes that only suggest trees. As was mentioned earlier, expressionistic qualities are found in some of Burningham's illustrations for *Mr. Gumpy's Outing,* including his striking drawing of a cat seen in Color Plate B.

Surrealism

Surrealism is another early twentieth-century phenomenon—although some examples can be found as far back as the Renaissance in Hieronymous Bosch's disturbing paintings. The surrealist draws with realistic details, sometimes almost photographically real, but the subject matter is entirely unrealistic, using jarring juxtapositions that often result in an unsettling, sometimes nightmarish, quality. This style is used frequently by Chris Van Allsburg (see *Jumanji,* Figure 7.1).

An artist rarely sets out deliberately to imitate a school of art—the very best will create a unique personal style, coalescing from the imagination, education, and life experience. Illustrators often do not fit neatly into one artistic style, and our inability to identify an artist's style should not diminish our enjoyment of the work. Nor does everyone always agree on an artist's style. However, recognizing the wide-ranging talents of illustrators of children's books does increase our appreciation and respect for the art of picture-book illustration.

Picture-Book Layout: Three Examples

A brilliant text or exquisite artwork will not guarantee a successful picture book, for the text and illustrations have to work together to form a pleasing and meaningful whole. Maurice Sendak's *Where the Wild Things Are* provides a good example of the way in which the layout of pictures and text can enrich each other. As the story opens, Max, a rather naughty boy, is causing all manner of havoc about his house. (It is significant that we do not actually see Max being destructive, for that might cause us to have less empathy for him—he is, instead, depicted just about to pound a nail into the wall or just about to pounce on the dog.) The first pictures are small with large white borders around them. Max is then sent to his room for his misbehavior (we never see his mother, for this is Max's story). Soon his room is transformed into a forest, and an ocean tumbles by. Each succeeding picture grows larger and larger on the page and the border recedes in size until it disappears altogether. Eventually the pictures overlap onto the facing page and finally become two-page spreads.

The accompanying text describes a magical event. Max steps into his private boat and sails to the land where the Wild Things are. There he becomes their king and presides over a "wild rumpus" during which the creatures all do whatever they like (the dream of every child?). During this rumpus the pictures completely cover the pages and there is no text whatever. In other words, when Max is thoroughly absorbed in his dream fantasy, the civilizing aspects of reality (represented by the text—language being a symbol of civilization—and the white border—symbolic of the necessary limitations society must impose) have vanished. Finally, Max tires of the rumpus and longs to be "where someone loved him best of all"—children really do want to have rules and order in their lives. So he sails back to the comfort of his bedroom where he finds his supper waiting for him, "and it was still hot."

The pictures depicting Max's return gradually recede in size and the border is restored—at the same time, order is also restored to Max (or his psyche) and his world (the trees vanish from his bedroom). At the end of the story, we see Max obviously awakening from a dream and looking very much like a vulnerable little boy, no longer the wild thing who terrorized the household at the story's beginning. The final words—"and it was still hot"—appear on a page without illustration, causing us to focus entirely on their meaning without pictorial assistance. We are left to ponder the statement, which signifies unconditional parental love and seems to contradict earlier statements in the book about the passage of time. (We are told, for instance, that Max's boat trip took "almost over a year.")

Perry Nodelman suggests that words in picture books accomplish three things, and we can find examples of all three in *Where the Wild Things Are*:

- Words indicate how we are to interpret the emotional and narrative content of the pictures. ("The night Max wore his wolf suit and made mischief of one kind and another, his mother called him 'wild thing' . . . and he was sent to bed without eating anything.")

- Words point out cause-and-effect relationships, either within parts of a single picture or within a series of pictures—for example, the words can indicate the passage of time between two pictures. ("That very night in Max's room a forest grew and grew . . . .")

- Words explain what is important and what is not. (". . . he found his supper waiting for him—and it was still hot.") (Nodelman 215)

So we see that the successful picture book is a true collaboration of words and pictures as reflected in the overall design of the book.

Another inventive use of picture-book layout is found in John Burningham's *Come Away from the Water, Shirley.* This book portrays a day at the beach for the imaginative Shirley and her humdrum parents (and don't most children think their parents are humdrum?). The layout is comprised of a series of double-page spreads, with the left side depicting the dull routine of the parents and the right side depicting the imaginative world of Shirley at play. The parents' world is drawn in sparse colors on a large white background; the naïve style is deliberately uninteresting. In contrast, Shirley's world is portrayed in rich colors suited to her lively imagination as she creates adventures on the beach (being captured by pirates, walking the plank, heroically escaping, and finding a buried treasure). Here the style is a form of expressionism—lively, vivid, with dramatic distortions. Our eyes, moving left to right, first see the dull adult world and then behold the wondrous world of childhood. The illustrations, then, create an irony in that the parents are illustrated with childlike drawings and the child is illustrated with a sophisticated artistic style (see Chapter 3 for a discussion of irony). The text consists entirely of the mother's words, which are either admonitions to Shirley (which she happily ignores) or empty promises. The contrasting illustrations and the incongruous text make for subtle ironies that will not be lost on many children. Even adult readers must lament the loss of imagination that often comes with maturity.

David Wiesner's *The Three Pigs* is an inventive take-off on the traditional folktale. Here the pigs are unexpectedly blown out of their own story and find themselves as characters in search of a story, wandering in and out of other storybooks. Wiesner uses a variety of artistic styles throughout the book, indicating the various kinds of stories the pigs find—a cartoonish nursery rhyme, a romantic tale of a knight and a dragon, and so on. Not only do the artistic styles change between the various stories, so do the typeface styles, each chosen to suit the story. The imaginative story invites us to explore the meaning of fiction and reality.

Of course, we do not always find such powerful symbolism in a book's layout. But the best books remind us that the size and placement of illustrations is not (or should not be) a random process, but rather a carefully conceived plan that carries out the overall intent of the book. Words and pictures work together in a good picture book, and the resulting sum is something far greater and more rewarding than the individual parts.

Graphic Novels

Some may be surprised to find this brief discussion of the graphic novel appended to a chapter on picture books. However, if we remember our definition of a picture book as one in which the illustrations and the text are equally important, then this is the perfect place. Comic books have been around for decades, but in the last 20 years a new phenomenon has arisen—the graphic novel, which is a novel in comic-book format. In Japan, people of all ages read comics called manga, and although manga technically refers to those comics of Japanese origin, the term is being rapidly adapted to any book-length work in graphic or comic-book format. (The term comic is highly problematic, since many of these works are not at all humorous, but at least it is a term everyone understands.) The comic-book format places illustrations in frames, with captions or dialogue bubbles, and in sequence. The sequencing conveys a specific meaning—it can suggest the passage of time or a shift of scenes, it can create suspense or shift the reader's attention, and so on.

Proponents of the graphic novel argue that it creates a bridge between the visual media (the media in which most young people are immersed) and the written media. The graphic novel can work very well with struggling readers—in much the same way that texts with pictures help students of a foreign language. Consequently, it can be argued that the graphic novel, rather than a distraction, is actually an enticement to reading. It is also argued that these works, in addition to developing visual literacy and getting young people to read, introduce such serious issues as philosophy, history, science, ethics, and others.

Certainly the reading of graphic novels is more intellectually demanding than watching television or texting messages to one's friends and relatives. And young people engrossed in graphic novels may be preferable to young people mesmerized by computer games or whiling away the hours on cell phones. Entire books have been written on the art of the graphic novel (see McCloud's *Understanding Comics* and *Reinventing Comics*). There is even an argument for the use of graphic novels in the classroom (see Yang, "Graphic Novels in the Classroom"). And in 2007, a graphic novel, Gene Luen Yang's *American Born Chinese*, was awarded the prestigious Michael Printz award for distinguished young adult literature. The graphic novel is here to stay, but we should regard it as a supplement to, not a replacement for, the beautifully designed picture book or the well-crafted novel.

Summary

Picture books, once thought of as objects of innocent amusement for toddlers, have metamorphosed into complex and sophisticated works of art that can be enjoyed by people of any age. The modern-day picture book represents a collaboration of both storytelling and visual art. It is a work in which the text and the illustrations share equally in the reading experience. This makes the picture book different from the illustrated book, in which the pictures merely decorate or elaborate on the text.

The text of the picture storybook is generally simple—but not simplistic. The good picture book contains an engaging plot and characters, it uses language that is both clear and evocative, and it is entertaining and, perhaps, thought provoking. Accompanying the text are the illustrations, which are examples of narrative art. That is, the illustrations must tell a story—specifically the same story revealed by the text. But the illustrations also contain the same elements we expect to find in any pictorial art—effective use of line, shape, space, texture, composition, and perspective.

Picture books, to be successful, depend on careful design, and that design must somehow reflect the story's meaning. We look for rhythm and movement in the pictures, as well as tension in the book's layout, to add interest. Page layout is also important, for this determines such things as the size and shape of pages, the placement of text and pictures, the typography, and so on. Borders, panels, and vignettes are also at the artist's disposal when designing pages.

The artistic medium—that is, oil, watercolor, pencil, woodblock prints, collage, photography, or digital graphics—is a choice the artist needs to make, as is the artistic style. The styles include everything from realism to expressionism, from naïve art to surrealism. Today's children can learn much about art simply by reading the many exquisite picture books available to them.

Finally, we should recognize that today the graphic novel has emerged as one of the most popular forms of children's and young adult literature. This offshoot of the comic book is regarded by many as a bridge between the two worlds of visual media and literature. As such, many believe it can be an effective means of encouraging reading in a society that at times seems besotted by electronic imagery. The field of picture-book art is dynamic and invigorating. As adults, one of our most enjoyable obligations is to make sure children are acquainted with the rich spectrum of the modern picture book.

For Reflection and Discussion

1. Read a number of children's picture books on a specific topic or theme—friendship, siblings, grandparents, first day of school, pets, and so on. Determine which are the most effective and why.

2. Read several (at least five or six) books illustrated by the same artist. Find some biographical information on the artist (try *Something About the Author* or *The Dictionary of Literary Biography* or *The Oxford Encyclopedia of Children's Literature* or other similar resources). What were the artist's specific artistic influences? Can you identify those aspects of the artist's style that seem to set him or her apart from others? What particularly about this artist's work appeals to you?

3. Choose any good picture book (you might start with the lists below) and carefully examine the book's layout and design. Try to explain the decisions made by the illustrator and how they affect your response to the book. What especially makes this an effective picture book? (Pick out specific pages that you find striking and try to determine exactly what techniques the illustrator used that make these good examples of picture-book art.)

4. Choose any good picture book (again, look at the lists below for starters) and consider how the illustrations add to and enrich the story. Do the illustrations affect our interpretation of the story? How? What mood do the illustrations establish and is it appropriate to the story?

5. Choose any graphic novel and read it. If you are already a fan of the graphic novel, explain what you look for in a good one. If this is your first experience, what is your response to the format? Try to find specific examples to support your responses.

● Works Cited

Nodelman, Perry. *Words About Pictures: The Narrative Art of Children's Picture Books.* Athens, GA: University of Georgia Press, 1988.

Stewig, John Warren. *Looking at Picture Books.* Fort Atkinson, WI: Highsmith Press, 1995.

● Recommended Readings

Alderson, Brian. *Looking at Picture Books 1973.* New York: Children's Book Council, 1974.

Bader, Barbara. *American Picturebooks from Noah's Ark to the Beast Within.* New York: Macmillan, 1976.

Barrett, Terry, and Kenneth Marantz. "Photographs as Illustrations." *The New Advocate* 17 (Fall 1989): 103–153.

Benedict, Susan, and Leonore Carlisle, eds. *Beyond Words: Picture Books for Older Readers and Writers.* Portsmouth, NH: Heinemann, 1992.

Cianciolo, Patricia. *Picture Books for Children,* 4th ed. Chicago: American Library Association, 1997.

Cummins, Julie, ed. *Children's Book Illustration and Design.* Glen Cove, NY: PBC International, 1992.

Dooley, Patricia. "The Window in the Book: Conventions in the Illustrations of Children's Books." *Wilson Library Bulletin* (October 1980): 108–112.

Gombrich, E. H. *The Image and the Eye: Further Studies in the Psychology of Pictorial Representation.* Ithaca, NY: Cornell University Press, 1982.

Kiefer, Barbara Z. *The Potential of Picturebooks: From Visual Literacy to Aesthetic Understanding.* Englewood Cliffs, NJ: Prentice-Hall, 1995.

Lacy, L. E. *Art and Design in Children's Books: An Analysis of Caldecott Award Winning Illustrations.* Chicago: American Library Association, 1986.

Matulka, Denise I. *A Picture Book Primer.* Santa Barbara, CA: Libraries Unlimited, 2008.

McCloud, Scott. *Reinventing Comics: How Imagination and Technology Are Revolutionizing an Art Form.* New York: Harper, 2000.

_____. *Understanding Comics: The Invisible Art.* New York: Harper, 1994.

Nikolajeva, Maria, and Carol Scott. *How Picture Books Work.* New York: Garland, 2000.

Nodelman, Perry. *Words About Pictures: The Narrative Art of Children's Picture Books*. Athens, GA: University of Georgia Press, 1988.

Roxburgh, Stephen. "A Picture Equals How Many Words? Narrative Theory and Picture Books for Children." *The Lion and the Unicorn* 7/8 (1983/84): 20–33.

Shulevitz, Uri. *Writing with Pictures: How to Write and Illustrate Children's Books*. New York: Watson-Guptin, 1985.

Spitz, Ellen Handler. *Inside Picture Books*. New Haven: Yale University Press, 1999.

Stewig, John Warren. *Looking at Picture Books*. Fort Atkinson, WI: Highsmith Press, 1995.

Yang, Gene. "Graphic Novels in the Classroom." *Language Arts* 85, 3 (January 2008): 185–192.

Selected Bibliography of Picture Storybooks

This list of children's picture storybooks includes timeless classics and more recent publications. The intended reader's age will vary from about 2 to 8 years old. For the most part, authors and illustrators are represented by only one title, so look for more books by these individuals. Also look at the lists of award-winning picture books in the appendix, especially the Caldecott and Greenaway winners.

Ackerman, Karen. *Song and Dance Man*. New York: Knopf, 1988.

Adoff, Arnold. *Black Is Brown Is Tan*. Illus. Emily McCully. New York: Harper, 1973.

Alexander, Lloyd. *The Fortune-Tellers*. Illus. Trina Schart Hyman. New York: Dutton, 1992.

Alexander, Martha. *Nobody Asked Me If I Wanted a Baby Sister*. New York: Dial, 1971.

Allard, Harry, and James Marshall. *Miss Nelson Is Missing*. Illus. James Marshall. Boston: Houghton Mifflin, 1977.

Allen, Jeffrey. *Mary Alice, Operator Number 9*. Illus. James Marshall. Boston: Little, Brown, 1975.

Ardizzone, Edward. *Little Tim and the Brave Sea Captain*. 1936. New York: Penguin, 1983.

Bang, Molly. *The Grey Lady and the Strawberry Snatcher*. New York: Four Winds, 1980.

Banks, Kate. *And If the Moon Could Talk*. Illus. Georg Hallensleben. New York: Farrar, Straus & Giroux, 1998.

Bemelmans, Ludwig. *Madeline*. New York: Viking, 1937.

Brooke, L. Leslie. *Johnny Crow's Garden*. 1903. London: Warne, 1978.

Brown, Margaret Wise. *Goodnight Moon*. Illus. Clement Hurd. New York: Harper, 1947.

Browne, Anthony. *Voices in the Park*. New York: DK Ink, 1998.

Burningham, John. *Come Away from the Water, Shirley*. New York: Harper, 1977.

Burton, Virginia L. *The Little House*. Boston: Houghton Mifflin, 1942.

Carrick, Carol. *In the Moonlight, Waiting*. Illus. Donald Carrick. New York: Clarion, 1990.

Chandra, Deborah, and Madeleine Comora. *George Washington's Teeth*. Illus. Brock Cole. New York: Farrar, Straus & Giroux, 2003.

Chorao, Kay. *Little Farm by the Sea*. New York: Holt, 1998.

Clifton, Lucille. *Some of the Days of Everett Anderson*. Illus. Evaline Ness. New York: Holt, 1970.

Clouse, Nancy L. *Puzzle Maps U.S.A.* New York: Holt, 1990.

Conrad, Pam. *The Tub People*. Illus. Richard Egielski. New York: Harper, 1989.

Cooney, Barbara. *Miss Rumphius*. New York: Viking, 1982.

Crews, Donald. *Sail Away*. New York: Greenwillow, 1995.

Cronin, Doreen. *Diary of a Spider*. Illus. Harry Bliss. New York: HarperCollins, 2005.

Cumpiano, Ina. *Quinito, Day and Night/Quinito, día y noche.* Illus. José Ramirez. San Francisco: Children's Book Press, 2008.

Daugherty, James. *Andy and the Lion.* New York: Viking, 1938.

de Angeli, Marguerite. *Thee Hannah!* New York: Doubleday, 1940.

de Brunhoff, Jean. *The Story of Babar, the Little Elephant.* 1933. New York: Knopf, 1989.

De Regniers, Beatrice Schenk. *May I Bring a Friend?* Illus. Beni Montressor. New York: Atheneum, 1964.

Domanska, Janina. *The Turnip.* New York: Atheneum, 1972.

Dunrea, Olivier. *Gossie.* New York: Houghton Mifflin Harcourt, 2002.

———. *The Painter Who Loved Chickens.* New York: Farrar, Straus & Giroux, 1995.

Duvoisin, Roger. *Petunia.* New York: Knopf, 1950.

Ehlert, Lois. *Leaf Man.* New York: Harcourt, 2005.

Ehrlich, Amy. *Parents in the Pigpen, Pigs in the Tub.* Illus. Steven Kellogg. New York: Dial, 1993.

Ets, Marie Hall. *Play with Me.* New York: Penguin, 1955.

Falconer, Ian. *Olivia.* New York: Simon and Schuster, 2000.

Fatio, Louise. *The Happy Lion.* Illus. Roger Duvoisin. 1954. New York: Scholastic, 1986.

Feiffer, Jules. *I Lost My Bear.* New York: Morrow, 1998.

Flack, Marjorie. *The Story about Ping.* Illus. Kurt Weise. New York: Penguin, 1933.

Freeman, Don. *Corduroy.* New York: Viking, 1968.

Gág, Wanda. *Millions of Cats.* New York: Coward, McCann, 1928.

Geisert, Arthur. *Lights Out.* Boston: Houghton Mifflin, 2005.

Gerstein, Mordicai. *The Man Who Walked Between the Towers.* Brookfield, CT: Millbrook, 2003.

Goble, Paul. *The Girl Who Loved Wild Horses.* New York: Bradbury, 1978.

Gramatky, Hardie. *Little Toot.* New York: Putnam, 1978.

Gravett, Emily. *Dogs.* New York: Simon and Schuster, 2010.

_____. *Little Mouse's Big Book of Fears.* New York: Simon and Schuster, 2008.

Hader, Berta, and Elmer Hader. *The Big Snow.* New York: Macmillan, 1948.

Hale, Lucretia. *The Lady Who Put Salt in Her Coffee.* Illus. and adapted by Amy Schwartz. New York: Harcourt, 1989.

Hall, Donald. *Ox-Cart Man.* Illus. Barbara Cooney. New York: Penguin, 1983.

Henkes, Kevin. *Kitten's First Full Moon.* New York: Scholastic, 2004.

Hoffman, Mary. *Amazing Grace.* Illus. Caroline Binch. New York: Dial, 1991.

Holub, Joan. *The Garden That We Grow.* Illus. Hiroe Nakata. New York: Viking, 2001.

Johnson, Crockett. *Harold and the Purple Crayon.* New York: Harper, 1955.

Joyce, William. *Rolie Polie Olie.* New York: Scholastic, 2001.

Keats, Ezra Jack. *The Snowy Day.* New York: Viking, 1962.

Keeping, Charles. *Joseph's Yard.* New York: Watts, 1969.

Kraus, Robert. *Leo the Late Bloomer.* Illus. Jose and Ariane Aruego. New York: Simon & Schuster, 1987.

Krauss, Ruth. *The Backward Day.* Illus. Marc Simont. New York: Harper, 1950.

Kuskin, Karla. *The Bear Who Saw the Spring.* New York: Harper, 1961.

Langstaff, John M. *A Frog Went a-Courtin'.* Illus. Feodor Rojankovsky. New York: Scholastic, 1985.

Leaf, Munro. *The Story of Ferdinand.* Illus. Robert Lawson. New York: Viking, 1936.

Lester, Julius. *Black Cowboy, Wild Horses: A True Story.* Illus. Jerry Pinkney. New York: Dial, 1998.

Lionni, Leo. *Fish Is Fish.* New York: Knopf, 1970.

Liwska, Renata. *Little Panda.* New York: Houghton, 2008.

Locker, Thomas. *Where the River Begins.* New York: Dial, 1984.

MacDonald, Golden (pseud. of Margaret Wise Brown). *The Little Island.* Illus. Leonard Wiesgard. New York: Doubleday, 1946.

Mahy, Margaret. *Bubble Trouble.* Illus. Polly Dunbar. New York: Clarion, 2009.

———. *The Horrendous Hullabaloo.* Illus. Patricia MacCarthy. New York: Viking, 1992.

Marshall, James. *George and Martha.* New York: Scholastic, 1972.

Martin, Bill. *Brown Bear, Brown Bear, What Do You See?* New York: Holt, 1983.

Mayer, Mercer. *There's a Nightmare in My Closet.* New York: Dial, 1968.

McCloskey, Robert. *Blueberries for Sal.* New York: Viking, 1948.

McCully, Emily Arnold. *Mirette on the High Wire.* New York: Putnam, 1992.

McPhail, David. *Farm Boy's Year.* New York: Atheneum, 1992.

Meddaugh, Susan. *Martha Speaks.* Boston: Houghton Mifflin, 1992.

Moss, Lloyd. *Zin! Zin! Zin! A Violin.* Illus. Marjorie Priceman. New York: Aladdin, 2000.

Murphy, Mary. *I Kissed the Baby.* New York: Candlewick, 2003.

Page, Robin. *What Do You Do With a Tail Like This?* Illus. Steve Jenkins. Boston: Houghton Mifflin, 2003.

Peet, Bill. *Encore for Eleanor.* Boston: Houghton Mifflin, 1985.

Piatti, Celestino. *The Happy Owls.* New York: Atheneum, 1964.

Pinkney, Brian. *JoJo's Flying Side Kick.* New York: Simon & Schuster, 1995.

Pinkney, Jerry. *The Lion & the Mouse.* New York: Little, 2009.

Potter, Beatrix. *The Tale of Peter Rabbit.* London: Warne, 1901.

Provensen, Alice, and Martin Provensen. *The Glorious Flight: Across the Channel with Louis Bleriot.* New York: Viking, 1983.

Rathman, Peggy. *Good Night, Gorilla.* New York: Putnam, 1994.

Rey, A. H. *Curious George.* Boston: Houghton Mifflin, 1973.

Robbins, Ken. *Tools.* New York: Macmillan, 1983.

Rockwell, Anne, and Harlow Rockwell. *Machines.* New York: Macmillan, 1972.

———. *The Supermarket.* New York: Macmillan, 1979.

Rylant, Cynthia. *When I Was Young in the Mountains.* Illus. Diane Goode. New York: Dutton, 1982.

Seder, Rufus Butler. *Gallop!* New York: Workman, 2007.

Seibold, J. Otto, and Vivian Walsh. *Mr. Lunch Takes a Plane Ride.* Illus. Otto Seibold. New York: Viking, 1993.

Sendak, Maurice. *Where the Wild Things Are.* New York: Harper, 1963.

Seuss, Dr. (pseud. of Theodore Geisel). *And to Think That I Saw It on Mulberry Street.* New York: Vanguard, 1973.

Shannon, David. *Duck on a Bike.* New York: Blue Sky Press, 2002.

Sheppard, Jeff. *Splash, Splash.* New York: Macmillan, 1994.

Shulevitz, Uri. *Rain, Rain, Rivers.* New York: Farrar, Straus & Giroux, 1969.

Sis, Peter. *Komodo!* New York: Greenwillow, 1993.

Small, David. *Imogene's Antlers.* New York: Crown, 2000.

Soto, Gary. *Chato's Kitchen.* Illus. Susan Guevara. New York: Putnam, 1995.

Steig, William. *Sylvester and the Magic Pebble.* New York: Windmill, 1969.

Steptoe, John. *My Daddy Is a Monster . . . Sometimes.* New York: Viking, 1980.

Stewart, Sarah. *The Library.* Illus. David Small. New York: Farrar, Straus & Giroux, 1995.

Tafuri, Nancy. *All Year Long.* New York: Penguin, 1984.

Testa, Fulvia. *If You Look Around You.* New York: Dial, 1983.

Thurber, James. *Many Moons.* Illus. Marc Simont. New York: Harcourt, 1990.

Tresselt, Alvin. *White Snow, Bright Snow.* Illus. Roger Duvoisin. New York: Lothrop, 1947.

Udry, Janice M. *The Moon Jumpers.* Illus. Maurice Sendak. New York: Harper, 1959.

Ungerer, Tonie. *The Beast of Monsieur Racine.* New York: Farrar, Straus & Giroux, 1971.

Van Allsburg, Chris. *The Polar Express.* Boston: Houghton Mifflin, 1985.

Viorst, Judith. *Alexander and the Terrible, Horrible, No Good, Very Bad Day.* Illus. Ray Cruz. New York: Atheneum, 1972.

Waber, Bernard. *Lyle, Lyle, Crocodile.* Boston: Houghton Mifflin, 1987.

Walsh, Melanie. *Do Monkeys Tweet?* Boston: Houghton Mifflin, 1997.

Ward, Lynd K. *The Biggest Bear.* Boston: Houghton Mifflin, 1952.

Wells, Rosemary. *Noisy Nora.* New York: Dial, 1980.

Wiesner, David. *Flotsam.* New York: Clarion, 2006.

Willard, Nancy. *A Visit to William Blake's Inn*. Illus. Alice and Martin Provensen. New York: Harcourt, 1981.

Willems, Mo. *Don't Let the Pigeon Drive the Bus*. New York: Hyperion, 2003.

_____. *Knuffle Bunny*. New York: Hyperion, 2004.

Zimmerman, Andrea, and David Clemesha. *Trashy Town*. Illus. Dan Yaccarino. New York: HarperCollins, 1999.

Williams, Vera B. *A Chair for My Mother*. New York: Greenwillow, 1982.

Willis, Val. *The Secret in the Matchbox*. Illus. John Shelley. New York: Farrar, Straus & Giroux, 1988.

Winthrop, Elizabeth. *That's Mine!* Illus. Emily McCully. New York: Holiday, 1977.

Wood, Audrey. *King Bidgood's in the Bathtub*. Illus. Don Wood. New York: Harcourt, 1985.

Yashima, Taro (pseud. of Jun Iwamatsu). *Crow Boy*. New York: Viking, 1955.

Yolen, Jane. *Owl Moon*. Illus. John Schoenherr. New York: Philomel, 1987.

Young, Ed. *Hook*. New York: Roaring Brook Press, 2009.

Yorinks, Arthur. *Hey Al*. Illus. Richard Egielski. New York: Farrar, Straus & Giroux, 1988.

Zemach, Margot. *Jake and Honeybunch Go to Heaven*. New York: Farrar, Straus & Giroux, 1982.

Zion, Gene. *Harry, the Dirty Dog*. Illus. Margaret Bloy Graham. New York: Harper, 1956.

Zolotow, Charlotte. *Mr. Rabbit and the Lovely Present*. Illus. Maurice Sendak. New York: Harper, 1962.

PEARSON
myeducationkit™

Go to the topic "Picture Books" on the MyEducationKit for this text, where you can:

- Search the Database of Children's Literature, housing more than 22,000 titles searchable in every genre by authors or illustrators, by awards won, by year published, and by topic and description.

- Explore genre-related Assignments and Activities, assignable exercises showing concepts in action through database use, video, cases, and student and teacher artifacts.

- Listen to podcasts and read interviews from some of the brightest and most enduring stars of children's literature in the Conversations.

- Discover Web Links that will lead you to sites representing the authors you learn about in these pages, classrooms with powerful children's literature connections, and literature awards.

Introduction

Perhaps no literary form evokes more decisive responses than poetry—people either think they love it or they hate it. This is curious, indeed, since our first exposure to literature is often the poetry of the nursery:

Rock-a-bye baby, on the treetop,
When the wind blows, the cradle will rock,
When the bough breaks, the cradle will fall,
And down will come baby, cradle and all.

Later we move on to the rollicking rhymes of Dr. Seuss and Ogden Nash, the outrageous humor of Shel Silverstein and Jack Prelutsky, and finally to the more reflective poems of Langston Hughes, Eve Merriam, Gwendolyn Brooks, Myra Cohn Livingston, and many others.

Sadly, except for broadly humorous verse, most poetry for readers in their teen years remains unread and unappreciated. For these readers, poetry has the reputation of being obscure or effete, appealing to a small cadre of "intellectuals." This is too bad because, in fact, poetry need not be stuffy or difficult. Rather, it can be one of the most beautiful, powerful, and memorable ways to communicate our feelings.

In this chapter we will lift the veil of mystery that seems to surround much of poetry that we might keep alive or rekindle its magic and joy in children. In Chapter 6 we looked at Mother Goose rhymes, which are typically a child's first introduction to poetry. The poems of the nursery hold much allure for toddlers and speaks to their love of the sounds of language and of the evocative (dare we say bizarre?) imagery. There is every reason to nurture this fascination as children grow older.

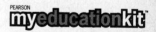

PEARSON

Visit the MyEducationKit for this course to enhance your understanding of chapter concepts with activities, web links, podcasts, and a searchable database of more than 22,000 children's literature titles.

Definition of Poetry

Poet Samuel Taylor Coleridge defined poetry as "the best words in their best order"; his good friend, poet William Wordsworth, called it "the spontaneous overflow of powerful feelings." And Robert Frost described a poem as "where an emotion has found its thought and the thought has found the words." These definitions demonstrate how elusive poetry is—the best is nothing less than our deepest feelings captured in a delicate balance of words. For practical purposes, we can argue that most poetry exhibits three qualities: economical language, metrical form, and a defined pattern. In other words, a poem packs a lot of meaning into a few words, it has a musical or rhythmical quality to it, and it is composed in a pattern of lines and stanzas. Here is the first stanza of one of the most famous poems in the language, "The Jabberwocky," found in Lewis Carroll's *Through the Looking-Glass and What Alice Found There:*

> Twas brillig, and the slithy toves
> Did gyre and gimble in the wabe;
> All mimsy were the borogoves,
> And the mome raths outgrabe.

This is what we call a nonsense poem—for obvious reasons. But we immediately recognize it as a poem just by looking at the arrangement of the words on the page—we don't even have to read them (here, they don't make sense, but most poems make a great deal of sense). Poems are organized into lines; frequently the lines are organized into stanzas, which are the paragraphs of poetry. When we read Carroll's words, it is impossible not to fall into the regular rhythm. Try moving the words about—for example, what if the first line read: "'Twas toves and the brillig slithy"? The sound just doesn't work as well—especially when we follow it with the second line. And, of course, we hear the end-rhyme and come to expect it—although not all poems have such regular rhythm and rhyme, and we'll discuss them later on.

Naturally, not all poetry rhymes or has a regular rhythmical pattern or is funny. The following poem by Ruth Whitman, "Listening to Grownups Quarreling," treats a very serious subject—the trauma experienced by young children when their parents quarrel—and is written in free verse. Notice that there is no regular rhyme, the lines are of varying lengths, and the rhythm is irregular, perhaps intending to capture a child's anguished state of mind. The poem's power comes from the dramatic comparisons that make us feel what the children are feeling:

Listening to grownups quarreling,

standing in the hall against the
wall with my little brother, blown

like leaves against the wall by their
voices, my head like a pingpong ball
between the paddles of their anger
I knew what it meant
to tremble like a leaf.

Cold with their wrath, I heard
the claws of the rain
pounce. Floods
poured through the city,
skies clapped over me,
and I was shaken, shaken
like a mouse
between their jaws.

> (*"Listening to Grownups Quarreling" from* The
> Marriage Wig and Other Poems, *compilation
> copyright © 1968 and renewed 1996 by Ruth
> Whitman, reprinted with permission of Houghton
> Mifflin Harcourt Publishing Company.*)

Whitman relies on a combination of similes and metaphors (these are explained later in the chapter) to convey the drama of this event. The poem consists of three sentences, each filled with word pictures intended to convey to the reader the speaker's feelings—the internal emotional stress becomes the atmospheric upheaval of storms and floods. The result is heartrending: What parents would argue in front of their children if they knew this?

The best poets show us fresh, new ways of thinking about things—and they express those ideas through a combination of sounds and images.

Sounds in Poetry

Part of the joy of reading poetry is listening to the combination of sounds the poet has created. Sound is a crucial part of every poem, and we usually think of poetic sound as having two features: rhyme and rhythm.

Rhyme

Rhyme is one of the first aspects of poetry children recognize. It is, simply put, the repetition of similar sounds. End-rhyme is perhaps the most widely acknowledged rhyme in poetry; it occurs when the last words of two or more lines repeat the same sounds. Too often, end-rhyme devolves into trite and unimaginative rhymes, as in that old jingle,

> Roses are red, violets are blue
> Sugar is sweet, and so are you.

And you probably know many variations on this rhyme. But end-rhyme is often most effective when it is unpredictable, as in this humorous example from Henry Wadsworth Longfellow:

> There was a little girl
> Who had a little curl
> Right in the middle of her forehead.
> When she was good
> She was very, very good,
> But when she was bad she was horrid.

For convenience, the pattern of a poem's end-rhyme is usually described by assigning the letter *a* to the first rhyme, *b* to the second rhyme, and so on. So Longfellow's poem has this rhyme scheme: *a-a-b-c-c-b*. As anyone who has tried to write poetry knows, making end-rhymes in English can be difficult, as this playful (and convoluted) nursery rhyme attests:

> What is the rhyme for porringer?
> The king he had a daughter fair,
> And gave the Prince of Orange her.

However, the repeated sound does not always have to be at the end of a word. For example, it is common in English to repeat the initial sounds of words. We call this alliteration. Indeed, early English poets were very fond of alliteration, as we see in this sixteenth-century verse with its repeated *w*'s, *f*'s, and *b*'s (incidentally, Boreas was the god of the north wind):

> This winter's weather it waxes cold,
> And frost it freezes on every hill,
> And Boreas blows his blast so bold
> That all our cattle are like to spill.

We find alliteration frequently in nursery rhymes and riddles ("Billy Button bought a buttered biscuit") and tongue-twisters ("The thistle sifter sifted seven thick thistles"). But as with most things, alliteration is best used in moderation. Listen to Alfred, Lord Tennyson's repetition of the consonant sounds *l*, and *w*, and hard *c* in "The Eagle":

> He clasps the crag with crooked hands;
> Close to the sea in lonely lands,
> Ring'd with the azure world, he stands.

The wrinkled sea beneath him crawls;
He watches from his mountain walls,
And like a thunderbolt he falls.

Repetition of sounds can also occur within words. When internal vowel sounds are repeated, it is called assonance, such as the long *a, e, i,* and *u* sounds in this line by Carl Sandburg: "Let me be the great nail holding a skyscraper through blue nights into white stars." Notice that it is the sound and not the spelling that we are concerned with. So "great," "nail," and "skyscraper" all share similar vowels sounds, as do "through" and "blue," even though their spellings are vastly different. Consonance is the repetition of consonant sounds within words. Listen, for example, to the way Robert Browning has sprinkled the "l" sounds throughout these lines from his poem, "Meeting at Night," describing the sea coast at night:

The gray sea and the long black land;
And the yellow half-moon large and low;
And the startled little waves that leap
In fiery ringlets from their sleep . . . .

Notice also that the repeated sounds—whether alliteration, assonance, or consonance—are only effective if they are reasonably close together, specifically within a line or two. A skillful poet carefully chooses words, not only for their meaning but also for the way they sound within the line and within the stanza.

Rhythm

Rhythm can provide a great deal of fun in a poem. English words are built on patterns of stressed and unstressed syllables. There are four common patterns, called metrical feet, which are easily demonstrated in the way we pronounce the following similar feminine names, each one representing one metrical foot:

Már-y (a stressed followed by an unstressed syllable—called a trochee)

Ma-**ríe** (an unstressed followed by a stressed syllable—called an iamb)

Már-i-an (a stressed syllable followed by two unstressed syllables—called a dactyl)

Mar-y-**ánne** (two unstressed syllables followed by a stressed one—called an anapest)

Experiment with your own name—can you determine which syllables should be stressed? Sometimes this takes practice. The trick is to speak the words naturally and not put an emphasis where there isn't one. Much of poetry is made up of these patterns. Listen to the stress patterns in these lines:

Mis-tress **Mar**-y **quite** con-**trar**-y

(This is in trochaic meter and consists of four trochees or trochaic feet.)

The **Queen** of **Hearts** she **made** some **tarts**

(Here we have iambic meter with four iambs or iambic feet.)

Ladybird, **Ladybird**, **fly** away **home**, your **house** is on **fire** and your **child**ren a**lone**

(This unusual line is in dactylic meter and consists of seven dactyls or dactylic feet—with an added iambic foot ["your house"] tucked in the middle.)

And the **taste** of the **ber**ries the **feel** of the **sun** I re**mem**ber

(This line, from Eleanor Farjeon's "It Was Long Ago," is a good example of anapestic meter, with five anapests or anapestic feet strung together—with an additional unstressed syllable ["-ber"] at the end.)

Very few poems maintain a consistent rhythmic pattern throughout—for that would be terrifically monotonous. Rhythm is usually subtler than that, but the rhythm is there. Rhythm—be it in nursery rhymes or in Shakespeare—is inseparable from poetry. We may not have to label it, but we do need to be aware of it when we read a poem.

Pictures in Poetry

A good poem creates a picture (or image) in our minds and makes us see something in a new way—if the image is not new and fresh, then the poem seems trite and dull (like "Roses are red, violets are blue"). Poets try to awaken our senses—all of our senses—by describing things we can see, hear, taste, feel, or smell. Contrary to what some seem to believe, a good poem does not have to be obscure or difficult to figure out. In fact, the best poems make us see things more clearly or feel things more deeply. The poet does this in one of two ways: directly, by describing the concept in sensory terms (sight, taste, touch, and so on), or indirectly, by comparing the concept to something else with which we are already familiar (using similes, metaphors, or personification).

Sensory Description

Let's begin by looking at those poetic descriptions that appeal directly to our physical senses—sight, touch, hearing, smell, taste, and motion.

SIGHT ● Poets frequently describe things that we can see. These grand lines by Alfred, Lord Tennyson, are not only musical but they contain an evocative word picture, the visual details describing a romantic sight:

The splendor falls on castle walls
And snowy summits old in story:

The long light shakes across the lakes,
And the wild cataract leaps in glory.

TOUCH • Sometimes poets describe things we can physically feel. Walter de la Mare is appealing to our tactile senses when he writes: "Through the green twilight of a hedge / I peered with cheek on the cool leaves pressed." De la Mare is trusting we have experienced the feel of cool leaves brushing against our skin.

HEARING • Another way a poet can help us respond to the world is by using words that describe or imitate sounds, as in these lines from John Keats's "To Autumn," describing the musical sounds of nature:

Hedge-crickets sing; and now with treble soft
The redbreast whistles from a garden-croft;
And gathering swallows twitter in the skies.

Perhaps one of the most famous allusions to sound is found in Edgar Allan Poe's *The Raven,* which opens with:

Once upon a midnight dreary, while I pondered, weak and weary,
Over many a quaint and curious volume of forgotten lore—
While I nodded, nearly napping, suddenly there came a tapping,
As of some one gently rapping, rapping at my chamber door.
"'Tis some visitor," I muttered, "tapping at my chamber door—Only this and
    nothing more."

SMELL • The sense of smell can be very evocative and call up past memories for us. Walt Whitman, a lover of nature, frequently uses the imagery of smell to stir our feelings: "The smell of apples, aromas from crush'd sage-plant, mint, birch-bark" or ". . . in the fragrant pines and the cedars dusk and dim."

TASTE • References to tastes can also be very suggestive, as in Mary O'Neill's description of the color brown: "Brown is cinnamon / and morning toast." And notice the combination of sensory images in these lines from a nineteenth-century poem titled "The Mouse and the Cake" by Eliza Cook:

A mouse found a beautiful piece of plum cake,
The richest and sweetest that mortal could make;
'Twas heavy with citron and fragrant with spice,
And covered with sugar all sparkling as ice.

(*Iona and Peter Opie.* The Oxford Book of Children's
    Verse. *Oxford: Oxford University Press, 1973.*)

MOTION ● Words also have the ability to convey the sense of movement. William Wordsworth uses movement to evoke the gentle sweetness of nature in his poem, "Daffodils":

> I wandered lonely as a cloud
> That floats on high o'er vales and hills,
> When all at once I saw a crowd,
> A host of golden daffodil
> Beside the lake, beneath the trees,
> Fluttering and dancing in the breeze.

Emily Dickinson creates an entirely differently feeling, using motion to suggest the locomotive's tremendous power in "The Railway Train":

> I like to see it lap the miles,
> And lick the valleys up,
> And stop to feed itself at tanks;
> And then, prodigious, step
>
> Around a pile of mountains,
> And, supercilious, peer
> In shanties by the sides of roads;
> And then a quarry pare
>
> To fit its sides, and crawl between,
> Complaining all the while
> In horrid, hooting stanza;
> Then chase itself down hill
>
> And neigh like Boanerges;
> Then, punctual as a star,
> Stop—docile and omnipotent—
> At its own stable door.

Comparative Description

In addition to describing the world through sight, sound, taste, touch, and smell, poets help us better understand their messages by making comparisons. The three most common types of comparison use similes, metaphors, and personification.

SIMILE ● A simile occurs when a poet makes a direct comparison using the words "like" or "as," such as the many examples in Ruth Whitman's poem included earlier in this chapter,

"Listening to grownups quarreling." Reread that poem and identify the four comparisons using the word "like." Also, in the final stanza of Emily Dickinson's "The Railway Train," we read that the train neighs "like Boanerges." Many modern readers would not understand this comparison. But Dickinson's nineteenth-century readers would likely know that Boanerges, which means "sons of thunder," was the name Jesus gave to James and John for their loud and fiery preaching. So a reference made in the nineteenth century may not work so well in the twenty-first—but this is true in all writing, not just poetry. In the next line, Dickinson describes the train as "punctual as a star," presumably because the stars seem to come out, as if on cue, each night. This is a much more enduring reference.

The opening line to James Elroy Flecker's poem, "The Old Ships," contains an interesting simile (not to mention a good example of alliteration): "I have seen old ships sail like swans asleep." We immediately think of old sailing ships, with their high masts, moved slowly along by a gentle wind. This is what the simile is supposed to do—make us think beyond the poem. As with rhyme, a simile is most effective if it is unexpected and fresh.

METAPHOR ● A metaphor is a little trickier because the comparison is not stated directly—without "like" or "as." A metaphor is an implied comparison. Again, turn to Ruth Whitman's poem on pages 148–149 and note her references to the "claws of the rain" and the floods pouring through the city—both intended to describe the impact on the child of the parents' quarreling. In the final stanza of Emily Dickinson's "The Railway Train," the locomotive is said to "neigh" (a reference to a horse) and finally arrives at "its own stable door." The poet is using a metaphor comparing the locomotive to a horse and the station as a stable. She has, in a single stanza, woven in both similes and metaphors.

In her poem "Time," Valerie Bloom compares time to a bird, a racing jockey, and a thief—all without the use of "like" or "as." These then are metaphors. Notice how she applies each metaphor to a different aspect of time, and notice how she works in other metaphors as well—such as comparing the sun and moon to racing horses:

> Time's a bird, which leaves its footprints
> At the corner of your eyes.
> Time's a jockey, racing horses,
> The sun and moon across the skies.
> Time's a thief, stealing your beauty,
> Leaving you with tears and sighs.
> But you waste time trying to catch him,
> Time's a bird and Time just flies.

> *("Time's A Bird" copyright © Valerie Bloom 2000,*
> *From* Hot Like Fire *published by Bloomsbury,*
> *reprinted by Permission of Valerie Bloom.)*

PERSONIFICATION ● **Personification** is just a form of either the simile or the metaphor, in which the poet gives human qualities to an inanimate object, an abstract idea, or a force of nature. We have already seen personification in the form of a simile when Emily Dickinson compares the locomotive to Boanerges (the followers of Christ). But throughout the poem, she personifies the locomotive through metaphors (that is, with no "like" or "as"). The locomotive laps, peers, complains, and so on. Notice how Robert Louis Stevenson gives human qualities to the winter sun in his poem, "Winter-Time":

> Late lies the wintry sun a-bed,
> A frosty, fiery sleepy-head;
> Blinks but an hour or two, and then,
> A blood-red orange, sets again.

Personification works well in children's poems because it appeals to the child's animistic view of the world, in which everything seems imbued with human attributes.

The effectiveness of all these forms of comparison depends in large part on what the reader brings to the poem. It is not entirely fair to fault the poet for our lack of knowledge. In fact, we could argue that the best poets are those who introduce us to new experiences, new ideas, and new ways of seeing things, and who challenge us to reach beyond our comfort zones.

Forms of Poetry

Poetry is a richly diverse genre that wears many clothes (to use a rather tired metaphor!). It can be divided into two broad categories: narrative poetry, which tells a story in verse, and lyric poetry, which is usually a short poem that expresses personal feelings (rather than telling a story).

Narrative Poetry

A **narrative poem** includes characters, action, and plot. Robert Browning's "The Pied Piper of Hamelin" and Henry Wadsworth Longfellow's "The Song of Hiawatha" are two nineteenth-century verse narratives still in print today. The early twentieth-century poet Alfred Noyes wrote "The Highwayman," a popular narrative poem that tells a tragic story of love and betrayal, concluding with the violent death of the highwayman and his beloved. "A Song of Sherwood," also by Noyes, is about the popular outlaw hero, Robin Hood.

For children, however, perhaps the most accessible narrative poems are ballads. Ballads are shorter narrative poems and usually include simple language—often dialect—and repeated refrains. They usually tell about a single event or they may recount the exploits of a hero. Tragic lovers and brave warriors are particular favorites among balladeers. Traditional ballads use the so-called ballad stanza, which contains four lines, each with eight syllables and with the second and fourth lines rhyming (that is, *a-b-c-b*), although many variations are found. One of the most famous ballads, "Barbara Allen," concerns tragic lovers and dates from the Middle Ages. The opening stanza sets the scene and introduces the main character:

In Scarlet town, where I was born,
There was a fair maid dwellin',
Made every youth cry Well-a-way!
Her name was Barbara Allen.

We learn that a young lad, Sweet William, is on his deathbed and begs to see Barbara Allen, but the hard-hearted maiden treats him with disdain and he dies. Soon she is overcome by remorse and she too dies. They are buried near each other and a red rose grows from his grave and a green briar grows from hers. The rose and briar grow from the two graves until

They grew and grew to the steeple top
Till they could grow no higher,
And there they twined in a true love's knot,
Red rose around green briar.

It should not be surprising that country and western songs were greatly influenced by the traditional ballad.

Lyric Poetry

Unlike a narrative poem, a lyric poem has no plot, it tells no tale, and it may or may not have characters. Instead, the lyric is a very personal poem describing the poet's innermost feelings or emotional response to something. In ancient Greece, these poems were typically sung to music played on a lyre—thus, they were called lyrics. Lyric poems come in an endless variety of forms—including cinquains, elegies, haiku, pastorals, odes, rondeaux, rondels, sestinas, sonnets, triolets, villanelles, and many more, with new ones still being created. Each form has its own rules for stanza length, line length, rhyme scheme, and so on. And we add to this large variety free verse, which ignores all the established rules.

What we look for in the lyric poem are fresh and thoughtful imagery, new ways of looking at things, and inventive use of rhyme and rhythm or language patterns. In other words, we want a pleasurable combination of sound and sense. What follows are but a few examples of lyric forms that children enjoy—and this only scratches the surface.

HAIKU ● Japanese in origin, haiku typically consists of 17 syllables (the number of words doesn't matter) divided into three lines and is usually on the subject of nature and our relationship to nature, such as this example by Ruby Lytle:

The moon is a week old—
A dandelion to blow
Scattering star seed.

(*From* What is the Moon? *By Ruby Lytle. Reprinted
with the permission of Tuttle Publishing.*)

In this haiku, the image of the stars as tiny seeds blown from the moon, like a whispery soft dandelion puff gone to seed, gives us a new way of thinking about the night sky and suggests a comforting pattern in creation. Haiku in English has a subtle rhythm but does not rhyme. Its strength lies in its evocative imagery. Successful haiku uses metaphor to give us a fresh and imaginative look at something we may view as quite ordinary.

CINQUAIN ● The cinquain is a five-line stanza apparently of medieval origin. The term once seems to have included any five-line poem (*cinq* is French for "five"), but Adelaide Crapsey, in her volume titled *Verse,* created more precise rules stipulating that the five lines should contain two, four, six, eight, and two syllables, respectively. No rhyming is necessary, but quite often the first and last lines contain related ideas, are synonymous, or mirror each other. Crapsey's cinquain, titled "November Night," plays on the double meaning of the last word (and, incidentally, notice the inverted simile in the third and fourth lines):

> Listen . . .
> With faint dry sound,
> Like steps of passing ghosts,
> The leaves, frost-crisp'd, break from the trees
> And fall.

VISUAL POETRY ● Also called concrete poetry or shape poetry, visual poetry consists of words arranged to form a pictorial representation of the poem's subject. Consequently, visual poetry is indeed a visual experience, rather than an auditory one—some visual poems even defy reading aloud. We can find visual poetry in English as far back as the seventeenth century. George Herbert, for example, wrote "The Altar" so that the lines form the shape of an altar, and his poem "Easter Wings" resembles angel wings. But Lewis Carroll is credited with the first visual poem for children—"The Mouse's Tale" from *Alice's Adventures in Wonderland,* in which the words of the poem take the shape of the mouse's tail, thus creating a pun on the title.

Today, visual poetry has become virtually a hybrid of literature and visual art. One of the most famous examples of modern visual poetry is Reinhard Döhl's poem titled "Pattern Poem with an Elusive Intruder." It consists of multiple repetitions of the word "apple", making up the shape of an apple. The intruder is the slyly placed word "worm," almost hidden in a lower corner. What is interesting about this poem is that it was originally written in German and the terms used are *apfel* and *wurm*—an example of a foreign-language poem that needs no translation. Robert Froman defines this poetry in his "A Seeing Poem" (see Figure 8.1), an example of a visual poem designed to be read.

Visual poetry is playful poetry—although that does not exclude it from being thoughtful poetry. It is appealing to children perhaps because it seems to be subversive, violating the sanctity of the text in favor of a collaboration between words as text and words as pictorial representations. Perhaps the best visual poems present interesting challenges to readers in very much the same way that poetic imagery does in a conventional poem.

Figure 8.1 ● Robert Froman's "A Seeing Poem"

Source: Robert Froman.

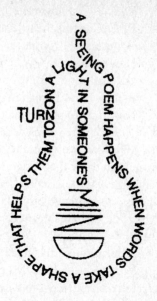

LIMERICK ● One of the most popular poetic forms among children is the limerick, a five-line humorous poem in which the first, second, and fifth lines rhyme and the third and fourth lines rhyme. The fun of the limerick lies in its rollicking rhythm and its broad humor—a limerick is always comical. The following limerick has been attributed to President Woodrow Wilson:

> I sat next to the Duchess at tea;
> It was just as I thought it would be;
> Her rumblings abdominal
> Were simply phenomenal,
> And everyone thought it was me.

The limerick's form is easily imitated (often in subversive and off-color ways), and young children can have a great deal of fun creating their own.

FREE VERSE ● Free verse, which became popular in the twentieth century, refers to poems that follow no established rules of form. Nineteenth-century American poet Walt Whitman is often credited with the popularization of free verse. He dramatically dispensed with traditional patterns of rhyme and rhythm. Here is Whitman's "When I Heard the Learn'd Astronomer," in which the poet suggests that the classroom is not always the best place to appreciate the wonders of the natural world:

> When I heard the learn'd astronomer,
> When the proofs, the figures, were ranged in columns before me,

When I was shown the charts and diagrams, to add, divide, and measure them,
When I, sitting, heard the astronomer, where he lectured with much applause in
 the lecture-room,
How soon, unaccountable, I became tired and sick,
Till rising and gliding out I wander'd off by myself,
In the mystical moist night-air, and from time to time,
Look'd up in perfect silence at the stars.

Whitman avoids all the restrictions of rhyme, rhythm, and line length, but it is a mistake to think that the good poet using free verse is not thinking about the sound of the language and the careful choice of words and images. Whitman's words are carefully chosen, his sentence (notice that there is only one) is perfectly constructed to reach the climax in the final line, which suggests that nature is the best teacher. Free verse does not imply "free-for-all"; the best free verse makes use of many poetic devices, including personification, simile, metaphor, alliteration, assonance, consonance, and repetition.

You can be assured that every word in this famous poem by Carl Sandburg was carefully considered—and not one was wasted. Try moving just one word and the effect of the entire poem is lost. Notice how Sandburg uses the metaphor of the fog as a creeping cat:

The fog comes
on little cat feet.
It sits looking
over harbor and city
on silent haunches
and then, moves on.

> (*From* Chicago Poems by *Carl Sandburg, copyright*
> *©1916 by Holt, Rinehart and Winston and renewed*
> *1944 by Carl Sandburg, reprinted by permission of*
> *Houghton Mifflin Harcourt Publishing Company.*)

Free verse, even its very name, suggests a subversive quality that may appeal to children—for it hints at a breaking of the rules, a challenging of the norms, a shattering of poetic taboos. Free verse finds its most ardent supporters among young teens, to whom its apparent flaunting of the rules must seem tantalizing. But we should not forget that both Whitman and Sandburg knew the rules and understood the traditions.

NONSENSE POETRY ● As with free verse, nonsense poetry is not so much a form of poetry as an approach. Nonsense verse, unlike free verse, usually depends heavily on regular rhyme and rhythm, but perhaps its most important rule is that it not make sense. In this regard, it is also subversive—which, we are learning, is irresistible to most children, for after all, childhood is about testing the waters, discovering what works, and finding out what is acceptable, how far one can go, and what the grown-ups are hiding.

Nonsense verse often hearkens back to the nursery rhymes, where, you will remember, words don't always have to be real—what on earth do "Diddle, diddle dumpling" and "Hickory dickory dock" mean anyway? Often, however, the nonsense is situational. Edward Lear, who lived in the nineteenth century, wrote an entire collection of nonsense verse. Perhaps his most famous poem begins with these lines:

> The Owl and the Pussy-Cat went to sea
>   In a beautiful pea-green boat,
> They took some honey, and plenty of money,
>   Wrapped up in a five-pound note.
> The Owl looked up to the stars above,
>   And sang to a small guitar,
> "O lovely Pussy! O Pussy, my love,
>   What a beautiful Pussy you are,
>   You are,
>   You are!
> What a beautiful Pussy you are!

The unlikely pair are married "by the Turkey who lives on the hill" and then

> . . . hand in hand, on the edge of the sand,
>   They danced by the light of the moon,
>   The moon,
>   The moon,
>   They danced by the light of the moon.

URCHIN POETRY ● Joseph T. Thomas Jr. uses the tantalizing term urchin poetry to describe the work of poets who are attempting to appeal to the earthier instincts in children that draw them to those forbidden topics of childhood, especially sex, bodily functions, and excretions. Urchin poetry—and the term presumably derives from the subjects of the poems and not the readers or the poets—is identified by its subject matter and treatment and not by any prescribed poetic pattern. It almost always rhymes and has a rhythmic beat and is, in those respects, quite conventional. However, it is characterized by its fixation on bodily excretions, the outrageous, and the grotesque. Naturally, all of these are fascinating to youth, perhaps largely because of the taboos associated with them.

The most famous poet in this vein is probably Shel Silverstein, whose *Where the Sidewalk Ends* and *The Light in the Attic* are filled with rollicking verses deliciously exploiting this material. With lines such this from "Messy Room"—"And his smelly old sock has been stuck to the wall,"—or his descriptions in "Sarah Cynthia Sylvia Stout"— "Gloppy glumps of cold oatmeal" and "Moldy melons, dried-up mustard"—Silverstein recognizes the value of a good "gross-out." Silverstein, in fact, is almost mainstream compared to the so-called "potty poets" whose obsessions with bodily excretions—always played for a laugh—have resulted in publications of many books of poetry (we will say nothing about the quality). The justification for all this, according to one website, is to provide "a gateway (albeit a rather wacky one!) into the world of books for many thousands of reluctant readers" (pottypoets.com).

PLAYGROUND POETRY ● As we have seen, free verse, nonsense verse, and the so-called urchin verse all seem to relish flaunting the rules, which at times seems to be a preoccupation of children in general. So it is not surprising that when children themselves experiment with poetry, they often challenge the status quo and break down social decorum. And where does this normally occur? On the playground—either literally or figuratively. Playground poetry (see Thomas) is the original urchin poetry, for it comes from the children themselves.

We have already suggested that children seem to have a natural affinity for poetry. Perhaps it is because the poetic form is one of the first literary forms introduced to them— in nursery rhymes, songs, and games. And it may have something to do with the fact that our bodies are tuned to natural rhythms—our heartbeats, for instance—and nature itself is filled with myriad patterns and rhythms. All this is speculative, but what is undeniable is that children, left to their own devices, are constantly reciting and creating poetry—and it is usually a communal experience. This jump-rope rhyme was a favorite playground verse of my own daughters when they were in early elementary school:

> Cinderella dressed in yella'
> Went to town to see her fella'
> On her way her girdle busted,
> How many people were disgusted?
> 1, 2, 3, . . . [etc. until the jumper misses]

For another example, see Chapter 6, "Fudge, Fudge, tell the judge." Playground poetry is very much like the traditional folktale in that it is passed along orally—often from child to child. And, since it not written down, it is easily altered in the transmission and readily adapted to changing times and circumstances—it is living poetry. Consequently, the children themselves become poets (of sorts) as they add their individual touches to the verses. The example of "Cinderella" is popular because it mentions an "unmentionable"—a girdle. References to undergarments invariably get a rise from first- and second-graders (although one wonders how much longer that term will hold meaning—it may be going the way of Boanerges in Dickinson's poem). The example of "Fudge, Fudge, tell the judge" is popular because of its fiendish violence.

But even these two poems are mild compared with what quite often is heard on the playground. I recall, for instance, this popular verse from my own childhood—and it is still in circulation:

> Great big gobs of greasy, grimy gopher guts,
> Mutilated monkey feet,

Dirty little birdy feet,
Great big gobs of greasy, grimy gopher guts,
And me without a spoon.

Playground poetry is recited out of earshot of adults and is therefore the product of childhood unleashed. Here children can throw off the yoke of adult domination and safely release the anxiety, hostility, and pent-up frustrations that are perfectly normal aspects of growing up (although many adults like to pretend otherwise). This contains all the language and imagery that are normally taboo for children. Profanity, sex, violence, and bodily functions are all typical features of this poetry—and I dare say that everyone reading this book can recall childhood favorites so I do not have to provide any further examples here. I am neither defending nor castigating these poetic offerings, only describing them.

Subversive poetry, including chants, parody, and the harmless cheers recited at sporting events, has always been, and always will be, an important part of childhood. Again, it serves as a much-needed outlet for pent-up childhood anxieties, doubt, fears, and frustrations. It is also an example of the creative process at work. Taste, refinement, and judgment will come with maturity, but art itself must begin with freedom of expression. I can only provide a personal testimonial—I once enjoyed singing along with my friends the words to "Great big gobs of greasy, grimy gopher guts" and I now enjoy the poetry of William Shakespeare, John Keats, Emily Dickinson, and Elizabeth Bishop. Go figure.

Sharing Poetry with Children

Studies of children's poetry preferences suggest, among other things, that (1) children prefer poetry that they can understand, (2) they prefer humorous poetry, (3) they prefer new poems to older ones, and (4) they do not like serious and contemplative poems (see Terry). However, such studies can be dangerous if we rely on them entirely to determine what poetry to share with children. This would result in a further narrowing of taste among children and deprive them of many fresh and imaginative poems that they just might enjoy.

For most elementary school children—and perhaps even older children—an oral approach to poetry makes the most sense. Because of its rhythmical and rhyming qualities, much of poetry begs to be read aloud. I would suggest doing it often—perhaps even a poem of the day or week. Go for the pleasure first, and then gradually work in the fundamental elements of poetry. In other words, pique the curiosity—tantalize them with good poems. Be sure to practice your own reading of poetry. These guidelines may be helpful when presenting poetry to children:

1. Read lots of poems of every shape and kind. We all like different types of poems. Variety is the only way you will eventually reach everyone. However, choose

poems that you personally like. It's hard to be enthusiastic about a work you don't care for. (However, if your tastes need to be broadened, then work on that!)

2. Before reading any poem aloud, read it over to yourself several times. Practice its rhythmic pattern, look up difficult-to-pronounce words, and so on. Be careful not to fall into a singsong pattern—and if the poem seems to require a singsong reading, maybe it's not such a good poem (unless it is just for fun).

3. Look closely at the punctuation and the spacing of the lines and stanzas on the page. Most inexperienced readers of poetry want to pause at the end of each line—but this can sound choppy and disjointed. If there is no punctuation at the end of the line, it may mean you should not pause. However, if the next line of poetry is indented or if it skips a space, that may suggest the poet wants you to pause a bit more. (Some poets use no punctuation at all and the spacing of words and lines is all we have to go on.) The following lines are from John Keats's *Endymion*. Read them through twice, first stopping at the end of each line, and then stopping only at the punctuation marks. See which makes the most sense:

> A thing of beauty is a joy forever:
> Its loveliness increases; it will never
> Pass into nothingness but still will keep
> A bower quiet for us, and a sleep
> Full of sweet dreams, and health, and quiet breathing

4. Think about the poem's meaning. What images does the poet use? What makes them effective? (If you don't find the images effective, maybe you should be looking for a different poem.)

5. Look for poems that invite participatory reading. See especially Paul Fleischman's *Joyful Noise: Poems for Two Voices* and *Big Talk: Poems for Four Voices,* and Sara Holbrook's *Wham! It's a Poetry Jam: Discovering Performance Poetry.*

Do not be afraid to have children memorize poems—yes, it is often considered old-fashioned and authoritarian, but that doesn't necessarily mean it's bad! Keep things informal and low key—perhaps using a poetry circle. Allow them to choose the poems they want to memorize.

The writing of original poetry may be encouraged and even required (but only after the children have caught the "poetry bug"), and some children will find it fun and rewarding. Again, some educators frown on this, but if practiced in the right spirit, it can prove to be very beneficial for many students. And it will certainly not harm the rest.

Finally, encourage children to form collections of their own favorite poems—and do so yourself. Poems can be copied into a notebook, illustrated, kept in a computer file, then given away as gifts. A simple exercise like this causes us to be on the lookout for good poems—and we will surely find them.

Summary

From the rhymes of Mother Goose to the jump-rope verse and limericks on the playground, poetry is a happy part of young children's lives. Perhaps, even in those formative years, children know instinctively what the eighteenth-century German philosopher, Novalis, said, "Poetry heals the wounds inflicted by reason." It is important that we nurture this initial love so that, as they grow older, children can appreciate the many facets of poetry—both the sound (the patterns of rhyme and rhythm) and the sense (including the exciting stories of narrative verse and the deep human emotion expressed in lyrics).

The poet is a visionary, one who sees the world in fresh and unusual ways and is capable of sharing that vision with the rest of us. It is important that we, as adults and teachers, overcome our own fears and apprehensions about poetry so that we can share its bounty. And the better we come to know poetry, the richer our experience will be. Although it is helpful to have some knowledge of poetic techniques and devices—rhythm, rhyme, metaphor, simile, and personification—it is important not to get bogged down by terminology. The best way to learn to enjoy poetry is to read and hear lots of it in all its rich variety. Most poetry is intended as an aural experience—that is, we need to hear it, not simply read it silently.

Children's tastes in poetry change over the years, evolving from the rhymes of Mother Goose to the playfully subversive poetry to the joyous verse of poets such as Silverstein and Prelutsky and eventually to the evocative visual poetry and the more intellectually and emotionally challenging work of poets such as Randall Jarrell (see especially *The Bat Poet,* a lovely tale in prose and poetry about the growth of an artist), Emily Dickinson, and Walt Whitman. The role of adults in all this is to see that all these options are available. Poetry presents many opportunities for creative activities through which we can explore and appreciate the richness of the art form—oral recitation, illustration, and writing, to name a few. Few literary forms offer so much in pleasure and knowledge as poetry. Lovers of poetry are not born, but made through patient and careful nurturing.

For Reflection and Discussion

1. Locate a collection of poems by a single poet. If possible, locate several collections by that poet. How would you describe this poetry to a friend? What are the poet's specific strengths? What are her or his specific weaknesses? If you have found several collections by the same poet, compare them. Has the poet exhibited any growth as a poet over the years?

2. Locate an anthology of poetry by several different poets and read through it. Which poems speak to you most clearly? What is it about those poems that seems to attract you? Is it form? The sound of the language? The meaning? Originality? A combination? From this experience, try to articulate your own feelings about poetry.

3. Memorize a favorite poem.

4. Write your own poem about a meaningful life experience. Try including some of the techniques of sound (rhyme and rhythm) and poetic form described in the chapter.

5. Find examples of what you would consider subversive poems—poems testing the boundaries of decorum or challenging the status quo. What is your response to them?

● Works Cited

Terry, Ann. *Children's Poetry Preferences: A National Survey of the Upper Elementary Grades.* Urbana, IL: National Council of Teachers of English, 1984.

Thomas, Joseph T., Jr. *Poetry's Playground: The Culture of Contemporary American Children's Poetry.* Detroit: Wayne State University Press, 2007.

● Recommended Readings

Ciardi, John, and Miller Williams. *How Does a Poem Mean?,* 2nd ed. Boston: Houghton Mifflin, 1975.

Higginson, William J., with Penny Harter. *The Haiku Handbook: How to Write, Share and Teach Haiku.* New York: McGraw-Hill, 1985.

Hopkins, Lee Bennet. *Pass the Poetry Please.* New York: Citation Press, 1972.

Hurst, Carol. "What to Do with a Poem." *Early Years* 11 (February 1980): 28–29, 68.

Kennedy, X. J. "'Go and Get Your Candle Lit!' An Approach to Poetry." *Horn Book Magazine* 57, 3 (June 1981): 273–279.

Livingston, Myra. *Climb into the Bell Tower: Essays on Poetry.* New York: HarperCollins, 1990.

——. *Poem-Making: Ways to Begin Writing Poetry.* New York: HarperCollins, 1991.

Oliver, Mary. *A Poetry Handbook: A Prose Guide to Understanding and Writing Poetry.* San Diego, CA: Harcourt, 1994.

Vardell, Sylvia M. *Poetry Aloud Here! Sharing Poetry with Children in the Library.* Chicago: ALA, 2006.

Selected Bibliography of Poetry Books for Children

The first list includes anthologies—collections that include poems by many different poets. The second list includes books by individual poets. Many of the poets have published several books, so you will want to look for other books by these writers.

Poetry Anthologies

Adoff, Arnold, ed. *I Am the Darker Brother: An Anthology of Modern Poems by African Americans.* Rev. ed. New York: Simon & Schuster, 1996.

Blishen, Edward, comp. *Oxford Book of Poetry for Children.* Illus. Brian Wildsmith. New York: Watts, 1963.

Carlson, Lori M., ed. *Cool Salsa: Bilingual Poems on Growing Up Latino in the United States.* New York: Holt, 1994.

De La Mare, Walter, ed. *Come Hither,* 3rd ed. Illus. Warren Chappell. New York: Knopf, 1957.

Demi, selector and illus. *In the Eyes of the Cat: Japanese Poetry for All Seasons.* Trans. Tze-si Huang. New York: Holt, 1992.

Dunning, Stephen, Edward Lueders, and Hugh Smith, comps. *Reflections on a Gift of Watermelon Pickle.* Glenview, IL: Scott, Foresman, 1967.

Elledge, Scott, ed. *Wider than the Sky: Poems to Grow Up With.* New York: Harper, 1990.

Esbensen, Barbara Juster, comp. *Swing around the Sun.* Illus. Khee Chee Cheng, Stephen Gammell, and Janice Lee Porter. Minneapolis: Carolrhoda, 2003.

Feelings, Tom, comp. and illus. *Soul Looks Back in Wonder.* New York: Dial, 1993.

Giovanni, Nikki, ed. *Hip Hop Speaks to Children.* Naperville, IL: Sourcebooks, 2008.

Harrison, Michael, and Christopher Stuart-Clark. *One Hundred Years of Poetry: For Children.* New York: Oxford University Press, 1999.

Hopkins, Lee Bennett, ed. *Sharing the Season: A Book of Poems.* New York: McElderry, 2010.

———. *Sky Magic.* Illus. Mariusz Stawarski. New York: Dutton, 2009.

Houston, James, ed. *Songs of the Dream People.* New York: Atheneum, 1972. (Eskimo and other Native American poems)

Janeczko, Paul B., ed. *A Kick in the Head: An Everyday Guide to Poetic Forms.* Illus. Chris Raschka. New York: Candlewick, 2005.

———. *A Poke in the I: A Collection of Concrete Poems.* Illus. Chris Raschka. Cambridge, MA: Candlewick, 2001.

Jones, Hettie, selector. *The Trees Stand Shining: Poetry of the North American Indians.* Illus. Robert Andrew Parker. New York: Dial, 1971.

Kennedy, X. J., and Dorothy Kennedy, eds. *Knock at a Star: A Child's Introduction to Poetry.* Rev. ed. Illus. Karen Lee Baker. Boston: Little, Brown, 1999.

Larrick, Nancy, ed. *Piping Down the Valleys Wild.* Illus. Ellen Raskin. 1968. New York: Dell, 1982.

Livingston, Myra Cohn, comp. *Dilly Dilly Piccalilli: Poems for the Very Young.* New York: McElderry, 1989. (Nonsense verse)

———. *Lots of Limericks.* New York: Simon & Schuster, 1991.

Michael, Pamela, ed. *River of Words.* Minneapolis: Milkweed, 2008.

Moore, Lilian, ed. *Sunflakes: Poems for Children.* Illus. Jan Ormerod. New York: Clarion, 1992.

Nye, Naomi Shihab, selector. *This Same Sky: A Collection of Poems from around the World.* New York: Macmillan, 1992.

Opie, Iona, and Peter Opie, eds. *The Oxford Book of Children's Verse.* New York: Oxford, 1973.

Orozco, José-Luis, selector-arranger. *De Colores and Other Latin-American Folk Songs for Children.* New York: Dutton, 1994.

Prelutsky, Jack, selector. *Read-Aloud Rhymes for the Very Young.* Illus. Marc Brown. New York: Knopf, 1987.

———. *The 20th Century Children's Poetry Treasury.* Illus. Meilo So. New York: Knopf, 1999.

Schwartz, Alvin, selector. *And the Green Grass Grew All Around: Folk Poetry from Everyone.* Illus. Sue Truesdell. New York: Harper, 1992.

Books by Individual Poets

Adoff, Arnold. *Street Music: City Poems.* Illus. Karen Barbour. New York: HarperCollins, 1995.

Agard, John. *Half-caste and Other Poems.* North Pomfret, VT: Hodder/Trafalgar Square, 2005.

Agee, Jon. *Orangutan Tongs: Poems to Tangle Your Tongue.* New York: Hyperion, 2009.

Berry, James. *Everywhere Faces Everywhere.* Illus. Reynold Ruffins. New York: Simon, 1997.

Bloom, Valerie. *The World Is Sweet*. London: Bloomsbury, 2000.

Brooks, Gwendolyn. *Bronzeville Boys and Girls*. Illus. Faith Ringgold. New York: Amistad/HarperCollins, 2007.

Chandra, Deborah. *Balloons and Other Poems*. Illus. Leslie Bowman. New York: Farrar, Straus & Giroux, 1990.

Ciardi, John. *You Read to Me, I'll Read to You*. Illus. Edward Gorey. New York: HarperCollins, 1987.

Coatsworth, Elizabeth. *Under the Green Willow*. Illus. Janina Domanska. New York: Macmillan, 1971.

cummings, e. e. *Hist Whist*. Illus. Deborah Kogan Ray. New York: Crown, 1989.

De La Mare, Walter. *Peacock Pie*. Illus. Barbara Cooney. New York: Knopf, 1961.

Dickinson, Emily. *My Letter to the World and Other Poems*. Toronto: Kids Can Press, 2008.

Eliot, T. S. *Old Possum's Book of Practical Cats*. Illus. Edward Gorey. New York: Harcourt, Brace, Jovanovich, 1982.

Fleischman, Paul. *Big Talk: Poems for Four Voices*. Illus. Beppe Giacobbe. New York: Candlewick, 2008.

———. *A Joyful Noise: Poems for Two Voices*. New York: Harper, 1987.

Florian, Douglas. *Lizards, Frogs, and Polliwogs*. New York: Harcourt, 2001.

Froman, Robert. *Seeing Things: A Book of Poems*. New York: Crowell, 1974.

Franco, Betsy. *Curious Collection of Cats*. Illus. Michael Wertz. San Francisco: Tricycle Press, 2009.

Frost, Robert. *Birches*. Illus. Ed Young. New York: Holt, 1988.

Giovanni, Nikki. *Spin a Soft Black Song*. Illus. George Martins. New York: Hill & Wang, 1985.

Greenberg, David T. *Bugs*. Illus. Lyn Munsinger. Boston: Little, Brown, 1997.

Greenfield, Eloise. *The Friendly Four*. Illus. Jan Spivey Gilchrist. New York: HarperColllins, 2006.

Hoberman, Mary Ann, and Linda Winston. *The Tree That Time Built: A Celebration of Nature, Science, and Imagination*. Naperville, IL: Sourcebooks, 2009.

Holbrook, Sara. *Wham! It's a Poetry Jam: Discovering Performance Poetry*. Honesdale, PA: Boyds Mills, 2002.

Hopkins, Lee Bennett. *City I Love*. Illus. Marcus Hall. New York: Abrams, 2009.

Hughes, Langston. *The Dream Keeper and Other Poems*. New York: Knopf, 1994.

Issa. *A Few Flies and I: Haiku by Issa*. Trans. R. H. Blyth and Nobuyaki Yuasa. Ed. Jean Merrill and Ronni Solbert. New York: Pantheon, 1969.

Janeczko, Paul B. *Brickyard Summer*. New York: Orchard, 1989.

Jarrell, Randall. *The Bat Poet*. Illus. Maurice Sendak. New York: Macmillan, 1964.

Kuskin, Karla. *Moon, Have You Met My Mother?* Illus. Sergio Ruzzier. New York: HarperCollins, 2003.

Lear, Edward. *The Complete Verse and Other Nonsense*. Ed. Vivian Noakes. New York: Penguin, 2006.

Lewis, J. Patrick. *The House*. Illus. Roberto Innocenti. Minneapolis: Creative Editions, 2009.

Livingston, Myra Cohn. *Calendar*. Illus. Will Hillebrand. New York: Holiday House, 2007.

McCord, David. *One at a Time: His Collected Poems for the Young*. Illus. Henry Kane. Boston: Little, Brown, 1977.

Mado, Michio. *The Magic Pocket*. Trans. Empress Michiko of Japan. Illus. Mitsumasa Anno. New York: McElderry, 1998.

Mahy, Margaret. *Nonstop Nonsense*. Illus. Quentin Blake. New York: McElderry, 1989.

Moore, Lilian. *Mural on Second Avenue and Other City Poems*. Illus. Roma Karas. New York: Candlewick, 2005.

Mordhorst, Heidi. *Pumpkin Butterfly: Poems from the Other Side of Nature*. Honesdale, PA: Wordsong/Boyds Mill Press, 2009.

Myers, Walter Dean. *Blues Journey*. Illus. Christopher Myers. New York: Holiday, 2003.

Nash, Ogden. *The Best of Ogden Nash*. Chicago: Ivan R. Dee, 2007.

Nye, Naomi Shihab. *19 Varieties of Gazelle: Poems of the Middle East*. New York: Greenwillow, 2002.

O'Neill, Mary. *Hailstones and Halibut Bones*. Illus. John Wallner. New York: Doubleday, 1989.

Prelutsky, Jack. *The Frog Wore Red Suspenders*. Illus. Petra Mathers. New York: Greenwillow, 2002.

———. *Ride a Purple Pelican*. New York: Greenwillow, 1986.

Richards, Laura. *Tirra Lirra: Rhymes Old and New.* 1932. Illus. Marguerite Davis. Boston: Little, Brown, 1955.

Roethke, Theodore. *Dirty Dinky and Other Creatures.* Selectors Beatrice Roethke and Stephen Lushington. New York: Doubleday, 1973.

Rosen, Michael J. *The Cuckoo's Haiku and Other Birding Poems.* Illus. Stan Fellows. Cambridge, MA: Candlewick, 2009.

Ruddell, Deborah. *A Whiff of Pine, a Hint of Skunk.* New York: Simon & Schuster, 2009.

Schertie, Alice. *Button Up! Wrinkled Rhymes.* Illus. Petra Mathers. New York: Houghton Mifflin Harcourt, 2009.

Shannon, George. *Busy in the Garden.* Illus. Sam Williams. New York: Greenwillow, 2006.

Sidman, Joyce. *Meow Ruff.* Illus. Michelle Berg. Boston: Houghton Mifflin, 2006.

Silverstein, Shel. *A Light in the Attic.* New York: Harper, 1981.

———. *Where the Sidewalk Ends.* New York: Harper, 1974.

Soto, Gary. *New and Selected Poems.* San Francisco: Chronicle Books, 1995.

Starbird, Kaye. *The Covered Bridge House.* Illus. Jim Arnosky. New York: Four Winds, 1979.

Stevenson, James. *Sweet Corn: Poems.* New York: Greenwillow, 1995.

Stevenson, Robert Louis. *A Child's Garden of Verses.* Illus. Jessie Willcox Smith. 1905. New York: Scribner's, 1969.

Swenson, May. *The Complete Poems to Solve.* New York: Macmillan, 1993.

Viorst, Judith. *If I Were in Charge of the World and Other Worries.* Illus. Lyn Cherry. New York: Atheneum, 1969.

Whitman, Walt. *Voyages: Poems by Walt Whitman.* Selector, Lee Bennett Hopkins. Illus. Charles Mikolaycak. New York: Harcourt, 1988.

Wilbur, Richard. *Opposites.* New York: Harcourt, 1973.

Willard, Nancy. *Household Tales of Moon and Water.* New York: Harcourt, 1982.

———. *A Visit to William Blake's Inn.* Illus. Alice and Martin Provensen. New York: Harcourt, 1981.

Williams, Vera B. *Amber Was Brave, Essie Was Smart.* New York: Greenwillow, 2001.

Wong, Janet S. *A Suitcase of Seaweed and Other Poems.* New York: Simon & Schuster, 1996.

Worth, Valerie. *All the Small Poems and Fourteen More.* Illus. Natalie Babbitt. New York: Farrar, Straus & Giroux, 1994.

PEARSON myeducationkit™

Go to the topic "Poetry" on the MyEducationKit for this text, where you can:

- Search the Database of Children's Literature, housing more than 22,000 titles searchable in every genre by authors or illustrators, by awards won, by year published, and by topic and description.

- Explore genre-related Assignments and Activities, assignable exercises showing concepts in action through database use, video, cases, and student and teacher artifacts.

- Listen to podcasts and read interviews from some of the brightest and most enduring stars of children's literature in the Conversations.

- Discover Web Links that will lead you to sites representing the authors you learn about in these pages, classrooms with powerful children's literature connections, and literature awards.

Folk Narratives

The Oldest Stories

Introduction

Folktales, legends, and myths are our oldest stories—and still some of the best. They contain gripping plots and exotic settings, and are filled with magic and wonder. They are at the core of all literature. In "Cinderella" we find the kernel of every romance. In "Hansel and Gretel" we find the essence of the coming-of-age story. In "Jack and the Beanstalk" we find the quintessential adventure story. In "Rumpelstiltskin" we find the mystery. And in "Little Red Riding Hood" we find the crucible of trickery and deceit. In the folktale, human emotions, desires, fears, and hopes are stripped to their bare bones. They bring us to the very heart of humanity.

The "folk" in folk narratives refers to the common people of a society—as opposed to professional writers, for example. Folk narratives, tradition tells us, are the stories the common people passed along by word of mouth, from generation to generation. The folk narratives were (and are) the products of societies in which most people could not read— societies without books, televisions, computers, and film. These are also societies whose wells of knowledge depended on the spoken word. Consequently, we can never know who created the first versions of "The Frog King" or "Rapunzel" or "The Three Billy Goats Gruff." And we can never speak of the author of a folktale—only the reteller.

The myths or sacred tales about the origins of the world, the gods and goddesses, and the cultural heroes began as oral narratives in the distant past. However, many of them (Homer's *Iliad,* Virgil's *Aeneid,* Ovid's *Metamorphoses, Beowulf,* and others) have long since been written down and become part of our literary culture. But most of the secular (or nonreligious) folk narratives (folktales, legends, tall tales, riddles, and so on) remained in the oral culture until fairly recently. It was only in the nineteenth century that collectors like Jacob and Wilhelm Grimm, Joseph Jacobs, Andrew Lang, Peter Asbjørnsen, Jørgen Moe, and others began to record the oral tales, chiefly from Europe. But soon collectors were gathering tales from native cultures the world over. And it was quickly discovered that tales from the far corners of the world bore striking similarities. African, Asian, and Native American cultures all had their own versions of "Cinderella" or "Little Red Riding Hood,"

PEARSON
myeducationkit™

Visit the MyEducationKit for this course to enhance your understanding of chapter concepts with activities, web links, podcasts, and a searchable database of more than 22,000 children's literature titles.

for example. What, scholars wondered, could explain this? Some speculated that all the stories had a common origin thousands of years ago when human beings were still largely concentrated in Africa and the Middle East. Then, when humanity migrated outward, the stories came with them and were eventually adapted to new environments and cultures. This theory is called monogenesis (that is, "one beginning"). Others disagreed and argued instead that the similarities in the stories were the natural results of the similarities in the human psyche. All human beings have essentially the same needs, anxieties, foibles, fears, desires, hopes, and dreams. The folktales address all these human concerns; they simply appear in different dress in different parts of the world. This theory is called polygenesis ("many beginnings"), and it is the most widely accepted explanation today. Of course, the truth probably lies somewhere in between—with some stories traveling from culture to culture over time, and others rising independently in multiple places all over the earth.

Today, of course, our chief exposure to all folk narratives is through the written word. We seldom get to experience them as they were intended—as communal storytelling events. Still, the oral origins of these tales are reflected in their style and content, and we should keep that in mind as we read them. To begin, we will look at the storytelling elements or conventions of the oral narrative and then we'll consider some of the more common types of oral narratives.

Storytelling Conventions in Folk Narratives

A convention is an established, agreed-on practice or technique or way of doing things. Folk narratives, over the years, have acquired many conventions that set them apart from other types of literature. The most important differences involve the setting, character, plot, theme, and style. Myths also differ from other forms of literature in several ways, which we will consider later.

Setting

"Once upon a time in a kingdom far, far away"—this is the conventional opening of many folktales. The time is the distant past; the place is a long way off—it is a setting where magical things can occur. Even so, the settings of most folk narratives retain the physical aspects of their place of origin. So, Scandinavian narratives have stark, cold, mountainous settings, surrounded by the sea; ancient Greek narratives describe sunny isles in the Aegean Sea and the rugged mountains of the Greek peninsula; Native American narratives are set in southwest deserts or eastern woodlands or Pacific coastlands or other places, depending on the tale's origin. The storytellers were describing what they—and their listeners—knew. Because the place was familiar to the audience, it required few descriptive details (a dark forest, a castle, a cottage—that's about all we get in the way of physical description). Because the time was long ago, it permitted the fantastic (talking animals, magical spells, enchanted objects)—it was, to paraphrase a popular lyric, a time when wishing made it so.

Character

If the settings are uncomplicated, so are the characters. In the folk narrative, everything is on the surface; consequently, characters do not internalize their feelings and are seldom plagued by mental torment. Motivation in folktale characters tends to be singular—that is, the characters are motivated by one overriding desire such as greed, love, fear, hatred, jealousy—unlike characters in novels where motivations are usually more complicated. Characters often function as symbols—representing generosity, faithfulness, greed, vanity, and so on.

Folktale characters do not develop the way that characters do in novels (see Chapters 3, 10, and 11). We find little self-discovery in folktales. A selfish or wicked character is not going to change—he or she will, instead, be punished. And goodness in a character is evident from the beginning—and will probably be rewarded in the end. Stereotypical characters abound—powerful, wicked stepmothers; weak-willed, ineffectual fathers; mean, jealous siblings; faithful friends; virtuous children; helpful animals; and simpletons or fools. A character is either good or evil, and it is usually not difficult for the audience to tell which is which. Physical appearance often gives away a character's nature—wicked witches are ugly, good princesses are beautiful, noble princes are fair, but enchanted disguises are common. The Beast in "Beauty and the Beast" has been transformed from his handsome self into a monstrosity by a jealous witch. In "The Frog Prince," a witch has transformed a handsome prince into a frog. When the spell is broken, the prince's pleasing appearance is restored. Only rarely do we find a truly beautiful character to be wicked. Snow White's stepmother is an example, but even her beauty is outshone by that of her virtuous stepdaughter, and she performs her most powerful magic when she assumes the disguise of an ugly hag. Truth cannot long remain hidden. (Figures 9.1 and 9.4 show illustrations for variants of "Snow White.")

The hero or heroine is often isolated and is usually cast out into the open world or is apparently without any human friends. Evil, on the other hand, seems overwhelming. Consequently, to offset the apparent imbalance, the hero/heroine must be aided by supernatural forces (such as a magical object or a fairy godmother). One reason young children are fascinated by folktales is that the heroes or heroines are very much like children picture themselves—the young, helpless victims of evil forces (sometimes appearing in the form of their parents!). And the evil characters symbolize all of their fears and frustrations. Most folk narratives are also wish fulfilling—or hopeful, depending on your point of view. And good generally triumphs over the evil—another reason these tales are so appealing to children.

Figure 9.1 ● Lancelot Speed's illustration for "Snowdrop," a variant of "Snow White."

Source: From *The Red Fairy Book*, edited by Andrew Lang, London, 1890.

Plot

The plot, or the sequence of events, is simple and straightforward in the folk narrative. Adventure and action are far more important to these tales than character development. Conflicts are quickly established and events move swiftly to their conclusion; although there may be subsidiary plots or the events may at times seem to get sidetracked, the action never slows down. Endings are almost always happy.

The oral nature of the folk narrative resulted in the use of formulaic patterns. We find, for instance, the pattern of three repeated in tale after tale—three brothers (or sisters), three tasks, three wishes, three obstacles, three tries, and so on. Incidentally, the ritual number three is a European feature—along with the numbers seven and twelve, all of which have cultural significance (the Holy Trinity, the seven days of creation, the twelve tribes of Judah, and so on). Tales from other cultures may use different ritual numbers. In Native American stories, for example, it is the number four—representing the four cardinal directions. In Russian tales, the sacred number three is often compounded—heroes are always going on far-off adventures to the "thrice-ninth land."

Another aspect of the formulaic plot is the motif, which is a repeated figure or element in a larger design. In visual arts, motifs might include repeated plant or animal designs or geometric designs that are used as decorative devices. Examples include seasonal motifs (such as hearts and cupids for Valentine's Day or shamrocks and leprechauns for St. Patrick's Day) and patriotic motifs (such as eagles, stars, and liberty bells for the United States or the maple leaf for Canada). In written literature, a motif can reinforce a theme, but in folk narratives it is more often a plot device. The folklorist Stith Thompson, who catalogued thousands of motifs, defines a folktale motif as "the smallest element in a tale having power to persist in tradition." Originally, folktale motifs may have been mnemonic devices or just easy ways to extend an oral tale. Examples of common folktale motifs include journeys through dark forests, enchanted transformations, magical cures or other spells, encounters with helpful animals or mysterious creatures, trickster antics, foolish bargains, impossible tasks, clever deceptions, and so on. Some motifs are accompanied by powerful visual images by which we readily identify many folktales— a glass slipper, a beanstalk and talking harp, a spinning wheel, a poisoned apple, a bloody handkerchief, a red riding hood. These stark visual elements contribute to the tales' enduring strength.

Surely one of the best-known aspects of folktale plots is the magic. Many folktale motifs consist of magical elements—helpful animals, transformations from human to beast and beast to human, granted wishes, and so on. Although magic is not a requirement of the folk narrative, it is fair to say that it is a ubiquitous feature—that is, it's found everywhere. It is notable that magic, when it does appear in the folk narrative, is always accepted by the characters with nonchalance or a matter-of-factness. No one is ever surprised when an animal starts talking or when a fairy godmother materializes out of thin air or when an elf suddenly appears and makes exotic promises. This acquiescent attitude toward magic further distances the folktale from reality, and it provides an important distinction between folk narratives and much of literary fantasy. In many literary fantasies (heroic fantasy being one of the exceptions), magical occurrences are not necessarily taken for granted, and may even be regarded with surprise, awe, and disbelief. Both Alice and Dorothy, those most famous of child travelers in literary fantasies, are in constant wonder at the characters and circumstances they encounter, whereas the folktale heroines Cinderella and Little Red Riding Hood accept fairy godmothers or talking wolves without batting an eye.

Theme

Themes in most folk narratives are usually quite simple, but serious and powerful. Commonly found themes include the following:

1. Everything in life comes at some cost. ("Rumpelstiltskin")
2. Goodness and generosity will ultimately triumph over wickedness and selfishness. ("Cinderella")
3. In life there are bargains we must keep, vows we must honor. ("Rapunzel," see Figure 9.5)
4. Wickedness can be overcome with cleverness and perseverance. ("Hansel and Gretel")
5. A person's inner qualities are what matter most. ("Beauty and the Beast")
6. Growing up is fraught with danger and pain. ("Little Red Riding Hood," see Figure 9.3)

These are not the only themes we find in folk narratives, but we can easily see why children might be drawn to tales that emphasize these issues, for they are at the very heart of growing up. If we had to make a general statement about themes in folk narratives, we might well turn to the great theme of Greek tragedy: Wisdom comes through suffering. For every benefit there is a condition; nothing in life comes without strings attached, responsibilities to be met, and bargains to be kept. And the themes of the folk narratives— especially in the Western tradition—espouse the virtues of compassion, generosity, and humility over the vices of greed, selfishness, and excessive or overweening pride.

Style

The predominant characteristic of a folk narrative's style is how it reflects its oral origins. As with the plots, the language of the folk narrative tends to be formulaic and economical—conventional openings and closings, for instance ("Once upon a time in a kingdom far, far away" and "They lived happily ever after") or formulaic commands or responses ("Mirror, Mirror, on the wall . . ." or "I'll huff and I'll puff and I'll blow your house down"). Repetitious phrases are mnemonic devices, of course, but they are also part of the ritual quality and the artistic nature of the folk narrative. They help create the magical or otherworldly aura of the tales—we are not listening to history but to poetry or to drama. Additionally, dialogue is a common feature of the folk narrative, and in the best-told tales the dialogue captures the nature of the character speaking; hence, a lowly peasant will speak in a folksy manner, whereas the speech of a king or princess will be more refined. (The English retellings of Joseph Jacobs admirably capture these differences in speech patterns.)

Folk narratives also use a technique known as stylized intensification, which occurs when, with each repetition, an element is further exaggerated or intensified—with each Billy Goat Gruff we get a larger, fiercer billy goat, for example, or with each visit Rumpelstiltskin's price for spinning straw into gold increases, or with each Little Pig's house the Wolf must work harder and harder (see Figure 9.2). This has the effect of increasing the tension and heightening the drama. It's just good storytelling.

Figure 9.2 ● H. J. Ford's illustration for "The Three Little Pigs."

Source: From *The Green Fairy Book,* edited by Andrew Lang, London, 1892.

Types of Folktales

Folktales from all over the world come in many different varieties. Let's look at some of the more commonly found types that especially appeal to children.

Talking Animal Tales and Fables

Many tales contain talking animals—including fables, wonder tales, merry tales, *pourquoi* tales, and trickster tales. So this is more of a motif than a tale type, but it is necessary to mention those stories in which talking animals are portrayed with human traits, a concept called **anthropomorphism.** The talking animals possess human strengths and weaknesses, human wisdom and folly. They talk. They may cook their food. They may live in houses. They may wear clothes. And they lead ordinary lives—although some are more like animals than others. Often these tales convey strong moral messages, particularly extolling the virtues of wisdom, hard work, and perseverance. Talking animal tales are among the favorites of very young children, who, we know, have no trouble imagining animals with personalities and emotions. Popular examples include "The Three Little Pigs" (where diligence and cleverness defeat a ravenous wolf—see Figure 9.2), "The Little Red Hen" (in which the title character's lazy companions refuse to help her make bread, but are more than willing to help eat it), and "The Three Billy Goats Gruff" (who behave very much like goats, except they can talk and they can outwit a disagreeable Troll). Incidentally, notice the repetitive pattern in the plot of each of these tales.

The story of "Henny Penny" is an animal tale that incorporates a cumulative plot (see the discussion of cumulative plots in Chapter 3) in which successive additions are made to a repetitive plot line. Henny Penny is a silly chicken who gets hit in the head with an acorn and decides the sky must be falling. She sets out to warn the king and on the way meets several other gullible animals (a duck, a goose, and a turkey) who join her in her journey. Unfortunately, they never reach the king, but instead fall victims to a wily fox.

As we see from these examples, talking animal stories are often quite serious. Let's take another example, "The Musicians of Bremen-town," about an assortment of over-the-hill farm animals who learn their masters are going to get rid of them (in one way or another) now that they are old and useless. Their mutual plight brings them together, and they decide to go to Bremen-town to become musicians (no, they have no musical talent that we are aware of). On their way, they come to a house occupied with thieves who are counting their treasure. The animals cleverly devise a scheme to scare off the thieves, and the animals move into their house and live happily ever after (never making it to Bremen-town).

Another popular tale, "Little Red Riding Hood" (see Figure 9.3), is a variation on the talking animal tale, except that it has only one talking animal (although we should point out that Little Red Riding Hood does not see anything unusual in that). But, like "The Three Little Pigs" and "The Musicians of Bremen-town," the tale is a serious one—and one

Figure 9.3 ● Gustave Doré's celebrated engraving for "Little Red Riding Hood" is typical of the drama—sometimes startling drama—with which he imbued all of his work.

Source: From *Perrault's Fairy Tales,* 1867, reprinted by Dover, 1969.

that would be more horrifying were the wolf a human being. Talking animal tales, then, become vehicles for conveying stories with important themes on a level easily comprehended by preschoolers. And the gripping plots, appealing characters, and powerful themes pleasingly cloak the underlying didactic purpose of the tales. These qualities make the talking animal tales among the most popular of all folk narratives.

One of the oldest types of talking animal tale is the fable. A *fable* is a short and blatantly didactic tale designed to teach specific lessons. An ancient Greek teacher named Aesop is credited with writing the most famous fables over 2,500 years ago, presumably as teaching tools for his students. Fables use animal characters as allegorical figures—that is, the animals represent specific human traits, such as greed, gullibility, selfishness, and so on. The fable is not known for its subtlety and it usually concludes with a statement like: "And the moral of the story is . . . ." The following fable is taken from those attributed to Aesop, and this particular tale is the origin of the well-worn expression "sour grapes":

A very hungry fox came upon a vineyard where hung many bunches of the most delicious, the most luscious grapes you could ever wish to see. However, the grapes were staked to a high trellis and the fox could not reach them no matter how hard he tried. After many vain leaps, the exhausted fox gave up, exclaiming, "Oh, those grapes look green and sour anyway. I don't even want them." And off he went.

The moral of the story is: It is easy to find an excuse for not wanting what we cannot have.

Moral Tales

Not all moral stories are talking animal tales. Didactic stories, designed to teach some moral or social lesson, are found in almost all cultures. The moral tale shows ordinary human beings going about their daily affairs and suddenly finding themselves in some dilemma. They always get out of it, but not without learning a frequently difficult lesson. The tales are usually quite simple, for if they were too complex they would lose their teaching effectiveness. And they often have a comic twist—the old storytellers knew the value of teaching through humor.

In one old Jewish tale, we find a very important lesson about justice and the folly of human nature—the judge's solution underscores the absurdity of the people's complaint. The story goes something like this.

For murdering one of his customers, the cobbler in the town of Chelm was sentenced to be hanged. However, when they heard the sentence the townspeople cried out to the judge to spare him, exclaiming that they only had one cobbler in town and if he were hanged they would have no one to mend their shoes. The judge, who was a careful and thoughtful man, took their pleadings to heart and finally decided that they were right, since there was only one cobbler, he should be spared. So, the judge declared that, since there were two roofers in town, one of them should be hanged instead.

Local Legends and Tall Tales

Legends are tales that claim to be based on true stories (except they seldom are). In the Middle Ages, legends grew up around religious figures, saints, and martyrs, about whom many miraculous stories were told. These saints' lives were used to teach children Christian morality. Both of these types celebrate the heroic feats by ordinary mortals—as opposed to gods, goddesses, or the great epic heroes. Certainly many legends once contained a kernel of truth, but as with all oral tales, they have, over the years, become hopelessly distorted and even fantastical. The following is the popular legend of William Tell, a fourteenth-century Swiss hero who defied the oppressive Austrian overlords in Switzerland:

William Tell was a man of enormous strength and he was the most skilled marksman in the county of Uri. The wicked Austrian governor, named Gessler, ordered that, as a sign of submission to Austrian rule, the Swiss people should bow to a hat propped up on a stick in the town square, a symbol of imperial authority. William Tell refused and was arrested. Gessler, who knew of the man's fame as a marksman, offered Tell his freedom if he could shoot an apple off his son's head with a crossbow from a hundred paces. The brave Tell took the bow in his hand and aimed it at the apple balanced on his young son's head. He let the arrow fly and it split the apple in two, sparing his son and freeing Tell. But then Tell boasted that he would have killed Gessler if the arrow had harmed his son. So Tell was immediately seized. While he was being transported across a lake to prison, a storm broke out and the crew needed Tell's great strength to help steer the boat. He was released, after which he found Gessler and shot an arrow through his heart.

Although there is no concrete evidence that Tell ever existed, the story has been told for generations and has been the subject of a play and an opera. And a statue of William Tell and his son stands today in the Swiss city of Altdorf.

Many American legends originated in the early days of the Republic, a result of nationalistic fervor. Fanciful stories quickly grew up around American frontiersmen David Crockett (who killed his first bear at the age of 3!), Daniel Boone, and Johnny Appleseed, among others. These were real people—it's just that their stories became exaggerated or even fabricated. But then, Americans are no strangers to exaggeration. How else do we explain tall tales?—those outrageous stories about fictional heroes performing extraordinary feats. Perhaps the most famous is Paul Bunyan, the giant logger, who performs miraculous feats of strength aided by his blue ox, Babe—creating rivers, canyons, leveling mountains, that sort of thing. Tall tales have a peculiarly American flavor—derived from the American love of bravado and the obsession with extremes (the biggest, the tallest, the costliest, the best).

Riddles and Dilemma Tales

A riddle asks for an answer to a puzzle—and the answer may be a trick and the riddle is often comical. A dilemma tale, on the other hand, poses an ethical problem that has no easy answer—nor does it normally supply one, leaving that up to the listeners. The following is famous riddle from India about the Mughal Emperor, Akbar, and his clever Hindu courtier, Birbal. It dates to the sixteenth century, in the reign of Akbar, an actual Indian ruler.

> *The Emperor Akbar one day took a stick and drew a straight line on the palace floor. He then asked if anyone could make the line shorter without touching any part of it. Everyone was baffled, except for clever Birbal, who simply picked up a stick and drew a longer line right next to the Emperor's—thus making Akbar's line shorter.*

Dilemma tales are found throughout the world, but they are especially popular in Africa. The tale summarized here is found in many variations throughout northern African and the Middle East:

> *Three brothers (or friends) set off on a search for the most valuable treasure in the world in order to win the hand of a lovely princess. The first finds a magic mirror that allows him to see anyone in the world. The second finds a magic carpet that can carry a person anywhere. The third finds a wondrous fruit that can restore life to a dying person. When they reunite, they use the magic*

mirror to discover that the princess is dying. They then take the magic carpet to reach her bedside, and use the magic fruit to bring her back to health. Which one should she marry?

Curiously, in several versions, answers are supplied—one says the fruit was the greatest sacrifice, because it could only be used once; or, in a Tunisian variation, their father actually takes the princess as his bride since had it not been for him, they would not have been born; or, in a Tajik variation, the princess herself brings out her two sisters, all look-alikes, and everyone can live happily ever after. Generally, however, the correct answer to a dilemma tale is not as important as the discussion that it invites. In oral cultures, such tales serve as instructional devices, asking the listeners to use their own wits to solve a conundrum.

Merry Tales

As the name suggests, merry tales are stories largely for fun and focus on foolish or gullible characters who are inevitably involved in some calamity or hilarity. Magic may be involved, but as often as not the plot revolves around mere silliness. The tales are also called simpleton tales or noodlehead tales for obvious reasons.

Unlike in the wonder tale (see the next section), where the hero usually ends up with lavish rewards, the heroes of the merry tale quite often end up exactly where they began— poor and down and out. But they seldom care. They accept life at face value and seem quite capable of making the best of a difficult situation—even when they themselves have caused the situation. Take this well-known example, sometimes referred to as "The Three Wishes":

A very poor couple were cutting wood for their fire one day when they heard a tiny voice cry, "Help me! Help me!" Lo and behold, it was a little imp caught beneath a great log. The couple lifted the log and released the poor imp.

It turns out the imp had magical powers and he said to them, "In gratitude for your kind assistance, I will grant you three wishes—but three only."

The poor couple returned to their meager cottage and pondered their good fortune. The husband said, "We could wish for a great fortune or servants or a team of horses." The wife said, "Or we could wish for a fine house or new clothes or jewels."

At last the husband said, "Right now I am exhausted and hungry. I just wish I had a pan full of sausages."

Instantly, on the fire appeared a frying pan full of juicy sausages.

The wife was furious. "You idiot! You have wasted one of our wishes on a pan of sausages! How I wish those sausages were on the end of your nose."

Instantly, on the end of the husband's nose, appeared the string of sausages, straight from the frying pan.

Despite all the couple's best efforts, the sausages would not be pulled from the man's nose.

They now had one wish left. They could wish for money, servants, houses, jewels, and much more, but could they enjoy them if the man had to live the rest of his life with a string of sausages attached to the end of his nose? They had but one choice.

They held each other's hand, closed their eyes, and, using their last wish, together wished the sausages back in the frying pan. And so it happened.

"At least," said the husband, "we got a fine supper of sausages out of it."

Although we may lament the foolishness of this poor couple, something tells us that they are much happier now than if they had wished for riches and houses and clothes. In a similar vein is the story of "The Three Sillies":

A girl goes to the cellar to draw beer for her parents and fiancé. Seeing a hatchet stuck in a beam overhead, she realizes she might marry her fiancé, and they might have a son who will grow up, come down to the cellar to draw beer, and be struck in the head by this very hatchet. She begins to weep at this prospect. Her parents come to the cellar to check on her and she tells them her fears. They also begin to weep. Her fiancé, finding the weeping trio, shakes his head in disbelief and vows to marry the girl if he can find three people sillier than these. And, naturally, he does find three sillier people and returns to marry the girl.

Wonder Tales or *Märchen*

Among the most familiar of folktales, thanks to Walt Disney, wonder tales are popularly referred to as fairy tales, but we are reserving that term for something else (in Chapter 10). They are also called by the German term *Märchen* (meaning "tale" and roughly pronounced "mer-ken" with a guttural emphasis). These are the stories of enchantment and magic in which a youthful hero (rarely is the hero old) confronts and (usually) overcomes some evil force. The heroes and heroines in wonder tales are typically young and beautiful and good (sometimes they are clever, but that is not a requirement, particularly if they have magical helpers on their side). The stories are highly formulaic and contain both ritualized language and repetitive patterns. Unlike moral tales, fables, or the merry tales, the wonder tales deal with very serious themes—treachery, deceit, avarice, pride. Most lack humor entirely—which is where the purists often find fault with the Disney versions, which always include comic relief (see Sayers and Weisenberg).

Wonder tales, especially those from Europe—"Snow White" (see Figures 9.1 and 9.4), "Rapunzel" (see Figure 9.5), "Sleeping Beauty" (see Figure 9.6), and so on—are remarkable for their emphasis on worldliness. The heroes and heroines acquire wealth and power; gold, silver, and precious jewels are frequently rewards or objects of desire. Poverty is seen as abhorrent, and wealth is an honorable goal. (Of course, we should remember that many of these tales come from a time when most people lived in poverty and on the brink of starvation.) Many of these tales end with marriages—the hero getting the girl, the gold, and the kingdom, and everyone lives happily ever after.

It is particularly interesting, in light of their appeal to very young children, that most of the heroes and heroines of the wonder tales are in late adolescence—and of marriageable age. The Grimm brothers actually gathered many of their tales from teenaged girls (and not

Figure 9.4 ● Walter Crane's illustration for "Snow White."

Source: From *Household Stories by the Brothers Grimm*, translated by Lucy Crane, London, 1886.

Figure 9.5 ● H. J. Ford's illustration for "Rapunzel."

Source: From *The Red Fairy Book,* edited by Andrew Lang, London, 1890.

from white-haired grandmothers), which would explain the interest in romance. So, we ask ourselves, why would a 5-year-old find such a story interesting? Of course, the answer is that the real story is not the romance but rather the conflict between good and evil (symbolized by innocent, beautiful youth and wicked, ugly witches or ogres). Young children are fascinated by the enchanted world, the strange creatures, and the fast-paced

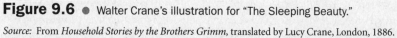

Figure 9.6 ● Walter Crane's illustration for "The Sleeping Beauty."

Source: From *Household Stories by the Brothers Grimm*, translated by Lucy Crane, London, 1886.

plots. These are hardly romances—they are adventure stories. That is not to say that some are not without sexuality (after all, Rapunzel does become pregnant in that tower—see Figure 9.5 in this chapter and Color Plate E in Chapter 7). But sexuality is treated with a combination of subtle inference and dispassion—a process called sublimation. Thus, the potentially steamy stories are rendered suitable for all audiences. The wonder tales are so well known that we need not recount one here.

Ghost Stories

Ghost stories are among the few folk narratives that are still commonly told orally. We enjoy ghost stories because we enjoy the adrenaline rush when we are frightened—in a safely controlled environment. They appeal to our latent superstitious natures, our longing to believe in a world beyond the visible landscape. And there may also be a sense of emotional achievement we experience, much as when we accomplish a daring act—a sense of triumph at having heard a blood-curdling, horrifying story and come away unscathed. Ghost stories are especially popular among adolescents, which suggests that these stories are, indeed, part of a rite of passage. The interactive ghost story—common around campfires and at pajama parties—involves the audience. The following tale, retold by Joseph Jacobs in the nineteenth century, is a form referred to as the Jump Tale, and you will see why:

Once upon a time there was a teeny-tiny woman who lived in a teeny-tiny house in a teeny-tiny village. Now, one day this teeny-tiny woman put on her teeny-tiny bonnet, and went out of her teeny-tiny house to take a teeny-tiny walk. And when this teeny-tiny woman had gone a teeny-tiny way, she came to a teeny-tiny gate; so the teeny-tiny woman opened the teeny-tiny gate, and went into a teeny-tiny churchyard. And when this teeny-tiny woman was in the teeny-tiny churchyard, she saw a teeny-tiny bone on a teeny-tiny grave, and the teeny-tiny woman said to her teeny-tiny self, "This teeny-tiny bone will make me some teeny-tiny soup for my teeny-tiny supper." So the teeny-tiny woman put the teeny-tiny bone into her teeny-tiny pocket, and went home to her teeny-tiny house.

Now when the teeny-tiny woman got home to her teeny-tiny house, she was a teeny-tiny bit tired, so she went up her teeny-tiny stairs to her teeny-tiny bed, and put the teeny-tiny bone into a teeny-tiny cupboard. And when this teeny-tiny woman had been sleeping a teeny-tiny time, she was awakened by a teeny-tiny voice from the teeny-tiny cupboard, which said: "Give me my bone!"

And this teeny-tiny woman was a teeny-tiny frightened, so she hid her teeny-tiny head under her teeny-tiny clothes and went to sleep again. And when she had been sleeping again a teeny-tiny time, the teeny-tiny voice again cried out from the teeny-tiny cupboard a teeny-tiny louder, "Give me my bone!"

This made the teeny-tiny woman a teeny-tiny more frightened, so she hid her teeny-tiny head a teeny-tiny further under the teeny-tiny clothes. And when the teeny-tiny woman had been asleep again a teeny-tiny time, the teeny-tiny voice from the teeny-tiny cupboard said again a teeny-tiny louder, "Give me my bone!"

And this teeny-tiny woman was a teeny-tiny bit more frightened, but she poked her teeny-tiny head out of the teeny-tiny clothes, and said in her loudest teeny-tiny voice, "TAKE IT!" (At this point, the storyteller shouts or perhaps grabs someone nearby in order to make the audience jump.)

Pourquoi Tales

Pourquoi (pronounced "por-kwah") is French for "why." The *pourquoi* tale is a story that explains the origins of some natural phenomenon and is closely related to myth or sacred narratives. A *pourquoi* tale might explain why certain animals look the way they do—why a zebra has stripes or why an elephant has a long trunk. It also may explain the cause of some geographic feature. An example is the Native American tale that explains the origin of the Sleeping Bear Dune, a large sand dune on the northwestern shore of Michigan's lower peninsula:

> *A mother bear and her two cubs were swimming east across Lake Michigan when, in the midst of a great storm, the cubs tired and could go no longer. Their mother, who had reached the shore, watched helplessly as her cubs drowned in the lake. Unable to take her eyes from the water where her cubs perished, she died of grief. The mother bear's body was transformed by the Great Spirit Manitou into the mighty sand dune, and her cubs became the two islands known today as North and South Manitou Islands.*

The *pourquoi* tale is a popular subject for many children's illustrated books.

Trickster Tales

Trickster tales are stories of a cultural figure who delights in creating havoc in the world. The hero (or anti-hero, depending on how the tale turns out) of the trickster tale is an irrepressible prankster. He (most are male, but female tricksters can be found) is chaos personified. Try as he may, he just cannot behave himself for long. The trickster is usually an animal, and the animal differs from culture to culture—in Africa he is often a spider or a rabbit or a parrot; in North America we find the coyote, as well as the rabbit, the mink, the blue jay, and the spider. (In fact, the popular cartoons of Wile E. Coyote and Brer Rabbit are modern versions of the trickster tale.) In European folktales we find the trickster Reynard the Fox.

The trickster, although often portrayed as a comic figure, is, in fact, an important mythological character, and in many cultures his stories appear in cycles. Mischievous, spirited, and irrepressible, the trickster reminds us that destruction is prerequisite for rebirth, that death is necessary for life. Consequently, the trickster, who appears to be a destroyer, turns out to be a creative force. He is in some places (particularly in Native American and African mythologies) elevated to near sacred status.

The role of the trickster is to challenge the status quo, to keep us from becoming too complacent, too comfortable in our ways. The trickster may cause us to re-examine our values. Quite often, he is the meek and lowly character who outwits a larger and more powerful character. Sometimes he is downright exasperating—vulgar, often a sexual figure (sexuality is a symbol of creation and creativity), a double-crosser, a cheater, a rogue, and a scoundrel. Nevertheless, at times we cannot help cheering on the trickster, even when he is being exasperating, because he takes on the establishment, upsetting the norm and challenging the dull and ordinary. He is doing what all of us would, at times, secretly like to do.

Myths and Traditional Epics

Myths are the sacred stories of a culture and they form the basis of most religions. In fact, the term myth does not mean "falsehood," but rather refers to a sacred narrative of origins and a mythology that is a compilation of tales of origins—the origins of the world, of natural phenomenon, of humankind, of sin, and of death. Myths are the stories of the gods and goddesses responsible for these beginnings and they help explain the role of human beings in the world. To people of Western cultures, the most familiar mythology outside the Judeo-Christian tradition is that of ancient Greece and Rome. Our daily lives are imbued with references to their extensive pantheon and their mythic heroes. The names we have given to the planets, stars, and galaxies, and, on a more mundane level, months of the year (January, March, May, and June), body parts (Achilles tendon), cleaning agents (Ajax), synthetic fibers (Herculon), automobiles (Mercury), mapbooks (Atlas), athletic games (Olympics), and spacecraft (Apollo and Gemini) all derive from Greek or Roman mythology. Knowledge of these myths makes us aware of our cultural debts. The Greeks, Romans and Norse, like the Hebrews, envisioned their deities in human form. Other cultures, however, have viewed their deities differently. For instance, the ancient Egyptian gods and goddesses were often unearthly combinations of human and animal form. The Hindu deities took on many unusual forms, some possessing multiple heads and limbs, some were part human–part animal, and some were blue in color. A culture's gods reveal much about its view of the universe and of humanity's role in that universe.

Another important influence on the Western tradition is Norse mythology, which reflects the harsh way of life engendered by the severe, yet dramatically beautiful, Scandinavian lands. In Norse mythology, the gods and goddesses were defenders of humanity against the mighty forces of evil. Like the Greek and Roman gods and goddesses, the Norse deities were anthropomorphic; that is, the gods and goddesses were conceived in human forms. But compared with the Greek deities, the Norse gods and goddesses were a much more serious lot, engaged in a perpetual struggle with the forces of evil—a struggle that they were destined eventually to lose. Individual codes of honor were highly esteemed in this war-conscious society. Among the most familiar images from Norse mythology is the god of thunder, Thor, who is remembered weekly in our own culture, for Thursday was named for him. Tuesday is named for Tiw (the Norse god of war), Wednesday for Woden (the father of the gods), and Friday for Fria (the goddess of fruits). This fascinating mythology still lingers with us.

Throughout the world we find cultures with compelling myths to tell—from the wondrous stories of the Native Americans, celebrating their belief in oneness with the natural world, to the deep well of tales from Africa and Asia, with their special brand of enchantment. Today these myths are becoming widely available in children's versions, and they are excellent methods of introducing world cultures. Many of the collections of folktales listed in the bibliography at the end of this chapter are retellings of mythological tales from around the world. And there are very beautiful picture-book versions of myths for younger children, such as Gerald McDermott's *Anansi the Spider* from West Africa and his *Arrow to the Sun* from the Pueblo Indians of the American Southwest.

Older children are drawn to the great adventures recounted in the traditional epics and heroic legends—stories that initially grew out of mythology. However, myths tend to focus on the gods and goddesses, whereas epics have human beings as their heroes. Among the most popular of the Greek and Roman heroes are Achilles, Odysseus, Hector, Jason, and Perseus. They were indeed the first superheroes, the prototypes of Superman, Batman, and Wonder Woman. Most were great warriors with superhuman strength. All had strong convictions and were charismatic leaders and were favored by the gods. Although Homer's *Iliad* and *Odyssey* were originally intended for adults, they have much appeal for young readers, for they are adventure-filled and abound with unworldly wonders. Excellent children's versions are available, such as Padraic Colum's *Children's Homer* and *The Golden Fleece.*

Medieval Europe saw the rise of a new type of hero tale—*Beowulf*, the legends of King Arthur and the Knights of the Round Table, the Quest for the Holy Grail, and the Life of Charlemagne being the most popular. These tales were influenced by Christianity and reflect the Christian values of humility, piety, charity, and valor—the heroes themselves are fierce defenders of their king (and their faith). *Beowulf*, one of the great medieval epics, is an old English tale about a valiant Danish hero who defeats a great monster called Grendel, Grendel's even more monstrous mother, and finally a dragon. Malory's *The Death of Arthur*, about a mythical king of Britain, and the French epic *The Song of Roland*, a tale set in the time of Charlemagne, are among the most famous. All of these tales have been successfully retold for young readers—for example, Rosemary Sutcliff's story of the Quest for the Holy Grail, *The Light Beyond the Forest*, and Michael Morpurgo's *Beowulf*.

The lasting influence of the great epics is evident in our modern-day fantasies—which is the subject of the next chapter. Anyone who has seen such popular films as George Lucas's *Star Wars* series or Peter Jackson's *The Lord of the Rings* series or James Cameron's *Avatar* has keenly felt that influence.

Summary

Folk narratives are among our oldest stories and many go back to ancient times, when stories were passed along by word of mouth. It is this oral quality of the folk narrative that most clearly separates it from the literary stories such as we find in novels. Consequently, the folk narrative is characterized by several storytelling conventions, including settings in a nonexistent past, stock characters, fast-paced and formulaic plots, and repetitive and ritualized language. Also common are motifs, small identifiable plot elements that tend to recur again and again in folktales from all over the world. Magic, too, is a feature pervasive in folk narratives throughout the world—but it is a magic that is as much a part of the folktale world as the landscape itself. If the tales are frequently fanciful, the themes are often quite serious and deal with subjects such as sacrifice, commitment, trust, and honor.

Folktales come in many types, including talking animal tales, moral tales and fables, tall tales, local legends, riddles and dilemma tales, merry (or noodlehead) tales, wonder tales (or *Märchen*), ghost stories, *pourquoi* tales, and trickster tales (the latter two being derived from mythology). Finally, there are the myths and epic legends that continue to inspire fantasy (in both book and film) to the present day. The folk narratives are an essential part of our cultural heritage and every child should know these great stories.

For Reflection and Discussion

1. Think of a favorite folktale you enjoyed in your childhood. Find a recent version of the tale and reread it. Is it how you remembered it? Explain. Now find three or four more versions and read them. What details tend to remain the same and what are likely to be changed? How does the inclusion or exclusion of certain details—such as characters, plot elements, and so on—affect the fundamental meaning of the story?

2. Locate at least three picture books of the same folktale—find three versions that are quite different from one another (it will be easier than you think). Read them carefully, listen to the language, and study the illustrations. Note the specific changes in plot, language, and characters—and, in many cases, the changes you find will be significant. Speculate on how these changes might affect a child's response to the story. Which retellings seem to work best for you? Why? If possible, share these books with a child (but remember that not all retellings will be for the same age group; you'll need to figure that out).

3. Locate a parody of a familiar folktale (Jon Scieszka is only one of many writers of folktale spoofs). In addition to "The Three Little Pigs," interesting parodies of "Hansel and Gretel," "Little Red Riding Hood," "The Princess and the Pea" (one of H. C. Andersen's literary fairy tales), "Cinderella," and many others exist. How does the parody change the tale's meaning and purpose? Does the parody work, in your opinion? Explain.

4. Locate a collection of trickster tales—try the tales of *Anansi the Spider* from West Africa or the Southwestern Native American trickster Kokopelli, or any one of a number of trickster figures from Native America (Nanabozo from the Northeast

Woodlands or Coyote from several Southwestern Native people). Read some of the tales. What do you find surprising? Anything shocking? How would you characterize the trickster figure? Why do you think he was so popular among the people? Do we have a counterpart in modern society?

● Works Cited

Ramanujan, A. K., ed. *Folktales from India.* New York: Pantheon, 1991.

Sayers, Frances Clarke, and Charles M. Weisenberg. "Walt Disney Accused." *Horn Book Magazine* 40 (December 1965): 602–611.

Schwartz, Alvin, ret. *Scary Stories to Tell in the Dark.* New York: HarperCollins, 1981.

Yolen, Jane, ed. *Favorite Folktales from Around the World.* New York: Pantheon, 1986.

● Recommended Readings

Armstrong, Karen. *A Short History of Myth.* Edinburgh: Cannongate, 2005.

Bernheimer, Kate, ed. *Mirror, Mirror on the Wall: Women Writers Explore Their Favorite Fairy Tales.* New York: Doubleday, 1998.

Bettelheim, Bruno. *The Uses of Enchantment: The Meaning and Importance of Fairy Tales.* New York: Knopf, 1976.

Bosma, Betty. *Fairy Tales, Fables, Legends, and Myths: Using Folk Literature in Your Classroom,* 2nd ed. New York: Teachers College Press, 1993.

Bottigheimer, Ruth, ed. *Fairy Tales and Society: Illusion, Allusion, and Paradigm.* Philadelphia: University of Pennsylvania Press, 1986.

———. *Grimms' Bad Girls and Bold Boys: The Moral and Social Vision of the Tales.* New Haven, CT: Yale University Press, 1987.

Campbell, Joseph. *The Hero with a Thousand Faces,* 2nd ed. Princeton, NJ: Princeton University Press, 1968.

Chase, Richard. *American Folk Tales and Songs.* New York: Dover, 1971.

Cook, Elizabeth. *The Ordinary and the Fabulous.* Cambridge: Cambridge University Press, 1969.

Hettinga, Donald R. *The Brothers Grimm: Two Lives, One Legacy.* New York: Clarion, 2001.

Levorato, Alessandra. *Language and Gender in the Fairy Tale Tradition: A Linguistic Analysis of Old and New Story Telling.* Houndmills, UK: Palgrave Macmillan, 2003.

Lieberman, Marcia R. "'Some Day My Prince Will Come': Female Acculturation through the Fairy Tale." *College English* 34, 3 (1972): 383–395.

Lüthi, Max. *The European Folktale: Form and Nature.* Bloomington: Indiana University Press, 1982.

———. *Once Upon a Time: On the Nature of Fairy Tales.* 1970. Bloomington: Indiana University Press, 1976.

Petrone, Penny. *Native Literature in Canada: From the Oral Tradition to the Present.* Oxford: Oxford University Press, 1990.

Stone, Kay. "Fairy Tales for Adults: Walt Disney's Americanization of the Märchen." *Folklore on Two Continents.* Ed. N. Burlakoff and C. Lindahl. Bloomington: Indiana University Press, 1980.

———. "The Misuses of Enchantment: Controversies on the Significance of Fairy Tales." *Women's Folklore, Women's Culture.* Ed. Rosan A. Jordan and Susan J. Kalicik. Philadelphia: University of Pennsylvania Press, 1985.

Storr, Catherine. "Folk and Fairy Tales." *Children's Literature in Education* 17 (Spring 1986): 63–70.

SurLaLuneFairytales.com This is a useful and accessible website that provides information and discussion opportunities on the topic of folktales.

Tatar, Maria. *Off with Their Heads*. Princeton, NJ: Princeton University Press, 1992. (Violence and cruelty in fairy tales.)

Thompson, Stith. *The Folktale*. New York: Holt, Rinehart and Winston, 1951.

Warner, Marina. *From the Beast to the Blonde: On Fairy Tales and Their Tellers*. New York: Farrar, Straus & Giroux, 1995.

Yolen, Jane. *Touch Magic*. New York: Philomel, 1981.

Zipes, Jack. *Breaking the Magic Spell: Radical Theories of Folk and Fairy Tales*. Austin: University of Texas Press, 1979.

————. *Don't Bet on the Prince: Contemporary Feminist Fairy Tales in North America and England*. London: Methuen, 1986.

————. *Fairy Tales and the Art of Subversion: The Classical Genre for Children and the Process of Civilization*. London: Heinemann, 1983.

————. *When Dreams Came True: Classical Fairy Tales and Their Tradition*. New York: Routledge, 1999.

————. *Why Fairy Tales Stick: The Evolution and Relevance of a Genre*. New York: Routledge, 2006.

Selected Bibliography of Folk Narratives

Picture-Book Versions

Aardema, Verna. *Bringing the Rain to Kapiti Plain*. Illus. Beatriz Vidal. New York: Dial, 1981.

————. *Subugugu, the Glutton: A Bantu Tale from Rwanda*. Illus. Nancy Clouse. Grand Rapids, MI: William B. Eerdmans, 1993.

————. *Why Mosquitoes Buzz in People's Ears*. Illus. Leo and Diane Dillon. New York: Dial, 1975.

Andersen, Hans Christian. *The Nightingale*. Trans. Eva LeGallienne. Illus. Nancy Ekholm Burkert. New York: Harper, 1965.

Ashley, Bryan. *Beautiful Blackbird*. New York: Atheneum, 2003.

Bishop, Claire Huchet. *The Five Chinese Brothers*. Illus. Kurt Wiese. New York: Coward, 1938.

Brown, Marcia. *Cinderella*. New York: Scribner's, 1954.

————. *Dick Whittington and His Cat*. New York: Scribner's, 1950.

————. *Once a Mouse*. New York: Scribner's, 1961.

Cendrars, Blaise. *Shadows*. Illus. Marcia Brown. New York: Scribner's, 1982.

Climo, Shirley. *The Egyptian Cinderella*. Illus. Ruth Heller. New York: Crowell, 1989.

Cooney, Barbara. *Chanticleer and the Fox*. New York: Crowell, 1958.

Demi. *The Firebird*. New York: Holt, 1994.

De Paola, Tomi. *Strega Nona*. New York: Prentice-Hall, 1975.

Domanska, Janina. *Little Red Hen*. New York: Macmillan, 1973.

Ehlert, Lois. *Mole's Hill: A Woodland Tale*. New York: Harcourt, 1994.

Emberley, Barbara. *Drummer Hoff*. Illus. Ed Emberley. New York: Prentice-Hall, 1967.

Galdone, Paul. *Hansel and Gretel*. New York: McGraw-Hill, 1982.

Geisert, Arthur. *After the Flood*. Boston: Houghton Mifflin, 1994.

Hodges, Margaret. *The Wave*. Illus. Blair Lent. Boston: Houghton Mifflin, 1964.

————. *Saint George and the Dragon*. Illus. Trina Schart Hyman. Boston: Little, Brown, 1984.

Hogrogian, Nonny. *One Fine Day*. New York: Macmillan, 1971.

Jarrell, Randall, reteller. *Snow White and the Seven Dwarfs*. Illus. Nancy Ekholm Burkert. New York: Farrar, Straus & Giroux, 1972.

Johari, Harish. *Little Krishna*. Illus. Pieter Weltevrede. New York: Bear Cub, 2002.

Johnston, Tony. *The Cowboy and the Black-eyed Pea*. Illus. Warren Ludwig. New York: Putnam, 1992.

Lester, Julius. *John Henry.* Illus. Jerry Pinkney. New York: Dial, 1994.

Louie, Ai-Ling. *Yeh-Shen: A Cinderella Story from China.* Illus. Ed Young. New York: Philomel, 1982.

Marshall, James. *Red Riding Hood.* New York: Dial, 1987.

McDermott, Gerald. *Anansi the Spider.* New York: Holt, 1972.

———. *Arrow to the Sun.* New York: Viking, 1974.

Minters, Frances. *Cinder-Elly.* Illus. G. Brian Karas. New York: Puffin, 1994.

———. *Sleepless Beauty.* Illus. G. Brian Karas. New York: Puffin, 1996.

Mosel, Arlene. *The Funny Little Woman.* Illus. Blair Lent. New York: Dutton, 1972.

———. *Tikki Tikki Tembo.* Illus. Blair Lent. New York: Holt, 1968.

Moser, Barry, reteller. *The Three Little Pigs.* Boston: Little, Brown, 2001.

Ness, Evaline. *Tom Tit Tot.* New York: Scribner's, 1965.

Nic Leodhas, Sorche (pseudonym of LeClaire G. Alger). *Always Room for One More.* Illus. Nonny Hogrogian. New York: Holt, 1965.

Novesky, Amy. *Elephant Prince: The Story of Ganesh.* Illus. Belgin K. Wedman. San Rafael, CA: Mandala, 2004.

Orgel, Doris, reteller. *The Bremen Town Musicians: And Other Animal Tales from Grimm.* Illus. Bert Kitchen. New Milford, CT: Roaring Brook, 2004.

Pinkney, Jerry, reteller. *Aesop's Fables.* New York: SeaStar/North-South, 2000.

Polacco, Patricia. *Babushka Baba Yaga.* New York: Philomel, 1993.

Ransome, Arthur. *The Fool of the World and the Flying Ship.* Illus. Uri Shulevitz. New York: Farrar, Straus & Giroux, 1968.

Robbins, Ruth. *Baboushka and the Three Kings.* Illus. Nicolas Sidjakov. Boston: Houghton Mifflin, 1960.

Root, Phyllis. *Big Momma Make the World.* Illus. Helen Oxenbury. New York: Candlewick, 2003.

San Souci, Robert D., adapter. *Cendrillon: A Caribbean Cinderella.* Illus. Brian Pinkney. New York: Simon & Schuster, 1998.

———. reteller. *Little Gold Star: A Spanish-American Cinderella.* Illus. Sergio Martinez. New York: HarperCollins, 2000.

Sawyer, Ruth. *Journey Cake, Ho!* Illus. Robert McCloskey. New York: Viking, 1953.

Scieszka, John. *The Stinky Cheese Man and Other Fairly Stupid Tales.* Illus. Lane Smith. New York: Viking, 1992.

———. *The True Story of the Three Little Pigs.* Illus. Lane Smith. New York: Viking, 1989.

Shepard, Aaron, reteller. *Master Man: A Tall Tale of Nigeria.* Illus. David Wisniewski. New York: HarperCollins, 2001.

Sierra, Judy. *The Gift of the Crocodile: A Cinderella Story.* Illus. Reynolds Ruffin. New York: Simon and Schuster, 2000.

Singer, Isaac Bashevis. *The Fearsome Inn.* Illus. Nonny Hogrogian. New York: Macmillan, 1984.

Steptoe, John. *Mufaro's Beautiful Daughters: An African Tale.* New York: Lothrop, 1987.

Tompert, Ann. *Grandfather Tang's Story.* Illus. Robert A. Parker. New York: Bantam, 1997.

Trivizas, Eugene. *The Three Little Wolves and the Big Bad Pig.* Illus. Helen Oxenbury. New York: Simon and Schuster, 1997.

Weisner, David. *The Three Pigs.* Boston: Houghton Mifflin, 2001.

Young, Ed. *Lon Po Po: A Red Riding Hood Story from China.* New York: Philomel, 1989.

Zelinsky, Paul O. *Rumpelstiltskin.* New York: Dutton, 1986.

Zemach, Harve, reteller. *Duffy and the Devil.* Illus. Margot Zemach. New York: Farrar, Straus & Giroux, 1973.

Zemach, Margot, reteller. *The Little Red Hen.* New York: Farrar, Straus & Giroux, 1983.

———. *The Three Little Pigs.* New York: Farrar, Straus & Giroux, 1988.

Folktale Collections

Aesop's Fables. Illus. Fritz Kredel. New York: Grosset, 1947.

Asbjørnsen, Peter, and Jørgen Moe. *East O' the Sun and West O' the Moon.* New York: Dover, 1970. (Scandinavian folktales)

Bierhorst, John, ed. *The Dancing Fox: Arctic Folktales.* New York: Morrow, 1997.

———. *Lightning Inside You: And Other Native American Riddles.* New York: Morrow, 1992.

———. *The White Deer and Other Stories Told by the Lenape.* New York: Morrow, 1995.

Bloch, Marie Halun. *Ukrainian Folk Tales.* New York: Coward, McCann, 1964.

Briggs, Katharine. *British Folk Tales.* New York: Pantheon, 1977.

Bushnaq, Inea, trans. *Arab Folktales.* New York: Pantheon, 1986.

Calvino, Italo, ed. *Italian Folktales.* New York: Pantheon, 1980.

Chandler, Robert, trans. *Russian Folk Tales.* New York: Shambhala/Random House, 1980.

Chase, Richard. *The Jack Tales.* Boston: Houghton Mifflin, 1971. (American tall tales)

Climo, Shirley. *Monkey Business: Stories from Around the World.* New York: Holt, 2005.

Cole, Joanna, selector. *Best-Loved Folktales of the World.* Garden City, NY: Doubleday, 1982.

Courlander, Harold. *The Crest and the Hide and Other African Stories of Heroes, Chiefs, Bards, Hunters, Sorcerers and Common People.* New York: Coward, McCann & Geoghegan, 1982.

Demi, adapter. *A Chinese Zoo: Fables and Proverbs.* New York: Harcourt, 1987.

de Wit, Dorothy. *The Talking Stone: An Anthology of Native American Tales and Legends.* New York: Greenwillow, 1979.

Dickinson, Peter, reteller. *City of Gold and Other Stories from the Old Testament.* Illus. Michael Foreman. London: Gollancz, 1992.

Fang, Linda, reteller. *The Ch'i-lin Purse: A Collection of Ancient Chinese Stories.* New York: Farrar, Straus & Giroux, 1995.

Finger, Charles. *Tales from Silver Lands.* New York: Doubleday, 1924. (Central America)

Fuller, O. Muriel. *The Book of Dragons: Tales and Legends from Many Lands.* New York: Dover, 2002.

Gág, Wanda. *Tales from Grimm.* New York: Coward, McCann & Geoghegan, 1981.

Glassie, Henry. *Irish Folk Tales.* New York: Pantheon, 1985.

Grimm, Jacob, and Wilhelm Grimm. *Household Stories.* Trans. Lucy Crane. New York: Dover, 1963. (One of many editions dating from 1812)

Gross, Ila Land. *Cinderella around the World.* New York: L.E.A.P., 2001.

Haley, Gail E., reteller-illustrator. *Mountain Jack Tales.* New York: Penguin, 1992.

Hausman, Gerald, collector-reteller. *How Chipmunk Got Tiny Feet: Native American Origin Stories.* New York: HarperCollins, 1995.

Haviland, Virginia. *Favorite Tales Told in India.* Boston: Little, Brown, 1973.

Hodges, Margaret, reteller. *Hauntings: Ghosts and Ghouls from Around the World.* Boston: Little, Brown, 1991.

Hoogasian-Villa, Susie. *One Hundred Armenian Tales.* Detroit: Wayne State University Press, 1966.

Hurston, Zora Neale, collector. *Lies and Other Tall Tales.* Adapted and illus. Christopher Myers. New York: HarperCollins, 2005.

Jacobs, Joseph. *Celtic Fairy Tales.* 1891. New York: Dover, 1968.

———. *English Fairy Tales.* 1890. New York: Dover, 1967.

Jaffe, Nina, and Steve Zeitlin. *While Standing on One Foot: Puzzle Stories and Wisdom Tales from the Jewish Tradition.* Illus. John Segal. New York: Holt, 1993.

Jaffrey, Madhur. *Seasons of Splendour: Tales, Myths & Legends of India.* Illus. Michael Foreman. Harmondsworth, UK: Puffin, 1987.

James, Grace, reteller. *Green Willow and Other Japanese Fairy Tales.* New York: Avenel, 1987.

Joseph, Lynn. *The Mermaid's Twin Sister: More Stories from Trinidad.* New York: Clarion, 1994.

Kherdian, David, reteller. *Feathers and Tails: Animal Fables from Around the World.* New York: Putnam, 1992.

Lang, Andrew. *The Blue Fairy Book.* 1889. New York: Dover, 1965. (The first of a series)

Lester, Julius. *Black Folktales.* New York: Richard W. Baron, 1969.

Lyons, Mary E., selector. *Raw Head, Bloody Bones: African-American Tales of the Supernatural.* New York: Scribners, 1991.

Manitonquat (Medicine Story), reteller. *The Children of the Morning Light: Wampanoag Tales.* Illus. Mary F. Arquette. New York: Macmillan, 1994.

Minford, John, trans. *Favourite Folktales of China.* Beijing, China: New World Press, 1983.

Neil, Philip, reteller. *Fairy Tales of Eastern Europe.* Boston: Houghton Mifflin, 1991.

Nic Leodhas, Sorche. *Thistle and Thyme: Tales and Legends from Scotland.* New York: Holt, Rinehart and Winston, 1962.

Opie, Iona, and Peter Opie. *The Classic Fairy Tales.* New York: Oxford University Press, 1974.

Perrault, Charles. *Perrault's Fairy Tales.* Illus. Gustave Doré. 1867. New York: Dover, 1969.

Phelps, Ethel Johnson. *The Maid of the North: Feminist Folk Tales from Around the World.* New York: Holt, Rinehart and Winston, 1981.

Ross, Gayle. *How Rabbit Tricked Otter and Other Cherokee Trickster Stories.* Illus. Murv Jacob. New York: HarperCollins, 1994.

Rounds, Glen. *Ol' Paul, the Mighty Logger.* New York: Holiday House, 1936.

Schwartz, Alvin, reteller. *Ghosts!: Ghostly Tales from Folklore.* New York: HarperCollins, 1991.

Schwarz, Howard, and Barbara Rush, retellers. *The Diamond Tree: Jewish Tales from Around the World.* New York: HarperCollins, 1991.

Singer, Isaac Bashevis. *Zlateh the Goat and Other Stories.* New York: Harper, 1966. (Yiddish folktales)

Stoutenburg, Adrien. *American Tall Tales.* New York: Viking, 1966.

Tehranchian, Hassan, adapter. *Kalilah and Dimnah: Fables from the Middle East.* New York: Harmony, 1985.

Thompson, Vivian L. *Hawaiian Tales of Heroes and Champions.* New York: Holiday House, 1971.

Vuong, Lynette Dyer. *The Golden Carp and Other Tales from Vietnam.* Illus. Manabu Saito. New York: Lothrop, 1993.

Wiggin, Kate Douglas, and Nora A. Smith, eds. *The Arabian Nights.* Illus. Maxfield Parrish. New York: Quality Paperback, 1996. (Originally published 1909)

Wolkstein, Diane. *The Magic Orange and Other Haitian Folktales.* New York: Knopf, 1978.

Yeats, W. B., and Lady Gregory. *A Treasury of Irish Myth, Legend, and Folklore.* New York: Avenel, 1986.

Yep, Laurence, reteller. *Tongues of Jade.* New York: HarperCollins, 1991. (Chinese)

Yolen, Jane, ed. *Favorite Folktales from Around the World.* New York: Pantheon, 1986.

Zipes, Jack, trans. *Beauties, Beasts, and Enchantment: Classic French Fairy Tales.* New York: Penguin, 1991.

Epics and Myths

Colum, Padraic. *The Children's Homer: The Adventures of Odysseus and the Tale of Troy.* 1919. New York: Macmillan, 1982.

———. *The Children of Odin: The Book of Northern Myths.* 1920. New York: Macmillan, 1984.

———. *The Golden Fleece and the Heroes Who Lived before Achilles.* 1921. New York: Macmillan, 1983.

Green, Roger Lancelyn. *Heroes of Greece and Troy: Retold from the Ancient Authors.* New York: Walck, 1961.

Hamilton, Virginia. *In the Beginning: Creation Stories from Around the World.* New York: Harcourt Brace Jovanovich, 1988.

———. *The People Could Fly.* New York: Knopf, 1985. (African American folktales)

Hastings, Selina, ret. *Sir Gawain and the Loathly Lady.* Illus. Juan Wijngaard. London: Walker Books, 1985.

Heany, Seamus, trans. *Beowulf.* New York: Farrar, Straus & Giroux, 2000.

Henderson, Kathy. *Lugalbanda: The Boy Who Got Caught Up in a War.* New York: Candlewick, 2006. (Ancient Sumeria)

Hieatt, Constance, reteller. *Sir Gawain and the Green Knight.* New York: Crowell, 1967.

Jendresen, Erik, reteller. *Hanuman: Based on Valmiki's Ramayana.* Illus. Ming Li. Berkeley, CA: Tricycle Press, 1998.

Kimmel, Eric A. *The Hero Beowulf.* New York: Farrar, Straus & Giroux, 2005.

Kingsley, Charles. *The Heroes.* New York: Dutton, 1963.

McCaughrean, Geraldine. *The Bronze Cauldron: Myths and Legends of the World.* New York: Margaret K. McElderry, 1998.

———. *The Crystal Pool: Myths and Legends of the World.* New York: Margaret K. McElderry, 1999.

———. *The Golden Hoard: Myths and Legends of the World.* New York: Margaret K. McElderry, 1996.

———. *The Silver Treasure: Myths and Legends of the World.* New York: Margaret K. McElderry, 1997.

Morpurgo, Michael. *Beowulf.* Cambridge, MA: Candlewick, 2006.

Philip, Neil. *The Tale of Sir Gawain.* Illus. Charles Keeping. New York: Philomel, 1987.

Sherwood, Merriam, trans. *The Song of Roland.* New York: McKay, 1938.

Sutcliff, Rosemary. *Beowulf.* London: Bodley Head, 1961. (Published in the United States as *Dragon Slayer*)

———. *Black Ships Before Troy: The Story of the Iliad.* New York: Delacorte, 1993.

———. *The Light Beyond the Forest: The Quest for the Holy Grail.* New York: Dutton, 1980.

———. *The Road the Camlann.* New York: Dutton, 1982.

———. *The Sword and the Circle: King Arthur and the Knights of the Round Table.* New York: Dutton, 1981.

———. *The Wanderings of Odysseus.* New York: Delacorte, 1995.

Tchana, Katrin Hyman, reteller. *Changing Woman and Her Sisters: Stories of Goddesses from Around the World.* Illus. Trina Schart Hyman. New York: Holiday House, 2006.

Thompson, Brian. *The Story of Prince Rama.* New York: Viking, 1985. (Ancient India)

Westwood, Jennifer, reteller. *Gilgamesh and Other Babylonian Tales.* New York: Coward McCann, 1970.

Williams, Marcia. *Greek Myths.* New York: Walker, 2006.

Zeitlin, Steve. *The Four Corners of the Sky: Creation Stories and Cosmologies from Around the World.* New York: Holt, 2000.

Go to the topic "Traditional Literature" on the MyEducationKit for this text, where you can:

- Search the Database of Children's Literature, housing more than 22,000 titles searchable in every genre by authors or illustrators, by awards won, by year published, and by topic and description.

- Explore genre-related Assignments and Activities, assignable exercises showing concepts in action

through database use, video, cases, and student and teacher artifacts.

- Listen to podcasts and read interviews from some of the brightest and most enduring stars of children's literature in the Conversations.

- Discover Web Links that will lead you to sites representing the authors you learn about in these pages, classrooms with powerful children's literature connections, and literature awards.

Fantasy
The World of Make-Believe

Introduction

The enduring figures of the great fantasies—Alice, Dorothy and her motley companions, the irrepressible Mr. Toad of Toad Hall, Peter Pan, Wilbur the pig, and Charlotte the spider—are fixed indelibly on the cultural consciousness of our society and have helped shape our imaginations. It is difficult to exaggerate the influence of reading fantasy in our lives.

Fantasy is one of two major types within the genre of fiction, the other being realism. A fantasy is an original work of fiction that contains an element of the supernatural—a contradiction to the laws of nature—whereas realism attempts to portray the world as it is. Fantasies differ wildly among themselves, however, and we recognize many kinds, including comic fantasy, talking animal fantasy, epic fantasy, miniature fantasy, horror fantasy, time-slip fantasy, and science fiction.

Modern fantasy has its roots in traditional folk narratives. However, fantasy differs from folk literature in that fantasy is a literary, not an oral, form. Each fantasy is a new creation coming from the pen of an individual writer. The fantasist's creation is original, derived from his or her own imagination. Consequently, the settings, characters, and plots of a fantasy tend to be much more complex than those of the folktales. Also, fantasies do not contain the conventions found in the folk narratives. Likewise, fantasy poses certain challenges to readers, often taking them outside their comfort zones. It is also this challenge in fantasy that attracts devoted readers.

History of Fantasy

Fantasy stories for adults, including *A Pilgrim's Progress* by John Bunyan and *Gulliver's Travels* by Jonathan Swift, have long been popular, and they were often appropriated by children in the days before they had their own books. However, in the eighteenth century, when the first written children's stories began to appear, fantasy for children was frowned upon. Writers, following in the wake of John Locke and Jean Jacque Rousseau, believed that all children's literature should be educational and tout high moral principles. To them, the folktales were frivolous at best and sacrilegious at worst. The very idea of talking animals seemed a perversion of God's laws. As we noted in Chapter 1, when Mrs. Trimmer wrote her *Story of the Robin* (1786), a moralistic tale that included a family of talking birds, she carefully explained to her child audience that animals could not, indeed, speak and did not have human feelings, but that this was only a story to illustrate a moral point. (Actually the fear that fantasy will confuse children, that they will grow up thinking animals can talk, witches exist, and so on, is still found in our society today. But this is largely nonsense based on a lack of faith in the abilities of children and on a limited understanding of child psychology.)

Despite their valiant efforts, these well-meaning and pious writers could not keep children and fantasy long separated. By the early nineteenth century, folktale collections began to circulate and then came the literary fairy tales of Hans Christian Andersen. In 1845, a German, Heinrich Hoffmann, published *Der Struwwelpeter,* a series of fanciful, if macabre, moral stories in which misbehavior results in disaster. (This book is an early example of parody for children, for it pokes fun at the moral tale.) One of the earliest fantasists in Great Britain was Charles Kingsley, whose *The Water Babies: A Fairytale for a Landbaby,* appeared in 1864. It is a story in the vein of the eighteenth-century moral tale, but in nineteenth-century dress. Kingsley uses the imaginative world of fairies and water babies to convey his religious message.

The great landmark in fantasy came with the publication in 1865 of *Alice's Adventures in Wonderland* (see Figure 10.1) by Lewis Carroll (a pseudonym for Charles Lutwidge Dodgson, an Oxford mathematician). An original work created by Carroll for the entertainment of the daughters of his college dean, this is considered one of the first children's books written for pure entertainment and without overt moral purpose. The story, even today, strikes us as delightfully bizarre in its defying of logic, its often caustic wit, and its outrageous and memorable characters. The weight of eighteenth-century didacticism had finally been lifted.

In a very short time, many imaginative children's fantasies cascaded onto the literary scene. It was an international phenomenon as well. From France came Jules Verne's popular works of science fiction (*From the Earth to the Moon* [1865] and *Twenty Thousand Leagues under the Sea* [1869], among others), and Italy gave us *The Adventures of Pinocchio* by Carlo Collodi(1881), about a puppet who wants to be real boy. George MacDonald was one of the most popular British fantasists of the nineteenth century, best remembered for works such as *The Light Princess* (1864), *At the Back of the North Wind* (1871), and *The Princess and the Goblin* (1872).

The talking animal story, that anathema of eighteenth-century moralists, became popular in the late nineteenth century. A story not actually written for children, but loved by them for generations, is Anna Sewell's *Black Beauty* (1877), the life story of a horse told by the horse itself. The book recounts the grueling life of a London cab horse and delivers

Figure 10.1 ● Sir John Tenniel's Illustration for Lewis Carroll's *Alice's Adventures in Wonderland*. Alice discovers a passage into Wonderland.

an undisguised moral message about the horrors of animal cruelty and the virtue of human kindness. Beatrix Potter's *Tale of Peter Rabbit* (1902) was the first of a series of popular picture books featuring animal characters. Other important fantasists of the early twentieth century include Kenneth Grahame, whose animal fantasy, *The Wind in the Willows*, appeared in 1908; Hugh Lofting, author of *The Story of Dr. Dolittle* (1920), and A. A. Milne, who wrote *Winnie-the-Pooh* (1926). In the United States, L. Frank Baum's *Wonderful Wizard of Oz* (1900) exhibited the traits of a truly American fantasy, with its midwestern setting, its simple agrarian values, and its celebration of individualism and ingenuity (old-fashioned American "know-how").

Fantasy remains a dynamic aspect of children's literature on all levels. The last half of the twentieth century and the early twenty-first century have witnessed a flowering of fantasy works in a wide variety of types, which we will examine more closely in this chapter.

Characteristics of Fantasy

Fantasy fiction contains certain characteristics that separate it from realism, and it is helpful to know something about these if we are to appreciate the fantasist's work.

Magic and Rules

Remember when, as a child, you played make-believe with your friends and perhaps invented fantasy worlds? The first thing you undoubtedly did was to establish "the rules." The rules determined what was and was not permissible. And they were crucial if the make-believe world was to be maintained. When people began to break the rules, the game fell apart. Without the rules, it was no longer fun. This is the very thing that operates in fantasy writing, the chief ingredient of which is magic, the supernatural. As readers of fantasy, we are being asked to abandon some (or all) of our preconceptions about how the universe operates. In the real world, we pretty much know the basic rules—we need air to breathe; plants and animals don't talk (except for a few birds talented in mimicry); our bodies have limitations; the past is irretrievable; the future unknown; death comes for everyone, and so on. But in fantasy, readers are asked to adapt to an entirely new set of rules. Animals may talk, characters may have superhuman powers, magic exists, time travel may occur—in fact, anything is possible.

Anything is possible—but not without limits. The fantasist creates these limits and invents the "rules," or "laws," that operate in the fantasy world. If it is to be a world where animals talk, or where witches ride on brooms, or where only one character is given magical powers, so be it. However, the fantasist must do two things for the readers: (1) make the rules clear and (2) stick to the rules. Just as we insisted during those childhood games, we expect the writer to play fairly with us—we want the magic, whatever it is, to be used consistently throughout the story. For example, the fantastical elements might be confined to a specific place—Wonderland, Oz, or Narnia. Or the fantasy may be confined to a particular time of day—such as during the nighttime, as in Philippa Pearce's *Tom's Midnight Garden*. Or only certain characters possess the magical powers—such as Pippi Longstocking with her superhuman strength. Or the wicked antagonist may be eliminated only by certain means—such as by pouring water over a witch causing her to melt.

Some fantasies seem to subvert the rules through the use of the dream device. Lewis Carroll's *Alice's Adventures in Wonderland* and *Through the Looking-Glass* are perhaps the most famous examples of dream world fantasies. In these stories the fantasy is depicted as a dream of the protagonist, Alice. When she awakes, the fantasy disappears. One of the presumed advantages of the dream world fantasy is that no explanation for the magical events is needed. Certainly this works well in Carroll's stories where the bizarre and illogical predominate; however, in fantasies of a more serious nature, readers may resent being told at the end that everything was but a dream. In other words, the dream device may seem like a cheap trick or the easy way out. Curiously, the popular film version of *The Wizard of Oz* portrays the adventures in Oz as only Dorothy's dream while she was recovering from an injury. However, in L. Frank Baum's original, Oz and its motley characters are presented as very real. Perhaps Baum realized that his young readers preferred to hold onto the fantasy, to be allowed to believe in it thoroughly and not have it taken away at the end. By turning a fantasy into a dream, we may deprive it of much of its enchantment, and that is not quite fair.

Fantasy Settings

The setting of a fantasy comes in one of three varieties. Some fantasies take place in our world, the primary world—as in Lindgren's *Pippi Longstocking* or Travers's *Mary Poppins* or E. B. White's *Charlotte's Web.* In these stories a magical element is introduced—a character with magical powers or talking animals, for example. Other fantasies take place in an alternative world, which exists apart from the primary world. The alternative world operates under its own set of rules. In some alternative world fantasies, no connection exists between the fantasy world and the primary world. We find this arrangement in J. R. R. Tolkien's *Lord of the Rings,* where no character comes from our world. A third type of fantasy creates a parallel world, which is a fantasy world that operates parallel to our own, and is reached through a portal from our world. The portal can take a variety of forms—a cyclone, a rabbit hole, a door at the back of an old wardrobe, a secret underground railway platform, and so on. Examples are found in Baum's *Wonderful Wizard of Oz,* Lewis's "Chronicles of Narnia" series, J. K. Rowling's "Harry Potter" series, and Philip Pullman's "His Dark Materials" trilogy. In the parallel world fantasy, at least one character will be transported from our world, the primary world, and experience the fantastic events, then usually returns to the primary world at the conclusion. Time-slip fantasies, in which characters are able to move forward or backward in time, are a variation on the parallel world fantasy.

Regardless of the setting, the writer is trying to make us believe in the fantasy—at least so long as we are reading it. Often the settings are described in elaborate detail to create the illusion of reality. In many fantasies, especially those set in alternative or parallel worlds, lengthy descriptions of place are necessary so we can envision the fantasy worlds. The following passage is taken from Kenneth Grahame's animal fantasy, *The Wind in the Willows* (see Figure 10.2), and describes the cozy kitchen of Mr. Badger, who lives in his comfortable underground bachelor pad:

> *The floor was well-worn red brick, and on the wide hearth burnt a fire of logs, between two attractive chimney-corners tucked away in the wall, well out of any suspicion of draught. A couple of high-backed settles, facing each other on either side of the fire, gave further sitting accommoda-tions for the sociably disposed. In the middle of the room stood a long table of plain boards placed on trestles, with benches down each side. At one end of it, where an arm-chair stood pushed back, were spread the remains of the Badger's plain but ample supper. Rows of spotless plates winked from the shelves of the dresser at the far end of the room, and from the rafters overhead hung*

Figure 10.2 ● Ernest H. Shepard's illustration for Kenneth Grahame's *The Wind in the Willows*. Mole and Water Rat go boating on the river.

hams, bundles of dried herbs, nets of onions, and baskets of eggs. It seemed a place where heroes could fitly feast after victory, where weary harvesters could line up in scores along the table and keep their Harvest Home with mirth and song, or where two or three friends of simple tastes could sit about as they pleased and eat and smoke and talk in comfort and contentment. The ruddy brick floor smiled up at the smoky ceiling; the oaken settles, shiny with long wear, exchanged cheerful glances with each other; plates on the dresser grinned at pots on the shelf, and the merry firelight flickered and played over everything without distinction. (Chapter 4)

We seldom find such minute detail in a folk narrative. The accumulation of detail such as Grahame's provides the fantasy with an illusion of reality.

Fantasy Characters

Unlike realistic fiction, where we expect characters to be lifelike and genuine, fantasy allows for an extraordinary range of characters—many of whom are not even human. Indeed, in fantasy a character may take on virtually any form—animal, vegetable, or mineral. For example, there are Audrey II, the voracious plant in the musical *Little Shop of Horrors;* "Hal," the diabolical computer in the Stanley Kubrick film *2001: A Space Odyssey;* and the more lovable R2-D2 and C-3PO, the droids in the *Star Wars* saga. But readers still insist that the characters, whatever shape they take, possess recognizable human qualities.

At the same time, readers want original, fresh, and boldly drawn characters. L. Frank Baum's *The Wonderful Wizard of Oz* and James Barrie's *Peter Pan* are not usually regarded as stylistic masterpieces, but who can forget the characters—the Scarecrow, the Tin Woodsman, the deliciously wicked Witch, the phony Wizard, Captain Hook, and the little boy who would not grow up. Carroll's *Alice's Adventures in Wonderland* and *Through the Looking-Glass* contain some of the most outrageous characters ever invented—the befuddled White Rabbit, the Mad Hatter, the March Hare, the crabby Duchess and her violent cook, the eerie Cheshire Cat, the quarrelsome Queen of Hearts. Where else can we find so rich and varied a cast than in a fantasy?

Perhaps the most important point about the characters in a good fantasy is that they have to be rooted in reality and human nature if readers are to develop any sort of feeling for them. Mr. Toad of Toad Hall, from *The Wind in the Willows,* may look like a toad, but he acts like a human and exhibits human weaknesses. He is rash, foolish, and vain. Winnie-the-Pooh, even though he is a toy, engages in human activities and exhibits very human emotions (despite his protest that he is only a "bear of little brain"). He is kind, considerate, and adventurous. And in fantasies such as *Charlotte's Web,* we see the protagonist, Wilbur, actually developing as a character—maturing from an insecure and self-centered pig into a courageous and loving friend.

It is difficult to imagine a successful fantasy in which the principal characters do not possess genuine human traits that either provoke our fear (like a power-hungry wicked witch or a berserk computer) or evoke our sympathy (like a gentle toy bear of "little brain" or a well-meaning robot).

Fantasy Journeys

As with any novel, plots of fantasies can be frivolous and absurd or they can be complex. They can be dramatic or episodic (see Chapter 3). However, one plot device deserves special attention. Journeys, as we have already noted, are metaphors for life and on journeys we encounter experiences that shape us and make us who we are. Journeys are common in both realistic fiction and in fantasy, but they seem especially prevalent in fantasy because they often provide a rationale for the fantasy elements (in other words, magic is often associated with specific places—it exists in Oz, but not in Kansas). The journey motif is especially useful in children's fantasy, for it can take the reader to a place where the rules of grownups no longer apply. Unshackled by the constraints of our world, the hero can encounter fantastic creatures, enchanted objects, miraculous powers, and harrowing adventures.

In many children's fantasies, the journey is a frequent plot device that contributes to the protagonist's maturation. In *The Wonderful Wizard of Oz* (see Figure 10.3), J. R. R. Tolkien's *Hobbit,* and C. S. Lewis's *The Lion, the Witch, and the Wardrobe,* the protagonists all return home wiser in the ways of the world. Fantasies use both circular and linear journeys. A primary world fantasy or a parallel world fantasy, which typically features a child or childlike protagonist, almost always brings the hero or heroine back home (as in *The*

Figure 10.3 ● Dorothy scolds the Cowardly Lion as the Scarecrow, the Tin Woodsman, and Toto look on.

Source: From W. W. Denslow's original illustrations for *The Wonderful Wizard of Oz*, New York: Hill, 1900.

Wonderful Wizard of Oz or *The Lion, the Witch, and the Wardrobe*). An alternative world fantasy, which frequently depicts a teenage protagonist engaged in a coming-of-age experience, may bring the hero or heroine to a new home, as in *A Wizard of Earthsea* by Ursula Le Guin.

One critic has noted that "reading fantasy is not so much an escape *from* something as a liberation *into* something, into openness and possibility and coherence" and that we as readers get perspective on our world "by exploring a strange fictional place and learning how its pieces fit together" (O'Keefe 11–12).The fantasy world is one of seemingly limitless possibilities. And the best fantasy causes us to come away with a fresh, new way of looking at our world.

Types of Fantasy

Fantasy is notoriously difficult to categorize—and there may be little need to do so. There are more important things than trying to determine in what class a particular fantasy belongs. But it is true that some readers prefer one type of fantasy over another—for example, science fiction, horror, and heroic fantasy are three types that attract specialized audiences. In that respect, it can be useful to be able to apply some broad labels. The chief intention of this classification is to suggest the wide range of fantasy writing. Keep in mind that some fantasies simply refuse to fit tidily into categories.

Literary Fairy Tales and Magical Fantasy

We begin with what is something of a *potpourri*—a catch-all. Many of the early fantasies for children were inspired by the traditional folk narratives (see Chapter 9). What these writers produced were literary fairy tales.These are stories that deliberately imitate the motifs and styles of the folk narratives but are the unique creations of individual writers. Perhaps the most famous writer of literary fairy tales is Hans Christian Andersen (1805–1875), whose stories, including "The Ugly Duckling," "The Little Mermaid," "The Emperor's New Clothes," and "The Princess and Pea," have become staples in Western culture. Even if Andersen based many of his stories on traditional folktales, he completely rewrote them, making them entirely his own. So, although we could never find the "original" tale of "Cinderella," for example, we can find Andersen's original of "The Little Mermaid" (which, incidentally, is rather drastically different from the sentimentalized Disney film).

George MacDonald's *Light Princess, The Princess and the Curdie*, and *The Princess and the Goblin* are among the most notable of the Victorian literary fairy tales. The major difference between these stories and the traditional folk narratives is, naturally, that MacDonald's full-length novels include far more character development—something a brief folktale cannot accomplish. L. Frank Baum, as we noted, deliberately set out to write an American fairy tale in *The Wonderful Wizard of Oz*. Although an unexceptional literary stylist, he accomplished what few writers do—he created a world filled with fantastical characters that we all want to believe in and not forget. Baum's tale espouses the American values of practical ingenuity and common sense. The heroes here are not of noble birth but common folk who want nothing more than simple down-home values—knowledge, love, courage, and family. And these they achieve through their adventure-filled, and now iconic, journey.

A modern incarnation of the literary fairy tale is the parody (see Chapter 3). Especially notable is James Thurber's delightful *Many Moons,* which contains comic twists on the traditional folktale form. The parodies of Jon Scieszka (*The True Story of the Three Little Pigs* and *The Stinky Cheese Man and Other Stupid Fairy Tales,* both illustrated by Lane Smith) are but the best-known of many examples found in today's picture books.

Comic Fantasy

Comic fantasy is admittedly comprehensive, including such wide-ranging works as Lewis Carroll's "Alice" books, Astrid Lindgren's *Pippi Longstocking,* Pamela Travers's *Mary Poppins,* and much of Roald Dahl's works (*Charlie and the Chocolate Factory, James and the Giant Peach,* and others). Like most categories of fiction, comic fantasy is a slippery one— here, I am using the term to include those humorous fantasies that do not fit tidily into another class and that are predominantly intended to entertain with their comedy. In some cases, they are absurdist or tall tales. *Pippi Longstocking,* for instance, is the fanciful story of a little girl with superhuman strength who lives alone (with her horse and monkey) and enjoys a fully independent life. In other words, she is every child's dream. The story succeeds because it is told with broad humor, often moving into slapstick, which reminds us that this is, after all, just a story—as any child knows.

As has already been pointed out (see Chapter 9), Americans have always been in love with the tall tale, that absurd story of egregious exaggeration—the search for the "extreme" (or, in the redundant parlance of modern television, "the most extreme"). Sid Fleischman's "McBroom" series for younger readers appeals directly to this fascination, and his stories for older readers, such as *The Ghost in the Noonday Sun* and *Chancy and the Grand Rascal,* are comical yarns set in nineteenth-century America and filled with eccentric characters and outrageous shenanigans. Lucretia Hale's *Peterkin Papers,* written in the nineteenth century about the misadventures of a completely inept family, has inspired modern imitators. Harry Allard's picture books, illustrated by James Marshall, are about a ridiculous family named the Stupids—*The Stupids Step Out, The Stupids Have a Ball,* and *The Stupids Die.* (Although many adults object to the repeated use of the word "stupid"in these books, Allard's intent may have been to rob the word of some of its sting. Consequently, instead of a being a tantalizingly forbidden word, it becomes just another overused term.) Similar to these are Peggy Parrish's beloved "Amelia Bedelia" books, about the befuddled maid who takes language too literally (imagine what she does when asked to "draw the drapes" or "dress the turkey").

A writer whose works are not easily pigeon-holed is Finland's Tove Jansson. Her stories of the Moomins, little creatures who look a bit like hippopotami (except they walk on two legs) and live in a magical place called Moominvalley, have enchanted readers around the world for over 50 years. (Incidentally, we cannot call these animal fantasies, because the creatures are largely entirely made up by Jansson—they are all rather strange beings inhabiting a marvelous world.) In their magical, alternative world, resembling Jansson's Scandinavia, extraordinary beings may pop up at any time, and wondrous things may occur—see *Comet in Moominland*. The Moomins take life as it comes and never fail to make the best of a difficult situation, be it a massive flood or a comet threatening to destroy the world. The stories are often thoughtful, even meditative, yet they are awash in gentle humor and pointed irony. They almost dare us to take them seriously, but we can't help enjoying them.

Some comic fantasies take a more serious turn. For example, Roald Dahl's works approach dark comedy. In *Charlie and the Chocolate Factory,* greedy, selfish, and proud children come to bizarre ends during their tour of Willy Wonka's factory. Dahl's work, peopled with rude, unruly children and vicious adults, and strewn with disturbing images, has met with much controversy. But most children grasp the dark humor and the ironic stances Dahl takes. Humor derives from tension (see Chapter 3)—from an incongruity between our expectations and reality. Comic fantasy, inviting us into the world of the absurd, liberates us, if only temporarily, from the bonds of society and propriety. Comedy levels the playing field, reminding us that we are all human. And so it is often through laughter that we become most humane.

Talking Animal (and Toy) Fantasy

This would seem to be another unwieldy category, but it is essentially the story of animals (or toys) behaving as humans. That is, they can talk and think and feel as humans. Beatrix Potter's picture books featuring small woodland and farm animals, beginning with *The Tale of Peter Rabbit,* have proved the staying power of a good talking animal story. They remain in print after a century. Peter and his family live in the woods, but they wear clothes, sleep in beds, and eat currant buns—that's anthropomorphism at its best. Kenneth Grahame's novel, *The Wind in the Willows,* published just a few years after *Peter Rabbit,* is the story of a water rat, a mole, a badger, and a toad residing in well-furnished houses along a riverbank, enjoying picnics (where they eat fried chicken!), taking harrowing rides in Mr. Toad's motor car, relaxing by the fireplace in the evening, living the good life (remember the description of Badger's kitchen quoted earlier). Each animal has his or her own distinctive character traits—none of which is very animal-like—and the interplay among them drives the plot.

An animal fantasy can be comic, such as Hugh Lofting's *Dr. Dolittle* (about a doctor who discovers he can communicate with animals) or Walter R. Brooks's stories of Freddy the pig (*Freddy the Detective* and many others) portraying the escapades of affable talking farm animals. Freddy lives in a pigpen, but he reads books and sometimes dresses up—in other words, he's really very unpiglike. But a surprising number of animal fantasies are really quite serious, such as E. B. White's *Charlotte's Web,* mentioned earlier, and Dick King-Smith's *Babe, the Gallant Pig,* in which a pig must learn the art of sheep herding to escape the slaughter house. Even Beatrix Potter's seemingly innocent tales have serious undercurrents—Peter's father has been eaten by humans and he himself narrowly escapes the same fate. Indeed, in animal fantasy, it is often human characters who are the antagonists.

Toy fantasies are not as common—although everyone knows the big ones—Carlo Collodi's *Adventures of Pinocchio,* Margery Williams's *Velveteen Rabbit,* and, of course, A. A. Milne's *Winnie-the-Pooh.* The toys, naturally, do not behave as toys. They behave as humans. It has been pointed out that the creatures in *Winnie-the-Pooh* behave like a large, dysfunctional family, each member with a different physical or psychological hang-up—a hyperactive tiger, a manic-depressive donkey, a paranoid pig, a dyslexic owl, and a feeble-minded bear (see Manlove 62). The allure of the stories is seeing how these creatures survive through love and loyalty.

Toy fantasies have become a cinematic phenomenon with Disney's *Toy Story,* which has made the name Buzz Lightyear a household word. In some, but by no means all, toy fantasies, the wish of the toy protagonist is to become real (Collodi's *Pinocchio* and Williams's *Velveteen Rabbit* spring to mind). The popularity of toy fantasies—which are primarily for preschoolers and early elementary children—lies in the child's conviction that all creation is imbued with a life spirit.

Miniature Fantasy

In miniature fantasy, the writer creates a miniature world. Swift did this in the eighteenth century in *Gulliver's Travels,* where he introduces Lilliput, a land of very tiny humans where the English traveler Gulliver looms as a giant. That story, although intended for adults, has proven a childhood favorite. A modern example of miniature fantasy is Mary Norton's series beginning with *The Borrowers,* about those little people who live in our walls and take all the things that go mysteriously missing from our houses. *The Gammage Cup,* by Carol Kendall, is about the struggles of the Minnipin society against their ancient enemies, the Mushroom People. This work contains many features of the heroic fantasy, just on a smaller scale. Children are fascinated by the concept of smallness—which is understandable in people to whom the world must seem overwhelmingly large. One story that defies classification is E. B. White's *Stuart Little,* in which a normal human family inexplicably ends up with a mouse as a child. Although not exactly a miniature fantasy and not exactly an animal fantasy, it contains elements of both. Still, however, the fascination lies in the tiny Stuart's struggle to survive in the larger world—which is alternately comical and terrifying.

In the miniature fantasy, the writer creates a world with which young readers can easily identify. It is gratifying for children to read stories in which the small creatures triumph over larger antagonists—usually through cleverness and perseverance. These stories portray the strengths and foibles of humanity in terms that young readers can readily understand.

Epic Fantasy

Also called heroic fantasy, high fantasy, or simply adventure fantasy—the epic fantasy was originally inspired by great traditional epics like *The Iliad* and *The Odyssey* of Homer, *The Aeneid* of Virgil, the anonymous Old English poem *Beowulf,* and the various medieval hero tales of King Arthur and the Knights of the Round Table. Modern epic fantasies remain enormously popular today. Few readers can resist their sweeping scope, their extraordinary adventures, their high themes, and their fierce battles. *The Hobbit,* Tolkien's prequel to *The Lord of the Rings,* is quite approachable for younger readers, and the great tales of the Rings, although not specifically written for children, make up one of the most famous of modern epic fantasies. The works of C. S. Lewis ("Chronicles of Narnia"), Lloyd Alexander ("Chronicles of Prydain"), Ursula Le Guin ("Earthsea" series), Susan Cooper ("The Dark Is Rising" series), and Philip Pullman ("His Dark Materials" trilogy) have wide followings among readers in the middle grades and older.

The scope of all these fantasies is on a grand scale. Everything about the epic is sublime. Its themes and its characters are larger than life—arch-villains plot against noble heroes, all of whom have some sort of magic at their disposal as well as an array of trusted supporters who would willingly sacrifice themselves for the cause. A world is at stake. Civilization hangs in the balance. And the value system in all these fantasies is familiar—goodness is defined as personal honor, compassion, generosity, and humility; evil is hatred, greed, pride, and selfishness. (Notice how similar these are to the values espoused in many of the folktales.) Most epic fantasies carry powerful moral and ethical messages. The epic fantasy portrays the great struggle between the forces of good and evil, and dramatic battle scenes are a staple.

Finally, the tone of epic fantasy is almost always serious—any humor is in the form of comic relief (usually in the minor characters). Here we see the strong influence of the traditional folk narratives (see Chapter 9). Tolkien was inspired by his reading of medieval literature in creating the world of Middle Earth; C. S. Lewis was also a scholar of medieval literature and borrowed heavily from the old stories; and Lloyd Alexander based his Prydain chronicles on ancient Welsh legends. The magic in epic fantasies is presented very much like that in the folk narratives—it is accepted as a part of the fantasy world—which is typically an alternative world (as in Tolkien) or a parallel world (as in Lewis). Even when the Pevensie children find themselves transplanted from 1940s England to Narnia (*The Lion, the Witch, and the Wardrobe*), they are essentially unsurprised by the talking animals, the magical charms, or even how they got there—once again, the mood of the story is weighty. This is quite a different attitude from that taken by, say, Dorothy, in *The Wonderful Wizard of Oz.*

One example of the overlap between fantasy types is the "Star Wars" film saga. Do not let their technological wizardry fool you. These are not really science fiction (discussed later in this chapter). The famous opening announcement—"A long time ago, in a galaxy far, far away"—was borrowed straight from the old folk narratives. Futuristic technology aside, this is high fantasy. The scope of epic fantasy has often resulted in the epic series—all the writers mentioned in this discussion have produced fantasy series. These writers have complex stories to tell—stories that cannot be contained in a single volume.

Horror Fantasy

Although some of the great epic fantasies of earlier times contain ghosts and frightful monsters (*Beowulf* is a good example), true horror fantasy began in the nineteenth century. Mary Shelley's *Frankenstein* (sometimes considered science fiction), the gruesome tales of Edgar Allan Poe, Robert Louis Stevenson's *The Strange Case of Dr. Jekyll and Mr. Hyde*, and Bram Stoker's *Dracula* are among the most famous—although none of these was particularly intended for children. Even very young children seem to enjoy reading about ghosts—Robert Bright's books about Georgie the shy ghost is a picture book for preschoolers, and the cartoon figure Casper the Friendly Ghost (also a popular film) has a long history. Witch stories for preschoolers abound, from Valerie Thomas's tales of Winnie the Witch (*Winnie the Witch, Winnie Flies Again*) to Norman Bridwell's *The Witch Next Door*. For elementary school readers, R. L. Stine's wildly successful "Goosebumps" series offers a sort of "horror fiction-light"—that is, scary but not too scary. Still, all these works form an introduction to the really scary stuff to come. Horror fantasy also claims a stake in modern adolescent literature best seen in the extraordinary popularity of the "Twilight" series about a family of vampires.

The friendly ghost and witch stories aside, horror fantasy is generally meant to scare the reader. Human beings seem to possess an innate desire to be frightened (or perhaps to be thrilled). This explains the popularity of not only horror films and books but also roller coaster rides, fun houses, and ghost stories shared around campfires and at pajama parties. Fear is one of our strongest emotions, and fear of the unknown is perhaps the most compelling fear. In most horror stories, it is the imagery of death that prevails—mummies, vampires, ghosts, zombies, monsters, and so on. Reading horror fiction gives the reader not only the thrill of facing the horror but also the satisfaction of seeing the hero overcome the horror—at least in most cases. So the horror story has something in common with survival fiction (see Chapter 11). We have met our fears and triumphed.

Not all horror stories are fantasies. Tales such as *The Texas Chainsaw Massacre* or the "Halloween" film series are ostensibly realistic, which in some ways makes them more frightening. However, all horror fiction seems to serve essentially the same purpose—to tantalize us with disturbing images and, usually, to reassure us at the end, when good triumphs over the horrific forces. Perhaps because its goal of terrorizing the reader overrides concerns such as character development and thematic subtlety, horror fantasy has rarely resulted in great literature. When it is not formulaic, it tends to be gimmicky, and modern readers seem to demand increasing gore and graphic violence—to the general detriment of the whole. Indeed, one of the common objections to R. L. Stine's books is that they include gratuitous violence, even though they are marketed for children in the middle to upper elementary grades.

Not all stories with ghosts are horror stories—some are just a bit chilling. Penelope Lively's *The Ghost of Thomas Kempe* and Lucy Boston's "Green Knowe" books are popular examples of the ghost story that is meant to intrigue rather than frighten. Devoid of any grisly horror, Lively's and Boston's novels explore the potentiality of ghosts from an earlier time invading the modern world.

Time-Slip Fantasy

Similar to the ghost story are those tales in which the protagonist from our world (that is, the primary world) is somehow transported to another time period. In 1889, Mark Twain published *A Connecticut Yankee in King Arthur's Court,* in which the nineteenth-century protagonist, having been hit on the head by a sledge hammer, wakes up in the time of King Arthur. His antics during his stay there cause him to alter history (always a consideration of any time traveler). H. G. Wells's famous novel, *The Time Machine,* published in 1895, crosses the boundaries between time-slip fantasy and science fiction, with the invention of a device that allows people to move back and forth in time. Most time-slip fantasies do not bother with a scientific explanation of the time travel; they simply accept that it is possible if the right conditions prevail. We find the time-slip device in Edith Nesbit's *Story of the Amulet* and in Rudyard Kipling's *Puck of Pook's Hill,* both first published in 1906. The next important example came in 1939 with *A Traveller in Time* by Alison Uttley, who was trained as a physicist and fascinated by the work of Einstein and his theories of time/space. Her story is about a girl who is able to move back and forth between the twentieth century and the sixteenth century, where she becomes involved in the famous Babington Plot to rescue Mary Queen of Scots from her imprisonment by Queen Elizabeth I—making it an interesting combination of historical fiction/time-slip fantasy.

Philippa Pearce's celebrated work, *Tom's Midnight Garden,* appearing in 1958, is about a young boy who discovers he can be transported back in time where he makes friends with children who lived decades before him. In his experiences, he comes to a new and richer understanding of human relationships. The time-slip fantasy remains popular as evidenced by Susan Cooper's *King of Shadows,* published in 2000, whose hero, Nat Field, a young boy about to play Puck in Shakespeare's comedy, *A Midsummer Night's Dream,* goes to sleep with a fever and wakes up 400 years earlier in Shakespeare's London. Time-slip novels raise several interesting questions. To what extent are the consequences of an action in the past felt in the future? Do travelers from another time period have the ability to change history? And, if so, should they?

A key element of the time-slip fantasy is that the passage of time in the alternative world (that is, where the time traveler visits) is not reflected in the primary world (where the time traveler actually lives). So, even if the traveler has spent days or years in the alternative world, no time at all will have passed once he or she returns home. Although his works are not time-slip fantasies but epic fantasies, C. S. Lewis uses this device in his Narnia books—in *The Lion, the Witch, and the Wardrobe,* the Pevensie children are transported to Narnia where they grow up and rule for years as kings and queens, only to go back through the wardrobe and find themselves exactly as they were when they left. This obviously eliminates a lot of embarrassing or difficult-to-answer questions from adults back home—like, "Where have you been for the past 20 years?"

Also not exactly a time-slip fantasy, Natalie Babbitt's *Tuck Everlasting* does deal with characters outside of their normal time period. It is about a family who inadvertently attains immortality by drinking from a magic spring. The theme of the story addresses the meaning of life, of immortality, and the importance of death, all in terms accessible to children.

Science Fiction or Speculative Fiction

As noted above, time-slip fantasy and science fiction sometimes cross paths, as in H. G. Wells's *The Time Machine*. We usually call Wells's novella science fiction because of his interest in the scientific or technological explanation; however, it is neither scientific nor technological. In the science fiction novel, we always find some scientific rationale for the fabulous. The science fiction writer often begins by asking what would happen if humans could colonize Mars? Be transported to distant galaxies? Exercise mind control over an entire society? Create artificial intelligence? And so on. Because of this, some prefer to call these works speculative fiction. Recall that Mary Shelley's *Frankenstein* (1819) is often credited with being the first true work in this field. She asks what would happen if humans could create life and uses ostensibly scientific explanations to answer the question. French author, Jules Verne, is famous for his *Twenty Thousand Leagues Under the Sea* and *From the Earth to the Moon*, both dating from the mid-nineteenth century. *The War of the Worlds* (1898), another work by H. G. Wells, was among the first science fiction novels to speculate on an invasion from outer space. In the twentieth century, many science fiction writers began to set their stories in alternative worlds and in the distant future. Science fiction is a product of the modern technological world, but it is really just fantasy that replaces magic with technology. As one critic notes, "How different, after all, is a wizard with a magic wand from a scientist with a microminiaturized matter-transformer? The reader does not know how either gadget works" (Roberts 90).

One writer of science fiction for young people, Sylvia Engdahl, prefers to call her work space fantasy, because she is little concerned with technology or science. Instead, she merely sets her stories (*Enchantress from the Stars, The Far Side of Evil,* and others) in the distant future and on faraway planets. These settings become merely the backdrops for her tales about the development of human civilization and its sociological and psychological implications. Indeed, a strong didactic strain runs through most science fiction, and many works deal with ethical problems facing humanity as science and technology outpace our development as human beings. The question as to whether technological discoveries will be used for humanity's benefit or its destruction frequently becomes a theme of science fiction. Madeleine L'Engle, best known for *A Wrinkle in Time*, addresses such issues in her science fiction.

Science fiction, whether it is set on distant planets in some unknown time or on our own Earth 100 years hence, often presents us with chilling prognostications. In *The Giver*, Lois Lowry offers a bleak picture of a future civilization that has attempted to curb all emotions—very much like Plato advocates in *The Republic*. Lowry's book has been criticized for its ambiguous ending, but she explores some very important ideas: How important are our emotions? What would happen to society if our feelings were suppressed? What would society be like if our futures were predetermined by the authorities? She presents all these ideas through the eyes of a youthful member of such a society. The result can be unsettling—and intensely thought provoking.

Summary

Fantasy, like all literature, changes with the tastes of a culture. Victorian fantasy—Lewis Carroll aside—was heavy with pointed morals and usually included magical element intruding on the real world. The early twentieth century was the heyday of escapist fantasy—animal fantasies, toy fantasies, and comic fantasies for younger readers—all perhaps a reaction to the upheaval caused by two World Wars and a great worldwide economic depression. Beginning in the 1950s came a shift toward fantasy for increasingly older children, with talking animal fantasies remaining popular in picture books for young children. More and more fantasies today deal with horrifying menaces. The rational fantasy world—such as that created by C. S. Lewis—has given way to a world in which irrational evil presents a constant threat. Psychological thrillers—done so successfully by the adult fantasist, Stephen King—are now common among fantasies for children (R. L. Stine has written dozens of these types of fantasies).

Fantasy holds many treasures for us, not the least of which is the stimulation of our imaginations. Fantasy writer Joan Aiken, in an essay entitled "On Imagination," has summarized what she sees to be the practical value of a developed imagination. In addition to amusing us, Aiken points out, our imagination keeps us hopeful, enabling us to see life's myriad possibilities. It helps us solve problems by allowing us to see things from a variety of perspectives. It helps us see the points of view of others and serves as a check to fanaticism. Aiken goes further to suggest that the imagination is a bit like a muscle—if we do not exercise it, it becomes weak and ineffectual. Reading is among the best ways to exercise our imagination. Although Aiken does not suggest that reading fantasy is a better exercise of the imagination than reading realism or nonfiction, we can say that fantasy does make special demands of readers. Fantasy creates not only its own characters and plots but also its own peculiar set of laws with which readers must become acquainted.

Through the medium of fantasy, writers are able to explore complex ideas on a symbolic level that would otherwise be difficult to convey to young readers. Fantasy is perfectly suited to the thoughtful exploration of philosophical issues at a level that can be understood and appreciated by the child reader. It deliberately challenges our perceptions of reality and forces us to explore new, uncharted realms of thought. But the readers who accept the challenge find whole new realms opened up for them and their lives enriched beyond measure.

The great psychologist, Carl Gustav Jung, wrote this of the importance of fantasy and its impact on the imagination and our lives:

The dynamic principle of fantasy is play, which belongs also to the child, and as such it appears to be inconsistent with the principle of serious work. But without this playing with fantasy no creative work has ever yet come to birth. The debt we owe to the play of the imagination is incalculable. (82)

For Reflection and Discussion

1. Read a fantasy novel—either of your choice or one assigned by the instructor—and as you read, keep a journal. Read a chapter or two at a time and then spend 15 to 20 minutes writing down your thoughts, observations, predictions—whatever comes to mind. Continue this process throughout the reading of the book. When you are finished, reread your journal entries and assess them. How accurate were you? How do you explain these results?

2. Invent a fantasy world. You may create any sort you wish, and populate it with whomever or whatever you wish. But you must also establish some fantasy rules—rules that are different from those in our world but that hold true in your fantasy world. Consider how these rules will affect any storyline.

3. Invent a fantasy character—not just an imaginary friend (although it may be), but a character out of a fantasy world. What do you call the character? What does the character look like? Describe the character's personality traits. What are the character's values? Likes? Dislikes? Habits? Special powers (the character is, after all, not human)? Try writing a very short story that features the character.

4. What is your favorite type of fantasy? Can you explain what about this type appeals to you? (You might try the reverse—what about some other type of fantasy does *not* appeal to you? Can you explain that?)

● Works Cited

Aiken, Joan. "On Imagination." *The Horn Book* (November/December 1984): 735–741.

Grahame, Kenneth. *The Wind in the Willows*. London: Methuen, 1908.

Jung, Carl Gustav. *Psychological Types.* New York: Harcourt, Brace, 1923.

Manlove, Colin. *From Alice to Harry Potter: Children's Fantasy in England*. Christchurch, New Zealand: Cybereditions, 2003.

O'Keefe, Deborah. *Readers in Wonderland: The Liberating Worlds of Fantasy Fiction*. New York: Continuum, 2003.

Roberts, Thomas J. "Science Fiction and the Adolescent." *Children's Literature: The Great Excluded* 2 (1973): 87–91.

Snyder, Zilpha Keatley. "Afterword." *Tom's Midnight Garden* by Philippa Pearce. New York: Dell, 1986, 230–232.

● Recommended Readings

Alexander, Lloyd. "High Fantasy and Heroic Romance." *Horn Book Magazine* 47, 6 (December 1971): 577–584.

Attebery, Brian. *The Fantasy Tradition in American Literature: From Irving to Le Guin*. Bloomington: Indiana University Press,1980.

Babbitt, Natalie. "Fantasy and the Classic Hero." *School Library Journal* (October 1987): 25–29.

Cameron, Eleanor. *The Green and Burning Tree*. Boston: Little, Brown, 1969.

Cooper, Susan. *Dreams and Wishes: Essays on Writing for Children*. New York: McElderry, 1996.

Dickinson, Peter. "Fantasy: The Need for Realism." *Children's Literature in Education* 17, 1 (1986): 39–51.

Egoff, Sheila. *Worlds Within: Children's Fantasy from the Middle Ages to Today.* Chicago: American Library Association, 1988.

Hume, Kathryn. *Fantasy and Mimesis.* New York and London: Methuen, 1984.

Johansen, K. V. *Quests and Kingdoms: A Grown-Up's Guide to Children's Fantasy Literature.* Sackville, New Brunswick: Sybertooth, 2005.

Kuznets, Lois. *When Toys Come Alive: Narratives of Animations, Metamorphosis and Development.* New Haven, CT: Yale University Press, 1994.

Le Guin, Ursula. *The Language of the Night.* Ed. Susan Wood. New York: G. P. Putnam's Sons, 1979.

Lynn, Ruth Nadelman. *Fantasy Literature for Children and Young Adults,* 5th ed. Santa Barbara, CA: Libraries Unlimited, 2005.

Marcus, Leonard S., ed. *The Wand in the Word: Conversations with Writers of Fantasy.* New York: Candlewick, 2006.

Mendelsohn, Farah. *The Inter-Galactic Playground: A Critical Study of Children's and Teens' Science Fiction.* Jefferson, NC: McFarland, 2009.

Mikkelsen, Nina. *Fantasy Literature for Children and Young Adults.* New York: Teachers College Press, 2005.

Raynor, Mary. "Some Thoughts on Animals in Children's Books." *Signal* 29 (May 1979): 81–87.

Sale, Roger. *Fairy Tales and After: From Snow White to E. B. White.* Cambridge, MA: Harvard University Press, 1978.

Smith, Karen Patricia. *The Fabulous Realm.* Lanham, MD: Scarecrow, 1993.

Sullivan, C. W. *Science Fiction for Young Readers.* New York: Greenwood, 1993.

Tolkien, J. R. R. *Tree and Leaf.* Boston: Houghton Mifflin, 1965.

Waggoner, Diana. *The Hills of Faraway: A Guide to Fantasy.* New York: Atheneum, 1978.

Westfahl, Gary. *Science Fiction, Children's Literature, and Popular Culture: Coming of Age in Fantasyland.* New York: Greenwood, 2000.

"World of Fantasy" (2000 ThinkQuest Internet Challenge Project). http://library.thinkquest.org.

Wullschläger, Jackie. *Inventing Wonderland: The Lives and Fantasies of Lewis Carroll, Edward Lear, J. M. Barrie, Kenneth Grahame, and A. A. Milne.* New York: Free Press, 1996.

Selected Bibliography of Fantasies for Children

Remember that some fantasy fiction does not fit neatly into a single category. In most cases, each author in a category is represented by a single book, so you may want to look for other books by these writers.

Literary Fairy Tales and Magical Fantasy

Andersen, Hans Christian. *The Complete Fairy Tales and Stories.* Trans. Erik Christian Haugaard. New York: Doubleday, 1974.

———. *The Emperor and the Nightingale.* Trans. Eva LeGallienne. Illus. Nancy Burkert. New York: Harper, 1965.

———. *The Steadfast Tin Soldier.* Illus. David Jorgensen. New York: Knopf, 1986.

Barrie, Sir James. *Peter Pan.* New York: Scribner's, 1950.

Baum, L. Frank. *The Wonderful Wizard of Oz.* 1900. Several modern editions.

Bomans, Godfried. *The Wily Witch and All the Other Fairy Tales and Fables.* Illus. Wouter Hoogendijk. Owings Mills, MD: Stemmer, 1977.

Gardner, John. *Dragon, Dragon, and Other Tales.* New York: Knopf, 1975.

MacDonald, George. *At the Back of the North Wind.* 1871. Several modern editions.

———. *The Light Princess.* 1864. Several modern editions.

———. *The Princess and the Curdie.* 1872. Several modern editions.

————. *The Princess and the Goblin*. 1883. Several modern editions.

Mekissack, Patricia C. *Porch Lies: Tales of Slicksters, Tricksters and Other Wily Characters*. New York: Schwartz and Wade, 2006.

Nesbit, E. *The Enchanted Castle*. 1907. Several modern editions.

————. *Five Children and It*. 1902. Several modern editions.

————. *The Phoenix and the Carpet*. 1904. Several modern editions.

————. *The Story of the Amulet*. 1906. Several modern editions.

Thurber, James. *Fables for Our Time*. New York: Harper & Row, 1939.

————. *Many Moons*. New York: Harbrace, 1943.

Comic Fantasy

Aiken, Joan. *Black Hearts in Battersea*. New York: Doubleday, 1964.

————. *The Wolves of Willoughby Chase*. New York: Doubleday, 1963.

Allard, Harry. *The Stupids Die*. Illus. James Marshall. Boston: Houghton Mifflin, 1981.

————. *The Stupids Step Out*. Illus. James Marshall. Boston: Houghton Mifflin, 1974.

Atwater, Richard, and Florence Atwater. *Mr. Popper's Penguins*. Illus. Robert Lawson. Boston: Little, Brown, 1938.

Babbitt, Natalie. *Kneeknock Rise*. New York: Farrar, Straus & Giroux, 1970.

————. *The Search for Delicious*. New York: Farrar, Straus & Giroux, 1969.

Carroll, Lewis. *Alice's Adventures in Wonderland*. Illus. John Tenniel. 1865. Several modern editions.

————. *Through the Looking-Glass and What Alice Saw There*. Illus. John Tenniel. 1871. Several modern editions.

Cresswell, Helen. *The Night-Watchmen*. London: Puffin, 1988.

Dahl, Roald. *Charlie and the Chocolate Factory*. New York: Knopf, 1964.

————. *James and the Giant Peach*. New York: Knopf, 1961.

DuBois, William Pene. *Twenty-One Balloons*. New York: Viking, 1947.

Fleischman, Sid. *Chancy and the Grand Rascal*. Boston: Little, Brown, 1966.

————. *The Ghost in the Noonday Sun*. Boston: Little, Brown, 1965.

————. *The Whipping Boy*. New York: Morrow, 1986.

Goudge, Elizabeth. *The Little White Horse*. 1946. New York: Dell, 1992.

Hale, Lucretia P. *The Peterkin Papers*. 1886. New York: Dover, 1963.

Janssen, Tove. *Comet in Moominland*. 1946. Trans. Elizabeth Portch. New York: Farrar, Straus & Giroux, 1959. (The beginning of a series that eventually included the following [the dates indicate the initial Finnish/Swedish publications]: *Finn Family Moomintroll*, 1948; *The Exploits of Moominpappa*, 1950 [later republished as *Moominpappa's Memoirs*, 1968]; *Moominsummer Madness*, 1954; *Moominland Midwinter*, 1957; *Tales from Moominvalley*, 1962; *Moominpappa at Sea*, 1965; and *Moominvalley in November*, 1970)

Jones, Diana Wynne. *Howl's Moving Castle*. New York: Greenwillow, 1986.

Juster, Norton. *The Phantom Tollbooth*. New York: Random, 1961.

Kendall, Carol. *The Gammage Cup*. New York: Harcourt, 1959.

Kipling, Rudyard. *Puck of Pook's Hill*. 1906. Various modern editions.

Lagerlof, Selma. *The Wonderful Adventures of Nils*. 1906. Several modern editions.

Lindgren, Astrid. *Pippi Longstocking*. New York: Viking, 1950.

McCaughrean, Geraldine. *A Pack of Lies*. New York: Scholastic, 1988.

Merrill, Jean. *The Pushcart War*. Reading, MA: Scott/Addison, 1964.

Norton, Mary. *The Borrowers*. New York: Harcourt, 1953.

———. *The Borrowers Afield*. New York: Harcourt, 1955.

———. *The Magic Bedknob*. 1945. New York: Odyssey, 2000. (With *Bonfires and Broomsticks*.)

Parish, Peggy. *Amelia Bedelia*. New York: Harper, 1963.

Pierce, Tamora. *Shatterglass*. New York: Scholastic, 2003.

Pratchett, Terry. *The Wee Free Man*. New York: HarperCollins, 2003.

Rodgers, Mary. *Freaky Friday*. New York: Harper, 1972.

Snicket, Lemony. (pseudonym for Daniel Handler). *A Series of Unfortunate Events: A Bad Beginning*. New York: HarperCollins, 1999. (First of a series of 13 books)

Snow, Alan. *Here Be Monsters!* New York: Atheneum, 2006.

Thomas, Shelley Moore. *Get Well, Good Knight*. Illus. Jennifer Plecar. New York: Dutton, 2002.

Travers, P. L. *Mary Poppins*. New York: Harcourt, 1934.

Umansky, Kaye. *The Silver Spoon of Solomon Snow*. New York: Candlewick, 2005.

Wyke-Smith, E. A. *The Marvelous Land of Snergs*. 1928. Baltimore: Old Earth, 1996.

Animal, Toy, and Miniature Fantasies

Adams, Richard. *Watership Down*. New York: Macmillan, 1974.

Bailey, Caroline Sherwin. *Miss Hickory*. New York: Viking, 1968.

Bond, Michael. *A Bear Called Paddington*. Boston: Houghton Mifflin, 1960.

Brooks, Walter R. *Freddy the Detective*. New York: Knopf, 1932.

Clarke, Pauline. *The Return of the Twelves*. New York: Coward-McCann, 1964. (British title: *The Twelve and the Genii*)

Cleary, Beverly. *Runaway Ralph*. New York: Morrow, 1970.

Collodi, Carlo (pseudonym for Carlo Lorenzini). *The Adventures of Pinocchio*. 1883. Several modern editions.

Corbett, W. J. *The Song of Pentecost*. New York: Dutton, 1983.

Delaney, Michael. *Birdbrain Amos*. New York: Philomel, 2002.

Ets, Marie Hall. *Mister Penny*. New York: Viking, 1935.

Field, Rachel. *Hitty, Her First Hundred Years*. New York: Macmillan, 1929.

Godden, Rumer. *The Doll's House*. New York: Viking, 1962.

Grahame, Kenneth. *The Wind in the Willows*. 1908. Several modern editions.

Hoban, Lillian. *Arthur's Birthday Party*. New York: HarperCollins, 1999.

Hoban, Russell. *The Mouse and His Child*. New York: Harper, 1967.

Jacques, Brian. *Marell of Redwall*. New York: Philomel, 1992. (These might also be considered epic fantasies, creating an entire alternative world.)

———. *Mattimeo*. New York: Philomel, 1990.

———. *Mossflower*. New York: Philomel, 1988.

———. *Redwall*. New York: Philomel, 1987.

Jarrell, Randall. *The Animal Family*. Illus. Maurice Sendak. New York: Pantheon, 1965.

———. *The Bat-Poet*. New York: Macmillan, 1964.

Jennings, Richard. *Orwell's Luck*. Boston: Houghton Mifflin, 2000.

King-Smith, Dick. *Babe, the Gallant Pig*. New York: Random House, 1983.

———. *The Water Horse*. New York: Crown, 1998.

Kipling, Rudyard. *Just So Stories*. 1902. Illus. Barry Moser. New York: Morrow, 1996.

Lawson, Robert. *Ben and Me*. Boston: Little, Brown, 1939.

———. *Rabbit Hill*. New York: Viking, 1944.

———. *The Tough Winter*. New York: Viking, 1970.

Lionni, Leo. *Alexander and the Wind-Up Mouse*. New York: Pantheon, 1969.

Lobel, Arnold. *Frog and Toad Are Friends*. New York: Harper, 1970.

———. *Frog and Toad Together*. New York: Harper, 1972.

Lofting, Hugh. *The Story of Dr. Dolittle*. New York: Stokes, 1920.

———. *The Voyages of Dr. Dolittle*. New York: Stokes, 1922.

Marshall, James. *Rats on the Roof and Other Stories*. New York: Dial, 1991.

Martin, Ann M., and Laura Godwin. *The Doll People*. New York: Hyperion, 2000.

Milne, A. A. *The House at Pooh Corner*. 1928. Illus. Ernest Shepard. New York: Dutton, 1961.

———. *Winnie-the-Pooh*. 1926. Illus. Ernest Shepard. New York: Dutton, 1961.

O'Brien, Robert. *Mrs. Frisby and the Rats of NIMH*. New York: Atheneum, 1971.

Proimos, James. *The Many Adventures of Johnny Mutton*. New York: Harcourt, 2001.

Reid Banks, Lynn. *The Indian in the Cupboard*. New York: Doubleday, 1981.

———. *The Magic Hare*. New York: Morrow, 1993.

Salton, Felix. *Bambi*. New York: Simon & Schuster, 1929.

Selden, George. *The Cricket in Times Square*. Illus. Garth Williams. New York: Farrar, Straus & Giroux, 1960.

Sharp, Margery. *Miss Bianca*. Boston: Little, Brown, 1962.

———. *The Rescuers*. Boston: Little, Brown, 1959.

Steig, William. *Abel's Island*. New York: Farrar, Straus & Giroux, 1976.

———. *Dominic*. New York: Farrar, Straus & Giroux, 1972.

Titus, Eve. *Basil in Mexico*. Illus. Paul Galdone. New York: McGraw-Hill, 1976.

White, E. B. *Charlotte's Web*. New York: Harper, 1952.

———. *Stuart Little*. New York: Harper, 1945.

———. *The Trumpet of the Swan*. New York: Harper, 1970.

Williams, Margery. *The Velveteen Rabbit*. 1922. Illus. Michael Hague. New York: Holt, Rinehart & Winston, 1983.

Winthrop, Elizabeth. *The Castle in the Attic*. New York: Holiday, 1985.

Epic and Adventure Fantasies

Alexander, Lloyd. *The Book of Three*. New York: Henry Holt, 1964. (First of the "Chronicles of Prydain" series, including *The Black Cauldron*, 1965; *The Castle of Llyr*, 1966; *Taran Wanderer*, 1967; *The High King*, 1968; and *The Foundling and Other Tales of Prydain*, 1970)

———. *Westmark*. New York: Penguin, 1981. (First of the "Westmark" trilogy, including *The Kestrel*, 1982, and *The Beggar Queen*, 1984)

Cooper, Susan. *Over Sea, Under Stone*. New York: Simon & Schuster, 1965. (First of the "Dark Is Rising" series, including *The Dark Is Rising*, 1973; *Greenwitch*, 1974; *The Grey King*, 1975; and *Silver on the Tree*, 1977)

Cross, Gillian. *The Dark Ground*. New York: Dutton, 2004. (First of the "Dark Ground" trilogy, including *The Black Room*, 2006, and *The Nightmare Game*, 2007)

Crossley-Holland, Kevin. *The Seeing Stone*. New York: Scholastic, 2001. (First of the "Arthur" trilogy, including *At the Crossing Places*, 2002, and *King of the Middle March*, 2004)

De Mari, Silvana. *The Last Dragon*. Trans. Shaun Whiteside. New York: Hyperion, 2006.

Doyle, Debra, and James D. Macdonald. *Knight's Wyrd*. New York: Harcourt, 1992.

Funke, Cornelia. *Dragon Rider*. Trans. Anthea Bell. New York: Scholastic, 2004.

Garner, Alan. *The Owl Service*. New York: Walck, 1968.

———. *The Weirdstone of Brisingamen*. London: Puffin, 1963.

Gee, Maurice. *Salt*. (Vol. 1 of the proposed "Salt" trilogy) Victoria, B.C.: Orca Publishing, 2009.

Jones, Diana Wynne. *Howl's Moving Castle*. St. Louis, MO: Turtleback, 2001.

Le Guin, Ursula. *A Wizard of Earthsea*. Boston: Houghton Mifflin, 1968. (First of the "Earthsea" series, including *The Tombs of Atuan,1971; The Farthest Shore*, 1972; *Tehanu*, 1990; and *Other Wind*, 2001)

Lewis, C. S. *The Lion, the Witch, and the Wardrobe*. 1950. New York: HarperCollins, various editions. (First of the "Chronicles of Narnia" series, including *Prince Caspian,* 1951; *The Voyage of the Dawn Treader,* 1952; *The Silver Chair,* 1953; *The Horse and His Boy,* 1954; *The Magician's Nephew,* 1955; and *The Last Battle,* 1956)

McCaffrey, Anne. *Dragondrums.* New York: Atheneum, 1979.

———. *Dragonsinger.* New York: Atheneum, 1977.

———. *Dragonsong.* New York: Atheneum, 1976.

McKinley, Robin. *The Blue Sword.* New York: Greenwillow, 1982.

———. *The Hero and the Crown.* New York: Greenwillow, 1985.

Mayne, William. *Antar and the Eagles.* New York: Delacorte, 1990.

Nicholson, William. *The Wind Singer.* New York: Hyperion, 2000. (First of the "Wind of Fire" trilogy, including *Slaves of the Mastery,* 2001, and *Firesong,* 2002)

Nix, Garth. *Sabriel.* New York: HarperCollins, 1996. (First of the "Old Kingdom" trilogy, also called the Abhorsen trilogy, including *Lireal,* 2001, and *Abhorsen,* 2003)

Pope, Elizabeth Marie. *The Perilous Gard.* New York: Puffin, 1962. (Historical fantasy)

Pullman, Philip. *The Golden Compass.* New York: Knopf, 1996. (First of the "His Dark Materials" trilogy, including *The Subtle Knife,* 1997, and *The Amber Spyglass,* 2000)

Rowling, J. K. *Harry Potter and the Philosopher's Stone.* (Released in U.S. as *Harry Potter and the Sorcerer's Stone.*) London: Bloomsbury, 1997. (First of the "Harry Potter" series, including *Harry Potter and the Chamber of Secrets,* 1998; *Harry Potter and the Prisoner of Azkaban,* 1999; *Harry Potter and the Goblet of Fire,* 2000; *Harry Potter and the Order of the Phoenix,* 2003; *Harry Potter and the Half-Blood Prince,* 2005; *Harry Potter and the Deathly Hallows,* 2007)

Snyder, Zilpha Keatley. *Song of the Gargoyle.* New York: Delacorte, 1991.

Stroud, Jonathan. *Heroes of the Valley.* New York: Hyperion, 2009.

Tolkien, J. R. R. *Fellowship of the Ring.* 1954. New York: Houghton Mifflin, Various editions. (First of the "Lord of the Rings" trilogy, including *The Two Towers,* 1955, and *The Return of the King,* 1955)

———. *The Hobbit, or There and Back Again.* London: George Allen &Unwin, 1937.

Townsend, John Rowe. *The Fortunate Isles.* New York: Lippincott, 1989.

Wein, Elizabeth E. *The Winter Prince.* New York: Atheneum, 1993.

Yolen, Jane. *Dragon's Blood.* New York: Delacorte, 1982. (First of the "Pit Dragon" series, including *Heart's Blood,* 1984; *A Sending of Dragons,* 1987; and *Dragon's Heart,* 2009)

Time-Slip and Horror Fantasy

Aiken, Joan. *A Foot in the Grave.* New York: Viking, 1992.

Babbitt, Natalie. *Tuck Everlasting.* New York: Farrar, Straus & Giroux, 1975.

Boston, Lucy. *The Children of Greene Knowe.* New York: Harcourt, 1964.

Cameron, Eleanor. *The Court of the Stone Children.* New York: Dutton, 1973.

Cobalt, Martin (pseudonym for William Mayne). *Pool of Swallows.* New York: Nelson, 1974.

Cooper, Susan. *King of Shadows.* New York: Margaret K. McElderry, 1999.

Dunlop, Eileen. *The Ghost by the Sea.* New York: Holiday, 1996.

Farmer, Penelope. *A Castle of Bone.* New York: Philomel, 1982.

———. *Charlotte Sometimes.* New York: Harcourt, 1969.

Garfield, Leon. *Mister Corbett's Ghost.* New York: Pantheon, 1968.

———. *The Restless Ghost: Three Stories.* New York: Pantheon, 1969.

Griffin, Peni R. *The Ghost Sitter.* New York: Dutton, 2001.

Hamilton, Virginia. *Sweet Whispers, Brother Rush.* New York: Philomel, 1982.

Hunter, Mollie. *The Haunted Mountain.* New York: Harper, 1972.

Ibbotson, Eva. *Dial-a-Ghost*. Illus. Kevin Hawkes. New York: Dutton, 2001.

Lindbergh, Anne. *Nick of Time*. Boston: Little, Brown, 1994.

Lively, Penelope. *The Ghost of Thomas Kempe*. Illus. Antony Maitland. New York: Dutton, 1973.

Lunn, Janet. *The Root Cellar*. New York: Scribner's, 1983.

Mayne, William. *Earthfasts*. New York: Dutton, 1967.

———. *A Game of Dark*. New York: Dutton, 1971.

———. *Over the Hills and Far Away*. (1968) London: Hodder, 1997.

Morgan, Helen. *The Witch Doll*. New York: Viking, 1992.

Norton, Mary. *Bed-Knob and Broomstick*. Illus. Erik Blegvad. New York: Harcourt, 1957.

Noyes, Deborah, ed. *Gothic!: Ten Original Dark Tales*. New York: Candlewick, 2004.

Pearce, Philippa. *Tom's Midnight Garden*. New York: Dell, 1986.

Pearson, Kit. *A Handful of Time*. New York: Viking, 1988.

Pratchett, Terry. *Wintersmith*. New York: Harper/Tempest, 2006.

Price, Susan. *Ghost Song*. New York: Farrar, Straus & Giroux, 1992.

Prince, Maggie. *The House on Hound Hill*. Boston: Houghton Mifflin, 1998.

Pullman, Philip. *Clockwork*. New York: Scholastic, 1998.

Rich, Susan, ed. *Half-Minute Horrors*. New York: HarperCollins, 2009.

Schmidt, Annie M. G. *Minnie*. New York: Milkweed, 1994.

VandeVelde, Vivian. *Ghost of a Hanged Man*. New York: Cavendish, 1998.

Walsh, Jill Paton. *A Chance Child*. New York: Farrar, Straus & Giroux, 1978.

Waugh, Sylvia. *The Mennyms*. New York: Random House, 1994.

Woodruff, Elvira. *The Magnificent Mummy Maker*. New York: Scholastic, 1994.

Yee, Paul. *Dead Man's Gold and Other Stories*. Toronto: Groundwood, 2002.

Yolen, Jane, and Martin H. Greenberg, eds. *Things That Go Bump in the Night: A Collection of Original Stories*. New York: Harper, 1989.

Science Fiction or Speculative Fiction

Cameron, Eleanor. *Wonderful Flight to the Mushroom Planet*. Illus. Robert Henneberger. Boston: Little, Brown, 1954.

Christopher, John. *Beyond the Burning Lands*. New York: Macmillan, 1971.

———. *When the Tripods Came*. New York: Dutton, 1988.

———. *The White Mountains*. New York: Macmillan, 1967.

Clarke, Arthur C. *Dolphin Island*. New York: Holt, 1963.

Conley, Jane Leslie. *The Rudest Alien on Earth*. New York: Holt, 2002.

Cooper, Susan. *King of Shadows*. 1999. New York: Aladdin.

Cresswell, Helen. *The Watchers: A Mystery of Alton Towers*. New York: Macmillan, 1994.

Del Rey, Lester. *The Runaway Robot*. Philadelphia: Westminster, 1965.

Dickinson, Peter. *Eva*. New York: Delacorte, 1989.

Engdahl, Sylvia. *Enchantress from the Stars*. New York: Macmillan, 1970.

———. *The Far Side of Evil*. New York: Macmillan, 1971.

Hamilton, Virginia. *Justice and Her Brothers*. New York: Greenwillow, 1978.

Hautman, Pete. *Hole in the Sky*. New York: Simon & Schuster, 2001.

Heinlein, Robert. *Have Space Suit—Will Travel*. New York: Scribner's, 1958.

Lanagan, Margo. *White Time*. New York: Eos/HarperCollins, 2006.

Lawrence, Louise. *Moonwind*. New York: Harper, 1986.

L'Engle, Madeleine. *A Ring of Endless Light*.New York: Farrar, Straus & Giroux, 1980.

———. *A Swiftly Tilting Planet*. New York: Farrar, Straus & Giroux, 1978.

———. *A Wrinkle in Time*. New York: Farrar, Straus & Giroux, 1962.

Lowry, Lois. *The Giver*. Boston: Houghton Mifflin, 1993. (First of a series, including *Gathering Blue*, 2000, and *The Messenger*, 2004)

Norton, Andre. *Moon of Three Rings*. New York: Viking, 1966.

Oppel, Kenneth. *Dead Water Zone*. New York: Joy Street, 1993.

Rubenstein, Gillian. *Beyond the Labyrinth*. New York: Watts, 1990.

Sleator, William. *Strange Attractors*. New York: Dutton, 1989.

Todd, Ruthven. *Space Cat*. Illus. Paul Galdone. New York: Scribner's, 1952.

Uttley, Alison. *The Traveler in Time*. 1939. Penguin Books Canada, 1977.

Verne, Jules. *Twenty Thousand Leagues Under the Sea*. 1864. New York: Penguin, 1987.

Waugh, Sylvia. *Earthborn*. New York: Delacorte, 2002.

Wells, H. G. *The Time Machine*. 1895. New York: Bantam, 1982.

———. *The War of the Worlds*. 1898. New York: Putnam, 1978.

Westall, Robert. *Future Track 5*. New York: Greenwillow, 1984.

Go to the topics "Picture Books" and "Modern Fantasy" on the MyEducationKit for this text, where you can:

- Search the Database of Children's Literature, housing more than 22,000 titles searchable in every genre by authors or illustrators, by awards won, by year published, and by topic and description.

- Explore genre-related Assignments and Activities, assignable exercises showing concepts in action through database use, video, cases, and student and teacher artifacts.

- Listen to podcasts and read interviews from some of the brightest and most enduring stars of children's literature in the Conversations.

- Discover Web Links that will lead you to sites representing the authors you learn about in these pages, classrooms with powerful children's literature connections, and literature awards.

Realistic Fiction

The Days of Our Lives

Introduction

Realism in children's literature, unlike fantasy, tries to portray the world as it is (or once was). The term "Realism" itself is problematic, since it also refers to a specific type of nineteenth-century American fiction. For our purposes, realistic fiction includes all those stories that attempt to depict life realistically—whether it be the world of the past or our contemporary world. The object in realistic fiction is to make the characters and situations as true to life as possible—something we call verisimilitude (literally, "resembling the truth"). True, some writers portray the world as a bit rosier than it probably is, whereas other writers portray it as far darker than we hope it is. However, realistic fiction contains nothing that is contrary to the laws of nature. Realism refers both to subject matter and treatment. So, chilling ghost, werewolf, and vampire stories we regard as fantasy (since we know they cannot actually happen), whereas the more horrific tales of the Holocaust are sadly realistic. Our interest in realistic fiction derives from an inherent interest in the human condition and in the varying ways people face life's challenges, defeats, joys, and sorrows.

The success of realistic fiction relies in no small part on the writer's ability to observe and interpret life and to transform these observations and interpretations into a believable fictional story. It is not too much of an exaggeration to suggest that most realistic novels read by young people (and a fair share of fantasies, we might add) are coming-of-age stories. In the coming-of-age story, the protagonist undergoes a series of experiences (emotional crises, trials, hardships, adventures) that result in the character's personal growth and development—the protagonist emerges a little bit older and a little bit wiser. Each coming-of-age story has its own theme, however, which expresses the writer's central idea about the subject. Certain broad themes keep reappearing (again, we find these themes in many fantasies as well). Some of the most important ones can be stated quite simply:

- "We're family and we're all in this together." (The importance of family)
- "Good friends are hard to find, so we need to stand by each other." (The importance of friendship)

- "The world's a tough place, but I am going to make it." (The importance of individual perseverance)
- "Through hard work and determination we can make this a better world." (The importance of community and the pursuit of social justice)
- "I won't like it, but I'll have to go on without you." (The acceptance of death)

These themes are found in both historical and contemporary realism—they only appear in different dress. In this chapter we will discuss both historical realism, which attempts to recreate an earlier time period, and contemporary realism, which seeks an accurate portrayal of the writer's own time.

Definitions

It is easy to say that historical realism refers to stories set in the past and that contemporary realism consists of stories set in the present day. But the distinction is not that simple. Eventually, all stories become stories set in the past. Does this mean that a realistic novel written and set in the 1960s is now to be considered historical realism? No, of course not. It is the writer who determines whether a book is historical or contemporary realism. Consider, for example, Louise Fitzhugh's popular novel, *Harriet the Spy*, published in 1964 and set in the same time. We still call this contemporary realism, even though close to 50 years have elapsed, because Fitzhugh's setting is contemporary with her writing. On the other hand, Christopher Paul Curtis's novel, *The Watsons Go to Birmingham—1963*, is set in almost the identical time period. However, this book was published in 1995—over 30 years after the events it describes—and so we call this historical realism. Curtis is writing about a time in the past and realizes that his readers may not be familiar with the 1960s. It is this awareness on the writer's part that distinguishes historical realism from contemporary realism. To give truth to his historical setting, Curtis includes very specific historical references, notably the infamous bombing of the Sixteenth Street Baptist Church in Birmingham that played such a key role in the civil rights struggle. Curtis is very conscious of describing a time and place in history. He fills his book with wonderful snippets of life in the 1960s, including a record player designed for use in an automobile in a time before CDs (or cassettes or even eight-track tapes), and the grim examples of segregation the African American family encounters on the journey to Birmingham.

So, we might generalize that contemporary realism assumes that the reader is familiar with the novel's time period and requires minimal cultural, social or political explanation.

Historical realism, on the other hand, is conscious of its setting in the past and therefore includes historical events, personages, and/or information that will bring the past to life. We will first look at the important features of historical realism and then move on to contemporary realism.

The History of Historical Realism

Sir Walter Scott (1771–1832) almost single-handedly invented historical realism in the early nineteenth century with such novels as *Ivanhoe*, a romantic tale of the Middle Ages, and *Waverley*, about a Scottish rebellion against the English in 1745. This early historical fiction sprang from the Romantic Movement of the late 1700s and early 1800s, and appealed to the Romantic desire to escape from the frantic pace of modern life (yes, even in the eighteenth century). In the later nineteenth century, historical fiction became popular with young readers who were drawn in by the exotic settings, colorful adventures, and heroic figures of the early historical novels. Popular historical novels included Charlotte Yonge's *The Dove in the Eagle's Nest* (1866), R. L. Stevenson's *The Black Arrow* (1883), and G. A. Henty's *With Clive in India* (1884). In the United States, nineteenth-century writers of historical fiction generally looked to American history for their inspiration; however, the most famous of them all, Howard Pyle, drew on medieval settings in *The Merry Adventures of Robin Hood* and *Otto of the Silver Hand* (see Figure 11.1).

With World War I, historical fiction fell into decline, perhaps because that conflict brought great disillusionment in the old ways and readers sought escape in fantasy, among other things. A revival of historical fiction occurred in the 1930s, and for the next 30 or more years historical fiction flourished. It became more eclectic, drawing on the histories of various cultures from ancient Ethiopia (Elizabeth Coatsworth's *The Princess and the Lion*) to Roman Britain (Rosemary Sutcliff's *The Lantern Bearers*) to the Spanish explorations of sixteenth-century America (Scott O'Dell's *The King's Fifth*). Many historical novels won major book awards and enjoyed great popularity during this period.

The 1970s saw the youth rebellion and the subsequent rejection of the past and an insistence on "relevance." All this cast shadows on history in general and on the historical novel in particular, which once again fell out of favor. The genre is now recovering its former popularity, and some very fine historical fiction is being written for children today, with an emphasis on reassessing and understanding the past, rather than extolling it. For example, in contrast to celebrating the patriotic glory of the Revolutionary War, Christopher and James Lincoln Collier paint a far more realistic (some would say cynical) picture in *My Brother Sam Is Dead*. Mildred Taylor reveals the ugliness of racial injustice in the South of the 1930s in *Roll of Thunder, Hear My Cry*. And many powerful stories about the monstrosities of World War II have been published, such as Lois Lowry's *Number the Stars* and Hans Richter's *Friedrich*.

Figure 11.1 ● This illustration is by Howard Pyle for his historical novel, *Otto of the Silver Hand,* an adventure romance set in the European Middle Ages.

Source: From Scribner's, New York, 1888.

Characteristics of Historical Realism

Re-Creating the Physical Background

In the mid-nineteenth century, Alessandro Manzoni pointed out that the difference between a historian and a historical novelist is that the historian must deal with the "bare bones of history" whereas the historical novelist's job is "to put the flesh back on the skeleton that is history" (67–68). Indeed, one reason readers turn to historical fiction is that they want to learn about life in the past—they want to be transported to another time. So the good historical novelist works for historical accuracy. At times, this means providing explanations for things with which modern readers might be unfamiliar. For instance, a writer of contemporary realism need not explain to us what a refrigerator is. But when writing about the American frontier of the mid-nineteenth century, the historical novelist might have to describe an ice house or the methods of preserving meat, such as salting or smoking. The more remote and unfamiliar the historical period, the more background the author may have to provide.

Because the readers are interested in the history—otherwise they would probably be reading contemporary fiction—the writer needs to take care to avoid anachronisms. An anachronism is anything that is out of place in a time period. For example, a character in a novel about the 1950s would not be using a cell phone, an ancient Roman would not be wearing eyeglasses, a medieval monk would not own a watch, and penicillin would not be used on a Civil War battlefield. An anachronism might work in a fantasy or a comic tale, but in serious historical realism, it suggests sloppiness and careless research, and it destroys the illusion that we are reading about another time period.

Re-Creating the Social Background

The science and technology should be accurate in good historical realism, but so too should the social attitudes. A story about the Middle Ages, such as Karen Cushman's *Midwife's Apprentice* or Marguerite de Angeli's *Door in the Wall,* would have to introduce the Catholic Church as the predominant social force of the time. The church played a role in virtually every aspect of society. Not mentioning religion at least in passing would misrepresent the period.

One danger that writers occasionally fall prey to is giving historical figures modern-day attitudes, for anachronisms can extend to behavior and ideas. An example is found in Avi's *True Confessions of Charlotte Doyle,* a Newbery Honor book. It is the story of a 13-year-old girl sailing to America in 1832. On the voyage, she outmaneuvers the ship's wicked captain and ultimately replaces him at the helm. Anne Scott MacLeod, although admitting the story is a "fine vicarious adventure story," calls it also "preposterous." MacLeod goes on to note that many recent historical novels are guilty of evading "the common realities of the societies they write about" (see MacLeod 29–31). This example reminds us that realistic fiction cannot seem to be too far-fetched. (We don't like fiction to be stranger than truth.)

Unobtrusive History

Historical fiction is not history, but it is literature. Readers want, first and foremost, a good story. Writers of historical fiction walk a fine line, for they have to provide enough historical background to prevent the reader from getting lost or being confused, but not so much as to impede or obscure the narrative flow of the story. So historical details are usually introduced in small, innocuous doses. In just a few words, Marguerite de Angeli sets the stage for her novel of medieval England, *The Door in the Wall:* "Robin drew the coverlet close about his head and turned his face to the wall. He covered his ears and shut his eyes, for the sound of the bells was deafening. All the bells of London were ringing the hour of

Nones" (7). The author's vocabulary—"coverlet" and "Nones"—evoke the Middle Ages, and yet we can reasonably guess at the meanings. A coverlet is a blanket or spread, and Nones refers to a time of day (it's actually three in the afternoon). The bell ringing, a daily occurrence in medieval times, may now seem romantic to us, but this passage suggests that it is commonplace—and even something of an annoyance. De Angeli gives us the historical flavor of the period without sounding like a history lesson. We don't, for example, need a theological discussion of the mass or a chronological listing of the popes.

Karen Hesse's Newbery winner *Out of the Dust* is the poetic journal of a young girl struggling in the Oklahoma Dust Bowl during the worst of the Depression in the mid-1930s. Through this device we learn a great deal about the relentless sandstorms and what the people had to endure—wetting sheets and blankets to place over windows and doors to absorb the blowing sand or stringing up ropes so people could find their way from house to barn in the blinding storms. And the vacillation between courage and desperation so characteristic of impoverished, struggling people is movingly portrayed. All is told in a child's simple, straightforward manner, engaging and moving. Like de Angeli, Hesse gives us enough information that we understand the plight, but not so much that we feel as if we were in a classroom.

Credible Dialogue

Part of the flavor of a period is the language the people speak. We know that nineteenth-century Americans did not speak the same way that Americans of today speak (indeed, teenagers of the 1950s did not speak like the teenagers of today). The following brief passage from Irene Hunt's Civil War story, *Across Five Aprils,* clearly shows how certain language is acceptable and even appropriate in historical fiction that would be out of place in a contemporary story:

> The young man got to his feet grinning. "Sure, Red, glad to oblige. Hear you been blowin' off at the mouth at some of the cracker-barrel heroes agin."
> Milton shrugged. "Word gets around fast."
> "Ben Harris was in fer a minute." The young man shook his head. "You jest ain't goin' to be happy till you git dressed up in tar and feathers, are you, Red?" (78)

The passage refers, of course, to an actual nineteenth-century practice of covering victims with tar and feathers—a not-too-subtle means of public chastisement. Employing words rarely used today (such as "oblige" and "cracker-barrel" heroes) as well as clipped and carelessly pronounced words lends an aura of realism to the scene and the characters.

Sensitivity and Objectivity

A historical novel for children is not the place for political propaganda or polemics. Instead, it is where balance, objectivity, and sensitivity should come into play. The day is past when we can excuse insensitive depictions of idealized cowboys pitted against savage, dehumanized Indians. No picture of the Old West is complete without showing us that some cowboys were frequently cruel and heartless and that Indians were frequently kind and noble. Portrayals of dastardly villains twisting their handlebar mustaches and innocent maidens all sweetness and light may make for acceptable melodrama, but they have no place in serious historical fiction. Good historical fiction is not painted with broad brushstrokes in black and white, but delicately in many shades of gray. The capable writer of historical fiction recognizes the realities of history and attempts an honest, balanced and intelligent viewpoint.

One notable example is Bette Greene's *Summer of My German Soldier,* set in Arkansas during World War II. It is the story of an unlikely friendship between Patty, a 12-year-old Jewish girl, and Anton, a 22-year-old escaped German POW. The subjects of prejudice and racism on several levels—Germans, African Americans, Jews—are treated with great sensitivity, but realistically. Nor does Greene sugarcoat or romanticize her story—Anton is shot and killed and Patty ends up in a reformatory.

Lois Lowry's *Number the Stars* presents another horrifying perspective of World War II. This is the story of Danish Christians rescuing Danish Jews from deportation and almost certain death in Nazi concentration camps. The inhumanity of the Nazi regime is indisputable—it cannot be sugarcoated. Neither should it be ignored. The responsible writer of historical fiction bears a moral obligation when writing about the past—the obligation to be honest and forthright. History is often not pretty. Things do not always end as we would like. Still, Lowry's tale of the heroic and selfless Danes, filled with sadness as it is, reminds us that, in adversity, the human spirit often rises to noble heights.

These works all represent historical fiction at its best—gripping stories, windows into a past time, profound and thought-provoking themes. Many teachers of history and social studies have discovered that a good work of historical fiction can be a great companion to a history text, for it can gives us a more intimate view of the past and make it come alive.

The History of Contemporary Realism

Nineteenth-Century Origins

Contemporary realism for children dates to the nineteenth century with works such as Charlotte Yonge's *The Daisy Chain* (1856), a long and occasionally rambling story of a large English family and their struggle to go on after the death of their mother. Louisa May Alcott's popular *Little Women* (1868) is an American family story about four sisters in New England in the 1860s. Other types of realistic fiction popular in the nineteenth century were school stories (usually set in boys' boarding schools) and adventure and survival stories (again, usually with male protagonists), all of which have survived into the present day in one form or another.

The granddaddy of school stories is Thomas Hughes's *Tom Brown's School-Days* (1857), which is set at Rugby School in England. The school story setting provides a venue for many youthful characters from many backgrounds to be together. And, of course, in boarding schools, the youth are not under the thumbs of their parents, giving them more personal freedom. (Family stories being the exception, most novels for young readers are compelled to push parents or other adults to the sidelines so that the youthful protagonists remain unfettered to pursue their adventures. Sending the children off to boarding school is one way to eliminate interfering parents.)

Another popular type that was aimed at boys was the adventure story. Robert Louis Stevenson's *Treasure Island* (1883) is an example of a story set in the past, but one not typically treated as historical fiction, for it contains few actual historical references (unlike his *Black Arrow* or *Kidnapped*). Adventures on the high seas, one-legged seamen (complete with parrots on their shoulders), buried treasure chests, and treasure maps (with "X" marking the spot)—all can be traced to this book. It is also notable for its lack of sentimentality and its portrayal of Long John Silver, perhaps the archetypal anti-hero, morally ambiguous and vastly intriguing. An anti-hero is a character who, despite being the ostensible villain, is attractive to us anyway—for guts, determination, cleverness, or other qualities. Often, an anti-hero is the most interesting character in the story.

In America, the most famous examples of adventure stories are Mark Twain's *The Adventures of Tom Sawyer* (1876) and *The Adventures of Huckleberry Finn* (1884). They contain intrigue, mayhem, and even murder—but they are so much more, for they are among the most insightful critiques on nineteenth-century American society ever written. And the character of Huck is one of the most memorable in literature. Of course, we have to notice that once again parental figures have been effectively eliminated—Tom is an orphan and Huck has been abandoned by his ne'er-do-well father.

A great many nineteenth-century American youths were also drawn to the so-called rags-to-riches story, exemplified by the books of Horatio Alger Jr. *Ragged Dick,* Alger's first book, appeared in 1868, and it established the formula for most of his books—a youth works long and hard to escape poverty. However, he is actually rescued by a wealthy benefactor who has been impressed by a brave act the boy performed. As you can see, the lesson is ambiguous, for apparently to be saved from dire poverty requires the help of a person of means. On the other hand, Alger's heroes never become wealthy themselves—just comfortable and self-reliant. Alger was one of the most widely read American writers of the nineteenth century. (My great-grandmother, born in 1872, was quite insistent that I read her copies of the Alger books when I was a youth. She thought they would do me good.)

A final type of realistic literature that grew popular in the nineteenth century was the survival story. Daniel Defoe's *Robinson Crusoe* (1719), although not intended for children, was the first great example of the survival story, in which the protagonist finds him- or herself stranded, away from society (and parents) and at the mercy of the elements. The Swiss writer Johann David Wyss in *The Swiss Family Robinson* (1812) introduced morality and sentimentality into the survival story—and kept the family intact, which is not very common in a survival story. Then, in 1857, R. M. Ballantyne's *The Coral Island* appeared—a story of three young boys stranded on a remote Pacific island who survive through perseverance and ingenuity. *The Coral Island* is the true progenitor of the modern survival story, which remains one of the most popular types of fiction for readers in the upper elementary grades.

Twentieth- and Twenty-First-Century Realism

Perhaps the most influential trend in realistic children's fiction in the twentieth century was the move away from sentimentalism (see the discussion in Chapter 3) toward honest, sometimes harsh, realism. Beginning in the 1960s the so-called New Realism surfaced, which introduced raw emotions, franker language, and bolder ideas to literature for children, and opened an entirely new range of subjects (leaving little that was taboo). Stories began to appear that addressed a wide variety of issues formerly avoided in children's literature: racial prejudice (works by Mildred Taylor and Virginia Hamilton), teenage gangs (S. E. Hinton's *The Outsiders* and Walter Dean Myers's *Scorpions*), drug abuse (Alice Childress's *A Hero Ain't Nothin' But a Sandwich*), homosexuality (M. E. Kerr's *"Hello," I Lied*), child abuse (Mirjam Pressler's *Halinka*), mental illness (James Bennett's *I Can Hear the Mourning Dove*), sexual abuse (Cynthia Voigt's *When She Hollers*), and many others.

An inevitable result of New Realism was a phenomenon known as the problem novel, which focuses on a single, "hot" issue that affects the protagonist. The problem novel is always set in contemporary times and aims at a naturalistic portrayal of an issue plaguing young teens—ranging from sexuality to drug abuse to parental problems to psychological disorders—the list is endless. Problem novels are directed at older readers and focus on the individual's emotional response to life's experience. Judy Blume's name has long been associated with the problem novel. Her *Forever* was one of the first books for young readers to deal frankly with sex (which also got it banned in many places), and her *Blubber* describes the cruelty inflicted by children on an overweight girl.

Too often problem novels contain predictable plots, shallow characters, and trite dialogue. Sometimes they are sensationalized and devolve into melodrama—they are the soap operas of young adult literature. At times they imply that teenage problems have simplistic solutions. Of course, their predictability and easy answers make them very popular with young readers, as evidenced by the success of the "Sweet Valley High" series and the "Babysitters Club" series. But at their best, problem novels explore significant psychological and sociological issues with sensitivity, and they give us vivid, complex characters. Judy Blume's *Tiger Eyes,* for young adult readers, is a good example.

Topics in Contemporary Realism

What follows is a brief discussion of some of the most popular topics we find in today's contemporary realism. As you might expect, many novels fit into more than one of these categories. And you may come up with others that are not here.

Family Life (and Problems)

Certainly this subject is among the oldest in realistic fiction, going back, as we have seen, to Louisa May Alcott (see Figure 11.2) and Charlotte Yonge. The protagonists face the complexities of coping with people in their daily lives, which for young people usually means family and friends. As we have seen, the earlier forms of these stories tended to be sentimentalized, touting the virtues of family relationships.

Figure 11.2 ● J. S. Eland's sentimental illustration for an early edition of Louisa May Alcott's popular domestic story, *Little Women,* depicts Amy playing dress-up, a typical pastime for middle-class, nineteenth-century girls.

Source: From George Routledge and Sons, London, n.d.

However, the great Russian novelist Leo Tolstoy was probably right: "All happy families are alike; each unhappy family is unhappy in its own way" (*Anna Karenina*). This, of course, is why it is more interesting to write about the unhappy ones. The current trend in family stories for children, unsurprisingly, is to focus on fractured, blended, and dysfunctional families, or families in crisis. Few children today grow up in homes in the suburbs with two parents, a sibling, and a dog. Single-parent homes are commonplace, and the vast majority of women now work outside the home. Modern children's books are at last coming to reflect this reality.

Beverly Cleary, famous for her humorous stories of Ramona Quimby and Henry Huggins, herself became part of this change in 1983 with the Newbery Medal–winning *Dear Mr. Henshaw,* written as a series of letters and journal entries by a young boy coming to terms with his parents' divorce. But some families are in even more dire straits. Bill and Vera Cleaver's *Where the Lilies Bloom,* portrays a family of orphaned siblings trying to make it on their own in their impoverished Appalachian home. And Cynthia Voigt's *Homecoming* and its sequels trace the difficulties faced by four siblings, abandoned by their emotionally unstable mother, making their way across several states in search of their grandmother whom they have never met—and who proves to be a hardened and difficult woman. In still a different vein is Patricia MacLachlan's *Baby,* the story of family, recently bereaved from the death of an infant, who find, on their doorstep, an abandoned baby. This poetic tale is one of healing and redemption.

If the message of the modern family story remains positive, it does suggest that the family is a diverse organism, intricately complicated, and ultimately worth fighting for.

Friends

This is a rather open category—very few books for young readers do not involve the forming of friendships. Indeed, as children grow older, friendships often become as important, and in many cases, more important, than family ties. Susan Patron's *The Higher Power of Lucky,* which won the 2007 Newbery Medal, bridges the narrow gap between stories of family and friends. It actually treats the disintegration of one family— Lucky's mother is dead and her father has deserted her—and the creation of a new family that includes, of all people, her father's second wife (now divorced). Stories about friendships include the subjects of making new friends, keeping old ones, disagreements among friends, and discovering unusual or unlikely friends. In many modern novels, it is with the support of good friends that young people cope with difficult home lives. An early example is Frances Hodgson Burnett's much-loved *The Secret Garden,* which describes the forming of a friendship between two children, one orphaned and one neglected. Lucy Maud Montgomery's equally popular *Anne of Green Gables* shows an orphan adapting to an unconventional family (an elderly brother and sister) and forming friendships in a new environment. In Eleanor Estes's *The Hundred Dresses,* a girl from an impoverished family and immigrant background is subjected to cruel taunts for being different, but is eventually embraced in friendship. One of the most popular modern children's stories on the subject of making new and unlikely friends is Kate DiCamillo's *Because of Winn-Dixie,* about a girl being raised by her father and adjusting to a new home in Florida, where she makes friends with an assortment of quirky characters and a dog.

But friendships have their rocky spots, and books dealing with friendship usually reveal the relationship being put to the test and emerging stronger. Louise Fitzhugh's *Harriet the Spy* is a good example. It is the story of a fiercely independent only child who has to learn the value of friendship the hard way—after she has done her best to drive all her friends away. Another popular trend in recent years is the novel about unusual friendships. E. L. Konigsburg's *The View from Saturday* describes a motley crew of youthful intellectuals who come from a wide variety of religious and ethnic backgrounds (and supported, incidentally, by a wheelchair-bound teacher). In all these stories, the message is that friendships do not just happen, they are forged with considerable effort and sacrifice—and that they come with inestimable rewards.

Outsiders

Stories in this category deal with individuals who must struggle to become part of society, and who are, for one reason or another, regarded as outside the mainstream. Mark Twain's irrepressible hero, Huckleberry Finn, is perhaps the original outsider—scorned by society and with only one true friend, Jim, he faces a difficult world with tenacity and bravery, and ultimately achieves acceptance (although by that time he is not sure he wants it—see Chapter 3).

Perhaps the quintessential twentieth-century outsider book is *The Outsiders,* a teenage gang story written by S. E. Hinton when she was still a teenager. It would be easy to argue that most fictional stories today are, to one degree or another, about "outsiders," including books such as Fitzhugh's *Harriet the Spy,* Burnett's *The Secret Garden,* DiCamillo's *Because of Winn-Dixie,* and many others. That they are outsiders is what makes the characters compelling. What has developed in recent years is an increased interest in those "outsiders" that have long been neglected in children's literature—people kept outside because they are troubled emotionally, disadvantaged physically, or challenged mentally. Katherine Paterson, in *The Great Gilly Hopkins,* portrays a troubled child placed in a foster home. *The Language of Goldfish* by Zibby Oneal describes a young girl plagued with mental illness and suicidal tendencies. *The Pigman* by Paul Zindel is about a developing relationship between two teenagers and an elderly man. Robert Cormier is probably the most famous writer of books about the darker side of life. In *The Chocolate War* he examines the questionable motives of the human heart and its penchant for corruption. In *I Am the Cheese,* he tells the chilling tale of a family in the witness protection program that ends in tragedy, with the young protagonist telling his story from a mental institution. A still later novel, *Tenderness,* is the portrait of a serial killer.

Sexuality

Once virtually ignored in children's books—indeed, many adults tried to pretend that it did not exist—sexuality in all its manifestations is now an important subject in children's and adolescent literature. Judy Blume was among the first popular writers to deal with this subject directly in books such as *Are You There, God? It's Me, Margaret*—about a young girl coping with the onset of menses. Frankly, one of the reasons for novels about sexuality is to provide children with necessary information that might help them through the very difficult period of puberty.

Today, few subjects for children at puberty are so delicate as homosexuality. Not only ignored—but taboo—in children's literature until the 1980s, sexual preference is now being recognized by many writers as an important social issue about which children need sensitive education. Pioneering works in this field include John Donovan's *I'll Get There. It Better Be Worth the Trip* and *The Man Without a Face* by Isabelle Holland. Other treatments of the subject include Marion Dane Bauer's *Am I Blue?: Coming Out from the Silence* (a selection of short stories on gay and lesbian themes by various writers) and M. E. Kerr's *Deliver Us from Evie* (about a teenage lesbian).

One more controversial subject we can add to this list is sexual abuse, movingly dealt with in books such as Laurie Halse Anderson's *Speak*. The trick with books on sexuality for young people is that they be honest and forthright and still avoid the lascivious. Without responsible writers creating sensitive and intelligent stories, many young people would learn about sexuality from ill-informed friends and neighbors—or worse. As with most topics, knowledge always trumps ignorance.

Mortality

This subject was broached briefly in Chapter 5, where it was suggested that children are quite capable of facing the subject of death with honesty and sensitivity. Certainly, this is not a new subject in children's literature—in fact, it is one of the oldest. In eighteenth-century children's books characters were always dying, the virtuous winging their way to heaven, the wicked consigned to the fires of hell. In the nineteenth century, the fire and brimstone were omitted and death became an object of sentimentalism (again, see Chapter 3). Perhaps earlier generations were better equipped emotionally to handle death than we are today—not because they had any answers, but because they simply were not afraid to face death as a fact of life. They were surrounded by death; they lived with it. Today, we confine it to institutions—impersonal hospitals and nursing homes. In addition, modern science has led us to believe in miracles, and has almost lulled us into a false sense of our own invulnerability. So when death does come, it seems an anomaly—an unwelcome stranger in our society. We deny it, bargain with it, rage against it—we can't even utter its name (people no longer "die," rather they "pass"). It is the difficulty of acceptance that is the subject of most children's books on the subject. (See Chapter 2 for a brief discussion of the treatment of death in books for very young children.)

Among the many superb writers treating the subject of death in contemporary realism are Mollie Hunter (*A Sound of Chariots*), Lois Lowry (*A Summer to Die*), Katherine Paterson (*Bridge to Terabithia*), and Paul Acampora (*Defining Dulcie*). And one further development has occurred, which is the introduction of a once-unspeakable subject—teen suicide (Richard Peck's *Remembering the Good Times* and John Green's *Looking for Alaska*). Once again we see the move in children's literature toward greater realism, more frankness and honesty, and greater intensity. In a curious way, like the writers of the eighteenth century, many of today's writers are again portraying death (although often without the religious overtones) as a natural part of the great circle of life.

Survival

If modern survival stories are descended from Daniel Defoe's *Robinson Crusoe,* few of them subscribe to Defoe's optimistic portrayal of a wild tropical paradise where the hero carves out a life of luxury. Instead, modern survival stories acknowledge the hardship and isolations that face most of the protagonists, who are usually humbled before the forces of nature. They adapt their lifestyles to their surroundings. Scott O'Dell's *Island of the Blue Dolphins,* a work of historical fiction based on an actual incident from the early nineteenth century, was one of the first modern survival stories to adopt this new and far more realistic approach to survival narratives. O'Dell wished to convey the message that, in real life, survival means sacrifice, suffering, adaptation, and often loneliness. Jean Craighead George (*Julie of the Wolves* and *My Side of the Mountain*) and Harry Mazer (*Snowbound* and *The Island Keeper*) are writers of survival stories who have followed O'Dell's example, portraying heroes and heroines who learn to live in harmony with the natural world and who often come to respect nature above the civilizing forces of humanity. In other words, they become aware of the ecosystem.

Felice Holman's *Slake's Limbo* portrays the hero surviving not in some isolated wilderness, but in the grim world of the New York City subway system. In a time when technology and impersonal bureaucracy threaten our identity and, it seems, even the nature of society and civilization as we know it, we may well feel that growing up in a city slum is as much a challenge as being abandoned on a desert island or in the reaches of the frozen Arctic. A key element in any survival story is its detailing of the means of survival—we see the protagonist gathering food, finding shelter from the elements, securing protection from threatening forces, and learning how to spend time alone. Survival stories depict the individual overcoming adversity and, in the process, achieving self-awareness, the recognition of one's strengths and shortcomings, an understanding of one's innermost character.

Mysteries and Puzzlers

Mysteries and puzzlers are often escapist fiction, creating a world somehow more exciting, more dangerous, and more interesting than we imagine our own to be. The mystery, first popularized in the early nineteenth century by Edgar Allan Poe and later refined by Arthur

Conan Doyle, the creator of Sherlock Holmes, has long been a favorite of young readers. Such serial detectives as Nancy Drew, the Hardy Boys, the Bobbsey Twins, and Donald Sobol's Encyclopedia Brown have been enormously popular over the years. The mystery always involves the solving of a puzzle—often a crime. The success of a mystery depends on the clever planting of clues and the ingenuity of the puzzle and its solution. The puzzle must not be too easily solved or the reader will lose interest. And the solution to the mystery must seem logical once all the pieces are put together or the reader will feel deceived. The mystery writer must keep a delicate balance, knowing just how much to reveal and when.

Among the fine mysteries for young readers is E. L. Konigsburg's *From the Mixed-Up Files of Mrs. Basil E. Frankweiler,* which recounts the exploits of young brother and sister detectives as they follow clues to the unraveling of a mystery, largely set in the Metropolitan Museum of Art. Likewise, Ellen Raskin's *The Westing Game* depicts a young detective searching out the word clues of a cleverly devised puzzle, containing numerous surprising twists.

Sports

Very popular among an important group of readers is the sports story, which actually has its origin in the boys' magazines of the nineteenth century. As full-blown books, however, they are a twentieth-century phenomenon.

One of the most popular of the early sports writers was Clair Bee—himself a noted athlete who lettered in three high school sports and went on to become a celebrated basketball coach and an inductee into the Basketball Hall of Fame. Bee's books, beginning with *Touchdown Pass* in 1948, are all about a high school athlete, Chip Hilton (who also letters in three sports). The stories promote high moral character and good sportsmanship. The series, updated for the modern reader, is still being reprinted today.

Sports tales are usually coming-of-age stories, particularly when the protagonist gains self-knowledge through participation in sports, as in the works of Matt Christopher (*The Fox Steals Home* and others). Most sports stories hinge on the excitement of the game, the necessity for teamwork and fair sportsmanship, and the interpersonal problems that develop between the players. The stories are popular because of their subject matter, although too often the plots are predictable, the characters are stereotyped, and the dialogue is trite—faults that do not deter eager fans. But in the hands of a talented writer such as Chris Crutcher (*Athletic Shorts* and others), the sports story can be a compelling study of human nature—the importance of sportsmanship and fair play, the striving for individual excellence, the challenge of meeting goals.

Animals

Animal stories in realistic fiction usually describe relationships between humans and animals, although we can find a few in which the animals themselves become the central figures. Realistic animal stories first appeared in the late nineteenth and early twentieth centuries, and they were most popular in North America. The Canadians Ernest Thompson

Seton (*Wild Animals I Have Known*) and Charles G. D. Roberts (*Red Fox*) wrote stories depicting animals realistically, but giving them personalities. Jack London's popular *White Fang* and *Call of the Wild* soon followed. The animals in these stories live as animals, behave as animals, and, of course, do not talk (although some readers may argue that the animals are given human emotions). A modern example of this type is Sheila Burnford's *The Incredible Journey*, in which a cat and two dogs undertake a hazardous trip across the Canadian wilderness. Some readers feel that Burnford oversteps the limits of credulity, with the animals assuming too much of human nature to be totally believable animals.

More common are those stories about humans who have developed attachments to animals—ranging from pets to wild animals. Some of the best known include *The Yearling* (the story about a fawn) by Marjorie Kinnan Rawlings, Mary O'Hara's *My Friend Flicka* (a horse), Eric Knight's *Lassie Come Home* (a heroic collie), and Marguerite Henry's *Misty of Chincoteague* (about the famous wild horses of Assateague and Chincoteague islands off the coast of Virginia). One of the most loved of all is Wilson Rawls's *Where the Red Fern Grows*, about two hunting dogs and their boy master. Unfortunately, animal stories have the reputation for being tearjerkers and lapsing into sentimentality. However, one serious theme recurring in many animal stories is that of animals falling prey to the savage insensitivity of human beings, as in Phyllis Reynolds Naylor's Newbery Award–winning *Shiloh*. A type of animal story we may see more of in the future is that dealing with environmental protection, as in Carl Hiaasen's *Hoot*, the story of two boys in Florida on a mission to save some endangered burrowing owls whose habitat is being threatened by a construction project.

These categories serve only as guidelines and we need to remember that the best books are probably the most difficult to pigeonhole. So, for instance, Hiassen's *Hoot* contains numerous themes, including the importance of making new friends, the difficulty of adapting to a new environment, the need to protect the environment, and the value of learning to stand up for oneself and for important principles. Also, we should note that realistic stories could be categorized according to their tones—from the broadly comic (Cleary's *Ramona the Pest*) to the sentimental (Montgomery's *Anne of Green Gables*) to the ironic (Fitzhugh's *Harriet the Spy*) to the serious and perhaps cynical (Cormier's *The Chocolate War*). The point is that contemporary realism is a rich field containing something for everyone—and it is perhaps the most popular type of reading among young people from the middle years and up.

Summary

Realistic fiction can be divided into two broad categories: historical and contemporary. Historical realism is a story written about a time in the author's past and contains actual historical references. Contemporary realism is set in the time it was written. We read realism—whether historical or contemporary—because we are interested in the lives of the characters: their loves, fears, likes, dislikes, struggles, and triumphs. Good historical realism not only entertains us with interesting and believable characters but it also broadens our horizons, taking us to times and places we have never been. Good historical realism can help us learn from the past. The philosopher George Santayana said, "Those who cannot remember the past are condemned to repeat it." This is why it is important for us to read about the ugliness of American slavery (Paula Fox's *The Slave Dancer*), the brutal treatment by the white Americans of the American Indians (Scott O'Dell's *Sing Down the Moon*), the racial bigotry in twentieth-century America (Mildred Taylor's *Roll of Thunder, Hear My Cry*), and the ghastly crimes of the Holocaust (Hans Richter's *Friedrich*). We read about them because covering up past sins will not erase them, and ignorance of the past only leaves us unprepared for the future.

But good historical fiction does much more than uncover the horrors of the past—it shows us its glory as well. Sometimes this shines in unexpected places, as revealed in Lowry's *Number the Stars* and its description of a heroic people in their struggle against bigotry and hatred. Our past, littered with violence and iniquity and the ridiculous, is also strewn with bright examples of honor and hope and the sublime.

On the other hand, a good work of contemporary realism—whether it comes from the nineteenth century or from last month—shows us human beings coping with the issues that have always confronted humanity. The broad subjects of family life, friendship, growing up, and socialization are familiar experiences to young people, and many people enjoy reading stories about others in the same fix as they themselves are. Whether they are school stories, teenage love stories, survival stories, mysteries, or sports stories, novels of contemporary realism deal with very similar messages—the importance of human connections, of assuming personal responsibility, of perseverance, of holding onto hope, and of realizing individual potential. Reading a good realistic novel is an excellent way to overcome our narrow prejudices, to get to know people different from us, and to under-stand human motivation and desire. Ironically, we invariably learn that people, wherever they are, whatever their history or heritage, are very much like us after all.

For Reflection and Discussion

1. Choose two works of historical fiction for children that deal with the same time period or same historical issue—for example, many historical novels have been written on various aspects of the Holocaust. Read and compare the novels on the basis of their specific subject matter, themes, style, character development, and so on. What are the fundamental differences? Does one seem more effective than the other? Why?

2. Choose one work of historical fiction on a time period or subject that interests you. Read the novel and then do some research into the actual history. For example, you

might look at a novel dealing with Native Americans, such as Scott O'Dell's *Walk Two Moons,* and then read something about the actual "Long Walk." Determine if the novelist has faithfully portrayed the spirit of the time. Be prepared to explain why or why not.

3. Choose a novel of contemporary realism and, as you read, keep an informal journal. Read a chapter or two at a time and then spend a few minutes writing down your thoughts, observations, or predictions—whatever comes to mind. Continue this process throughout the reading of the book. When you are finished, reread your journal entries and assess them. Were your predictions and assessments of the characters accurate? Did the author pull any surprises? If so, did this help the story?

4. Choose one of the so-called problem novels—books for middle and high school readers that focus on one particular problem of growing up (physical, social, psychological, and so on), and read it with attention to how the problem is portrayed and what resolution finally occurs. How would you assess the book on its depiction of the problem and the credibility of the resolution? (Is it oversimplified? Inaccurate? Didactic or preachy?)

● Works Cited

de Angeli, Marguerite. *The Door in the Wall.* New York: Doubleday, 1949.

Hunt, Irene. *Across Five Aprils.* New York: Follett, 1964.

MacLeod, Anne Scott. "Writing Backward: Modern Models in Historical Fiction." *The Horn Book Magazine* (January/February 1998): 26–33.

Manzoni, Alessandro. *On the Historical Novel.* 1850. Trans. Sandra Bermann. Lincoln: University of Nebraska, 1984.

Nodelman, Perry. "How Typical Children Read Typical Books." *Children's Literature in Education* 12 (Winter 1981): 177–185.

Repplier, Agnes. "Little Pharisees in Fiction." *Scribner's Magazine* (December 1896).

Twain, Mark (pseudonym for Samuel Langhorne Clemens). *The Adventures of Huckleberry Finn.* New York: Bantam, 1981.

● Recommended Readings

Alston, Anne. *The Family in English Children's Literature.* New York: Routledge, 2008.

Connelly, Mark. *The Hardy Boys Mysteries, 1927–1979: A Cultural and Literary History.* Jefferson, NC: McFarland, 2008.

Cornelius, Michael G., and Melanie E. Gregg, eds. *Nancy Drew and Her Sister Sleuths: Essays on the Fiction of Girl Detectives.* Jefferson, NC: McFarland, 2008.

Crowe, Chris. *More Than a Game, Sports Literature for Young Adults.* Lanham, MD: Scarecrow, 2003.

Gavin, Adrienne, and Christopher Routledge, eds. *Mystery in Children's Literature: From the Rational to the Supernatural.* New York: Palgrave Macmillan, 2001.

Gillespie, John T. *Historical Fiction for Young Readers (Grades 4–8): An Introduction.* Santa Barbara, CA: Libraries Unlimited, 2008.

Hinton, S. E. "Teenagers Are for Real." *New York Times Book Review* 27 (August 1967): 26–29.

Nixon, Joan Lowry. "Clues to the Juvenile Mystery." *The Writer* 90 (February 1977): 23–26.

Paterson, Katherine. *Gates of Excellence: On Reading and Writing Books for Children.* New York: Elsevier/Nelson, 1981.

Rees, David. *The Marble in the Water.* Boston: The Horn Book, 1980.

——. *Painted Desert, Green Shade: Essays on Contemporary Writers for Children and Young Adults.* Boston: The Horn Book, 1984.

Thiel, Elizabeth. *The Fantasy of Family: Nineteenth-Century Children's Literature and the Myth of the Domestic Ideal.* New York: Routledge, 2007.

Wilkin, Binnie Tate. *Survival Themes in Fiction for Children and Young People.* New York: Scarecrow, 1978.

Selected Bibliography of Historical Realism

The following list offers a sampling of the many novels of historical realism available for young readers. Most of these works are accessible to readers from about fourth or fifth grade and above. The books have been categorized according to the historical time period in which they are set.

Ancient, Medieval, and Renaissance European History

Avi. *Crispin: The Cross of Lead.* New York: Hyperion, 2002. (Medieval England)

Brennan, J. H. *Shiva: An Adventure of the Ice Age.* New York: Lippincott, 1989.

Cheaney, J. B. *The True Prince.* New York: Knopf, 2002. (Renaissance England)

Curry, Jane Louise. *The Black Canary.* New York: Margaret K. McElderry, 2005. (Elizabethan England)

Cushman, Karen. *Catherine, Called Birdy.* New York: Clarion, 1994. (Medieval England)

——. *Matilda Bone.* New York: Random House, 2000. (Medieval England)

de Angeli, Marguerite. *The Door in the Wall.* New York: Doubleday, 1949. (Medieval England)

Dines, Carol. *The Queen's Soprano.* New York: Harcourt, 2006. (Renaissance Italy)

Ellis, Deborah. *A Company of Fools.* Markham, Ontario: Fitzhenry and Whiteside, 2002. (Medieval England)

Gray, Elizabeth Janet. *Adam of the Road.* New York: Viking, 1942. (Medieval England)

Haugaard, Erik Christian. *Leif the Unlucky.* Boston: Houghton Mifflin, 1982. (Medieval Norse)

Hawes, Louise. *The Vanishing Point.* Boston: Houghton Mifflin, 2004. (Renaissance Italy)

Hunter, Mollie. *The Spanish Letters.* New York: Funk, 1967. (Renaissance England)

——. *The Stronghold.* New York: Harper, 1974. (The Bronze Age)

Kelly, Eric P. *The Trumpeter of Krakow.* New York: Macmillan, 1928. (Medieval Poland)

Leeds, Constance. *The Silver Cup.* New York: Viking, 2007. (Middle Ages)

McGraw, Eloise Jarvis. *Mara, Daughter of the Nile.* New York: Coward, 1961. (Ancient Egypt)

Oliver, Jane. *Faraway Princess.* New York: St. Martin's, 1962. (Medieval Britain)

Pilar, Molina Llorente. *The Apprentice.* New York: Farrar, Straus & Giroux, 1993. (Renaissance Florence)

Pyle, Howard. *Men of Iron.* (1890). Various modern editions. (Medieval England)

——. *Otto of the Silver Hand.* (1888) Various modern editions. (Medieval Germany)

Speare, Elizabeth George. *The Bronze Bow.* Boston: Houghton Mifflin, 1961. (Ancient Rome)

Stolz, Mary. *Zekmet the Stone Carver: A Tale of Ancient Egypt*. Illus. by Deborah Nourse Lattimore. New York: Harcourt, 1988.

Sutcliff, Rosemary. *The Eagle of the Ninth*. New York: Walck, 1954. (Roman Britain)

———. *The Mark of the Horse Lord*. New York: Walck, 1965. (Roman Britain)

Tarr, Judith. *His Majesty's Elephant*. New York: Harcourt, 1993. (Early Medieval France)

Tingle, Rebecca. *Far Traveler*. New York: Putnam, 2005. (Eleventh-century England)

Treace, Geoffrey. *The Red Towers of Granada*. New York: Vanguard, 1967. (Medieval Spain)

Treece, Henry. *The Centurion*. Illus. Mary Russon. New York: Meredith, 1967. (Ancient Rome)

Vining, Elizabeth Gray. *Adam of the Road*. New York: Viking, 1942. (Medieval England)

Walsh, Jill Paton. *The Emperor's Winding Sheet*. New York: Farrar, Straus & Giroux, 1974. (Medieval Constantinople)

Wein, Elizabeth E. *A Coalition of Lions*. New York: Viking, 2003. (Very early Britain)

Yolen, Jane, and Robert J. Harris. *Girl in a Cage*. New York: Philomel, 2002. (Medieval Scotland)

Modern European History Since the Renaissance

Anderson, Rachel. *Black Water*. New York: Holt, 1995. (Victorian England)

Avery, Gillian. *Maria Escapes*. New York: Simon, 1992. (Originally published in 1957 in England as *The Warden's Niece*) (Victorian England)

Avi. *The True Confessions of Charlotte Doyle*. New York: Orchard, 1990. (Nineteenth-century high seas)

Burton, Hester. *Time of Trial*. Cleveland: World, 1964. (Eighteenth-century England)

Dumas, Alexandre. *The Three Musketeers*. 1844. Several modern editions. (Seventeenth-century France)

Durbin, William. *The Darkest Evening*. New York: Orchard, 2004. (1930s Russia)

Garfield, John. *Smith*. New York: Pantheon, 1967. (Eighteenth-century England)

———. *The Sound of Coaches*. New York: Viking, 1974. (Eighteenth-century England)

Hesse, Karen. *Letters from Rifka*. New York: Holt, 1992. (Russian immigrants to U.S., early twentieth century)

Holman, Felice. *The Wild Children*. New York: Scribner's, 1983. (Russian revolution)

Holub, Josef. *An Innocent Soldier*. Trans. Michael Hoffmann. New York: Scholastic, 2005. (Napoleonic Wars)

Hughes, Dean. *Soldier Boys*. New York: Atheneum, 2001. (World War II)

Kerr, Judith. *When Hitler Stole Pink Rabbit*. New York: Coward, 1972. (World War II)

Lasky, Kathryn. *Broken Song*. New York: Viking, 2005. (Nineteenth- to early twentieth-century Russia)

Lowry, Lois. *Number the Stars*. Boston: Houghton Mifflin, 1989. (World War II)

McCaughrean, Geraldine. *The Pirate's Son*. New York: Scholastic, 1998. (Eighteenth-century England)

Minard, Rosemary. *Long Meg*. New York: Pantheon, 1982. (Sixteenth-century Holland)

Monjo, Ferdinand. *The Sea Beggar's Son*. New York: Coward, 1975. (Seventeenth-century Holland)

O'Dell, Scott. *The Hawk That Dare Not Hunt by Day*. Boston: Houghton Mifflin, 1975. (Sixteenth-century Europe)

Orczy, Baroness Emmuska. *The Scarlet Pimpernel*. 1905. Several modern editions. (French Revolution)

Orlev, Uri. *The Island on Bird Street*. Trans. Hillel Halkin. Boston: Houghton Mifflin, 1984. (World War II)

Pelgrom, Els. *The Winter When Time Was Frozen*. Trans. Maryka and Rafael Rudnik. New York: Morrow, 1980. (World War II)

Peyton, K. M. *Flambards*. Oxford: Oxford University Press, 1967. (Pre–World War I England)

Pressler, Mirjam. *Malka*. Trans. Brian Murdoch. New York: Philomel, 2003. (Holocaust)

Richter, Hans Peter. *Friedrich.* New York: Holt, 1970. (World War II)

Schmidt, Gary D. *Anson's Way.* New York: Clarion, 1999. (Eighteenth-century Ireland)

Serraillier, Ian. *The Silver Sword.* New York: Criterion, 1959. (World War II)

Stevenson, Robert Louis. *Kidnapped.* 1886. Several modern editions. (Eighteenth-century Scotland)

Suhl, Yuri. *The Merrymaker.* New York: Four Winds, 1975. (Early twentieth-century Eastern Europe)

Whelan, Gloria. *Burying the Sun.* New York: HarperCollins, 2004. (World War II Russia)

Wilson, John. *Four Steps to Death.* Toronto: Kids Can Press, 2005. (World War II Russia)

North American and Native American History

Anderson, Laurie Halse. *Fever 1793.* New York: Simon and Schuster, 2000. (Eighteenth-century America)

Armer, Laura Adams. *Waterless Mountain.* New York: McKay, 1931. (Navajo)

Avi. *The Barn.* New York: Jackson, 1994. (Nineteenth century)

———. *Encounter at Easton.* New York: Pantheon, 1980. (Eighteenth century)

Banks, Sara Harrell. *Abraham's Battle: A Novel of Gettysburg.* New York: Atheneum, 1999. (Civil War)

Bawdin, Nina. *Carrie's War.* New York: Lippincott, 1973. (World War II)

Beatty, Patricia. *Jayhawker.* New York: Morrow, 1991. (Civil War)

Blos, Joan. *A Gathering of Days.* New York: Scribner's, 1979. (Early nineteenth century)

Brink, Carol Ryrie. *Caddie Woodlawn.* 1936. Various modern editions. (Nineteenth century)

Bruchac, Joseph. *Code Talker: A Novel About the Navajo Marines of World War Two.* New York: Penguin, 2005.

Bulla, Clyde. *A Lion to Guard Us.* New York: Crowell, 1978. (Seventeenth century)

Cannon, A. E. *Charlotte's Rose.* New York: Random House, 2002. (Nineteenth-century Mormons in Utah)

Carbone, Elisa. *Blood on the River: Jamestown 1607.* New York: Viking, 2006.

Chibarro, Julie. *Redemption.* New York: Atheneum, 2004. (Sixteenth-century English settlers in America)

Collier, James Lincoln, and Christopher Collier. *My Brother Sam Is Dead.* New York: Four Winds Press, 1974. (American Revolution)

Curtis, Christopher Paul. *The Watsons Go to Birmingham—1963.* New York: Doubleday, 1996.

Donnelly, Jennifer. *A Northern Light.* San Diego, CA: Harcourt, 2003. (Early twentieth century)

Dorris, Michael. *Guests.* New York: Hyperion, 1994. (Pre-Columbian America)

———. *Morning Girl.* New York: Hyperion, 1992. (Pre-Columbian America)

Fleischman, Paul. *The Borning Room.* New York: Harper, 1991. (Nineteenth century)

Forbes, Esther. *Johnny Tremain.* Boston: Houghton Mifflin, 1946. (American Revolution)

Fox, Paula. *The Slave Dancer.* New York: Bradbury, 1973. (Early nineteenth century)

Fritz, Jean. *The Cabin Faced West.* New York: Coward, 1958. (Late eighteenth century)

Frost, Helen. *Crossing Stones.* New York: Foster/Farrar, 2009. (Early twentieth-century)

Giff, Patricia Reilly. *Lily's Crossing.* New York: Delacorte, 1997. (World War II)

Greene, Bette. *Summer of My German Soldier.* New York: Dial, 1973. (1940s anti-Semitism)

Hahn, Mary Downing. *Hear the Wind Blow: A Novel of the Civil War.* New York: Clarion, 2003.

Hearn, Julie. *The Minister's Daughter.* New York: Atheneum, 2005. (Colonial America)

Hesse, Karen. *Out of the Dust.* New York: Scholastic, 1997. (1930s Dust Bowl)

Hickman, Janet. *Susannah.* New York: Greenwillow, 1998. (Nineteenth century)

Hudson, Jan. *Sweetgrass*. New York: Philomel, 1989. (Native Canadian)

Hunt, Irene. *Across Five Aprils*. New York: Follett, 1964. (Civil War)

Hurwitz, Johanna. *Faraway Summer*. Illus. Mary Azarian. New York: Morrow, 1998. (Late nineteenth century)

Isaacs, Anne. *Treehouse Tales*. New York: Dutton, 1997. (The 1880s)

Kerr, M. E. *Slap Your Sides*. New York: HarperCollins, 2001. (World War II)

Klages, Ellen. *The Green Glass Sea*. New York: Viking, 2006. (World War II)

Lasky, Kathryn. *Beyond the Burning Time*. New York: Scholastic, 1994. (Colonial)

Leviton, Sonia. *Clem's Chances*. New York: Scholastic, 2001. (Nineteenth century)

Lyons, Mary E. *Letters from a Slave Girl: The Story of Harriet Jacobs*. New York: Scribner's, 1992. (Nineteenth century)

Myers, Walter Dean. *The Glory Field*. New York: Scholastic, 1994. (Eighteenth century to the present)

O'Dell, Scott. *Island of the Blue Dolphins*. Boston: Houghton Mifflin, 1960. (Early nineteenth-century Native American)

———. *The King's Fifth*. Boston: Houghton Mifflin, 1966. (Sixteenth-century Spanish America)

Paterson, Katherine. *Jip: His Story*. New York: Lodestar, 1996. (Nineteenth-century New England)

Peck, Richard. *Fair Weather*. New York: Dial, 2001. (Late nineteenth century)

———. *A Long Way from Chicago*. New York: Dial, 1998. (The Great Depression)

———. *A Year Down Yonder*. New York: Dial, 2000. (The Great Depression)

Pellowski, Anne. *Winding Valley Farm: Annie's Story*. New York: Philomel, 1982. (Late nineteenth century)

Perez, N. A. *The Slopes of War: A Novel of Gettysburg*. Boston: Houghton Mifflin, 1984. (Civil War)

Perkins, Lynne Rae. *Criss Cross*. New York: Greenwillow, 2005. (The 1970s)

Petry, Ann. *Tituba of Salem Village*. New York: Crowell, 1964. (Colonial)

Pinkney, Andrea Davis. *Silent Thunder: A Civil War Story*. New York: Hyperion, 1999.

Reeder, Carolyn. *Shades of Gray*. New York: Macmillan, 1989. (Civil War)

Richter, Conrad. *The Light in the Forest*. New York: Knopf, 1953. (Nineteenth century)

Rostokowski, Margaret I. *After the Dancing Days*. New York: Harper, 1986. (World War I)

Salisbury, Graham. *Under the Blood-Red Sun*. New York: Delacorte, 1994. (World War II Pacific Islands)

Sebestyen, Ouida. *Words by Heart*. Boston: Little, Brown, 1979. (Early twentieth century)

Speare, Elizabeth George. *The Sign of the Beaver*. Boston: Houghton Mifflin, 1983. (Eighteenth century)

———. *The Witch of Blackbird Pond*. Boston: Houghton Mifflin, 1958. (Colonial)

Taylor, Mildred. *Let the Circle Be Unbroken*. New York: Dial, 1981. (The 1930s racial prejudice)

———. *Roll of Thunder, Hear My Cry*. New York: Dial, 1976. (The 1930s racial prejudice)

Thor, Annika. *A Faraway Island*. Trans. Linda Schenck. New York: Delacorte, 2009. (World War II)

Watts, Leander. *Stonecutter*. Boston: Houghton Mifflin, 2002. (Early nineteenth century)

Wilder, Laura Ingalls. *Little House in the Big Woods*. New York: Harper, 1932. (First of a series about growing up in the nineteenth century, followed by *Little House on the Prairie*, 1932; *Farmer Boy*, 1933; *On the Banks of Plum Creek*, 1937; *By the Shores of Silver Lake*, 1939; *The Long Winter*, 1940; *Little Town on the Prairie*, 1941; *These Happy Golden Years*, 1943; and *The First Four Years*, 1971)

Wolf, Virginia Euwer. *Bat 6*. New York: Scholastic, 1998. (The 1940s)

Other Times and Places

Aldridge, James. *The True Story of Spit MacPhee*. New York: Viking, 1986. (1920s Australia)

Bosse, Malcolm. *The Examination*. New York: Farrar, Straus & Giroux, 1994. (Medieval China)

Choi, Sook-Nyul. *Year of Impossible Goodbyes*. Boston: Houghton Mifflin, 1991. (World War II Korea)

De Jenkins, Lyll Becerra. *The Honorable Prison*. New York: Lodestar, 1988. (South America)

DeJong, Meindert. *The House of Sixty Fathers*. New York: Harper, 1956. (China)

Dickinson, Peter. *The Dancing Bear*. Boston: Little, Brown, 1972. (Byzantium)

Disher, Gary. *The Bamboo Flute*. Boston: Houghton Mifflin, 1993. (1930s Australia)

Fleischman, Sid. *The White Elephant*. New York: Greenwillow, 2006. (Ancient Siam)

Hautzig, Esther. *The Endless Steppe: A Girl in Exile*. New York: Harper, 1968.

Ho, Minfong. *The Clay Marble*. New York: Farrar, Straus & Giroux, 1991. (Cambodia)

Holman, Felice. *Wild Children*. New York: Scribner's, 1983. (Russia)

Kaplan, Kathy Walden. *The Dog of Knots*. Grand Rapids, MI: Eerdmans, 2004. (Israel, 1970s)

Lewis, Elizabeth Foreman. *Young Fu of the Upper Yangtze*. New York: Holt, 1932. (China)

Maruki, Toshi. *Hiroshima No Pika*. New York: Lothrop, 1982. (World War II Japan)

Mead, Alice. *Dawn and Dusk*. New York: Farrar, Straus & Giroux, 2007. (Iran/Iraq, 1980s)

Namioka, Lensey. *Island of Ogres*. New York: Harper, 1989. (Japan)

———. *Village of the Vampire Cat*. New York: Delacorte, 1981. (Medieval Japan)

Napoli, Donna Jo. *Bound*. New York: Atheneum, 2004. (Medieval China)

O'Dell, Scott. *My Name Is Not Angelica*. Boston: Houghton Mifflin, 1989. (Eighteenth-century West Indies)

Park, Linda Sue. *A Single Shard*. New York: Dell, 2001. (Twelfth-century Korea)

———. *When My Name Was Keoko*. Boston: Houghton Mifflin, 2002. (World War II Korea)

Paterson, Katherine. *The Master Puppeteer*. New York: T. Crowell, 1976. (Japan)

———. *Of Nightingales That Weep*. New York: T. Crowell, 1974. (Japan)

———. *Rebels of the Heavenly Kingdom*. New York: T. Crowell, 1983. (China)

———. *The Sign of the Chrysanthemum*. New York: T. Crowell, 1973. (Japan)

Ritchie, Rita. *The Golden Hawks of Genghis Khan*. New York: Dutton, 1958.

———. *Secret Beyond the Mountains*. New York: Dutton, 1960. (China)

———. *The Year of the Horse*. New York: Dutton, 1957. (China)

Ruby, Lois. *Shanghai Shadows*. New York: Holiday House, 2006. (World War II China)

Sayres, Meghan Nuttall. *Anahita's Woven Riddle*. New York: Amulet, 2006. (Early twentieth-century Persia)

Williams, Susan. *Wind Rider*. New York: Laura Geringer/HarperCollins, 2006. (Prehistoric Asia)

Yep, Laurence. *Hiroshima*. New York: Scholastic, 1995. (World War II Japan)

———. *The Serpent's Children*. New York: Harper, 1984. (China)

Selected Bibliography of Contemporary Realism

The following lists are merely representative of the wealth of realistic fiction for young readers. The best books are not easily classified into tidy pigeonholes and the classifications are suggestive only. These lists may be supplemented by the lists at the end of Chapter 5.

Family and Friendship

Aiken, Joan. *Cold Shoulder Road*. New York: Delacorte, 1996.

Alcott, Louisa May. *Little Women*. 1868–1869. Several modern editions.

Bawden, Nina. *The Real Plato Jones*. New York: Clarion, 1993.

Blume, Judy. *Tales of a Fourth Grade Nothing*. New York: Dutton, 1972.

————. *Tiger Eyes*. Scarsdale, NY: Bradbury, 1981.

Burnett, Frances Hodgson. *The Secret Garden*. 1909. Various modern editions.

Byars, Betsy. *The Blossoms Meet the Vulture Lady*. New York: Delacorte, 1986.

————. *The Night Swimmers*. New York: Delacorte, 1980.

Cleary, Beverly. *Dear Mr. Henshaw*. New York: Morrow, 1983.

————. *Henry Huggins*. New York: Morrow, 1950.

————. *Ramona the Brave*. New York: Morrow, 1975.

————. *Ramona the Pest*. New York: Morrow, 1968.

Cleaver, Bill, and Vera Cleaver. *Where the Lilies Bloom*. Philadelphia: Lippincott, 1969.

Cole, Brock. *Celine*. New York: Farrar, Straus & Giroux, 1989.

————. *The Goats*. New York: Farrar, Straus & Giroux, 1987.

Creech, Sharon. *Walk Two Moons*. New York: Harper, 1994.

————. *Chasing Redbird*. New York: HarperCollins, 1997.

————. *Granny Torrelli Makes Soup*. New York: Harper, 2003.

————. *The Not-Just-Anybody Family*. New York: Delacorte, 1986.

————. *Wanted . . . Mud Blossom*. New York: Delacorte Press, 1991.

Dorris, Michael. *The Window*. New York: Hyperion, 1997.

Ellis, Sarah. *Out of the Blue*. New York: McElderry, 1995.

Enright, Elizabeth. *Thimble Summer*. New York: Holt, 1938.

Estes, Eleanor. *The Moffats*. New York: Harcourt, 1941.

Fine, Anne. *Alias, Madame Doubtfire*. Boston: Little, Brown, 1988.

————. *Flour Babies*. Boston: Little, 1994.

Fitzhugh, Louise. *Harriet the Spy*. New York: Harper, 1964.

Gates, Doris. *Blue Willow*. New York: Viking, 1940.

Gautier, Gail. *A Year with Butch and Spike*. New York: Putnam, 1998.

Greene, Bette. *Philip Hall Likes Me. I Reckon Maybe*. New York: Dial, 1974.

Henkes, Karen. *The Birthday Room*. New York: Greenwillow, 1999.

Hermes, Patricia. *Mama, Let's Dance*. Boston: Little, 1991.

Hickman, Janet. *Jericho*. New York: Greenwillow, 1994.

Horvath, Polly. *The Pepins and Their Problems*. New York: Farrar, 2004.

Hunt, Irene. *Up a Road Slowly*. New York: Follett, 1967.

Kerrin, Jessica Scott. *Martin Bridge, Ready for Takeoff!* Toronto: Kids Can, 2005.

————. *Martin Bridge, on the Lookout!* Toronto: Kids Can, 2006.

Klein, Norma. *Mom, the Wolfman and Me*. New York: Pantheon, 1972.

Konigsburg, E. L. *Jennifer, Hecate, Macbeth, William McKinley, and Me, Elizabeth*. New York: Atheneum, 1967.

————. *The View from Saturday*. New York: Atheneum, 1996.

L'Engle, Madeleine. *Meet the Austins*. New York: Vanguard, 1960.

Lowry, Lois. *Anastasia Krupnik*. Boston: Houghton Mifflin, 1979.

McCloskey, Robert. *Centerburg Tales*. New York: Viking, 1951.

————. *Homer Price*. New York: Viking, 1943.

————. *Lentil*. New York: Viking, 1940.

MacLachlan, Patricia. *Baby*. New York: Delacorte, 1993.

————. *Cassie Binegar*. HarperCollins, 1982.

————. *Journey*. New York: Delacorte, 1991.

————. *Sarah, Plain and Tall*. New York: Harper, 1985.

Martin, Ann M. *A Corner of the Universe*. New York: Scholastic, 2002.

Mason, Simon. *The Quigleys in a Spin*. New York: Random, 2006.

Montgomery, L. L. *Anne of Green Gables*. 1908. Several modern editions.

Myers, Walter Dean. *Street Love*. New York: HarperCollins, 2006.

Naylor, Phyllis Reynolds. *Alice in Rapture, Sort Of*. New York: Atheneum, 1989.

Parry, Rosanne. *Heart of a Shepherd*. New York: Random House, 2009.

Paterson, Katherine. *The Great Gilly Hopkins*. New York: Crowell, 1978.

Peck, Robert. *A Day No Pigs Would Die*. New York: Knopf, 1972.

Perkins, Lynne Rae. *All Alone in the Universe.* New York: Greenwillow, 1999.

Pinkwater, Daniel. *The Education of Robert Nifkin.* New York: Farrar, Straus & Giroux, 1998.

Potok, Chaim. *Zebra and Other Stories.* New York: Knopf, 1998.

Raskin, Ellen. *Figgs & Phantoms.* New York: Dutton, 1974.

Sachar, Louis. *Holes.* New York: Farrar, Straus & Giroux, 1998.

Salisbury, Graham. *Lord of the Deep.* New York: Delacorte, 2001.

Sawyer, Ruth. *Roller Skates.* New York: Viking, 1936.

Sidney, Margaret. *The Five Little Peppers and How They Grew.* 1880. Various modern editions.

Sorenson, Virginia. *Miracles on Maple Hill.* New York: Harcourt, 1956.

Spinelli, Jerry. *Maniac Magee.* Boston: Little, Brown, 1990.

Taylor, Sidney. *All-of-a-Kind Family.* New York: Follett, 1951.

Twain, Mark. *The Adventures of Tom Sawyer.* 1876. Several modern editions.

———. *The Adventures of Huckleberry Finn.* 1884. Several modern editions.

Voigt, Cynthia. *Dicey's Song.* New York: Atheneum, 1982.

Wojciechowska, Maia. *Shadow of a Bull.* New York: Atheneum, 1964.

Wynne-Jones, Tim. *Some of the Kinder Planets.* New York: Kroupa, 1995.

———. *The Uninvited.* New York: Candlewick, 2009.

Outsiders and Personal Challenges

Anderson, Laurie Halse. *Speak.* New York: Farrar, Straus & Giroux, 1999. (Sexual abuse)

Bawden, Nina. *Humbug.* New York: Clarion, 1992. (Aging)

Bennett, James. *I Can Hear the Mourning Dove.* Boston: Houghton Mifflin, 1990. (Emotional illness)

Blue, Rose. *Me and Einstein.* New York: Human Sciences, 1979. (Learning disability—dyslexia)

Brooks, Jerome. *Uncle Mike's Boy.* New York: Harper, 1973. (Emotional illness)

Bunting, Eve. *Summer Wheels.* San Diego: Harcourt Brace Jovanovich, 1992. (Aging)

Carrick, Carol. *Stay Away from Simon.* New York: Clarion, 1985. (Mental retardation)

Childress, Alice. *A Hero Ain't Nothin' but a Sandwich.* New York: Coward, 1973. (Drugs)

Clymer, Eleanor. *The Get-Away Car.* New York: Dutton, 1978. (Aging)

Cormier, Robert. *Beyond the Chocolate War.* New York: Knopf, 1985. (Social corruption)

———. *The Chocolate War.* New York: Pantheon, 1974. (Social corruption)

———. *I Am the Cheese.* New York: Bell, 1987. (Government corruption)

———. *Tenderness.* New York: Delacorte, 1997. (Serial murderer)

Crutcher, Chris. *Staying Fat for Sarah Byrnes.* New York: Morrow, 1993. (Child abuse)

Foreman, Michael. *Seal Surfer.* Orlando: Harcourt Brace, 1997. (Physical disability)

Hamilton, Virginia. *The Planet of Junior Brown.* New York: Macmillan, 1971. (Emotional problems)

Hanson, Joyce. *Yellow Bird and Me.* New York: Houghton, 1986. (Learning disability)

Hinton, S. E. *The Outsiders.* New York: Viking, 1967. (Teenage gangs)

Howe, James. *The Watcher.* New York: Atheneum, 1997. (Child abuse)

Johnston, Julie. *The Only Outcast.* Toronto: Tundra, 1998. (Physical disability)

Koss, Amy Goldman. *Side Effects.* New Milford, CT: Roaring Brook Press, 2006. (Fighting cancer)

Levoy, Myron C. *A Shadow Like a Leopard.* New York: Harper, 1981. (Aging)

Lipsyte, Robert. *One Fat Summer.* New York: Harper, 1977. (Obesity)

Marek, Margot. *Different, Not Dumb.* New York: Watts, 1985. (Learning disability)

Meyer, Carolyn. *Killing the Kudu.* New York: Macmillan, 1990. (Disability—mobility)

Myers, Walter Dean. *It Ain't All for Nothin'.* New York: Viking, 1978. (Crime)

———. *Scorpions.* New York: Harper, 1988. (Gangs)

Oneal, Zibby. *The Language of Goldfish.* New York: Random House, 1980. (Emotional illness)

Peck, Richard. *Secrets of the Shopping Mall.* New York: Delacorte, 1979. (Running away)

———. *Those Summer Girls I Never Met.* New York: Delacorte, 1988. (Aging)

Pressler, Mirjam. *Halinka.* Trans. Elizabeth D. Crawford. New York: Holt, 1998. (Child abuse)

Rapp, Adam. *The Buffalo Tree.* Arden, NC: Front Street, 1997. (Juvenile detention center)

Skinner, David. *The Wrecker.* New York: Simon, 1995. (Social misfit)

Vaught, Susan. *Trigger.* New York: Bloomsbury, 2006. (Brain-damaged youth; attempted suicide)

Voigt, Cynthia. *Izzy Willy-Nilly.* New York: Simon & Schuster, 1986. (Debilitating accident)

———. *When She Hollers.* New York: Scholastic, 1994. (Sexual abuse)

Wolf, Virginia Euwer. *Make Lemonade.* New York: Holt, 1993. (Inner-city youth)

Woodson, Jacqueline. *I Hadn't Meant to Tell You This.* New York: Delacorte, 1994. (Sexual abuse)

Wright, Betty Ren. *Getting Rid of Marjorie.* New York: Holiday House, 1981. (Aging)

Zindel, Paul. *The Pigman.* New York: Harper, 1968. (Aging)

Sexuality

Bauer, Marion Dane. *Am I Blue?: Coming Out of the Silence.* New York: HarperCollins, 1994. (Homosexuality)

Block, Francesca Lia. *Weetzie Bat.* New York: Harper Collins, 1989. (Alternative lifestyles in a work of surrealism)

Blume, Judy. *Are You There, God? It's Me, Margaret.* New York: Bradbury, 1970. (Sexuality)

Brooks, Martha. *True Confessions of a Heartless Girl.* New York: Farrar, Straus & Giroux, 2003. (Teenage pregnancy and relationships)

Daly, Maureen. *Seventeenth Summer.* New York: Dodd, 1942.

Danziger, Paula. *The Cat Ate My Gymsuit.* New York: Delacorte, 1974.

Donovan, John. *I'll Get There. It Better Be Worth the Trip.* New York: Harper, 1969. (Homosexuality)

Fox, Paula. *The Eagle Kite.* New York: Jackson/Orchard, 1995. (Homosexuality)

Garden, Nancy. *Annie on My Mind.* New York: Farrar, Straus & Giroux, 1982. (Lesbianism)

Jacobson, Jennifer Richard. *Stained.* New York: Atheneum, 2005. (Homosexuality)

Kerr, M. E. *Deliver Us from Evie.* New York: HarperCollins, 1994. (Homosexuality)

———. *"Hello," I Lied.* New York: HarperCollins, 1997. (Homosexuality)

Koja, Kathe. *Talk.* New York: Farrar, Straus & Giroux, 2005. (Homosexuality)

Murrow, Liza Ketchum. *Twelve Days in August.* New York: Holiday House, 1993. (Sexuality)

Naylor, Phyllis Reynolds. *Reluctantly Alice.* New York: Atheneum, 1991. (Sexuality)

Nelson, Theresa. *Earthshine.* New York: Jackson, 1994. (AIDS)

Ryan, Sara. *Empress of the World.* New York: Viking, 2001. (Lesbianism)

Rylant, Cynthia. *A Couple of Kooks and Other Stories about Love.* New York: Orchard, 1990. (Love and sexuality)

Sanchez, Alex. *Rainbow Boys.* New York: Simon & Schuster, 2001. (Homosexuality)

———. *Rainbow Road.* New York: Simon, 2005. (Homosexuality)

Scoppettone, Sandra. *Trying Hard to Hear You.* New York: Harper, 1981. (Homosexuality)

Mortality

Acampora, Paul. *Defining Dulcie.* New York: Dial, 2006. (Death of a father)

Byars, Betsy. *The Summer of the Swans.* New York: Viking, 1970. (Death of a sibling)

Cormier, Robert. *The Bumblebee Flies Anyway.* New York: Pantheon, 1983. (Terminal illness)

Green, John. *Looking for Alaska.* New York: Dutton, 2005. (Death of a friend)

Hest, Amy. *Remembering Mrs. Rossi.* New York: Candlewick, 2007. (Death of a mother)

Hobbs, Valerie. *Defiance.* New York: Farrar, Straus & Giroux, 2004. (Death of a friend)

Hunter, Mollie. *A Sound of Chariots.* New York: Harper, 1972. (Death of a father)

Kadohata, Cynthia. *Kira-Kira.* New York: Atheneum, 2004. (Death of a sibling)

Lowry, Lois. *A Summer to Die.* Boston: Houghton Mifflin, 1977. (Death of a sibling)

Oneal, Zibby. *In Summer Light.* New York: Viking, 1985. (Death of a mother)

Paterson, Katherine. *Bridge to Terabithia.* New York: Crowell, 1977. (Death of a friend)

Peck, Richard. *Remembering the Good Times.* New York: Delacorte, 1985. (Suicide of a friend)

Rylant, Cynthia. *Missing May.* New York: Scholastic, 1992. (Death of a foster mother)

Smith, Doris Buchanan. *A Taste of Blackberries.* New York: Crowell, 1973. (Death of a friend)

Tolan, Stephanie S. *Listen!* New York: HarperCollins, 2006. (Death of a mother)

Wiles, Deborah. *Each Little Bird That Sings.* Orlando, FL: Gulliver Books, 2005. (Growing up in a funeral home)

Survival, Mystery, Animal, and Sports Stories

Bee, Clair. *Touchdown Pass.* New York: Grosset and Dunlap, 1948. (Sports)

Brooks, Bruce. *The Moves Make the Man.* New York: Harper & Row, 1984. (Sports)

Christopher, Matt. *Football Fugitive.* Boston: Little, Brown, 1976. (Sports)

———. *The Fox Steals Home.* Boston: Little, Brown, 1978. (Sports)

Corcoran, Barbara. *A Star to the North.* Philadelphia: Lippincott, 1970. (Survival)

Creech, Sharon. *The Wanderer.* New York: Harper, 2000. (Adventure/survival)

Cross, Gillian. *On the Edge.* New York: Holiday House, 1985. (Mystery, suspense)

Crutcher, Chris. *Athletic Shorts.* New York: Greenwillow, 1991. (Sports)

Dyer, T. A. *A Way of His Own.* Boston: Houghton Mifflin, 1981. (Survival)

Fenner, Carol. *The King of Dragons.* New York: Simon & Schuster, 1998. (Survival)

George, Jean Craighead. *Julie of the Wolves.* New York: Harper, 1972. (Survival)

———. *My Side of the Mountain.* New York: Dutton, 1959. (Survival)

Hiaasen, Carl. *Scat.* New York: Knopf, 2010. (Mystery)

Holman, Felice. *Slake's Limbo.* New York: Scribner's, 1974. (Survival)

Houston, James. *Frozen Fire.* New York: Atheneum, 1977. (Survival)

———. *Long Claw: An Arctic Adventure.* New York: Atheneum, 1981. (Survival)

Key, Watt. *Alabama Moon.* New York: Farrar, Straus & Giroux, 2006. (Survival)

Konigsburg, E. L. *From the Mixed-Up Files of Mrs. Basil E. Frankweiler.* New York: Atheneum, 1967. (Mystery)

Mazer, Harry. *The Island Keeper.* New York: Delacorte, 1981. (Survival)

———. *Snowbound.* New York: Dell, 1973. (Survival)

Morpurgo, Michael. *Kensuke's Kingdom.* New York: Scholastic, 2003. (Survival)

Paulsen, Gary. *Hatchet.* New York: Bradbury, 1987. (Survival)

Phipson, Joan. *Hit and Run.* New York: Atheneum, 1985. (Survival)

Powell, Randy. *My Underrated Year.* New York: Farrar, Straus & Giroux, 1988. (Sports)

Raskin, Ellen. *The Mysterious Disappearance of Leon (I Mean Noel).* New York: Dutton, 1971. (Mystery)

———. *The Westing Game.* New York: Dutton, 1978. (Mystery)

Shecter, Ben. *Inspector Rose.* New York: Harper, 1969. (Mystery)

Slote, Alfred. *The Trading Game.* Philadelphia: Lippincott, 1990. (Sports)

Sobol, Donald. *Encyclopedia Brown Saves the Day.* Nashville, TN: Nelson, 1970. (Mystery)

Speare, Elizabeth George. *The Sign of the Beaver.* Boston: Houghton Mifflin, 1983. (Survival)

Stead, Rebecca. *When You Reach Me.* New York: Random House, 2009. (Mystery)

Stevenson, Robert Louis. *Treasure Island.* 1883. Various modern editions. (Mystery, adventure)

Streiber, Whitley. *Wolf of Shadows.* New York: Knopf, 1985. (Survival)

Taylor, Theodore. *The Cay.* New York: Doubleday, 1969. (Survival)

Westall, Robert. *The Kingdom by the Sea.* New York: Farrar, 1991. (Mystery)

———. *A Place to Hide.* New York: Scholastic, 1994. (Mystery)

Wynne-Jones, Tim. *The Maestro.* New York: Orchard, 1996. (Survival)

Animal Stories for All Ages

Burnford, Sheila. *The Incredible Journey.* Boston: Little, Brown, 1961.

Byars, Betsy. *The Midnight Fox.* New York: Viking, 1968.

Cleary, Beverly. *Socks.* New York: Morrow, 1973.

DeJong, Meindert. *Hurry Home, Candy.* New York: Harper, 1953.

Eckert, Allan W. *Incident at Hawk's Hill.* Boston: Little, Brown, 1971.

Farley, Walter. *The Black Stallion.* New York: Random House, 1944.

———. *The Black Stallion Returns.* New York: Random House, 1945.

Fleischman, Sid. *The White Elephant.* Illus. Robert McGuire. New York: Greenwillow, 2006.

Gates, Doris. *Little Vic.* New York: Viking, 1951.

George, Jean. *The Cry of the Crow.* New York: Harper, 1980.

Gipson, Fred. *Old Yeller.* New York: Harper, 1956.

Griffiths, Helen. *The Greyhound.* New York: Doubleday, 1964.

———. *The Wild Heart.* New York: Doubleday, 1963.

Henry, Marguerite. *King of the Wind.* New York: Rand, 1948.

———. *Misty of Chincoteague.* New York: Rand, 1947.

Hiaasen, Carl. *Hoot.* New York: Bantam, 2005.

James, Will. *Smoky, the Cow Horse.* New York: Scribner's, 1926.

Kjelgaard, Jim. *Big Red.* New York: Holiday, 1956.

Knight, Eric. *Lassie Come Home.* Philadelphia: Winston, 1940.

London, Jack. *The Call of the Wild.* 1903. Various modern editions.

Mowat, Farley. *Owls in the Family.* Boston: Little, Brown, 1962.

Mukerji, Dhan Gopal. *Gay-Neck.* New York: Dutton, 1927.

Naylor, Phyllis Reynolds. *Shiloh.* New York: Atheneum, 1991.

O'Hara, Mary. *My Friend Flicka.* New York: Lippincott, 1941.

Rawlings, Marjorie Kinnan. *The Yearling.* New York: Scribner's, 1938.

Rawis, Wilson. *Where the Red Fern Grows.* New York: Doubleday, 1961.

Reaver, Chap. *Bill.* New York: Delacorte, 1994.

Rodowsky, Colby. *Not My Dog.* New York: Farrar, Straus & Giroux, 1999.

Rylant, Cynthia. *Every Living Thing*. Illus. S. D. Schindler. New York: Simon & Schuster, 1988.

Schlitz, Laura Amy. *A Drowned Maiden's Hair: A Melodrama*. New York: Candlewick, 2006.

Sewell, Anna. *Black Beauty: The Autobiography of a Horse*. 1877. Various modern editions.

Taylor, William. *Agnes the Sheep*. New York: Scholastic, 1991.

PEARSON
myeducationkit™

Go to the topics "Contemporary Realistic Fiction" and "Historical Fiction" on the MyEducationKit for this text, where you can:

- Search the Database of Children's Literature, housing more than 22,000 titles searchable in every genre by authors or illustrators, by awards won, by year published, and by topic and description.

- Explore genre-related Assignments and Activities, assignable exercises showing concepts in action through database use, video, cases, and student and teacher artifacts.

- Listen to podcasts and read interviews from some of the brightest and most enduring stars of children's literature in the Conversations.

- Discover Web Links that will lead you to sites representing the authors you learn about in these pages, classrooms with powerful children's literature connections, and literature awards.

Nonfiction

Telling It Like It Is

CHAPTER 12

Introduction

A famous television detective from the 1950s, Joe Friday of *Dragnet,* was fond of remarking, "All we want are the facts, ma'am." And a nineteenth-century English physician, Peter Mere Latham, defined a good book as containing "important facts, duly arranged, and reasoned upon with care." Both of these remarks hit at the heart of nonfiction. The purpose of nonfiction is, of course, to convey factual information; however, as Dr. Latham tells us, the facts have to be well organized and they have to be used carefully and thoughtfully. The good work of nonfiction is not a mere catalogue of information or an almanac of data. It is interestingly written, designed to engage us, even entertain us, as well as inform us.

In Chapter 6 we saw examples of the inventive concept books, nonfiction works for preschoolers, appearing in recent years. Equally imaginative nonfiction is being written for older readers, and those works are the subject of this chapter. We will first consider biography and autobiography and then examine the broader spectrum of children's nonfiction—books dealing with history, politics, travel, the arts, sports, science, technology, and so on. In this survey we will see that today's nonfiction can be every bit as gripping as the best fiction.

History of Children's Nonfiction

Most consider Commenius's *Orbis Pictus,* which first appeared in 1658, to be the first children's picture book (see Chapter 1). If this is so, then the first picture book was a nonfiction book instructing young children in Latin vocabulary. Unfortunately, during most of the intervening three and a half centuries, much nonfiction for children consisted of dreary tomes prepared for use in the schoolroom. They often contained rather dry catalogues of facts and figures for young readers to absorb, master, or memorize.

Thankfully, beginning in the mid-twentieth century, a new attitude toward nonfiction emerged. This was the notion that a work of nonfiction could be just as interesting, just as beautiful, just as inspiring as a work of fiction.

Biography was one of the first types of nonfiction that began to transform. Some well-written biographies appeared in the 1930s, especially the works of husband and wife, Ingri and Edgar Parin d'Aulaire. Their beautifully illustrated biographies of figures such as George Washington, Abraham Lincoln, Pocahontas, and Buffalo Bill were very popular. By today's standards, these early biographies appear overly romanticized. Their heroes were glorified and thus tended to lack a flesh-and-blood quality. It was perhaps the civil unrest of the 1960s and 1970s that helped change all that. Writers turned away from romantic biographies in favor of more realistic, if less glamorous, portraits. Russell Freedman's outstanding biographies—on Abraham Lincoln, Franklin Delano Roosevelt, and Eleanor Roosevelt, among others—are perfect examples.

High-quality nonfiction works on a wide variety of subjects soon followed. Books on history focused on subjects such as the Chicago Fire of 1871 (James Murphy's *Great Chicago Fire*), the history of burial practices (Penny Colman's *Corpses, Coffins, and Crypts*), and the Ice Age (Ilene Cooper's *Exploring the Ice Age*). Science and technology began to receive more attention, especially after the Russians launched *Sputnik*, the first orbiting spacecraft, in 1957. It would be several years, though, before the influence finally reached children's books. By the 1970s and 1980s, such fine science writers as the prolific Millicent Selsam (*Birth of an Island*), Franklin Branley (*Light and Darkness)*, Laurence Pringle (*The Hidden World: Life Under a Rock)*, and, more recently, Gail Gibbons (*The Vegetables We Eat)* and Seymour Simon (*Our Solar System)*, and others began to bring high-quality nonfiction books to young readers. Gibbons writes and illustrates nonfiction picture books for younger children and is noted for her clear, straightforward style and striking illustrations. Simon, a former science teacher, is considered by some to be the dean of children's nonfiction. He has written more than 200 science books for young readers (typically in the early elementary years)—and on a wide variety of topics from anatomy to nature to outer space. He prefers to illustrate his books with photographs.

Nature books, always favorites with children of all ages, remained popular, but now they began to emphasize ecology (Pringle's *Living in a Risky World,* for example*)*. Books on the solar system and outer space took advantage of the satellite and space probe explorations (the works of Simon, mentioned previously, and others). And modern nonfiction books have benefitted from technological advances in computer graphics and microscopic and telescopic photography (Robin Kerrod and David Hughes's *Visual Encyclopedia of Space*). On the whole, today's nonfiction has become known for its inventiveness, with many well-written and superbly illustrated books on the market that are both informative and entertaining.

Characteristics of Nonfiction

Nonfiction has its own special criteria for excellence. The best nonfiction contains (1) a clear purpose suited to the audience, (2) factual information that is accurate and objectively balanced, (3) a style that is clear and engaging, and (4) a format or design that effectively conveys the material.

Purpose and Audience

Every work of nonfiction has a specific instructional goal—from teaching the sounds of the alphabet to explaining the cycles of life or the movement of the stars. Each work also has a specific audience and the author needs to ask: How much do they know? How much can I expect them to grasp? Naturally, the intended audience (preschoolers, elementary schoolers, middle schoolers, teenagers) will determine the contents and the approach of the nonfiction work. *The King's Day* by Aliki is a picture book about Louis XIV of France, but it is for readers in the early elementary grades. Clearly, Aliki's purpose is not to provide a history of France during the reign of Louis XIV, nor is it to provide a biography of the king. Second- and third-graders have little interest in politics or court intrigue or warfare. So how does Aliki make her subject appealing to her young audience? She decides to describe a typical day in the king's life, showing us the customs, clothing, manners, daily rituals and so on. These are details that can be easily absorbed by her readers. Accompanying the simple text are richly detailed and colorful pictures.

It goes without saying that a science book for preschoolers can probably do little more than make children aware of the subject. Ruth Heller's popular *Chickens Aren't the Only Ones* is about animals who lay eggs, including birds, snakes, lizards, crocodiles, fish, and many more. This may, at first, seem like a peculiar focus, but its purpose is to get young children (preschoolers love this book) interested in the natural world. Heller's striking realistic illustrations and her eloquent text make this a perfect introduction to the biological sciences. Obviously, older audiences are going to want more text, and the illustrations are going to be less decorative and more informative. It is important to keep in mind the intended audience and the author's purpose when evaluating a nonfiction book—and remember, it is unfair to criticize a book for not doing something it never intended to do.

Factual Information

When reading fiction, we don't have to worry so much about whether the facts are accurate—most of them are made up anyway. But it goes without saying that in nonfiction, accuracy is crucial. But "facts" themselves can be tentative things. For example, in *The Reason for a Flower*, a beautiful picture book about plants first published in 1983 and still in print,

Ruth Heller refers to fungi as plants. But in 2007, fungi were reclassified and put into their own kingdom—neither plant nor animal. The "facts" have changed. Moreover, it is not just science where new discoveries are being made. Historians, for example, also keep uncovering new materials—forgotten letters, secret memos, newly discovered artifacts. Nothing is static.

Also, every writer must make choices about what to include and what to omit. Every work of nonfiction reflects the writer's individual judgment. This goes back to Dr. Latham's notion that the facts must be "reasoned upon with care." A survey of children's biographies of Christopher Columbus reveals a marked change in society's attitude over time. Early books (such as Ingri and Edgar Parin d'Aulaire's *Columbus,* 1955) depict Columbus in an unabashedly heroic light, whereas more recent studies (notably David Adler's *Christopher Columbus, Great Explorer,* 1991, and Milton Meltzer's *Christopher Columbus and the World Around Him,* 1990) emphasize Columbus's greedy, mercenary side as well as his heinous treatment of the native population. History itself may not change, but what we know about it and how we view it does.

Especially in books for older children, we are now finding fewer sweeping generalizations and more solid evidence—in the form of figures, data, charts, and so on. This helps young readers understand that facts are needed to support claims. Many nonfiction books for older children are now including resource material and bibliographies showing where the author got the information, and this helps give integrity to the work itself—it provides evidence that the writer just didn't make up this stuff. And finally, we need to take note of the date of the writing (which may be different from the date of publication). This doesn't mean that the more recent a nonfiction book is the better. But we have to keep in mind what facts and/or attitudes may have changed since a book's writing (as we have seen in the preceding examples).

Style

Millicent Selsam, a noted science writer for children, once said, "A good science book is not just a collection of facts" (62). A good science book conveys, in Selsam's words, "something of the beauty and excitement of science" (65). She is referring to style—the writer's choice of words, the construction of sentences and paragraphs, and the organization of the material. Perhaps the first rule of style is that the writing be clear. It does not matter how accurate the text is if we cannot understand what it's saying. Terms need to be identified in a language young readers can grasp. Here is where the language of metaphor comes in handy. When Selsam describes the white spots on a baby deer's coat as looking "like spots of sunlight on the forest floor" (*Hidden Animals*), she is making a comparison (a simile, in fact) to help us visualize the subject.

Jim Arnosky, in *Watching Desert Wildlife,* shares with the reader his detailed observations about birds, snakes, lizards, deer, and other desert wildlife. At the conclusion of his work, he is able to beautifully sum up his experience and its meaning:

> *I went to the desert to feel the heat of the desert sun and breathe the dry air. I went to the desert*
> *to see its wide open places. I went with my eyes open wide, watchful for snakes and scorpions,*

and alert, ready to see all the wonderful wild animals who make their homes amid the thorns and spines.

   I came home from the desert with a fresh new outlook on nature and wildlife. I felt bigger and broader, happy in the knowledge that I had discovered another world. (n. p.)

The good writer of nonfiction is often something of a poet—sharing in beautiful words the wondrous things of life.

Format

Format refers to the way the material is presented in the book and how the pages are laid out. A book filled with facts can be overwhelming unless the writer has found a clever way to present them. In Chapter 7 we discussed David Macaulay's *The New Way Things Work,* a monumental encyclopedia of the physical sciences describing how all sorts of gadgets operate—from simple inclined planes to computers. Macaulay is skilled in organizing the information in small snippets and providing carefully detailed drawings to illustrate his points. A book that is well laid out and provides helpful illustrations can make difficult information less intimidating. This could mean historical illustrations or engaging photographs interestingly positioned on the page (as you will see in Figure 12.1) or light-hearted cartoons (much like you saw in Figure 7.5) or richly detailed drawings (as you will see in Figure 12.2). The format also includes such matters as chapter and division headings and the various auxiliary features often found in a work of nonfiction. And we will turn to those now.

Apparatus of Nonfiction

Unlike a novel, which stands on its own without need for any supporting materials, a work of nonfiction typically includes both text and auxiliary matter. This auxiliary matter—we might call it the apparatus of nonfiction—may include a table of contents, footnotes or endnotes, a glossary, a list of references or resources, and an index. Except for footnotes and endnotes, this textbook contains examples of each kind of apparatus mentioned below. Browse through the book to see how these features are used.

Table of Contents

This is an outline of the chapters, sometimes broken down into their various parts, along with the corresponding page numbers. It is placed at the beginning of the book, and looking at the table of contents often lets us know whether the book covers the information we need. The most helpful table of contents contains clear headings (rather than merely clever ones) and is not so detailed that it is exhausting to read. It should give us an overview of the book and its layout, clearly and simply.

Footnotes/Endnotes

Many nonfiction books include footnotes, which are placed at the bottom of the page, or endnotes, which are placed at the end of each chapter or at the back of the book. These notes provide us with additional information the author found interesting and useful, but not necessarily crucial to the content of the book. Sometimes these notes contain suggestions for additional readings or fascinating tidbits of extraneous information. (Footnotes and endnotes are occasionally more interesting than the text!)

Glossary

A nonfiction work may include a glossary, which is a specialized dictionary of important terms used throughout the book. A glossary defines terms as they are used specifically in the text. This is very helpful if the book uses a lot of technical terms or is about a topic unfamiliar to most people. See the Glossary at the back of this book.

Bibliography

To further help readers explore the subject, many works of nonfiction contain a bibliography or a list of resources, which identifies materials (books, articles, films, and so on) on a specific subject. Usually in nonfiction for children and adolescents, the bibliography consists of a reading list of relevant books children might find interesting. However, some also contain reference lists, which include the works actually used by the author in writing the book.

Index

Except in books for the very young, most nonfiction works contain an index. An index, which appears at the very end of a book, lists key words and tells us on which pages of the book we can find them. The purpose of the index is so the book can be used as a reference source—that is, if we want to find out something specific, we can locate the topic in the index without having to read through the entire book. See the Index to this book.

Illustrations in Nonfiction

The illustrations in a nonfiction book form another important part of the apparatus, and they need to be treated in greater detail. Virtually all works of nonfiction for young readers contain illustrations, which may include drawings, photographs, diagrams, graphs, charts, or any other nontextual matter used to explain key ideas.

Drawings

Drawings in ink or pencil are among the oldest form of illustration in nonfiction works. They remain popular and useful today, as well. For example, cartoons depicting aspects of human anatomy and sexuality are used in Babette Cole's book on human reproduction, *Mommy Laid an Egg; Or, Where Do Babies Come From?* The book has faced some controversy for its frank explanations of human sexuality, but the hilarious cartoons present important concepts in a way that many parents find acceptable—it is, after all, a book intended for parents to share with their children. (This is a good example of a case where photographs would just not be advisable.) Tony De Saulles's cartoon drawing for Nick Arnold's *The Body Owner's Handbook* is another example where comical illustrations can serve as effective teaching tools. In other cases, drawings are used where photographs are either impossible to come by or would not explain the concepts adequately. David Macaulay, in *Cathedral,* describes the process of building a medieval cathedral, and his exquisite pen-and-ink drawings (an example is shown later in this chapter) more than make up for the absence of photographs, which, of course, do not exist.

Photographs

Today, in our highly visual society, photography is often the medium of choice. It has become popular in recent years for history books and biographies to use period photographs (i.e., photographs taken during the specific historical era covered in the book). Russell Freedman uses period photographs in his histories and biographies, thereby demonstrating that photographs do not have to be in color to be interesting. Since photography was only developed in the nineteenth century, we can't expect to find period photos in a biography of George Washington.

In the sciences and the arts, photography has become indispensable. For example, remarkable photographs of wildlife are found in books such as Celia Bland's *Bats,* a book in the "Eyes on Nature" series. Another science series, Dorling Kindersley's "Eyewitness Junior," features a combination of detailed photographs and careful drawings, all labeled with informative captions (see Figure 12.1).

The "Eyewitness Juniors" series seems inspired by television and electronic media, containing, as they do, information in small doses on pages filled with an array of illustrations. They serve as stimulating introductions and springboards to meatier treatments. Similarly, Seymour Simon's *Out of Sight: Pictures of Hidden Worlds* contains a series of stunning photographs, all produced through technologically sophisticated means showing us such things as the interior of a living human heart or the head of a ladybug or the formation of new stars in a galaxy 7,000 light years away.

Maps, Charts, Diagrams, and Tables

A history or geography book might require maps of the areas discussed. Janis Herbert's *The Civil War for Kids,* for example, includes several maps, including battlefield maps. Map

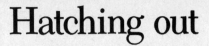

Hatching out

Most reptiles lay eggs. Some eggs have leathery shells, and others have hard shells, like hens' eggs. And some reptiles don't lay eggs at all. They give birth to live young, just like humans do.

1 When it's time to break out, the baby hog-nosed viper's egg shrivels, because the baby has used up all the yolk inside.

2 The baby snake makes the first cut in its shell with a special tiny egg tooth. Pushing with its snout, it pokes its head out.

4 The baby snake is a miniature version of its parents. Once it's hatched, it does not need to be looked after by Mom.

3 The snake stays inside its safe shell for hours, or even days, before it finally crawls out.

Empty shell

Figure 12.1 ● In this illustration from Mary Ling's *Amazing Crocodiles & Reptiles* we see the hatching of a viper, with four stages of the process captured in photography by Jerry Young and carefully labeled.

Source: From *Amazing Crocodiles and Reptiles* by Mary Ling. Copyright © Dorling Kindersley, 1991. Reproduced by permission of Dorling Kindersley Ltd.

reading itself is an important skill too easily overlooked in this day of global positioning systems, and young readers might need the help of such works as Scot Ritchie's picture storybook, *Follow That Map! A First Book of Mapping Skills,* and Sara Finelli's *My Map Book.*

A biography, on the other hand, might include a genealogy, a chart illustrating the family tree of the subject. A genealogy can go backward—identifying parents, grandparents, and so on—or it can go forward—identifying children, grandchildren, and so on. To include all these names in a paragraph would be very confusing and difficult to read. Science books might include a diagram, which is simply a labeled drawing. A book on dance might include a diagram of a dance movement—something very difficult to capture in a photograph. A table is a means of organizing information into rows and columns to make it more accessible or to help compare items—for example, a table might be used to show how various kinds of animals differ in their diet, habitat, life span, and so on. Tables can pack a lot of information into a small space.

The key to all these visual aids is that they are clear, unambiguous, and easy to follow and that they help us understand the subject. In a good piece of nonfiction, the illustrations are clearly labeled—the label is called a caption. Illustrations without captions leave us guessing about what were looking at. That's not helpful. Each illustration should have a point and the point should be very clear. Illustrations should not be mere decoration.

Now let's look more closely at some of the more common types of nonfiction, beginning with biography and autobiography.

Biography and Autobiography

A biography is a book about the life—or part of the life—of another person. When someone writes the story of his or her own life, we call the work an autobiography. In addition to giving us fascinating stories, biographies can inspire us with portraits of the indomitable human spirit or arouse us from complacency with portraits of human malice and insensitivity. Biographies are also reminders of the common thread of humanity running through us all.

Early biographies for children were, not surprisingly, didactic in nature. Charlotte Yonge's *Book of Golden Deeds of All Time* (1864) is one of the earliest examples and its title suggests its purpose. Children were given biographies of the saints and great men and women so they could learn from their example. Unfortunately, these early biographies tended to be very one-sided, portraying untouchable heroes or dastardly villains, with little aim toward creating real-life characters. Children's biography, as we noted earlier, remained like this for many years.

Today, most readers prefer a biography that shows the whole person—warts and all. We are all human. We all make errors in judgment. We all have personality flaws, peculiar habits, and eccentric ideas. This does not mean that we want our heroes debunked—it is very disconcerting to learn about the unsavory escapades our favorite sports figures, actors, or politicians. Young people want heroes or heroines to believe in. But they also want to read about flesh-and-blood human beings, people with whom they can empathize. Abraham Lincoln, for instance, was self-conscious about his appearance. Russell Freedman opens his book, *Lincoln: A Photobiography,* with this:

> *At first glance, most people thought he was homely. Lincoln thought so too, referring once to his "poor, lean, lank face." As a young man he was sensitive about his gawky looks, but in time, he learned to laugh at himself. When a rival called him "two-faced" during a political debate, Lincoln replied, "I leave it to my audience. If I had another face, do you think I'd wear this one?" (1)*

What sets heroes apart from everyone else is not that they have no weaknesses, but that they succeed despite their weaknesses. Doesn't that make their triumph more impressive?

Biography for children takes one of three forms: authentic biography, which sticks only to facts; fictionalized biography, which adds invented, but believable, dialogue to otherwise factual material; and biographical fiction, which plays fast and loose with facts and is, as the name implies, fiction.

Authentic Biography

An authentic biography, such as Freedman's *Lincoln: A Photobiography,* uses only facts that can be supported by evidence. Consequently, if dialogue is used (which is not common in authentic biography), it has to be supported by historical documents (such as letters or diaries) or verifiable personal recollections. The above quotation from Lincoln is drawn from material of the period—it is not made up.

This does not mean that an authentic biography is nothing but a series of boring facts, as we can see in this passage from Robert Quackenbush's *Mark Twain? What Kind of Name Is That?* The author opens with a folksy, light-hearted tone that is quite appropriate in a book about America's favorite humorist:

> *Samuel Langhorne Clemens—river pilot, gold miner, frontier reporter, humorist, and this nation's best-loved author—claimed that two important events took place on November 30, 1835. One was the appearance in the night sky of Halley's Comet—an event that comes only once every seventy-five years—and the other was his birth in Florida, Missouri. Sam loved telling jokes and playing tricks. He claimed that he couldn't remember what his first lie was, but he told his second lie when he was only nine days old. He had pretended that a diaper pin was sticking him, and he'd hollered as loud as he could. This brought him extra loving attention—until his trickery was found out, that is. Sam's mother thought he might get hit by a bolt of lightning one day, on account of all the mischief he caused as he was growing up in Hannibal, Missouri, with his older brother Orion, his older sister Pamela, his younger brother Henry, and nineteen cats. (9)*

Yes, much is omitted about young Sam Clemens' childhood, but in this short paragraph we learn several facts, we get a good idea of his character, and we want to read on. It is just what we want from good biography.

The most thorough and honest biographer tries to be objective and free from bias. However, every choice a writer makes is a judgment, and by ignoring some facts and highlighting others, writers impose their own points of view on their subjects. It is good to question everything we read.

Fictionalized Biography

Some biographers have found it inviting to dramatize certain events—to make up lively dialogue or to invent dramatic scenes—presumably to make the story more interesting. The writer may fabricate scenes and conversations, and speculate on details for dramatic effect. Fictionalized biographies are often easily recognized by their use of dialogue. That is, if we are reading a biography of Benjamin Franklin and find extended conversations between young Franklin and his brother or his parents, such as we find in Augusta Stevenson's *Benjamin Franklin: Young Printer*, we can be pretty sure that the dialogue is made up. Or, if the writer conveys the intimate thoughts of a character, we may rightly wonder how the author knows these things. A sound fictionalized biography, however, such as Jean Lee Latham's Newbery Award–winning *Carry On, Mr. Bowditch*, will not tamper with the basic facts. And the truth of the matter is that these books often capture the attention of more reluctant readers—readers who may think reading about an artist or president or inventor might be boring.

Biographical Fiction

It is important to understand that this type is not really biography, but fiction—in some cases, even fantasy. This doesn't mean they are not well written or fun to read—they're just not history. Robert Lawson is famous for his fanciful biographies—of the pirate Captain Kidd (*Captain Kidd's Cat*), of Christopher Columbus (*I Discover Columbus*), of Benjamin Franklin (*Ben and Me*)—all told by animals who knew them. They are purely delightful, which is just what they were intended to be. And, who knows? Perhaps they will inspire a young reader to seek out authentic biographies of these people.

Complete, Partial, and Collective Biographies

In addition to these differences in approach, biographies differ in the range of biographical coverage. A complete biography covers a subject's entire life, from cradle to grave. It may be simple—such as Aliki's charming picture-book biographies (*The Story of Johnny Appleseed*, for example)—or it may be more extensive as in the Freedman's *Lincoln: A Photobiography*.

A partial biography covers only one phase of the subject's life and allows the author to focus more clearly on a specific theme or issue. For instance, Johanna Johnston's fictional-ized biography of Harriet Beecher Stowe, *Harriet and the Runaway Book*, focuses chiefly on Mrs. Stowe's writing of *Uncle Tom's Cabin*. Younger children enjoy partial biographies that describe the childhoods of famous people (first- and second-graders readers often care little about grown-ups' lives). One very popular biographical series, "The Childhood of Famous Americans," includes fictionalized biographies that focus chiefly on the subject's childhood and teen years. One goal of these books is to pique the interest of young readers so that, in time, they will want to read full-length biographies of their favorite people.

A collective biography provides sketches of the lives of several people who are linked by a common thread: scientists, first ladies, sports figures, musicians, and so on. Typically, these books are organized into chapters or parts, each devoted to a different person. Henrietta Buckmaster's *Women Who Shaped History* deals with such influential women as Dorothea Dix, Harriet Tubman, and Mary Baker Eddy. One of the most famous of all collective biographies is President John F. Kennedy's best-selling *Profiles in Courage,* which has been edited for younger audiences. Such books make good introductions to the lives of famous people, and may encourage readers to find more thorough biographies.

Autobiography

An autobiography is a book written about one's own life and, it goes without saying, it is written before the end of one's life—and therefore is not "complete." Sometimes, an autobiographer will write about only one part of his or her life—childhood and adolescence, for example, or early adult years, or specific career experiences. Autobiographies are usually more informal than biographies, often in the form of memoirs or reminiscences. Many individuals believe they don't have to research their own lives (after all, who should know their lives better than they do?), and so they rely on their recollections of events. Consequently, specific dates are frequently missing from autobiographies, and seldom do we find any documentation. Not only are facts suspect in an autobiography, but so is the interpretation. In other words, what is more important to the writer of an autobiography— the truth or the subject's image?

Nevertheless, what famous people say about themselves can be both enlightening and entertaining. An autobiography can also be a great source for discovering an individual's character traits, likes and dislikes, innermost feelings—things that are not so easily hidden. Autobiographies for children include a series of picture books about famous children's illustrators, such as *Self-Portrait: Margot Zemach* and *Self-Portrait: Eric Blegvad,* in which the artists not only tell their life stories but they also illustrate them. Several children's authors have written their autobiographies for young readers, including Betsy Byars's *The Moon and I,* Phyllis Reynolds Naylor's *How I Came to Be a Writer,* Jean Fritz's *Homecoming: My Own Story,* and Roald Dahl's *Boy: Tales of Childhood.*

General Nonfiction

Nonfiction books cover the breadth of human knowledge. Today it is possible to find children's books on virtually any subject under the sun (and beyond). For the sake of economy, this overview divides nonfiction (beyond biography and autobiography) into four immense categories: History and Culture, Science and Nature, Art and Leisure, and Human Growth and Development. Remember that concept books were discussed in Chapter 6 and these are a type of nonfiction as well.

History and Culture

This is a very large category, but most books fit into one of the following subcategories: political and social history, geography, or religion.

As we have seen in the preceding chapters, we can learn a great deal about people and places through well-written realistic fiction or through the traditional folktales. However, along with these fictional works, we need to know certain facts to gain a fuller understanding of and appreciation for a culture. Even children in the early elementary years can be drawn into historical subjects. We have already mentioned Aliki, whose picture books on historical and cultural subjects are ideally suited to young readers. One of their favorites is *Mummies Made in Egypt,* which describes the complicated process by which the ancient Egyptians embalmed their dead. Also on an Egyptian subject is James Cross Giblin's *Secrets of the Sphinx,* which includes stunning artwork by Bagram Ibatoulline. It is filled with information about one of the most intriguing monuments of the ancient world, all presented for readers in the middle grades.

Books for older readers generally have longer texts and fewer illustrations (most are illustrated books rather than picture books). The best writers of history try to depict the past faithfully, including the unpleasant, the controversial, and the vile. Milton Meltzer is one writer who has been committed to portraying the past accurately, and he has tackled some difficult facets of American history. His books include *In Their Own Words: A History of the American Negro; Brother Can You Spare a Dime? The Great Depression: 1929–1933;* and *Bread and Roses: The Struggle of American Labor, 1865–1915.* Meltzer's works are distinguished by their thorough scholarship. He treats his young readers respectfully, never condescending to them; he includes bibliographies and indexes; and he prefers to use period photographs to illustrate his works, giving them an authentic flavor.

Jim Murphy is noted for his compelling books on American history, such as *Across America on an Emigrant Train* (based on author Robert Louis Stevenson's harrowing experience traversing the United States in 1879 on a low-budget train for poor emigrants); *The Great Fire* (about the Chicago fire of 1871); and *An American Plague: The True and Terrifying Story of the Yellow Fever Epidemic of 1793.* Like Freedman's works mentioned earlier, Murphy's books include all the apparatus of nonfiction (bibliography, index, archival illustrations, and so on). Books such as Walter Dean Myers's *Now Is Your Time!: The African-American Struggle for Freedom* bring to light both the struggles of African Americans and their contribution to American society. Unfortunately, is it still difficult to find good historical nonfiction for children on non-Western cultures—Asian, African, South American, even European. The works of Adeline Yen Mah (including *China: Land of Dragons and Emperors,* an acclaimed history of China for young readers) and the works of Suzanne Strauss Art (*The Story of Ancient China* and others) are examples that need to be emulated.

Religion is a sensitive area for many people, and writers on religious subjects are wise to be mindful of the delicate nature of this topic. In other words, there is a difference between informing and preaching. If approached purely from an informational point of view, books on religion can help children learn about their own heritage as well as about religions and cultures around the world. Given the widespread misunderstandings between faiths today, we can all benefit from books such as Howard Greenfield's *Passover* and *Rosh Hashanah and Yom Kippur* and Karla Kuskin's *Jerusalem, Shining Still,* all about Judaism. Anton Powell's *The Rise of Islam* describes the earlier history of that important world religion. And Elizabeth Seeger's *Eastern Religions* explores the religious faiths of Asia. Books such as Franz Metcalf's *Buddha in Your Backpack: Everyday Buddhism for Teens* and Diana Winston's *Wide Awake: A Buddhist Guide for Teens* introduce the tenets of Buddhism in accessible and refreshing ways. A knowledge of religion—our own beliefs aside—is crucial to understanding history, art, cultural mores, and social customs. And knowledge is the key to tolerance.

Science and Nature

Books about science and nature include many topics: the life sciences (animals and plants), the earth sciences (rocks, minerals, the weather, the environment), astronomy, mathematics, and technology.

As might be expected, books about animals are among the most popular of the science books, particularly with younger readers. We are told that the most frequently consulted entry in a young people's encyclopedia is "dogs." Even the youngest children find almost any book about animals appealing. In recent years a number of fine books have been written on unusual or threatened animal species, including the puffin, the panda, the bald eagle, and obscure species, such as the hoiho (Adele Vernon's *The Hoiho: New Zealand's Yellow-Eyed Penguin*). Catherine Paladino's *Our Vanishing Farm Animals* describes several breeds of American farm animals close to extinction. Typically these books describe the animals' life cycles, habits, and importance in the larger frame of the natural world (again, see Figure 12.1).

Gail Gibbons's *From Seed to Plant* and Ruth Heller's *Reason for a Flower* (mentioned earlier) illustrate one of nature's most elemental tales, the growth of a plant from a tiny seed, and they invite hands-on experiences. Plants, of course, are not naturally cuddly, nor do they have expressive personalities (except possibly for the Venus flytrap). So a writer must emphasize other qualities, such as a plant's beauty, its uniqueness, and its importance to us and our ecosystem. It is not only the animal world that is threatened with extinction, and we are beginning to see books alerting young children to the potential disappearance of our plant life as well. Barbara Taylor's series, including *Coral Life, Desert Life, Pond Life,* and *Rain Forests,* introduces the very young to the concept of the ecosystem—plants and animals working together to maintain the balance of nature and ensure the survival of the planet.

Astronomy is an exciting, if challenging, subject for children, one that requires a great deal of ingenuity in order to make it understandable for the reader. In *Exploring the Night*

Sky, science writer Terence Dickinson describes the immense size of the solar system using an extended metaphor:

> *A model of the solar system gives an idea of its size and the sizes of its various members. Let's use a major-league baseball stadium located in the centre of a large city for the model. The sun, the size of a baseball, rests on home plate. Mercury, Venus, Earth and Mars, each about the dimensions of the ball in a ballpoint pen, are, respectively, 1/8, 1/5, 1/3 and 1/2 of the way to the pitcher's mound. A pea near second base is Jupiter. In shallow centre field is a smaller pea, Saturn. Uranus, the size of this letter O, is at the fence off in deep centre field. Neptune and Pluto, a letter O and a grain of salt in our model, are just outside the park. (26)*

He continues with the baseball field metaphor, noting that the nearest star to our solar system "would be a baseball in another city more than 1,000 miles away" (26).

This passage includes another example of outdated nonfiction. When first published in 1987, the details were deemed accurate. However, as most people know, the scientific community has downgraded Pluto to the status of a dwarf planet, since recent data reveal that it does not possess all of the properties to qualify it as a planet—particularly, it is not big enough to clear other things out of its orbit. In addition to Pluto, other dwarf planets include Ceres, Eris, Make Make, and Haumea (and incidentally, the latter two are among the first celestial bodies to be named for Polynesian, rather than Greek or Roman, deities). Such is the fate of all nonfiction, relying as it does on the never-ending process of collecting new information and on the ever-changing human perspectives that analyze that information.

Laurence Pringle's *Living in a Risky World* encourages young readers to think about modern civilization and the implications of our lifestyle, particularly the effects of human pollutants (acid rain, carcinogens, and other environmental hazards). Pringle shows us that science is not divorced from our everyday world or from the complicated ethical issues that face humanity. His work pointedly examines the ethics of science and technology in the modern world—the title suggests both the substance and the theme. People have an ethical responsibility to the earth. Pollution, overpopulation, and reckless development have taken their toll, and children need to learn about the delicate ecosystem on which we all depend. This is the world they, too, have to live in.

An unusual series of science books produced in Great Britain by Nick Arnold is fiendishly called "Horrible Science." It is referred to in the cover material as "Science with the squishy bits left in!" It now includes numerous titles on all aspects of science and each book includes cartoonish and often outrageous drawings by Tony De Saulles. The titles themselves are tantalizing, including *Chemical Chaos, Fatal Forces,* and *Nasty Nature.* In *The Body Owner's Handbook* Arnold describes in detail the functions of our organs, what can go wrong, and how to best care for our bodies—it is billed as "the guide you simply can't live without." It reads like a manual for auto care, and the author delights in giving his teen audience the gruesome, the unsavory, and the indelicate they love so much. Although the texts and illustrations are light-hearted in tone, the subjects and explanations are quite serious and the books provide a great deal of interesting and useful information.

One book of scientific explanations that is not to be missed is David Macaulay's near monumental *The Way Things Work* (originally published in 1988 and expanded and updated in 1998 in *The New Way Things Work*). This hefty volume explores all the realms of the earth sciences—mechanics, physics (even nuclear physics), electronics, and chemistry. With amazing clarity and simplicity and with the help of hundreds of clever drawings, Macaulay explains a phenomenal number of complex ideas and processes. He ties the entire work together by using cartoon figures of woolly mammoths to demonstrate the various properties and scientific principles involved. For example, the mammoths are used to represent "force" or "effort." (The cartoon figures, incidentally, do not trivialize the subject matter in this case; instead, they clarify complex ideas—such as jet propulsion and the operation of computers.) In this way, Macaulay uses metaphor to illustrate an abstract concept and humor to make his explanations understandable and enjoyable. This book has enormous appeal for adults as well as young people.

Even abstract mathematical subjects have been successfully presented in children's books, such as Mitsumasa Anno's imaginatively illustrated *Anno's Math Games* in two volumes and Jane Jonas Srivastava's *Statistics*, an introduction for children in middle elementary school. Given the highly publicized math deficiency of most American children, this is a field ripe for imaginative writers and illustrators.

Arts and Leisure

This category includes a wide variety of books covering everything from cooking to watching movies to playing football. We may roughly categorize them into four broad subject areas: performing arts (music, dance, theater), graphic arts (drawing, painting, photography), plastic arts (sculpture, architecture), and sports and entertainment.

Unfortunately, modern society has typically regarded these activities as luxuries or pastimes. When school budgets are cut, art programs are often the first to go. But art feeds the soul as well as the mind and it is an indispensable part of a child's education. As with anything else, most people find art more meaningful when they can participate in it—perform the music or the dance, act in the play, paint the picture, or form the sculpture. Nevertheless, books can expand experiences, pique curiosity, and develop taste. Historical surveys of the various art forms provide useful perspectives—it is always important to know what has gone before us. Marc Aronson's *Art Attack: A Short Cultural History of the Avant-Garde,* for example, describes a specific modern movement in art. Some books instruct on various aspects of the art, such as Cheryl Walsh Bellville's *Theater Magic: Behind the Scenes at a Children's Theater*. And some books actually teach the techniques of the art form, such as Miriam Cooper's *Snap! Photography*.

David Macaulay, already mentioned for his science book, *The Way Things Work,* has further distinguished himself by bringing the complex world of architecture and construc-tion to young readers. His picture books, which bridge science, history, and art, describe the building of some of the world's great monuments, from the Egyptian pyramids (*Pyramid*) to medieval castles (*Castle*) to cathedrals (*Cathedral;* see Figure 12.2) to modern skyscrapers

Figure 12.2 ● David Macaulay's dramatic ink drawing of a medieval cathedral from his information picture book, *Cathedral,* emphasizes the triumph of both faith and engineering in the Middle Ages. The human figures and even the city wall and houses appear diminutive in comparison to the monumental structure that took several lifetimes to complete. Macaulay's drawings are at once meticulous and expressionistic, which helps them capture both the spiritual and technological aspects of the achievement.

Source: Cathedral: The Story of Its Construction by David Macaulay. Copyright © 1973 by David Macauley. Reprinted by permission of Houghton Mifflin Publishing Company. All rights reserved.

(*Unbuilding*). In addition to their attention to technical detail, Macaulay's books also convey information about human society, including lifestyles and cultural beliefs. His book *Mosque* attempts to narrow the gap that has long existed between the Judeo-Christian and Muslim cultures, and provides the kind of understanding needed to help mend the wounds of generations of misunderstanding. Obviously, Macaulay's books straddle our categories—perhaps the sure sign of a good book.

Leisure activities and sports consume a great deal of a child's time, and many books have been written to introduce and explain the history, techniques, and importance of these subjects. For example, ice skating, as described in Jonah and Laura Kalb's *The Easy Ice Skating Book,* has developed into a highly refined performing art. One sport in particular has long captured the imagination of writers, and that is fishing. Jim Arnosky's *Fish in a Flash?: A Personal Guide to Spin-Fishing* is just one of the more recent in a long line of books for fishing enthusiasts, reaching back to Renaissance England. Combining sports and the art of writing is William Jaspersohn's *Magazine: Behind the Scenes at Sports Illustrated,* describing the writing, editing, illustrating, and printing of a magazine.

Human Growth and Development

Books about human growth and development are the most recent additions to nonfiction books for children. They include such psychological and sociological concerns as family relationships, friendship and human interaction, sexual growth and development, physical and emotional challenges, and death and dying.

As you might imagine, books on sexuality are in high demand. Gail Saltz's *Changing You: A Guide to Body Changes and Sexuality,* includes a straightforward text with cartoon drawings by Lynne Avril Cravath and is perfectly suited to children in the upper elementary grades. Along similar lines is Jacqui Bailey's *Sex, Puberty, and All That Stuff: A Guide to Growing Up.* But as children reach puberty, the need arises for books especially aimed at either males or females. Jeremy Daldry's *The Teenage Guy's Survival Guide: The Real Deal on Girls, Growing Up and Other Guy Stuff* sets out to assuage some of the teenage angst that plagues every boy. And for teenage girls there are books such as Debra Beck's *My Feet Aren't Ugly!: A Girl's Guide to Loving Herself from the Inside Out,* among others. We also find books on very specific sensitive matters, such as Susan Terkel and Janice Rench's *Feeling Safe, Feeling Strong: How to Avoid Sexual Abuse and What to Do If It Happens to You.* It is unfortunate that such books are necessary, but ignoring unpleasant issues does not make them go away.

Our society's penchant for therapy has at last spilled over into the realm of children's books, and although we may regret the need for such books for children, we should be glad that capable and sensitive writers have risen to the task. One popular approach is the book that recounts the experiences of real people. In Jill Krementz's *How It Feels When Parents Divorce,* children of divorced parents share their emotional responses to this childhood trauma. The book is illustrated with sensitive photographs of people, which seems appropriate to the serious nature of the work. Eda Le Shan's *What Makes Me Feel This Way?*

is written for upper elementary-aged children and deals with personal emotions. Physical disabilities, which for decades were virtually ignored in books for children, are now finding voices. Ron Roy's *Move Over, Wheelchairs Coming Through!* helps to fill a significant gap. Subtitled *Several Young People in Wheelchairs Talk About Their Lives,* the book treats the subject with both candor and sensitivity.

In Chapter 5 we briefly discussed the treatment of death in books for children, pointing out that sometimes a well-written fictional work can provide comfort and understanding in experiencing loss. And sometimes, young people simply need to hear the facts. Earl A. Grollman's *Straight Talk about Death for Teenagers: How to Cope with Losing Someone You Love* is an example of a thorough and straightforward discussion of the many facets of this very difficult topic. Regardless of the subject matter, young readers need honesty, sensitivity, and accuracy in their nonfiction.

Summary

Fiction and nonfiction have similar ends—to help us understand, just a little bit better, the world we live in. The difference is that fiction does it through story, whereas nonfiction sticks to factual evidence. Nonfiction books, once thought of as chiefly dull, utilitarian works, have risen to a higher stature in recent years, some even having received children's literature's most prestigious awards.

The best nonfiction writers impart the facts in a way that sparks our interest and stirs our imagination. They know that truth, as the old expression goes, is "stranger than fiction." There is nothing dull about facts—only in the method by which they are conveyed. Nonfiction writers have to combine the spellbinding skills of the storyteller with the scholar and researcher's knowledge.

This is no easy task; for nonfiction, like fiction, is judged on its ability to keep our interest. But unlike fiction, nonfiction is also judged on the quality of its research, the accuracy of its facts, and the integrity of its explanations. Nonfiction also requires a clear purpose and audience, balance and objective, as well as accuracy and sufficient detail— as well as being enjoyable to read. Most nonfiction for children includes illustrations that should extend our knowledge, explain the complicated, and unravel the mysterious. They should not be mere ornamentation. Most nonfiction books include supplementary materials, such as a table of contents, a glossary, a list of references, and an index—all designed to help the reader use the book more effectively.

Topics in nonfiction range from biography and autobiography to works about history and culture, science and nature, arts and leisure, and human growth and development. Regardless of the topic, a well-constructed nonfiction work is not simply a loose collection of facts (something like a *Guinness Book of Records*—interesting to read in bits and pieces but hardly a gripping story). The best nonfiction is well crafted, carefully designed, and precisely written. It helps us understand our world and ourselves, and it urges us to read on, to learn more. In the end, like the best fiction, nonfiction speaks to the strength and resilience of the human spirit and to the unending wonder of the universe.

For Reflection and Discussion

1. Choose any biography written for children (of any age). After reading the book, locate some factual information about the individual—from reliable online sources, biographical dictionaries or encyclopedias, adult biographies, and so on. Be sure to examine more than one source so that you can verify the facts. Now evaluate the children's biography for its accuracy, its thoroughness, and its effectiveness in capturing the personality of the subject. In light of your research, what are the book's strengths and weaknesses?

2. Locate and read at least three or four information books on the same topic but for different age levels—a picture book for preschoolers, a picture book for early elementary, and a chapter book for children in the middle grades, for example. First, determine the specific audience and purpose for each book. What are the chief differences in treatment among the books? Consider the factual differences, the differences in tone, and the differences in layout and presentation. How successful is each book given its specific audience and purpose?

3. Try your hand at writing an explanation of a concept for young children. For example:

   a. What makes night and day?

   b. What is the difference between a solid, a liquid, and a gas?

   c. What are the seasons? What makes them?

   d. Who is George Washington and why is he important?

   e. What happens when our heart beats?

   Be sure to determine your audience's age level: Are you writing for preschoolers? For early elementary, middle schoolers? This will determine the extent of the detail, your choice of vocabulary, and so on. You may want to include illustrations—don't worry, if you're not an artist, you can pull materials off the Web. When you're finished, try it out on a child. How successful was your explanation?

● Works Cited

Arnosky, Jim. *Watching Desert Wildlife*. Washington, DC: National Geographic Society, 1998.

Dickinson, Terence. *Exploring the Night Sky*. Willowdale, Ontario: Firefly, 1987.

Ford, Danielle. "More than the Facts: Reviewing Science Books." *The Horn Book Magazine* 78, 3 (May/June 2002): 265–271.

Freedman, Russell. *Lincoln: A Photobiography.* New York: Clarion, 1987.

Fritz, Jean. *And Then What Happened, Paul Revere?* New York: Coward, McCann & Geoghegan, 1973.

Gottleib, Robin. "On Nonfiction Books for Children: Tradition & Dissent." *Wilson Library Journal* (October 1974): 174–177.

Quackenbush, Robert. *Mark Twain? What Kind of Name Is That?: A Story of Samuel Langhorne Clemens.* New York: Simon and Schuster, 1984.

Selsam, Millicent E. "Writing about Science for Children." In *Beyond Fact: Nonfiction for Children and Young People.* Ed. Jo Carr. Chicago: American Library Association, 1982, pp. 61–65.

Recommended Readings

Aiken, Joan. "Interpreting the Past." *Children's Literature in Education* 16 (Summer 1985): 67–83.

Baxter, Kathleen A., and Marcia Agness Kochel. *Gotcha Good!: Nonfiction Books to Get Kids Excited About Reading.* Santa Barbara, CA: Libraries Unlimited, 2008.

Burton, Hester. "The Writing of Historical Novels." In *Children and Literature: Views and Reviews.* Ed. Virginia Haviland. Glenview, IL: Scott, Foresman, 1973, pp. 299–304.

Carr, Jo, ed. *Beyond Fact: Nonfiction for Children and Young People.* Chicago: American Library Association, 1982.

Carter, Betty, and Richard F. Abrahamson. *Nonfiction for Young Adults: From Delight to Wisdom.* Phoenix: Oryx Press, 1991.

Cianciolo, Patricia. *Informational Picture Books for Children.* Chicago: American Library Association, 2000.

Epstein, William H. "Introducing Biography." *Children's Literature Association Quarterly* 12 (Winter 1987): 177–179.

Fisher, Margery. *Matters of Fact: Aspects of Non-fiction for Children.* New York: Crowell, 1972.

Fraser, Elizabeth. *Reality Rules!: A Guide to Teen Nonfiction Reading Interests.* Santa Barbara, CA: Libraries Unlimited, 2008.

Garfield, Leon. "Historical Fiction for Our Global Times." *The Horn Book* (November/December 1988): 736–742.

Kendall, Paul Murray. *The Art of Biography.* 1965. New York: Norton, 1985.

Mallet, Margaret. *Making Facts Matter: Reading Non-fiction 5–11.* London: Paul Chapman, 1992.

Marcus, Leonard. "Life Drawing: Some Notes on Children's Picture Book Biographies." *The Lion and the Unicorn* 4 (Summer 1980): 15–31.

Moore, Ann W. "A Question of Accuracy: Errors in Children's Biographies." *School Library Journal* 31 (February 1985): 34–35.

Segel, Elizabeth. "In Biographies for Young Readers, Nothing Is Impossible." *The Lion and the Unicorn* 4 (Summer 1980): 4–14.

Weinberg, Steve. "Biography: Telling the Untold Story." *The Writer* (February 1993): 23–25.

Wilms, Denise M. "An Evaluation of Biography." In *Jump Over the Moon.* Ed. Pamela Barron and Jennifer Burley. New York: Holt, Rinehart & Winston, 1984, pp. 220–225.

Selected Bibliography of Biographies and Autobiographies

Since many writers specialize in biographical writing, look for other biographies by a number of the writers represented on this list. If the subject of the biography is not obvious from the title, it has been supplied in parentheses next to the entry.

Adler, David A. *Christopher Columbus, Great Explorer.* New York: Holiday House, 1991.

———. *Lou Gehrig: The Luckiest Man Alive.* Illus. Terry Widener. New York: Harcourt, 1997.

Adoff, Arnold. *Malcolm X.* Illus. John Wilson. New York: Crowell, 1970.

Aliki (pseud. of Aliki Brandenburg). *The Story of Johnny Appleseed.* Englewood Cliffs, NJ: Prentice-Hall, 1963.

———. *A Weed Is a Flower: The Life of George Washington Carver.* Englewood Cliffs, NJ: Prentice-Hall, 1965.

———. *William Shakespeare and the Globe.* New York: HarperCollins, 1999.

Allen, Thomas B. *Harriet Tubman, Secret Agent: How Daring Slaves and Free Blacks Spied for the Union During the Civil War.* Washington, DC: National Geographic, 2006.

Anderson, M. T. *Handel, Who Knew What He Liked.* Illus. Kevin Hawkes. Cambridge, MA: Candlewick, 2001.

———. *Strange Mr. Satie.* Illus. Peter Mathers. New York: Viking, 2003. (Composer Erik Satie)

Andronik, Catherine M. *Hatshepsut, His Majesty, Herself.* New York: Atheneum, 2001. (Ancient Egypt's only female pharaoh)

Asimov, Isaac. *Breakthroughs in Science.* Boston: Houghton Mifflin, 1960.

Bitton-Jackson, Livia. *I Have Lived a Thousand Years: Growing Up in the Holocaust.* New York: Simon & Schuster, 1997.

Blegvad, Erik. *Self-Portrait: Erick Blegvad.* Reading, MA: Addison-Wesley, 1979.

Bolliger, Max. *David.* Illus. Edith Schindler. New York: Delacorte, 1967.

Brooks, Polly Schoyer. *Queen Eleanor: Independent Spirit of the Medieval World.* Philadelphia: Lippincott, 1983.

Bruchac, Joseph. *A Boy Called Slow: The True Story of Sitting Bull.* New York: Philomel, 1995.

Burleigh, Robert. *Flight: The Journey of Charles Lindbergh.* New York: Philomel, 1991.

Carlson, Laurie. *Boss of the Plains: The Hat That Won the West.* New York: DK Ink, 1998. (Hatmaker John Stetson)

Christensen, Bonnie. *Woody Guthrie: Poet of the People.* New York: Knopf, 2001.

Clayton, Ed. *Martin Luther King: The Peaceful Warrior.* Englewood Cliffs, NJ: Prentice-Hall, 1968.

Clouse, Nancy L. *Perugino's Path: The Journey of a Renaissance Painter.* Grand Rapids, MI: Wm. B. Eerdmans, 1997.

Dahl, Roald. *Boy: Tales of Childhood.* New York: Farrar, Straus & Giroux, 1984.

Daugherty, James. *Abraham Lincoln.* New York: Viking, 1943.

d'Aulaire, Ingri, and Edgar Parin d'Aulaire. *Abraham Lincoln.* New York: Doubleday, 1939.

Davidson, Margaret. *The Story of Eleanor Roosevelt.* New York: Four Winds, 1969.

De Trevino, Elizabeth Borton. *I, Juan de Pareja.* New York: Farrar, Straus & Giroux, 1965.

Demi. *Ghandi.* New York: McElderry, 2001.

———. *Mother Teresa.* New York: Margaret K. McElderry, 2005.

Duncan, Lois. *Chapters: My Growth as a Writer.* Boston: Little, Brown, 1982.

Engle, Margarita. *The Poet Slave of Cuba: A Biography of Juan Francisco Manzano.* New York: Holt, 2006.

Faber, Doris. *Eleanor Roosevelt: First Lady of the World.* New York: Viking, 1985.

Ferris, Jeri. *Native American Doctor: The Story of Susan LaFlesche Picotte.* Minneapolis: Carolrhoda, 1991.

Fisher, Leonard Everett. *Galileo.* New York: Macmillan, 1992.

Fleischman, Sid. *The Abracadabra Kid: A Writer's Life.* New York: Greenwillow, 1996.

———. *Escape!: The Story of the Great Houdini.* New York: Greenwillow, 2006.

Frank, Anne. *The Diary of a Young Girl: The Definitive Edition.* Ed. Otto H. Frank and Mirjam Pressler. Trans. Susan Massotty. New York: Doubleday, 1995.

Freedman, Russell. *Eleanor Roosevelt: A Life of Discovery.* New York: Clarion, 1993.

———. *Lincoln: A Photobiography.* New York: Clarion, 1987.

Fritz, Jean. *Bully for You, Teddy Rooseelt!* New York: Putnam, 1991.

———. *The Double Life of Pocahontas.* New York: Putnam, 1983.

———. *Homesick: My Own Story.* New York: Putnam, 1982. (Autobiography)

Gerstein, Mordicai. *What Charlie Heard.* New York: Farrar, Straus & Giroux, 2002. (American Composer Charles Ives)

Gibbin, James Cross. *Charles A. Lindbergh: A Human Hero.* New York: Clarion, 1998.

Giovanni, Nikki. *Rosa.* Illus. Bryan Collier. New York: Holt, 2005. (Rosa Parks)

Gish, Lillian, and Selma Lanes. *An Actor's Life for Me.* New York: Viking, 1987.

Greenfield, Eloise. *Mary McLeod Bethune.* New York: Crowell, 1977.

Hamilton, Virginia. *W. E. B. DuBois: A Biography.* New York: Crowell, 1972.

Heiligman, Deborah. *Charles and Emma: The Darwins' Leap of Faith.* New York: Holt, 2009.

Hyman, Trina Schart. *Self-Portrait: Trina Schart Hyman.* (1981). New York: HarperCollins, 1989.

Johnson, Johanna. *Harriet and the Runaway Book: The Story of Harriet Beecher Stowe and Uncle Tom's Cabin.* New York: Harper, 1977.

Judson, Clara Ingram. *Abraham Lincoln, Friend of the People.* Chicago: Wilcox and Follett, 1950.

Kherdian, David. *The Road from Home: The Story of an Armenian Girl.* New York: Greenwillow, 1979.

Konigsburg, E. L. *A Proud Taste for Scarlet and Miniver.* New York: Dell, 1973. (Fictionalized account of the life of Eleanor of Aquitaine)

Krull, Kathleen. *Lives of the Artists: Masterpieces, Messes (and What the Neighbors Thought).* Illus. Kathryn Hewitt. Orlando: Harcourt, 1995.

———. *Lives of the Presidents: Fame, Shame (and What the Neighbors Thought).* Illus. Kathryn Hewitt. Orlando: Harcourt, 1998.

Lanier, Shannon, and Jane Feldman. *Jefferson's Children: The Story of One American Family.* New York: Random House, 2000.

Latham, Jean Lee. *Carry On, Mr. Bowditch.* Boston: Houghton Mifflin, 1955.

Lawrence, Jacob. *Harriet and the Promised Land.* New York: Windmill, 1968. (One-time slave and heroine of the underground railroad Harriet Tubman)

Marrin, Albert. *George Washington and the Founding of a Nation.* New York: Dutton, 2001.

Matthews, Elizabeth. *Different Like Coco.* New York: Candlewick, 2007. (Fashion designer Coco Chanel)

McKissack, Patricia C. *Jesse Jackson: A Biography.* New York: Scholastic, 1989.

Monjo, F. N. *The One Bad Thing about Father.* New York: Harper, 1970. (Theodore Roosevelt)

———. *Poor Richard in France.* New York: Holt, 1973. (Benjamin Franklin)

Mora, Pat. *A Library for Juana: The World of Sor Juana Inéz.* Illus. Beatriz Vidal. New York: Knopf, 2002. (Seventeenth-century woman scholar of Mexico)

Myers, Walter Dean. *At Her Majesty's Request: An African Princess in Victorian England.* New York: Scholastic, 1999. (The story of an orphaned West African princess raised in England under the protection of Queen Victoria)

Parks, Rosa, with Jim Haskins. *I Am Rosa Parks.* Illus. Wil Clay. New York: Dial, 1997.

Poole, Josephine. *Joan of Arc.* Illus. Angela Barret. New York: Knopf, 1998.

Provensen, Alice, and Martin Provensen. *The Glorious Flight: Across the Channel with Louis Bleriot.* New York: Viking, 1983.

Raboff, Ernest. *Pablo Picasso.* New York: Doubleday, 1968.

Rappaport, Doreen. *John's Secret Dreams: The Life of John Lennon.* Illus. Bryan Collier. New York: Hyperion, 2004.

Redsand, Anna. *Viktor Frankl: A Life Worth Living.* New York: Clarion, 2006. (Holocaust survivor and renowned psychiatrist)

Reef, Catherine. *Walt Whitman.* New York: Clarion, 1995.

Reich, Susanna. *Clara Schumann: Piano Virtuoso.* New York: Clarion, 1999. (About one of the few celebrated women composers and musicians of the nineteenth century)

Rylant, Cynthia. *Best Wishes.* Photographs by Carlo Ontal. Katonah, NY: Richard C. Owen, 1992. (Autobiography)

Severance, John B. *Gandhi: Great Soul.* New York: Clarion, 1997. (Mahatma Gandhi)

———. *Winston Churchill.* New York: Clarion, 1996.

Shiels, Barbara. *Winners: Women and the Nobel Prize.* Minneapolis: Dillon, 1985.

Shippen, Katherine. *Leif Eriksson: First Voyager to America*. New York: Harper, 1951.

Siegal, Aranka. *Upon the Head of a Goat: A Childhood in Hungary, 1939–1944*. New York: Farrar, Straus & Giroux, 1985.

Sills, Leslie. *Inspirations: Stories about Women Artists*. Morton Grove, IL: Whitman, 1989. (A collective biography)

Singer, Isaac Bashevis. *A Day of Pleasures: Stories of a Boy Growing Up in Warsaw*. New York: Farrar, Straus & Giroux, 1969. (Autobiographical reminisences of a Nobel Prize winning author)

Sis, Peter. *Starry Messenger: Galileo Galilei*. New York: Farrar, Straus & Giroux, 1996.

———. *The Tree of Life: Charles Darwin*. New York: Farrar, Straus & Giroux, 2003.

Stanley, Diane. *Joan of Arc*. New York: Morrow, 1998.

———. *Leonardo da Vinci*. New York: Morrow, 1996.

Stanley, Diane, and Peter Vennema. *Good Queen Bess: The Story of Elizabeth I of England*. New York: Four Winds, 1990.

———. *Shaka: King of the Zulus*. New York: Morrow, 1988.

Stanley, Fay. *The Last Princess: The Story of Princess Ka'iulani of Hawai'i*. New York: Four Winds, 1991.

Steig, William. *When Everybody Wore a Hat*. New York: HarperCollins, 2003.

Stevenson, Augusta. *Benjamin Franklin: Young Printer*. "Childhood of Famous Americans" series. 1941. New York: Aladdin, 1986.

Szabo, Corinne. *Sky Pioneer: A Photobiography of Amelia Earhart*. Washington, DC: National Geographic, 1997.

Thomas, Jane Resh. *Behind the Mask: The Life of Queen Elizabeth I*. New York: Clarion, 1998.

Tillage, Leon Walter. *Leon's Story*. Illus. Susan L. Roth. New York: Farrar, Straus & Giroux, 1997. (Autobiographical account of an African American's struggle in the mid-twentieth century)

Turner, Robyn Montana. *Georgia O'Keeffe*. Boston: Little, Brown 1991.

van der Rol, Ruud, and Rian Verhoeven. *Anne Frank: Beyond the Diary*. New York: Viking, 1993.

Venezia, Mike. *Beatles*. New York: Scholastic, 1997.

———. *Johann Sebastian Bach*. New York: Scholastic, 1998.

Wadsworth, Ginger. *Rachel Carson: Voice for the Earth*. Minneapolis: Lerner, 1992.

Wallner, Alexander. *Laura Ingalls Wilder*. New York: Holiday, 1997.

Weidhorn, Manfred. *Jackie Robinson*. New York: Atheneum, 1993.

Yates, Elizabeth. *Amos Fortune, Free Man*. New York: Dutton, 1950. (Story of a nineteenth-century American slave who manages to buy his freedom)

Yolen, Jane. *A Letter from Phoenix Farm*. Photographs by Jason Stemple. Katonah, NY: Richard C. Owens, 1992. (Autobiography)

Zemach, Margot. *Self-Portrait: Margot Zemach*. Reading, MA: Addison-Wesley, 1978.

Selected Bibliography of Nonfiction

The books are categorized according to the four broad classifications outlined in this chapter; however, these are only general guidelines and books frequently cross boundaries.

History and Culture

Aliki (pseudonym for Aliki Brandenburg). *Corn Is Maise—The Gift of the Indians*. New York: Crowell, 1976.

———. *Mummies Made in Egypt*. New York: Crowell, 1979.

Armstrong, Carol. *Women of the Bible*. New York: Simon & Schuster, 1998.

Art, Suzanne Strauss. *The Story of Ancient China*. Lincoln, MA: Pemblewick, 2001.

Ashabranner, Brent. *Children of the Maya.* New York: Dodd, Mead, 1986.

———. *Land of Yesterday, Land of Tomorrow: Discovering Chinese Central Asia.* New York: Cobblehill, 1992.

Atkin, S. Beth. *Voices from the Streets: Young Former Gang Members Tell Their Stories.* Boston: Little, Brown, 1996.

Bach, Alice, and J. Cheryl Exum. *Miriam's Well: Stories about Women in the Bible.* New York: Delacorte, 1991.

Bartoletti, Susan Campbell. *Black Potatoes: The Story of the Great Irish Famine.* Boston: Houghton Mifflin, 2001.

———. *Growing Up in Coal Country.* Boston: Houghton Mifflin, 1996.

Baylor, Byrd. *When Clay Sings.* Illus. Tom Bakhi. New York: Scribner's, 1972.

Bealer, Alex W. *Only the Names Remain: The Cherokees and the Trail of Tears.* Boston: Little, Brown, 1972.

Berck, Judith. *No Place to Be: Voices of Homeless Children.* Boston: Houghton Mifflin, 1991.

Bial, Raymond. *Cajun Home.* Boston: Houghton Mifflin, 1998.

Caselli, Giovanni. *The First Civilizations.* New York: Bedrick, 1985.

Chaikin, Miriam. *Clouds of Glory.* Illus. David Frampton. New York: Clarion, 1998.

———, adapter. *Exodus.* Illus. Charles Mikolaycak. New York: Holiday, 1987.

Chang, Ina. *A Separate Battle: Women and the Civil War.* New York: Dutton, 1991.

Colman, Penny. *Corpses, Coffins, and Crypts: A History of Burial.* New York: Holt, 1997.

———. *Rosie the Riveter: Women Working on the Home Front in World War II.* New York: Crown, 1995.

Cooper, Ilene. *The Dead Sea Scrolls.* Illus. John Thompson. New York: Morrow, 1997.

Cooper, Margaret. *Exploring the Ice Age.* New York: Atheneum, 2001.

DK Publishing. *World War I.* ("DK Eyewitness Books") New York: DK, 2001.

———. *World War II.* ("DK Eyewitness Books") New York: DK, 2000.

Finelli, Sara. *My Map Book.* New York: Harper, 1995.

Fisher, Leonard Everett. *The Hospitals.* New York: Watts, 1980.

Foster, Genevieve. *The World of William Penn.* New York: Scribner's, 1973.

Frank, John. *The Tomb of the Boy King.* Illus. Tom Pohrt. New York: Farrar, Straus & Giroux, 2001. (Tutankhamen)

Freedman, Russell. *Cowboys of the Wild West.* New York: Tickner & Fields, 1985.

———. *Immigrant Kids.* New York: Dutton, 1980.

Ganeri, Anita, and Chris Oxlade. *DK First Atlas.* ("DK First Reference" series) New York: DK, 2004.

Giblin, James Cross. *Secrets of the Sphinx.* Illus. Bagram Ibatoulline. New York: Scholastic, 2004.

Greenfeld, Howard. *The Hidden Children.* New York: Clarion, 1993.

Herbert, Janis. *The Civil War for Kids: A History with 32 Activities.* Chicago: Chicago Review Press, 1999.

Herbst, Judith. *The Mystery of UFOs.* Illus. Greg Clarke. New York: Atheneum, 1997.

Hoyt-Goldsmith, Diane. *Celebrating Ramadan.* Photographs by Lawrence Migdale. New York: Holiday, 2001.

Ippisch, Hanneke. *Sky: A True Story of Resistance During World War II.* New York: Simon & Schuster, 1996.

Jacobs, Francine. *The Tainos: The People Who Welcomed Columbus.* New York: Putnam, 1992.

Kantar, Andrew. *29 Missing: The True and Tragic Story of the Disappearance of the S. S. Edmund Fitzgerald.* East Lansing: Michigan State University Press, 1998.

Keegan, Marcia. *Pueblo Boy: Growing Up in Two Worlds.* New York: Dutton, 1991.

Kimmel, Eric A. *Bar Mitzvah: A Jewish Boy's Coming of Age.* New York: Viking, 1995.

Kuskin, Karla. *Jerusalem, Shining Still.* New York: Harper, 1987.

Levine, Ellen. *Darkness Over Denmark: The Danish Resistance and the Rescue of the Jews.* New York: Holiday House, 2000.

McWhorter, Diane. *A Dream of Freedom: The Civil Rights Movement from 1954 to 1968.* New York: Scholastic, 2004.

Meltzer, Milton, ed. *The Black Americans: A History in Their Own Words, 1619–1983.* New York: Crowell, 1984.

———. *Brother Can You Spare Dime? The Great Depression: 1929–1933*. New York: New American Library, 1977.

———. *Columbus and the World Around Him*. New York: Watts, 1990.

———. *The Hispanic Americans*. New York: Crowell, 1982.

Metcalf, Franz. *Buddha in Your Backpack: Everyday Buddhism for Teens*. Berkeley, CA: Ulysses Press, 2002.

Morimoto, Junko. *My Hiroshima*.1987. New York: Puffin, 1990.

Murphy, Jim. *Across America on an Emigrant Train*. New York: Clarion, 1993.

———. *An American Plague: The True and Terrifying Story of the Yellow Fever Epidemic of 1793*. New York: Clarion, 2003.

———. *The Great Fire*. New York: Scholastic, 1995. (The Chicago fire)

Myers, Walter Dean. *Now Is Your Time!: The African-American Struggle for Freedom*. New York: HarperCollins, 1991.

National Geographic Society. *National Geographic Our World, Updated Edition: A Child's First Picture Atlas*. Washington, DC: National Geographic Society, 2006.

Philbrick, Nathaniel. *Revenge of the Whale: The True Story of the Whaleship* Essex. New York: Putnam, 2002.

Ritchie, Scot. *Follow That Map! A First Book of Mapping Skills*. Toronto: Kids Can Press, 2009.

Rylant, Cynthia. *Appalachia: The Voices of Sleeping Birds*. New York: Harcourt, 1991.

Smith, David J. *If the World Were a Village: A Book about the World's People*. Illus. Shelagh Armstrong. Toronto: Kids Can, 2002.

Snelling, John. *Buddhism*. New York: Watts, 1986.

Stanley, Jerry. *I Am an American: A True Story of Japanese Internment*. New York: Crown, 1994.

Van Loon, Hendrik Willem. *The Story of Mankind*. 1921. Updated by John Merriman. New York: Liveright, 1999.

Winston, Diana. *Wide Awake: A Buddhist Guide for Teens*. New York: Perigee Trade, 2003.

Yen Mah, Adeline. *China: Land of Dragons and Emperors*. 2004. New York: Delacorte, 2009.

Science and Nature

Anderson, Joan. *Earth Keepers*. New York: Harcourt, 1993.

Anno, Mitsumasa. *Anno's Math Games*. New York: Philomel, 1987.

———. *Anno's Math Games II*. New York: Philomel, 1987.

Arnold, Nick. *The Body Owner's Handbook*. ("Horrible Science" series) Illus. Tony De Saulles. New York: Scholastic, 2002.

———. *Chemical Chaos*. ("Horrible Science" series) Illus. Tony De Saulles. (1999) New York: Scholastic, 2008.

———. *Nasty Nature*. ("Horrible Science"series) Illus. Tony De Saulles.(1999) New York: Scholastic, 2006.

———. *The Stunning Science of Everything*. ("Horrible Science" series) Illus. Tony De Saulles. New York: Scholastic, 2005.

Arnosky, Jim. *Secrets of a Wildlife Watcher*. New York: Lothrop, 1983.

———. *Watching Desert Wildlife*. Washington, DC: National Geographic, 1998.

Bang, Molly. *Common Ground: The Water, Earth, and Air We Share*. New York: Scholastic, 1997.

Bland, Celia. *Bats*. ("Eyes on Nature" series) Chicago: Kidsbooks, 1997.

Brandenburg, Jim. *An American Safari: Adventures on the North American Prairie*. New York: Walker, 1995.

Branley, Franklyn. *Air Is All Around You*. New York: Crowell, 1986.

———. *The International Space Station*. Illus. True Kelley. New York: HarperCollins, 2000.

Brown, Laurie Krasny, and Marc Brown. *Dinosaurs to the Rescue!: A Guide to Protecting Our Planet*. Boston: Little, Brown, 1992.

Cobb, Vicki. *I Face the Wind*. New York: HarperCollins, 2003.

Cole, Joanna. *The Magic School Bus and the Electric Field Trip*. Illus. Bruce Degen. New York: Scholastic, 1997.

————. *The Magic School Bus: Inside the Earth.* Illus. Bruce Degen. New York: Scholastic, 1987.

Cowley, Joy. *Red-Eyed Tree Frog.* Photographs by Nic Bishop. New York: Scholastic, 1999.

Curlee, Lynn. *Brooklyn Bridge.* New York: Simon & Schuster, 2001.

Dickinson, Terence. *Exploring the Night Sky.* Buffalo, NY: Firefly, 1987.

Ehlert, Lois. *Waiting for Wings.* San Diego: Harcourt, 2001.

Facklam, Margery. *Bugs for Lunch.* Illus. Sylvia Long. Watertown, MA: Charlesbridge, 1999.

————. *Spiders and Their Web Sites.* Boston: Little, Brown, 2001.

Farrell, Jeanette. *Invisible Enemies: Stories of Infectious Disease.* New York: Farrar, Straus & Giroux, 1998.

First Space Encyclopedia. ("DK First Reference" series) New York: DK Publishing, 2008.

Floca, Brian. *Moonshot: The Flight of* Apollo 11. New York: Atheneum, 2009.

Gibbons, Gail. *Exploring the Deep, Dark Sea.* Boston: Little, Brown, 1999.

————. *From Seed to Plant.* New York: Holiday, 1991.

————. *The Vegetables We Eat.* New York: Holiday, 2008.

Heller, Ruth. *Chickens Aren't the Only Ones.* ("World of Nature" series) St. Louis, MO: Turtleback, 1999.

————. *The Reason for a Flower.* New York: Scholastic, 1983.

Henderson, Douglas. *Asteroid Impact.* New York: Penguin, 2001.

Herbst, Judith. *The Mystery of UFOs.* Illus. Greg Clarke. New York: Simon, 1997.

Hopkinson, Deborah. *Sky Boys: How They Built the Empire State Building.* New York: Schwartz & Wade, 2006.

Jenkins, Martin. *Fly Traps!: Plants That Bite Back.* Illus. David Parkins. New York: Candlewick, 1996.

Jenkins, Steve. *Life on Earth: The Story of Evolution.* Boston: Houghton Mifflin, 2002.

Kerrod, Robin, and David Hughes. *Visual Encyclopedia of Space.* New York: DK Children, 2006.

Krautwurst, Terry. *Night Science for Kids: Exploring the World After Dark.* Asheville, NC: Lark Books, 2003.

Lauber, Patricia. *Summer of Fire: Yellowstone 1988.* New York: Watts, 1991.

————. *Tales Mummies Tell.* New York: Crowell, 1985.

Lewin, Ted. *Tooth and Claw: Animal Adventures in the Wild.* New York: HarperCollins, 2003.

Ling, Mary. *Amazing Crocodiles & Reptiles.* ("Eyewitness Juniors") Photographs by Jerry Young. New York: Knopf, 1991.

Llewellyn, Claire. *My First Book of Time.* Boston: Houghton Mifflin, 1992.

Macaulay, David. *The New Way Things Work.* Boston: Houghton Mifflin, 1998.

Markle, Sandra. *Outside and Inside Bats.* New York: Atheneum, 1992.

Masoff, Joy. *Fire!* New York: Scholastic, 1998.

Montgomery, Sy. *The Man-Eating Tigers of Sundarbans.* Photographs by Eleanor Briggs. Boston: Houghton Mifflin, 2001.

Paladino, Catherine. *Our Vanishing Farm Animals: Saving America's Rare Breeds.* Boston: Little, Brown, 1991.

Patent, Dorothy Hinshaw. *Quetzel: Sacred Bird of the Cloud Forest.* Illus. Neil Waldman. New York: Morrow, 1996.

————. *Where the Bald Eagles Gather.* Photographs by William Munoz. Boston: Houghton Mifflin, 1984.

Peters, Lisa Westberg. *Water's Way.* New York: Arcade, 1991.

Petersen, Christine. *Solar Power.* New York: Children's Press, 2004.

————. *Wind Power.* New York: Children's Press, 2004.

Pringle, Laurence. *City and Suburbs: Exploring Ecosystems.* New York: Macmillan, 1975.

————. *The Hidden World: Life Under a Rock.* New York: Macmillan, 1977.

————. *Living in a Risky World.* New York: Morrow, 1989.

Resnick, Jane. *Snakes.* ("Eyes on Nature" series) Chicago: Kidsbooks, 1996.

Ride, Sally, and Susan Okie. *To Space and Back.* New York: Lothrop, 1986.

Romanek, Trudee. *Switched On, Flushed Down, Tossed Out: Investigating the Hidden Workings of Your House.* Illus. Stephen MacEachern. Willowdale, Ontario: Annik Press, 2005.

St. George, Judith. *The Brooklyn Bridge: They Said It Couldn't Be Built.* New York: Putnam, 1982.

Schwartz, David M. *Millions to Measure.* Illus. Steven Kellogg. New York: HarperCollins, 2003.

Scott, Elaine. *Close Encounters: Exploring the Universe with the Hubble Space Telescope.* New York: Hyperion, 1998.

Selsam, Millicent. *The Birth of an Island.* New York: Scholastic, 1972.

Simon, Seymour. *The Heart: Our Circulatory System.* New York: Collins, 2006.

———. *Oceans.* New York: Collins, 2006.

———. *Our Solar System.* Rev. ed. New York: Collins, 2007.

———. *Penguins.* (Smithsonian) New York: Collins, 2009.

———. *Tropical Rainforests.* New York: Collins, 2010.

Skurzynski, Gloria. *Waves: The Electromagnetic Universe.* Washington, DC: National Geographic, 1996.

Srivastava, Jane Jonas. *Statistics.* New York: Crowell, 1973.

Taylor, Barbara. *Coral Reef.* Boston: Houghton, 1992.

Turner, Pamela S. *The Frog Scientist.* New York: Houghton Mifflin, 2009.

Vernon, Adele. *The Hoiho: New Zealand's Yellow-Eyed Penguin.* New York: Putnam, 1991.

Walker, Sally M. *Fossil Fish Found Alive: Discovering the Coelacanth.* Minneapolis: Carolrhoda, 2002.

Webb, Sophie. *My Season with Penguins: An Antarctic Journal.* Boston: Houghton Mifflin, 2000.

Wick, Walter. *Walter Wick's Optical Tricks.* New York: Scholastic, 1998.

YES Magazine Editors. *Fantastic Feats and Failures.* Toronto: Kids Can Press, 2004.

Zoehfeld, Kathleen Weidner. *What Is the World Made of?: All about Solids, Liquids, and Gases.* Illus. Paul Meisel. New York: Harper, 1998.

Arts and Leisure

Aliki. *Ah, Music!* New York: HarperCollins, 2003.

Ancona, George. *Cutters, Carvers, and the Cathedral.* New York: Lothrop, 1995. (St. John the Divine, New York City)

Anderson, Dave. *The Story of Golf.* New York: Morrow, 1998.

Arnosky, Jim. *Fish in a Flash!: A Personal Guide to Spin-Fishing.* New York: Bradbury, 1991.

———. *Sketching Outdoors in Spring.* New York: Lothrop, 1987.

Aronson, Marc. *Art Attack: A Short Cultural History of the Avant-Garde.* New York: Clarion, 1998.

Banks, Kate. *Max's Words.* Illus. Boris Kulikov. New York: Farrar, Straus & Giroux, 2006.

Beardsley, John. *Pablo Picasso.* New York: Abrams, 1991.

Bellville, Cheryl Walsh. *Theater Magic: Behind the Scenes at a Children's Theater.* Minneapolis: Carolrhoda, 1986.

Bierhorst, John. *A Cry from the Earth: Music of the North American Indians.* New York: Four Winds, 1979.

Brown, Marc. *Your First Garden Book.* Boston: Little, Brown, 1981.

Carter, David A., and James Diaz. *The Elements of Pop-Up.* New York: Simon & Schuster, 1999.

Cleary, Brian P. *Pitch and Throw, Grasp and Know: What Is a Synonym?* Illus. Brian Gable. Minneapolis, MN: Carolrhoda, 2004.

Cone, Ferne Geller. *Crazy Crocheting.* Illus. Rachel Osterlof. Photographs by J. Morton Cone. New York: Atheneum, 1981.

Cooper, Elisha. *Dance!* New York: Greenwillow, 2001.

Cooper, Miriam. *Snap! Photography.* New York: Messner, 1981.

Duncan, Lois. *The Circus Comes Home: When the Greatest Show on Earth Rode the Rails.* New York: Doubleday, 1993.

Evans, Dilys. *Show and Tell: Exploring the Fine Art of Children's Book Illustration.* San Francisco: Chronicle Books, 2008.

Fisher, Leonard Everett. *Alphabet Art.* New York: Four Winds, 1978.

Florian, Douglas. *A Carpenter.* New York: Greenwillow, 1991.

Green, Jared, ed. *D. J. Dance, and Rave Culture.* Detroit, MI: Greenhaven Press, 2005.

Greenberg, Jan, and Sandra Jordan. *The Painter's Eye: Learning to Look at Contemporary American Art.* New York: Delacorte, 1991.

Heller, Ruth. *A Cache of Jewels and Other Collective Nouns.* New York: Grosset, 1987.

Hofsinde, Robert (Gray-Wolf). *Indian Arts.* New York: Morrow, 1971.

Hughes, Langston. *The First Book of Jazz.* New York: Watts, 1955.

Jaspersohn, William. *Magazine: Behind the Scenes at Sports Illustrated.* Boston: Little, Brown, 1983.

Jones, Bill T., and Susan Kuklin. *Dance.* Photographs by Susan Kuklin. New York: Hyperion, 1998.

Kalb, Jonah, and Laura Kalb. *The Easy Ice Skating Book*. Illus. Sandy Kossin. Boston: Houghton Mifflin, 1981.

Kohl, Herbert. *A Book of Puzzlements: Play and Invention with Language*. New York: Schocken, 1981.

Lasky, Kathryn. *Puppeteer*. New York: Macmillan, 1985.

Macaulay; David. *Castle*. Boston: Houghton Mifflin, 1983.

———. *Cathedral: The Story of Its Construction*. Boston: Houghton Mifflin, 1974.

———. *Mosque*. Boston: Houghton Mifflin, 2003.

Marks, Mickey K. *OP-Tricks: Creating Kinetic Art*. Philadelphia: Lippincott, 1972.

Naylor, Penelope. *Black Images: The Art of West Africa*. New York: Doubleday, 1973.

Pulver, Robin. *Punctuation Takes a Vacation*. Illus. Lynn Rowe Reed. New York: Holiday, 2003.

Rodari, Florian. *A Weekend with Picasso*. New York: Rizzoli, 1991.

Skira-Venturi, Rosabianca. *A Weekend with Van Gogh*. New York: Rizzoli, 1994.

Streatfield, Noel. *A Young Person's Guide to Ballet*. London: Warne, 1985.

Thomson, Peggy, with Barbara Moore. *The Nine-Ton Cat: Behind the Scenes at an Art Museum*. Boston: Houghton Mifflin, 1997.

Tinkelman, Murray. *Rodeo: The Great American Sport*. New York: Greenwillow, 1982.

Weiss, Harvey. *How to Make Your Own Books*. New York: Crowell, 1974.

Wolf, Diane. *Chinese Writing*. New York: Holt, Rinehart & Winston, 1975.

Yolen, Jane, and Heidi E. Y. Stemple. *The Barefoot Book of Ballet Stories*. Santa Rosa, CA: Barefoot Books, 2004.

Human Growth and Development

Aliki. *Feelings*. New York: Greenwillow, 1984.

———. *We Are Best Friends*. New York: Greenwillow, 1982.

Anholt, Catherine, and Laurence Anholt. *All about You*. New York: Viking, 1992.

Bailey, Jacqui. *Sex, Puberty, and All That Stuff: A Guide to Growing Up*. Illus. Jan McCafferty. Hauppauge, NY: Barron's Educational, 2004.

Banish, Roslyn. *A Forever Family*. New York: HarperCollins, 1992.

Beck, Debra. *My Feet Aren't Ugly!: A Girl's Guide to Loving Herself from the Inside Out*. New York: Beaufort Books, 2007.

Bernstein, Joanne, and Stephen Gullo. *When People Die*. New York: Dutton, 1977.

Bode, Janet. *Death Is Hard to Live With: Teenagers and How They Cope with Loss*. New York: Delacorte, 1993.

Brown, Laurie Krasny, and Marc Brown. *How to Be a Friend: A Guide to Making Friends and Keeping Them*. Boston: Little, Brown, 1998.

———. *What's the Big Secret?: Talking about Sex with Girls and Boys*. Illus. Marc Brown. Boston: Little, 1997.

———. *When Dinosaurs Die: A Guide to Understanding Death*. Illus. Marc Brown. Boston: Little, Brown, 1996.

Cho, Shinta. *The Gas We Pass: The Story of Farts*. Trans. Amanda Mayer Stinchecum. La Jolla, CA: Kane/Miller, 1994.

Cole, Babette. *Mommy Laid an Egg! Or Where Do Babies Come From?* New York: Chronicle, 1996.

Cole, Joanna. *The New Baby at Your House*. New York: Morrow, 1985.

Daldry, Jeremy. *The Teenage Guy's Survival Guide: The Real Deal on Girls, Growing Up and Other Guy Stuff*. Boston: Little, Brown, 1999.

Dee, Catherine. *The Girls' Guide to Life: How to Take Charge of the Issues That Affect You*. Illus. Cynthia Jabar. Photographs by Carol Palmer. Boston: Little, Brown, 1997.

Engel, Joel. *Handwriting Analysis Self-Taught*. New York: Elsevier/Nelson, 1980.

Fujikawa, Gyo. *Let's Play!* New York: Grosset, 1975.

Giblin, James Cross. *From Hand to Mouth: Or How We Invented Knives, Forks, Spoons, and Chopsticks & the Table Manners to Go with Them*. New York: Crowell, 1987.

Girard, Linda Walvoord. *Alex, the Kid with AIDS*. Morton Grove, IL: A. Whitman, 1990.

———. *We Adopted You, Benjamin Koo*. Morton Grove, IL: A. Whitman, 1989.

Gomi, Taro. *Everyone Poops*. Trans. Amanda Mayer Stinchecum. La Jolla, CA: Kane/Miller, 1993.

Gravelle, Karen, and Nick and Chava Castro. *What's Going on Down There?: Answers to Questions Boys Find Hard to Ask*. Illus. Robert Leighton. New York: Walker, 1997.

Grollman, Earl A. *Straight Talk about Death for Teenagers: How to Cope with Losing Someone You Love*. Boston: Beacon Press, 1993.

Harris, Robie H. *It's Perfectly Normal: A Book about Changing Bodies, Growing Up, Sex, and Sexual Health*. Cambridge, MA: Candlewick, 1994.

Jennes, Aylette. *Families: A Celebration of Diversity, Commitment, and Love*. Boston: Houghton Mifflin, 1990.

Kamien, Janet. *What If You Couldn't . . . ?* New York: Scribner's, 1979.

LeShan, Eda. *What's Going to Happen to Me? When Parents Separate or Divorce*. New York: Four Winds, 1978.

Macaulay, David. *The Way We Work*. New York: Houghton Mifflin, 2008.

Machotka, Hana. *Breathtaking Noses*. New York: Morrow, 1992.

———. *What Neat Feet!* New York: Morrow, 1991.

Maestro, Betsy, and Giulio Maestro. *Where Is My Friend?* New York: Crown, 1976.

Meltzer, Milton. *The Landscape of Memory*. New York: Viking, 1987.

———. *When a Parent Is Very Sick*. New York: Atlantic, 1986.

Levy, Janice. *Finding the Right Spot: When Kids Can't Live with Their Parents*. Illus. Whitney Martin. Washington, D. C.: APA, 2004.

Pardes, Bronwen. *Doing It Right: Making Smart, Safe, and Satisfying Choices about Sex*. New York: Simon Pulse, 2007.

Perl, Lila. *The Great Ancestor Hunt: The Fun of Finding Out Who You Are*. Boston: Houghton Mifflin, 1989.

Rofes, Eric E. *The Kids' Book About Death and Dying*. Boston: Little, Brown, 1985.

Rosen, Michael. *Michael Rosen's Sad Book*. Illus. Quentin Blake. New York: Candlewick, 2005.

Saltz, Gail. *Changing You: A Guide to Body Changes and Sexuality*. Illus. Lynne Avril Cravath. New York: Dutton, 2007.

Schwartz, Alvin. *Telling Fortunes: Love Magic, Dream Signs, and Other Ways to Learn the Future*. Philadelphia: Lippincott, 1987.

Stickney, Doris. *Water Bugs & Dragonflies: Explaining Death to Children*. Cleveland: Pilgrim Press, 2004.

Sutton, Roger. *Hearing Us Out: Voices from the Gay and Lesbian Community*. Boston: Little, Brown, 1994.

Terkel, Susan N., and Janice Rench. *Feeling Safe, Feeling Strong: How to Avoid Sexual Abuse and What to Do If It Happens to You*. Minneapolis: Lerner, 1984.

Zolotow, Charlotte. *The Quarreling Book*. Illus. Arnold Lobel. New York: HarperCollins, 1982.

Go to the topic "Nonfiction" on the MyEducationKit for this text, where you can:

- Search the Database of Children's Literature, housing more than 22,000 titles searchable in every genre by authors or illustrators, by awards won, by year published, and by topic and description.

- Explore genre-related Assignments and Activities, assignable exercises showing concepts in action

through database use, video, cases, and student and teacher artifacts.

- Listen to podcasts and read interviews from some of the brightest and most enduring stars of children's literature in the Conversations.

- Discover Web Links that will lead you to sites representing the authors you learn about in these pages, classrooms with powerful children's literature connections, and literature awards.

Children's Book Awards

Every year numerous book awards are presented to works of children's literature, both for writing and for illustration. These awards are sponsored by various organizations, each with its own set of criteria. In addition, several awards are presented to individuals recognizing lifetime achievement in children's literature. Included here are some, but not all, of the more prestigious awards. The award-selection process is not infallible, and often some very excellent works have been overlooked, whereas some award-winning works have not altogether successfully stood the test of time. In general, these lists can suggest—in addition to specific titles—authors and illustrators who produce works of high quality, but we should by no means be slaves to book award lists.

Included in the following lists are awards presented to writers in English, as well as some international awards. It is important that we make a concerted effort to acquaint ourselves not only with American and English children's authors, but with writers the world over. Perhaps in time, more of these foreign language books for children will be available in translation as we realize how important intercultural communication is to global understanding.

American Book Awards

The Newbery Medal

The Newbery Medal was named for John Newbery, the British entrepreneur who pioneered children's book publishing in the eighteenth century. The award is, however, an American award, presented annually by the American Library Association to the most distinguished contribution to children's literature published in the United States. Runners-up are termed Honor Books. As with any such award, there has not always been general agreement with the decisions. However, the list does include some of the finest writing for young people in the past century.

1922   *The Story of Mankind* by Hendrik Willem van Loon, Liveright
Honor Books: *The Great Quest* by Charles Hawes, Little, Brown; *Cedric the Forester* by Bernard Marshall, Appleton; *The Old Tobacco Shop: A True Account of What Befell a Little Boy in Search of Adventure* by William Bowen, Macmillan; *The Golden Fleece and the Heroes Who Lived before Achilles* by Padraic Colum, Macmillan; *Windy Hill* by Cornelia Meigs, Macmillan

1923   *The Voyages of Doctor Dolittle* by Hugh Lofting, Lippincott
Honor Books: No record

1924   *The Dark Frigate* by Charles Hawes, Little, Brown
Honor Books: No record

1925   *Tales from Silver Lands* by Charles Finger, Doubleday
Honor Books: *Nicholas: A Manhattan Christmas Story* by Anne Carroll Moore, Putnam; *Dream Coach* by Anne Parrish, Macmillan

1926   *Shen of the Sea* by Arthur Bowie Chrisman, Dutton
Honor Book: *Voyagers: Being Legends and Romances of Atlantic Discovery* by Padraic Colum, Macmillan

1927   *Smoky, The Cowhorse* by Will James, Scribner's
Honor Books: No record

1928   *Gayneck, The Story of a Pigeon* by Dhan Gopal Mukerji, Dutton
Honor Books: *The Wonder Smith and His Son: A Tale from the Golden Childhood of the World* by Elia Young, Longmans; *Downright Dencey* by Caroline Snedeker, Doubleday

1929   *The Trumpeter of Krakow* by Eric P. Kelly, Macmillan
      Honor Books: *Pigtail of Ah Lee Ben Loo* by John Bennett, Longmans, Green (McKay); *Millions of Cats* by Wanda Gág, Coward, McCann & Geoghegan; *The Boy Who Was* by Grace Hallock, Dutton; *Clearing Weather* by Cornelia Meigs, Little, Brown; *Runaway Papoose* by Grace Moon, Doubleday; *Tod of the Fens* by Elinor Whitney, Macmillan

1930   *Hitty, Her First Hundred Years* by Rachel Field, Macmillan
      Honor Books: *Daughter of the Seine: The Life of Madame Roland* by Jeanette Eaton, Harper; *Pran of Albania* by Elizabeth Miller, Doubleday; *Jumping-off Place* by Marian Hurd McNeely, Longmans, Green (McKay); *Tangle-coated Horse and Other Tales: Episodes from the Fionn Saga* by Ella Young, Longmans, Green (McKay); *Vaino: A Boy of New England* by Julia Davis Adams, Dutton; *Little Blacknose* by Hildegarde Swift, Harcourt Brace Jovanovich

1931   *The Cat Who Went to Heaven* by Elizabeth Coatsworth, Macmillan
      Honor Books: *Floating Island* by Anne Parrish, Harper; *The Dark Star of Itza: The Story of a Pagan Princess* by Alida Malkus, Harcourt Brace Jovanovich; *Queer Person* by Ralph Hubbard, Doubleday; *Mountains Are Free* by Julia Davis Adams, Dutton; *Spice and the Devil's Cave* by Agnes Hewes, Knopf; *Meggy MacIntosh* by Elizabeth Janet Gray, Doubleday; *Garram the Hunter: A Boy of the Hill Tribes* by Herbert Best, Doubleday; *Ood-Le-Uk the Wanderer* by Alice Lide and Margaret Johansen, Little, Brown

1932   *Waterless Mountain* by Laura Adams Armer, Longmans, Green (McKay)
      Honor Books: *The Fairy Circus* by Dorothy P. Lathrop, Macmillan; *Calico Bush* by Rachel Field, Macmillan; *Boy of the South Seas* by Eunice Tietjens, Coward, McCann & Geoghegan; *Out of the Flame* by Eloise Lownsbery, Longmans, Green (McKay); *Jane's Island* by Marjorie Allee, Houghton Mifflin; *Truce of the Wolf and Other Tales of Old Italy* by Mary Gould Davis, Harcourt Brace Jovanovich

1933   *Young Fu of the Upper Yangtze* by Elizabeth Foreman Lewis, Winston
      Honor Books: *Swift Rivers* by Cornelia Meigs, Little, Brown; *The Railroad to Freedom: A Story of the Civil War* by Hildegarde Swift, Harcourt Brace Jovanovich; *Children of the Soil: A Story of Scandinavia* by Nora Burglon, Doubleday

1934   *Invincible Louisa: The Story of the Author of* Little Women by Cornelia Meigs, Little, Brown
      Honor Books: *The Forgotten Daughter* by Caroline Snedeker, Doubleday; *Swords of Steel* by Elsie Singmaster, Houghton Mifflin; *ABC Bunny* by Wanda Gág, Coward, McCann & Geoghegan; *Winged Girl of Knossos* by Erik Berry, Appleton; *New Land* by Sarah Schmidt, McBride; *Big Tree of Bunlaby: Stories of My Own Countryside* by Padraic Colum, Macmillan; *Glory of the Seas* by Agnes Hewes, Knopf; *Apprentice of Florence* by Ann Kyle, Houghton Mifflin

1935   *Dobry* by Monica Shannon, Viking
      Honor Books: *Pageant of Chinese History by* Elizabeth Seeger, Longmans, Green (McKay); *Davy Crockett* by Constance Rourke, Harcourt Brace Jovanovich; *Day on Skates: The Story of a Dutch Picnic* by Hilda Van Stockum, Harper

1936   *Caddie Woodlawn* by Carol Ryrie Brink, Macmillan
      Honor Books: *Honk, the Moose* by Phil Strong, Dodd, Mead; *The Good Master* by Kate Seredy, Viking; *Young Walter Scott* by Elizabeth Janet Gray, Viking; *All Sail Set: A Romance of the* "Flying Cloud" by Armstrong Sperry, Winston

1937   *Roller Skates* by Ruth Sawyer, Viking
      Honor Books: *Phoebe Fairchild: Her Book* by Lois Lenski, Stokes; *Whistler's Van* by Idwal Jones, Viking; *Golden Basket* by Ludwig Bemelmans, Viking; *Winterbound* by Margery Bianco, Viking; *Audubon* by Constance Rourke, Harcourt Brace Jovanovich; *The Codfish Musket* by Agnes Hewes, Doubleday

1938   *The White Stag* by Kate Seredy, Viking
      Honor Books: *Pecos Bill* by James Cloyd Bowman, Little, Brown; *Bright Island* by Mabel Robinson, Random House; *On the Banks of Plum Creek* by Laura Ingalls Wilder, Harper

1939   *Thimble Summer* by Elizabeth Enright, Holt, Rinehart & Winston
      Honor Books: *Nino* by Valenti Angelo, Viking; *Mr. Popper's Penguins* by Richard and Florence Atwater, Little, Brown; *"Hello the Boat!"* by Phillis Crawford, Holt, Rinehart & Winston; *Leader by Destiny: George Washington, Man and Patriot* by Jeanette Eaton, Harcourt Brace Jovanovich; *Penn* by Elizabeth Janet Gray, Viking

1940   *Daniel Boone* by James Daugherty, Viking
Honor Books: *The Singing Tree* by Kate Seredy, Viking; *Runner of the Mountain Tops: The Life of Louis Agassiz* by Mabel Robinson, Random House; *By the Shores of Silver Lake* by Laura Ingalls Wilder, Harper; *Boy with a Pack* by Stephen W Meader, Harcourt Brace Jovanovich

1941   *Call It Courage* by Armstrong Sperry, Macmillan
Honor Books: *Blue Willow* by Doris Gates, Viking; *Young Mac of Fort Vancouver* by Mary Jane Carr, Crowell; *The Long Winter* by Laura Ingalls Wilder, Harper; *Nansen* by Anna Gertrude Hall, Viking

1942   *The Matchlock Gun* by Walter D. Edmonds, Dodd, Mead
Honor Books: *Little Town on the Prairie* by Laura Ingalls Wilder, Harper; *George Washington's World* by Genevieve Foster, Scribner; *Indian Captive: The Story of Mary Jemison* by Lois Lenski, Lippincott; *Down Ryton Water* by Eva Roe Gaggin, Viking

1943   *Adam of the Road* by Elizabeth Janet Gray, Viking
Honor Books: *The Middle Moffat* by Eleanor Estes, Harcourt Brace Jovanovich; *Have You Seen Tom Thumb?* by Mabel Leigh Hunt, Lippincott

1944   *Johnny Tremain* by Esther Forbes, Houghton Mifflin
Honor Books: *These Happy Golden Years* by Laura Ingalls Wilder, Harper; *Fog Magic* by Julia Sauer, Viking; *Rufus M.* by Eleanor Estes, Harcourt Brace Jovanovich; *Mountain Born* by Elizabeth Yates, Coward, McCann & Geoghegan

1945   *Rabbit Hill* by Robert Lawson, Viking
Honor Books: *The Hundred Dresses* by Eleanor Estes, Harcourt Brace Jovanovich; *The Silver Pencil* by Alice Dalgliesh, Scribner's; *Abraham Lincoln's World* by Genevieve Foster, Scribner's; *Lone Journey: The Life of Roger Williams* by Jeanette Eaton, Harcourt Brace Jovanovich

1946   *Strawberry Girl* by Lois Lenski, Lippincott
Honor Books: *Justin Morgan Had a Horse* by Marguerite Henry, Rand McNally; *The Moved-Outers* by Florence Crannell Means, Houghton Mifflin; *Bhimsa, the Dancing Bear* by Christine Weston, Scribner; *New Found World* by Katherine Shippen, Viking

1947   *Miss Hickory* by Carolyn Sherwin Bailey, Viking
Honor Books: *Wonderful Year* by Nancy Barnes, Messner; *Big Tree* by Mary and Conrad Buff, Viking; *The Heavenly Tenants* by William Maxwell, Harper; *The Avion My Uncle Flew* by Cyrus Fisher, Appleton; *The Hidden Treasure of Glaston* by Eleanore Jewett, Viking

1948   *The Twenty-One Balloons* by William Pene du Bois, Viking
Honor Books: *Pancakes-Paris* by Claire Huchet Bishop, Viking; *Le Lun, Lad of Courage* by Carolyn Treffinger, Abingdon; *The Quaint and Curious Quest of Johnny Longfoot, The Shoe-King's Son* by Catherine Besterman, Bobbs-Merrill; *The Cow-Tail Switch, and Other West African Stories* by Harold Courlander, Holt, Rinehart & Winston; *Misty of Chincoteague* by Marguerite Henry, Rand McNally

1949   *King of the Wind* by Marguerite Henry, Rand McNally
Honor Books: *Seabird* by Holling C. Holling, Houghton Mifflin; *Daughter of the Mountains* by Louise Rankin, Viking; *My Father's Dragon* by Ruth S. Gannett, Random House; *Story of the Negro* by Arna Bontemps, Knopf

1950   *The Door in the Wall* by Marguerite de Angeli, Doubleday
Honor Books: *Tree of Freedom* by Rebecca Caudill, Viking; *The Blue Cat of Castle Town* by Catherine Coblentz, Longmans, Green (McKay); *Kildee House* by Rutherford Montgomery, Doubleday; *George Washington* by Genevieve Foster, Scribner's; *Song of the Pines: A Story of Norwegian Lumbering in Wisconsin* by Walter and Marion Havighurst, Winston

1951   *Amos Fortune, Free Man* by Elizabeth Yates, Aladdin
Honor Books: *Better Known as Johnny Appleseed* by Mabel Leigh Hunt, Lippincott; *Gandhi, Fighter without a Sword* by Jeanette Eaton, Morrow; *Abraham Lincoln, Friend of the People* by Clara Ingram Judson, Follett; *The Story of Appleby Capple* by Anne Parrish, Harper

1952   *Ginger Pye* by Eleanor Estes, Harcourt Brace Jovanovich
Honor Books: *Americans before Columbus* by Elizabeth Baity, Viking; *Minn of the Mississippi* by Holling C. Holling, Houghton Mifflin; *The Defender* by Nicholas Kalashnikoff, Scribner's; *The Light at Tern Rock* by Julia Sauer, Viking; *The Apple and the Arrow* by Mary and Conrad Buff, Houghton Mifflin

1953   *Secret of the Andes* by Ann Nolan Clark, Viking
Honor Brooks: *Charlotte's Web* by E. B. White, Harper; *Moccasin Trail* by Eloise McGraw, Coward, McCann & Geoghegan; *Red Sails to Capri* by Ann Well, Viking; *The Bears on Hemlock Mountain* by Alice Dalgliesh, Scribner; *Birthdays of Freedom, Vol. 1*, by Genevieve Foster, Scribner

1954   *. . . and Now Miguel* by Joseph Krumgold, Crowell
Honor Books: *All Alone* by Claire Huchet Bishop, Viking; *Shadrach* by Meindert DeJong, Harper; *Hurry Home Candy* by Meindert DeJong, Harper; *Theodore Roosevelt, Fighting Patriot* by Clara Ingram Judson, Follett; *Magic Maize* by Mary and Conrad Buff, Houghton Mifflin

1955   *The Wheel on the School* by Meindert DeJong, Harper
Honor Books: *The Courage of Sarah Noble* by Alice Dalgliesh, Scribner's; *Banner in the Sky* by James Ullman, Lippincott

1956   *Carry On, Mr. Bowditch* by Jean Lee Latham, Houghton Mifflin
Honor Books: *The Secret River* by Marjorie Kinnan Rawlings, Scribner's; *The Golden Name Day* by Jennie Linquist, Harper; *Men, Microscopes, and Living Things* by Katherine Shippen, Viking

1957   *Miracles on Maple Hill* by Virginia Sorensen, Harcourt Brace Jovanovich
Honor Books: *Old Yeller* by Fred Gipson, Harper; *The House of Sixty Fathers* by Meindert DeJong, Harper; *Mr. Justice Holmes* by Clara Ingram Judson, Follett; *The Corn Grows Ripe* by Dorothy Rhoads, Viking; *Black Fox of Lorne* by Marguerite de Angeli, Doubleday

1958   *Rifles for Watie* by Harold Keith, Crowell
Honor Books: *The Horsecatcher* by Mari Sandoz, Westminster; *Gone-Away Lake* by Elizabeth Enright, Harcourt Brace Jovanovich; *The Great Wheel* by Robert Lawson, Viking; *Tom Paine, Freedom's Apostle* by Leo Gurko, Crowell

1959   *The Witch of Blackbird Pond* by Elizabeth George Speare, Houghton Mifflin
Honor Books: *The Family under the Bridge* by Natalie Savage Carlson, Harper; *Along Came a Dog* by Meindert DeJong, Harper; *Chúcaro: Wild Pony of the Pampas* by Francis Kalnay, Harcourt Brace Jovanovich; *The Perilous Road* by William O. Steele, Harcourt Brace Jovanovich

1960   *Onion John* by Joseph Krumgold, Crowell
Honor Books: *My Side of the Mountain* by Jean George, Dutton; *America Is Born* by Gerald W. Johnson, Morrow; *The Gammage Cup* by Carol Kendall, Harcourt Brace Jovanovich

1961   *Island of the Blue Dolphins* by Scott O'Dell, Houghton Mifflin
Honor Books: *America Moves Forward* by Gerald W. Johnson, Morrow; *Old Ramon* by Jack Schaefer, Houghton Mifflin; *The Cricket in Times Square* by George Selden, Farrar, Straus & Giroux

1962   *The Bronze Bow* by Elizabeth George Speare, Houghton Mifflin
Honor Books: *Frontier Living* by Edwin Tunis, World; *The Golden Goblet* by Eloise McCraw, Coward, McCann & Geoghegan; *Belling the Tiger* by Mary Stolz, Harper

1963   *A Wrinkle in Time* by Madeline L'Engle, Farrar, Straus & Giroux
Honor Books: *Thistle and Thyme: Tales and Legends from Scotland* by Sorche Nic Leodhas, Holt, Rinehart & Winston; *Men ofAthens* by Olivia Coolidge, Houghton Mifflin

1964   *It's Like This, Cat* by Emily Cheney Neville, Harper
Honor Books: *Rascal* by Sterling North, Dutton; *The Loner* by Ester Wier, McKay

1965   *Shadow of a Bull* by Maia Wojciechowska, Atheneum
Honor Book: *Across Five Aprils* by Irene Hunt, Follett

1966   *I, Juan de Pareja* by Elizabeth Borten de Trevino, Farrar, Straus & Giroux
Honor Books: *The Black Cauldron* by Lloyd Alexander, Holt, Rinehart & Winston; *The Animal Family* by Randall Jarrell, Pantheon; *The Noonday Friends* by Mary Stolz, Harper

1967   *Up a Road Slowly* by Irene Hunt, Follett
Honor Books: *The King's Fifth* by Scott O'Dell, Houghton Mifflin; *Zlateh the Goat and Other Stories* by Isaac Bashevis Singer, Harper; *The Jazz Man* by Mark H. Weik, Atheneum

1968   *From the Mixed-Up Files of Mrs. Basil E. Frankweiler* by E. L. Konigsburg, Atheneum
Honor Books: *Jennifer, Hecate, Macbeth, William McKinley, and Me, Elizabeth* by E. L. Konigsburg, Atheneum; *The Black Pearl* by Scott O'Dell, Houghton Mifflin; *The Fearsome Inn* by Isaac Bashevis Singer, Scribner; *The Egypt Game* by Zilpha Keatley Snyder, Atheneum

1969   *The High King* by Lloyd Alexander, Holt, Rinehart & Winston
Honor Books: *To Be a Slave* by Julius Lester, Dial Press; *When Shlemiel Went to Warsaw and Other Stories* by Isaac Bashevis Singer, Farrar, Straus & Giroux

1970   *Sounder* by William H. Armstrong, Harper
Honor Books: *Our Eddie* by Sulamith Ish-Kishor, Pantheon; *The Many Ways of Seeing: An Introduction to the Pleasures of Art* by Janet Gaylord Moore, World; *Journey Outside* by Mary Q. Steele, Viking

1971   *Summer of the Swans* by Betsy Byars, Viking
Honor Books: *Kneeknock Rise* by Natalie Babbitt, Farrar, Straus & Giroux; *Enchantress from the Stars* by Sylvia Louise Engdahl, Atheneum; *Sing Down the Moon* by Scott O'Dell, Houghton Mifflin

1972   *Mrs. Frisby and the Rats of NIMH* by Robert C. O'Brien, Atheneum
Honor Books: *Incident at Hawk's Hill* by Allan W Eckert. Little, Brown; *The Planet of Junior Brown* by Virginia Hamilton, Macmillan; *The Tombs of Atuan* by Ursula K. Le Guin, Atheneum; *Annie and the Old One* by Miska Miles, Little, Brown; *The Headless Cupid* by Zilpha Keatley Snyder, Atheneum

1973   *Julie of the Wolves* by Jean Craighead George, Harper
Honor Books: *Frog and Toad Together* by Arnold Lobel, Harper; *The Upstairs Room* by Johanna Reiss, Crowell; *The Witches of Worm* by Zilpha Keatley Snyder, Atheneum

1974   *The Slave Dancer* by Paula Fox, Bradbury
Honor Book: *The Dark Is Rising* by Susan Cooper, Atheneum

1975   M. C. Higgins, the Great by Virginia Hamilton, Macmillan
Honor Books: *Figgs & Phantoms* by Ellen Raskin, Dutton; *My Brother Sam Is Dead* by James Lincoln Collier and Christopher Collier, Four Winds; *The Perilous Gard* by Elizabeth Marie Pope, Houghton Mifflin; *Philip Hall Likes Me, I Reckon Maybe* by Bette Greene, Dial Press

1976   *The Grey King* by Susan Cooper, Atheneum
Honor Books: *The Hundred Penny Box* by Sharon Bell Mathis, Viking; *Dragonwings* by Laurence Yep, Harper

1977   *Roll of Thunder, Hear My Cry* by Mildred D. Taylor, Dial Press
Honor Books: *Abel's Island* by William Steig, Farrar, Straus & Giroux; *A String in the Harp* by Nancy Bond, Atheneum

1978   *Bridge to Terabithia* by Katherine Paterson, Crowell
Honor Books: *Ramona and Her Father* by Beverly Cleary, Morrow; *Anpao: An American Indian Odyssey* by Jamake Highwater, Lippincott

1979   *The Westing Game* by Ellen Raskin, Dutton
Honor Book: *The Great Gilly Hopkins* by Katherine Paterson, Crowell

1980   *A Gathering of Days: A New England Girl's Journal 1830–32* by Joan Blos, Scribner's
Honor Book: *The Road from Home: The Story of an Armenian Girl* by David Kherdian, Greenwillow (Morrow)

1981   *Jacob Have I Loved* by Katherine Paterson, Cromwell
Honor Books: *The Fledgling* by Jane Langton, Harper; *A Ring of Endless Light* by Madeleine L'Engle, Farrar, Straus & Giroux

1982   *A Visit to William Blake's Inn: Poems for Innocent and Experienced Travelers* by Nancy Willard, Harcourt Brace Jovanovich
Honor Books: *Ramona Quimby, Age 8* by Beverly Cleary, Morrow; *Upon the Head of the Goat: A Childhood in Hungary, 1939–1944* by Aranka Siegal, Farrar, Straus & Giroux

1983   *Dicey's Song* by Cynthia Voigt, Atheneum
Honor Books: *Blue Sword* by Robin McKinley, Morrow; *Dr. DeSoto* by William Steig, Farrar, Straus & Giroux; *Graven Images* by Paul Fleischman, Harper; *Homesick: My Own Story* by Jean Fritz, Putnam; *Sweet Whisper, Brother Rush* by Virginia Hamilton, Philomel (Putnam)

1984   *Dear Mr. Henshaw* by Beverly Cleary, Morrow
Honor Books: *The Wish Giver* by Bill Brittain, Harper; *Sugaring Time* by Kathryn Lasky, Macmillan; *The Sign of the Beaver* by Elizabeth George Speare, Houghton Mifflin; *A Solitary Blue* by Cynthia Voigt, Atheneum

1985   *The Hero and the Crown* by Robin McKinley, Greenwillow (Morrow)
Honor Books: *The Moves Make the Man* by Bruce Brooks, Harper; *One-Eyed Cat* by Paula Fox, Bradbury; *Like Jake and Me* by Mavis Jukes, Knopf

1986   *Sarah, Plain and Tall* by Patricia MacLachlan, Harper
Honor Books: *Commodore Perry in the Land of the Shogun* by Rhoda Blumberg, Lothrop; *Dogsong* by Gary Paulsen, Bradbury

1987   *The Whipping Boy* by Sid Fleischman, Greenwillow (Morrow)
Honor Books: *On My Honor* by D. Bauer, Clarion; *Volcano: The Eruption and Healing of Mount St. Helens* by Patricia Lauber, Bradbury; *A Fine White Dust* by Cynthia Rylant, Bradbury

1988   *Lincoln: A Photobiography* by Russell Freedman, Clarion/Houghton Mifflin
Honor Books: *After the Rain* by Norma Fox Mazer, Morrow; *Hatchet* by Gary Paulsen, Bradbury

1989   *Joyful Noise: Poems for Two Voices* by Paul Fleischman, Harper
Honor Books: *In the Beginning* by Virginia Hamilton, Harcourt Brace Jovanovich; *Scorpions* by Walter Dean Myers, Harper

1990   *Number the Stars* by Lois Lowry, Houghton Mifflin
Honor Books: *Afternoon of the Elves* by Janet Taylor Lisle, Orchard Books/Watts; *The Winter Room* by Gary Paulsen, Orchard Books/Watts; *Shabanu: Daughter of the Wind* by Suzanne Fisher Staples, Knopf

1991   *Maniac Magee* by Jerry Spinelli, Little, Brown
Honor Book: *The True Confessions of Charlotte Doyle* by Avi, Orchard

1992   *Shiloh* by Phillis Reynolds Naylor, Atheneum
Honor Books: *Nothing But the Truth* by Avi, Orchard; *The Wright Brothers: How They Invented the Airplane* by Russell Freedman, Holiday

1993   *Missing May* by Cynthia Ryland, Orchard
Honor Books: *The Dark-Thirty: Southern Tales of the Supernatural* by Patricia McKissack, Knopf; *Somewhere in the Darkness* by Walter Dean Myers, Scholastic; *What Hearts* by Bruce Brooks, HarperCollins

1994   *The Giver* by Lois Lowry, Houghton Mifflin
Honor Books: *Eleanor Roosevelt: A Life of Discovery* by Russell Freedman, Clarion/Houghton Mifflin; *Dragon's Gate* by Laurence Yep, HarperCollins; *Crazy Lady* by Jane Leslie Conly, HarperCollins

1995   *Walk Two Moons* by Sharon Creech, HarperCollins
Honor Books: *Catherine, Called Birdy* by Karen Cushman, Clarion; *The Ear, the Eye, and the Arm* by Nancy Farmer, Orchard

1996   *The Midwife's Apprentice* by Karen Cushman, Houghton Mifflin
Honor Books: *What Jamie Saw* by Carolyn Coman, Front Street; *The Watsons Go to Birmingham—1963* by Christopher Paul Curtis, Delacorte; *Yolanda's Genius* by Carol Fenner, Simon; *The Great Fire* by Jim Murphy, Scholastic

1997   *The View from Saturday* by E. L. Konigsburg, Atheneum
Honor Books: *A Girl Named Disaster* by Nancy Farmer, Orchard; *Moorchild* by Eloise McGraw, McElderry; *The Thief* by Whalen Turner, Greenwillow; *Belle Prater's Boy* by Ruth White, Farrar

1998   *Out of the Dust* by Karen Hesse, Scholastic
Honor Books: *Ella Enchanted* by Gail Carson Levine, HarperCollins; *Lily's Crossing* by Patricia Reilly Giff, Delacorte; *Wringer* by Jerry Spinelli, HarperCollins

1999   *Holes* by Louis Sachar, Farrar, Straus & Giroux
Honor Book: *A Long Way Home* by Richard Peck, Dial

2000   *Bud, Not Buddy* by Christopher Paul Curtis, Delacorte
Honor Books: *Getting Near to Baby* by Audrey Couloumbis, Putnam; *26 Fairmount Avenue* by Tomie de Paola, Putnam; *Our Only May Amelia* by Jennifer L. Holm, HarperCollins

2001   *A Year Down Yonder* by Richard Peck, Dial
       Honor Books: *Hope Was Here* by Joan Bauer, Putnam; *The Wanderer* by Sharon Creech, HarperCollins; *Because of Winn-Dixie* by Kate DiCamillo, Candlewick; *Joey Pigza Loses Control* by Jack Gantos, Farrar

2002   *A Single Shard* by Linda Sue Park, Houghton Mifflin
       Honor Books: *Everything on a Waffle* by Polly Horvath, Farrar, Straus & Giroux; *Carver: A Life in Poems* by Marilyn Nelson, Front Street

2003   *Crispin: The Cross of Lead* by Avi, Hyperion
       Honor Books: *The House of the Scorpion* by Nancy Farmer, Atheneum; *Pictures of Hollis Woods* by Patricia Reilly Giff, Random House; *Hoot* by Carl Hiaasen, Knopf; *A Corner of the Universe* by Ann M. Martin, Scholastic; *Surviving the Applewhites* by Stephanie S. Tolan, HarperCollins

2004   *The Tale of Despereaux: Being the Story of a Mouse, a Princess, Some Soup, and a Spool of Thread* by Kate DiCamillo, Candlewick Press
       Honor Books: *Olive's Ocean* by Kevin Henkes, Greenwillow; *An American Plague: The True and Terrifying Story of the Yellow Fever Epidemic of 1793* by Jim Murphy, Clarion

2005   *Kira-Kira* by Cynthia Kadohata, Atheneum
       Honor Books: *Al Capone Does My Shirts* by Gennifer Choldenko, Putnam; *The Voice that Challenged a Nation: Marion Anderson and the Struggle for Equal Rights* by Russell Freedman, Clarion; *Lizzie Bright and the Buckminster Boy* by Gary D. Schmidt, Clarion

2006   *Criss Cross* by Lynne Rae Perkins, Greenwillow
       Honor Books: *Whittington* by Alan Armstrong, Random House; *Hitler Youth: Growing Up in Hitler's Shadow* by Susan Campbell Bartoletti, Scholastic; *Princess Academy* by Shannon Hale, Bloomsbury; *Show Way* by Jacqueline Woodson, Putnam

2007   *The Higher Power of Lucky* by Susan Patron, Simon & Schuster
       Honor Books: *Penny from Heaven* by Jennifer L. Holm, Random House; *Hattie Big Sky* by Kirby Larson, Delacorte; *Rules* by Cynthia Lord, Scholastic

2008   *Good Masters! Sweet Ladies! Voices from a Medieval Village* by Laura Amy Schlitz, Candlewick
       Honor Books: *Elijah of Buxton* by Christopher Paul Curtis, Scholastic; *The Wednesday Wars* by Gary D. Schmidt, Clarion; *Feathers* by Jacqueline Woodson, Putnam

2009   *The Graveyard Book* by Neil Gaiman, illus. by Dave McKean, HarperCollins
       Honor Books: *The Underneath* by Kathi Appelt, illus. by David Small, Atheneum; *The Surrender Tree: Poems of Cuba's Struggle for Freedom* by Margarita Engle, Henry Holt; *Savvy* by Ingrid Law, Dial/Walden Media; *After Tupac & D Foster* by Jacqueline Woodson, G.P. Putnam's Sons

2010   *When You Reach Me* by Rebecca Stead, Random House
       Honor Books: *Claudette Colvin: Twice Toward Justice* by Phillip Hoose, Farrar, Straus and Giroux; *The Evolution of Calpurnia Tate* by Jacqueline Kelly, Henry Holt; *Where the Mountain Meets the Moon* by Grace Lin, Little, Brown; *The Mostly True Adventures of Homer P. Figg* by Rodman Philbrick, Scholastic, Inc.

The Caldecott Medal

Named for the British illustrator Randolph Caldecott, the Caldecott Medal has been awarded annually since 1938 by the American Library Association to the most distinguished picture book published in the United States. Runners-up are given Honor Awards. Although the passage of time has not always validated the awards and many fine books have been overlooked, the awards list does provide a roll call of some of the best in children's books. The Caldecott Award is given to the illustrator and honors the pictorial art rather than the text. Unless indicated otherwise, the illustrator is the author.

1938   *Animals of the Bible* by Helen Dean Fish, illustrated by Dorothy P. Lathrop, Stokes
       Honor Books: *Seven Simeons: A Russian Tale* by Boris Artzybasheff, Viking; *Four and Twenty Blackbirds: Nursery Rhymes of Yesterday Recalled for Children of To-Day* by Helen Dean Fish, illustrated by Robert Lawson, Stokes

1939   *Mei Li* by Thomas Handforth, Doubleday
       Honor Books: *The Forest Pool* by Laura Adams Arner, Longmans, Green (McKay); *Wee Gillis* by Munro Leaf, illustrated by Robert Lawson, Viking; *Snow White and the Seven Dwarfs* by Wanda Gág, Coward, McCann &

Geoghegan; *Barkis* by Clare Newberry, Harper; *Andy and the Lion: A Tale of Kindness Remembered or the Power of Gratitude* by James Daugherty, Viking

1940 *Abraham Lincoln* by Ingri and Edgar Parin d'Aulaire, Doubleday
Honor Books: *Cock-a-Doodle Doo: The Story of a Little Red Rooster* by Berta and Elmer Hader, Macmillan; *Madeline* by Ludwig Bemelmans, Simon & Schuster; *The Ageless Story* by Lauren Ford, Dodd, Mead

1941 *They Were Strong and Good* by Robert Lawson, Viking
Honor Book: *April's Kittens* by Clare Newberry, Harper

1942 *Make Way for Ducklings* by Robert McCloskey, Viking
Honor Books: *An American ABC* by Maud and Miska Petersham, Macmillan; *In My Mother's House* by Ann Nolan Clark, illustrated by Velino Herrera, Viking; *Paddle-to-the-Sea* by Holling C. Holling, Houghton Mifflin; *Nothing at All* by Wanda Gág, Coward, McCann & Geoghegan

1943 *The Little House* by Virginia Lee Burton, Houghton Mifflin
Honor Books: *Dash and Dart* by Mary and Conrad Buff, Viking; *Marshmallow* by Clare Newberry, Harper

1944 *Many Moons* by James Thurber, illustrated by Louis Slobodkin, Harcourt Brace Jovanovich
Honor Books: *Small Rain: Verses from the Bible* selected by Jessie Orton Jones, illustrated by Elizabeth Orton Jones, Viking; *Pierre Pigeon* by Lee Kingman, illustrated by Arnold E. Bare, Houghton Mifflin; *The Mighty Hunter* by Berta and Elmer Hader, Macmillan; *A Child's Good Night Book* by Margaret Wise Brown, illustrated by Jean Charlot, W. R. Scott; *Good Luck Horse* by Chih-Yi Chan, illustrated by Plato Chan, Whittlesey

1945 *Prayer for a Child* by Rachel Field, illustrated by Elizabeth Orton Jones, Macmillan
Honor Books: *Mother Goose: Seventy-Seven Verses with Pictures*, illustrated by Tasha Tudor, Walck; *In the Forest* by Marie Hall Ets, Viking; *Yonie Wondernose* by Marguerite de Angeli, Doubleday; *The Christmas Anna Angel* by Ruth Sawyer, illustrated by Kate Seredy, Viking

1946 *The Rooster Crows . . .*, illustrated by Maud and Miska Petersham, Macmillan
Honor Books: *Little Lost Lamb* by Golden MacDonald, illustrated by Leonard Weisgard, Doubleday; *Sing Mother Goose* by Opal Wheeler, illustrated by Marjorie Torrey, Dutton; *My Mother Is the Most Beautiful Woman in the World* by Becky Reyher, illustrated by Ruth Gannett, Lothrop; *You Can Write Chinese* by Kurt Wiese, Viking

1947 *The Little Island* by Golden MacDonald, illustrated by Leonard Weisgard, Doubleday
Honor Books: *Rain Drop Splash* by Alvin Tresselt, illustrated by Leonard Weisgard, Lothrop; *Boats on the River* by Marjorie Flack, illustrated by Jay Hyde Barnum, Viking; *Timothy Turtle* by Al Graham, illustrated by Tony Palazzo, Viking; *Pedro, The Angel of Olvera Street* by Leo Politi, Scribner's; *Sing in Praise: A Collection of the Best Loved Hymns* by Opal Wheeler, illustrated by Marjorie Torrey, Dutton

1948 *White Snow, Bright Snow* by Alvin Tresselt, illustrated by Roger Duvoisin, Lothrop
Honor Books: *Stone Soup: An Old Tale* by Marcia Brown, Scribner's; *McElligot's Pool* by Dr. Seuss, Random House; *Bambino the Clown* by George Schreiber, Viking; *Roger and the Fox* by Lavinia Davis, illustrated by Hildegard Woodward, Doubleday; *Song of Robin Hood* edited by Anne Malcolmson, illustrated by Virginia Lee Burton, Houghton Mifflin

1949 *The Big Snow* by Berta and Elmer Hader, Macmillan
Honor Books: *Blueberries for Sal* by Robert McCloskey, Viking; *All Around the Town* by Phyllis McGinley, illustrated by Helen Stone, Lippincott; *Juanita* by Leo Politi, Scribner's; *Fish in the Air* by Kurt Wiese, Viking

1950 *Song of the Swallows* by Leo Politi, Scribner's
Honor Books: *America's Ethan Allen* by Stewart Holbrook, illustrated by Lynd Ward, Houghton Mifflin; *The Wild Birthday Cake* by Lavinia Davis, illustrated by Hildegard Woodward, Doubleday; *The Happy Day* by Ruth Krauss, illustrated by Marc Simont, Harper; *Bartholomew and the Oobleck* by Dr. Seuss, Random House; *Henry Fisherman* by Marcia Brown, Scribner's

1951 *The Egg Tree* by Katherine Milhouse, Scribner's
Honor Books: *Dick Whittington and His Cat* by Marcia Brown, Scribner's; *The Two Reds* by William Lipkind, illustrated by Nicholas Mordvinoff, Harcourt Brace Jovanovich; *If I Ran the Zoo* by Dr. Seuss, Random House; *The Most Wonderful Doll in the World* by Phyllis McGinley, illustrated by Helen Stone, Lippincott; *T-Bone, the Baby Sitter* by Clare Newberry, Harper

1952   *Finders Keepers* by William Lipkind, illustrated by Nicholas Mordvinoff, Harcourt Brace Jovanovich
Honor Books: *Mr. T. W. Anthony Woo: The Story of a Cat and a Dog and a Mouse* by Marie Hall Ets, Viking; *Skipper John's Cook* by Marcia Brown, Scribner's; *All Falling Down* by Gene Zion, illustrated by Margaret Bloy Graham, Harper; *Bear Party* by William Pene du Bois, Viking; *Feather Mountain* by Elizabeth Olds, Houghton Mifflin

1953   *The Biggest Bear* by Lynd Ward, Houghton Mifflin
Honor Books: *Puss in Boots* by Charles Perrault, illustrated and translated by Marcia Brown, Scribner's; *One Morning in Maine* by Robert McCloskey, Viking; *Ape in a Cape: An Alphabet of Odd Animals* by Fritz Eichenberg, Harcourt Brace Jovanovich; *The Storm Book* by Charlotte Zolotow, illustrated by Margaret Bloy Graham, Harper; *Five Little Monkeys* by Juliet Kepes, Houghton Mifflin

1954   *Madeline's Rescue* by Ludwig Bemelmans, Viking
Honor Books: *Journey Cake, Ho!* by Ruth Sawyer, illustrated by Robert McCloskey, Viking; *When Will the World Be Mine?* by Miriam Schlein, illustrated by Jean Charlot, W. R. Scott; *The Steadfast Tin Soldier* by Hans Christian Andersen, illustrated by Marcia Brown, Scribner's; *A Very Special House* by Ruth Krauss, illustrated by Maurice Sendak, Harper; *Green Eyes* by A. Birnbaum, Capitol

1955   *Cinderella, or the Little Glass Slipper* by Charles Perrault, translated and illustrated by Marcia Brown, Scribner's
Honor Books: *Book of Nursery and Mother Goose Rhymes,* illustrated by Marguerite de Angeli, Doubleday; *Wheel on the Chimney* by Margaret Wise Brown, illustrated by Tibor Gergely, Lippincott; *The Thanksgiving Story* by Alice Dalgliesh, illustrated by Helen Sewell, Scribner's

1956   *Frog Went A-Courtin* edited by John Langstaff, illustrated by Feodor Rojankovsky, Harcourt Brace Jovanovich
Honor Books: *Play with Me* by Marie Hall Ets, Viking; *Crow Boy* by Taro Yashima, Viking

1957   *A Tree Is Nice* by Janice May Udry, illustrated by Marc Simont, Harper
Honor Books: *Mr. Penny's Race Horse* by Marie Hall Ets, Viking; *1 is One* by Tasha Tudor, Walck; *Anatole* by Eve Titus, illustrated by Paul Galdone, McGraw-Hill; *Gillespie and the Guards* by Benjamin Elkin, illustrated by James Daugherty, Viking; *Lion* by William Pene du Bois, Viking

1958   *Time of Wonder* by Robert McCloskey, Viking
Honor Books: *Fly High, Fly Low* by Don Freeman, Viking; *Anatole and the Cat* by Eve Titus, illustrated by Paul Galdone, McGraw-Hill

1959   *Chanticleer and the Fox* adapted from Chaucer and illustrated by Barbara Cooney, Crowell
Honor Books: *The House That Jack Built: A Picture Book in Two Languages* by Antonio Frasconi, Harcourt Brace Jovanovich; *What Do You Say, Dear?* by Sesyle Joslin, illustrated by Maurice Sendak, Scott; *Umbrella* by Taro Yashima, Viking

1960   *Nine Days to Christmas* by Marie Hall Ets and Aurora Labastida, illustrated by Marie Hall Ets, Viking
Honor Books: *Houses from the Sea* by Alice E. Goudey, illustrated by Adrienne Adams, Scribner's; *The Moon Jumpers* by Janice May Udry, illustrated by Maurice Sendak, Harper

1961   *Baboushka and the Three Kings* by Ruth Robbins, illustrated by Nicolas Sidjakov, Parnassus
Honor Book: *Inch by Inch* by Leo Lionni, Obolensky

1962   *Once a Mouse . . .* by Marcia Brown, Scribner's
Honor Books: *The Fox Went Out on a Chilly Night: An Old Song* by Peter Spier, Doubleday; *Little Bear's Visit* by Else Holmelund Minarik, illustrated by Maurice Sendak, Harper; *The Day We Saw the Sun Come Up* by Alice E. Goudey, illustrated by Adrienne Adams, Scribner's

1963   *The Snowy Day* by Ezra Jack Keats, Viking
Honor Books: *The Sun Is a Golden Earring* by Natalia M. Belting, illustrated by Bernarda Bryson, Holt, Rinehart & Winston; *Mr. Rabbit and the Lovely Present* by Charlotte Zolotow, illustrated by Maurice Sendak, Harper

1964   *Where the Wild Things Are* by Maurice Sendak, Harper
Honor Books: *Swimmy* by Leo Lionni, Pantheon Books; *All in the Morning Early* by Sorche Nic Leodhas, illustrated by Evaline Ness, Holt, Rinehart & Winston; *Mother Goose and Nursery Rhymes* illustrated by Philip Reed, Atheneum

1965   *May I Bring a Friend?* by Beatrice Schenk de Regniers, illustrated by Beni Montresor, Atheneum
Honor Books: *Rain Makes Applesauce* by Julian Scheer, illustrated by Marvin Bileck, Holiday; *The Wave* by Margaret Hodges, illustrated by Blair Lent, Houghton Mifflin; *A Pocketful of Cricket* by Rebecca Caudill, illustrated by Evaline Ness, Holt, Rinehart & Winston

1966   *Always Room for One More* by Sorche Nic Leodhas, illustrated by Nonny Hogrogian, Holt, Rinehart & Winston
       Honor Books: *Hide and Seek Fog* by Alvin Tresselt, illustrated by Roger Duvoisin, Lothrop; *Just Me* by Marie Hall Ets, Viking; *Tom Tit Tot* by Evaline Ness, Scribner's

1967   *Sam, Bangs & Moonshine* by Evaline Ness, Holt, Rinehart & Winston
       Honor Book: *One Wide River to Cross* by Barbara Emberley, illustrated by Ed Emberley, Prentice-Hall

1968   *Drummer Hoff* by Barbara Emberley, illustrated by Ed Emberley, Prentice-Hall
       Honor Books: *Frederick* by Leo Lionni, Pantheon; *Seashore Story* by Taro Yashima, Viking; *The Emperor and the Kite* by Jane Yolen, illustrated by Ed Young, World

1969   *The Fool of the World and the Flying Ship* by Arthur Ransome, illustrated by Uri Shulevitz, Farrar, Straus & Giroux
       Honor Book: *Why the Sun and the Moon Live in the Sky: An African Folktale* by Elphinstone Dayrell, illustrated by Blair Lent, Houghton Mifflin

1970   *Sylvester and the Magic Pebble* by William Stieg, Windmill (Simon & Schuster)
       Honor Books: *Goggles!* by Ezra Jack Keats, Macmillan; *Alexander and the Wind-Up Mouse* by Leo Lionni, Pantheon; *Pop Corn and Ma Goodness* by Edna Mitchell Preston, illustrated by Robert Andrew Parker, Viking; *Thy Friend, Obadiah* by Brinton Turkle, Viking; *The Judge: An Untrue Tale* by Harve Zemach, illustrated by Margot Zemach, Farrar, Straus & Giroux

1971   *A Story—A Story: An African Tale* by Gail E. Haley, Atheneum
       Honor Books: *The Angry Moon* by William Sleator, illustrated by Blair Lent, Little, Brown; *Frog and Toad Are Friends* by Arnold Lobel, Harper; *In the Night Kitchen* by Maurice Sendak, Harper

1972   *One Fine Day* by Nonny Hogrogian, Macmillan
       Honor Books: *If All the Seas Were One Sea* by Janina Domanska, Macmillan; *Moja Means One: Swahili Counting Book* by Muriel Feelings, illustrated by Tom Feelings, Dial Press; *Hildilid's Night* by Cheli Duran Ryan, illustrated by Arnold Lobel, Macmillan

1973   *The Funny Little Woman* retold by Arlene Mosel, illustrated by Blair Lent, Dutton
       Honor Books: *Anansi the Spider: A Tale from the Ashanti* adapted and illustrated by Gerald McDermott, Holt, Rinehart & Winston; *Hosie's Alphabet* by Hosea Tobias and Lisa Baskin, illustrated by Leonard Baskin, Viking; *Snow White and the Seven Dwarfs* translated by Randall Jarrell, illustrated by Nancy Elkholm Burkert, Farrar, Straus & Giroux; *When Clay Sings* by Byrd Baylor, illustrated by Tom Bahti, Scribner's

1974   *Duffy and the Devil* by Harve Zemach, illustrated by Margot Zemach, Farrar, Straus & Giroux
       Honor Book: *Three Jovial Huntsmen* by Susan Jeffers, Bradbury; *Cathedral: The Story of Its Construction* by David Macaulay, Houghton Mifflin

1975   *Arrow to the Sun* adapted and illustrated by Gerald McDermott, Viking
       Honor Book: *Jambo Means Hello: A Swahili Alphabet Book* by Muriel Feelings, illustrated by Tom Feelings, Dial Press

1976   *Why Mosquitoes Buzz in People's Ears* retold by Verna Aardema, illustrated by Leo and Diane Dillon, Dial Press
       Honor Books: *The Desert Is Theirs* by Byrd Baylor, illustrated by Peter Parnall, Scribner's; *Strega Nona* retold and illustrated by Tomie de Paola, Prentice-Hall

1977   *Ashanti to Zulu: African Traditions* by Margaret Musgrove, illustrated by Leo and Diane Dillon, Dial Press
       Honor Books: *The Amazing Bone* by William Stieg, Farrar, Straus & Giroux; *The Contest* retold and illustrated by Nonny Hogrogian, Greenwillow (Morrow); *Fish for Supper* by M. B. Goffstein, Dial Press; *The Golem: A Jewish Legend* by Beverly Brodsky McDermott, Lippincott; *Hawk, I'm Your Brother* by Byrd Baylor, illustrated by Peter Parnall, Scribner's

1978   *Noah's Ark* by Peter Spier, Doubleday
       Honor Books: *Castle* by David Macaulay, Houghton Mifflin; *It Could Always Be Worse* retold and illustrated by Margot Zemach, Farrar, Straus & Giroux

1979   *The Girl Who Loved Wild Horses* by Paul Goble, Bradbury
       Honor Books: *Freight Train* by Donald Crews, Greenwillow (Morrow); *The Way to Start a Day* by Byrd Baylor, illustrated by Peter Parnall, Scribner's

1980   *Ox-Cart Man* by Donald Hall, illustrated by Barbara Cooney, Viking
       Honor Books: *Ben's Trumpet* by Rachel Isadora, Greenwillow (Morrow); *The Treasure* by Uri Shulevitz, Farrar, Straus & Giroux; *The Garden of Abdul Gasazi* by Chris Van Allsburg, Houghton Mifflin

1981   *Fables* by Arnold Lobel, Harper
        Honor Books: *The Bremen-Town Musicians* by Ilse Plume, Doubleday; *The Grey Lady and the Strawberry Snatcher* by Molly Bang, Four Winds; *Mice Twice* by Joseph Low, Atheneum; *Truck* by Donald Crews, Greenwillow (Morrow)

1982   *Jumanji* by Chris Van Allsburg, Houghton Mifflin
        Honor Books: *A Visit to William Blake's Inn: Poems for Innocent and Experienced Travelers* by Nancy Willard, illustrated by Alice and Martin Provensen, Harcourt Brace Jovanovich; *Where the Buffaloes Begin* by Olaf Baker, illustrated by Stephen Gammell, Warne; *On Market Street* by Arnold Lobel, illustrated by Anita Lobel, Greenwillow (Morrow); *Outside Over There* by Maurice Sendak, Harper

1983   *Shadow* by Blaise Cendrars, illustrated by Marcia Brown, Scribner's
        Honor Books: *When I Was Young in the Mountains* by Cynthia Rylant, illustrated by Diane Goode, Dutton; *Chair for My Mother* by Vera B. Williams, Morrow

1984   *The Glorious Flight: Across the Channel with Louis Blériot July 25, 1909* by Alice and Martin Provenson, Viking
        Honor Books: *Ten, Nine, Eight* by Molly Bang, Greenwillow (Morrow) ; *Little Red Riding Hood* by Trina Schart Hyman, Holiday House

1985   *Saint George and the Dragon* by Margaret Hodges, illustrated by Trina Schart Hyman, Little, Brown
        Honor Books: *Hansel and Gretel* by Rika Lesser, illustrated by Paul O. Zelinsky, Dodd, Mead; *The Story of the Jumping Mouse* by John Steptoe, Lothrop; *Have You Seen My Duckling?* by Nancy Tafuri, Greenwillow (Morrow)

1986   *The Polar Express* by Chris van Allsburg, Houghton Mifflin
        Honor Books: *The Relatives Came* by Cynthia Rylant, illustrated by Stephen Gammell, Bradbury; *King Bidgood's in the Bathtub* by Audrey Wood, illustrated by Don Wood, Harcourt Brace Jovanovich

1987   *Hey, Al* by Arthur Yorinks, illustrated by Richard Egielski, Farrar, Straus & Giroux
        Honor Books: *The Village of Round and Square Houses* by Ann Grifalconi, Little, Brown; *Alphabatics* by Suse MacDonald, Bradbury; *Rumpelstiltskin* by Paul O. Zelinsky, Dutton

1988   *Owl Moon* by Jane Yolen, illustrated by John Schoenherr, Philomel (Putnam)
        Honor Book: *Mufaro's Beautiful Daughters* by John Steptoe, Lothrop

1989   *Song and Dance Man* by Karen Ackerman, illustrated by Stephen Gammell, Knopf
        Honor Books: *Goldilocks* by James Marshall, Dial Press; *The Boy of the Three-Year Nap* by Dianne Snyder, illustrated by Allen Say; *Mirandy and Brother Wind* by Patricia McKissack, illustrated by Jerry Pinkney, Knopf; *Free Fall* by David Wiesner, Lothrop

1990   *Lon Po Po: A Red-Riding Hood Story from China* by Ed Young, Philomel (Putnam)
        Honor Books: *Hershel and the Hanukkah Goblins* by Eric Kimmel, illustrated by Trina Schart Hyman, Holiday; *Color Zoo* by Lois Ehlert, Lippincott; *Bill Peet: An Autobiography* by Bill Peet, Houghton Mifflin; *The Talking Eggs* retold by Robert D. San Souci, illustrated by Jerry Pinkney, Dial

1991   *Black and White* by David Macaulay, Houghton Mifflin
        Honor Books: *Puss'n Boots* by Charles Perrault, illustrated by Fred Marcellino, Farrar, Straus & Giroux; *"More, More, More," Said the Baby: 3 Love Stories* by Vera Williams, Greenwillow

1992   *Tuesday* by David Wiesner, Clarion
        Honor Book: *Tar Beach* by Faith Ringgold, Crown

1993   *Mirette on the High Wire* by Emily Arnold McCully, Putnam
        Honor Books: *Seven Blind Mice* by Ed Young, Philomel; *The Stinky Cheese Man and Other Fairly Stupid Tales* by Jon Scieszka, illustrated by Lane Smith, Viking; *Working Cotton* by Sherley Anne Williams, illustrated by Carole Byard, Harcourt Brace Jovanovich

1994   *Grandfather's Journey* by Allen Say, Houghton Mifflin
        Honor Books: *Peppe the Lamplighter* by Elisa Bartone, illustrated by Ted Lewin, Lothrop; *In the Small, Small Pond* by Denise Fleming, Holt; *Owen* by Keven Henkes, Greenwillow; *Raven: A Trickster Tale from the Pacific Northwest* by Gerald McDermott, Harcourt; *Yo! Yes?* by Chris Raschka, Orchard

1995   *Smoky Night* by Eve Bunting, illustrated by David Diaz, Harcourt
        Honor Books: *Swamp Angel* by Anne Isaacs, illustrated by Paul O. Zelinsky, Dutton; *John Henry* retold by Julius Lester, illustrated by Jerry Pinkney, Dial; *Time Flies* by Eric Rohmann, Crown

1996   *Officer Buckle and Gloria* by Peggy Rathmann, Putnam
Honor Books: *Alphabet City* by Stephen T. Johnson, Viking Penguin; *Zin! Zin! Zin! A Violin!* by Lloyd Moss, illustrated by Marjorie Priceman, Simon & Schuster; *The Faithful Friend* by Robert D. San Souci, illustrated by Brian Pinkney, Simon & Schuster; *Tops & Bottoms* by Janet Stevens, Harcourt Brace Jovanovich

1997   *Golem* by David Wisniewski, Clarion
Honor Books: *Hush! A Thai Lullaby* by Holly Meade, Orchard; *The Paperboy* by Dav Pilkey, Orchard; *Starry Messenger* by Peter Sis, Farrar, Straus & Giroux; *The Graphic Alphabet* by David Pelletier, Orchard

1998   *Rapunzel* by Paul O. Zelinsky, Dutton
Honor Books: *The Gardener* by Sarah Stewart, illustrated by David Small, Farrar; *Harlem* by Walter Dean Myers, illustrated by Christopher Myers, Scholastic; *There Was an Old Woman Who Swallowed a Fly* by Simms Taback, Viking

1999   *Snowflake Bentley* by Jacquelline Briggs Martin, illustrated by Mary Azarian, Houghton Mifflin
Honor Books: *Duke Ellington: The Piano Prince and His Orchestra* by Andrea Davis Pinkney, illustrated by Brian Pinkney, Simon & Schuster; *No, David!* by David Shannon, Scholastic; *Snow* by Uri Shulevitz, Farrar; *Tibet: Through the Red Box* by Peter Sis, Farrar, Straus & Giroux

2000   *Joseph Had a Little Overcoat* by Simms Taback, Viking
Honor Books: *Sector 7* by David Weisner, Clarion; *The Ugly Duckling* by Jerry Pinkney, Morrow; *When Sophie Gets Angry—Really, Really Angry...* by Molly Bang, Scholastic; *A Child's Calendar* by John Updike, illustrated by Trina Schart Hyman, Holiday

2001   *So You Want to Be President?* by Judith St. George, illus. by David Small, Philomel
Honor Books: *Casey at the Bat* by Ernest Thayer, illus. Christopher Bing, Handprint; *Click, Clack, Moo: Cows That Type* by Doreen Cronin, illus. Betsy Lewin, Simon & Schuster; *Olivia* by Ian Falconer, Atheneum

2002   *The Three Pigs* by David Wiesner, Clarion/Houghton Mifflin
Honor Books: *The Dinosaurs of Waterhouse Hawkins* by Barbara Kerley, illus. by Brian Selznick, Scholastic; *Martin's Big Words: The Life of Dr. Martin Luther King, Jr.* by Doreen Rappaport, illus. Bryan Collier, Hyperion; *The Stray Dog* by Marc Simont, HarperCollins

2003   *My Friend Rabbit* by Eric Rohmann, Roaring Brook
Honor Books: *The Spider and the Fly* by Mary Howitt, illus. by Tony DiTerlizzi, Simon & Schuster; *Hondo and Fabian* by Peter McCarty, Holt; *Noah's Ark* by Jerry Pinkney, Seastar/North-South

2004   *The Man Who Walked Between the Towers* by Mordicai Gerstein, Roaring Brook Press
Honor Books: *Ella Sarah Gets Dressed* by Margaret Chodos-Irvine, Harcourt; *What Do You Do with a Tail Like This?* by Steve Jenkins and Robin Page, Houghton Mifflin; *Don't Let the Pigeon Drive the Bus* by Mo Willems, Hyperion

2005   *Kitten's First Full Moon* by Kevin Henkes, Greenwillow
Honor Books: *The Red Book* by Barbara Lehman, Houghton Mifflin; *Coming on Home Soon* by Jacqueline Woodson, illustrated by E. B. Lewis, Putnam; *Knuffle Bunny: A Cautionary Tale* by Mo Willems, Hyperion

2006   *The Hello, Goodbye Window* by Norton Juster, illustrated by Chris Raschka, Hyperion
Honor Books: *Rosa* by Nikki Giovanni, illustrated by Bryan Collier; *Zen Shorts* by Jon J. Muth, Scholastic; *Hot Air: The (Mostly) True Story of the First Hot-Air Balloon Ride* by Marjorie Priceman, Simon & Schuster; *Song of the Water Boatman and Other Pond Poems* by Joyce Sidman, illustrated by Beckie Prange, Houghton Mifflin

2007   *Flotsam* by David Wiesner, Clarion
Honor Books: *Gone Wild: An Endangered Animal Alphabet* by David McLimans, Walker; *Moses: When Harriet Tubman Led Her People to Freedom* by Carole Boston Weatherford, Hyperion

2008   *The Invention of Hugo Cabret* by Brian Selznick, Scholastic Press
Honor Books: *Henry's Freedom Box: A True Story from the Underground Railroad* by Ellen Levine, illustrated by Kadir Nelson, Scholastic; *First the Egg* by Laura Vaccaro Seeger (Roaring Brook/Neal Porter); *The Wall: Growing Up Behind the Iron Curtain* by Peter Sis (Farrar/Frances Foster); *Knuffle Bunny Too: A Case of Mistaken Identity* by Mo Willems (Hyperion)

2009   *The House in the Night* by Susan Marie Swanson, illustrated by Beth Krommes, Houghton Mifflin
Honor Books: *A Couple of Boys Have the Best Week Ever* by Marla Frazee, Harcourt; *How I Learned Geography* by Uri Shulevitz, Farrar, Straus & Giroux; *A River of Words: The Story of William Carlos Williams* by Jen Bryant, illustrated by Melissa Sweet, Eerdmans

2010 *The Lion & the Mouse* by Jerry Pinkney, Little, Brown
Honor Books: *All the World* by Liz Garton Scanlon, illustrated by Marla Frazee, Beach Lane Books; *Red Sings from Treetops: A Year in Colors* by Joyce Sidman, illustrated by Pamela Zagarenski, Houghton Mifflin Harcourt

Boston Globe–Horn Book Awards

Awarded annually since 1967 and sponsored jointly by *The Boston Globe* and *The Horn Book Magazine,* two prizes originally were given—one to recognize the outstanding text and one the outstanding illustration. Beginning in 1976, the categories were redefined: Outstanding Fiction or Poetry, Outstanding Nonfiction, and Outstanding Illustration. In 1996, the Fiction category was expanded to include poetry.

1967 Text: *The Little Fishes* by Erik Haugaard, Houghton Mifflin
Illustration: *London Bridge Is Falling Down* by Peter Spier, Doubleday

1968 Text: *The Spring Rider* by John Lawson, Crowell
Illustration: *Tikki Tikki Tembo* by Arlene Mosel, illustrated by Blair Lent, Holt

1969 Text: *A Wizard of Earthsea* by Ursula K. Le Guin, Houghton Mifflin
Illustration: *The Adventures of Paddy Pork* by John S. Goodall, Harcourt

1970 Text: *The Intruder* by John Rowe Townsend, Lippincott
Illustration: *Hi, Cat!* by Ezra Jack Keats, Macmillan

1971 Text: *A Room Made of Windows* by Eleanor Cameron, Little, Brown
Illustration: *If I Built a Village* by Kazue Mizumura, Crowell

1972 Text: *Tristan and Iseult* by Rosemary Sutcliff, Dutton
Illustration: *Mr. Gumpy's Outing* by John Burningham, Holt, Rinehart & Winston

1973 Text: *The Dark Is Rising* by Susan Cooper, McElderry/Atheneum
Illustration: *King Stork* by Trina Schart Hyman, Little, Brown

1974 Text: *M. C. Higgins, The Great* by Virginia Hamilton, Macmillan
Illustration: *Jambo Means Hello* by Muriel Feelings, illustrated by Tom Feelings, Dial

1975 Text: *Transport 7-41-R* by T. Degens, Viking
Illustration: *Anno's Alphabet* by Mitsumasa Anno, Crowell

1976 Fiction: *Unleaving* by Jill Paton Walsh, Farrar, Straus & Giroux
Nonfiction: *Voyaging to Cathay: Americans in the China Trade* by Alfred Tamarin and Shirley Glubok, Viking
Illustration: *Thirteen* by Remy Charlip and Jerry Joyner, Parents

1977 Fiction: *Child of the Owl* by Laurence Yep, Harper
Nonfiction: *Chance, Luck and Destiny* by Peter Dickinson, Little, Brown
Illustration: *Granfa' Grig Had a Pig and Other Rhymes* by Wallace Tripp, Little, Brown

1978 Fiction: *The Westing Game* by Ellen Raskin, Dutton
Nonfiction: *Mischling, Second Degree: My Childhood in Nazi Germany* by Ilse Koehn, Greenwillow
Illustration: *Anno's Journey* by Mitsumasa Anno, Philomel

1979 Fiction: *Humbug Mountain* by Sid Fleischman, Little, Brown
Nonfiction: *The Road From Home: The Story of an Armenian Girl* by David Kherdian, Greenwillow
Illustration: *The Snowman* by Raymond Briggs, Random House

1980 Fiction: *Conrad's War* by Andrew Davies, Crown
Nonfiction: *Building: The Fight Against Gravity* by Mario Salvadori, McElderry/Atheneum
Illustration: *The Garden of Abdul Gasazi* by Chris Van Allsburg, Houghton Mifflin

1981 Fiction: *The Leaving* by Lynn Hall, Scribner's
Nonfiction: *The Weaver's Gift* by Kathryn Lasky, Warne
Illustration: *Outside Over There* by Maurice Sendak, Harper

1982 Fiction: *Playing Beatie Bow* by Ruth Park, Atheneum
Nonfiction: *Upon the Head of the Goat: A Childhood in Hungary, 1939–1944* by Aranka Siegal, Farrar, Straus & Giroux
Illustration: *A Visit to William Blake's Inn: Poems for Innocent and Experienced Travelers* by Nancy Willard, illustrated by Alice and Martin Provensen

1983   Fiction: *Sweet Whispers, Brother Rush* by Virginia Hamilton, Philomel
Nonfiction: *Behind Barbed Wire: The Imprisonment of Japanese Americans During World War II* by
Daniel S. David, Dutton
Illustration: *A Chair for My Mother* by Vera B. Williams, Greenwillow

1984   Fiction: *A Little Fear* by Patricia Wrightson, McElderry/Atheneum
Nonfiction: *The Double Life of Pocahontas* by Jean Fritz, Putnam
Illustration: *Jonah and the Great Fish* retold and illustrated by Warwick Hutton, McElderry/Atheneum

1985   Fiction: *The Moves Make the Man* by Bruce Brooks, Harper
Nonfiction: *Commodore Perry in the Land of the Shogun* by Rhoda Blumberg, Lothrop
Illustration: *Mama Don't Allow* by Thatcher Hurd, Harper

1986   Fiction: *In Summer Light* by Zibby Oneal, Viking/Kestrel
Nonfiction: *Auks, Rocks and the Odd Dinosaur* by Peggy Thompson, Crowell
Illustration: *The Paper Crane* by Molly Bang, Greenwillow

1987   Fiction: *Rabble Starkey* by Lois Lowry, Houghton Mifflin
Nonfiction: *Pilgrims of Plymouth* by Marcia Sewall, Atheneum
Illustration: *Mufaro's Beautiful Daughters* by John Steptoe, Lothrop

1988   Fiction: *The Friendship* by Mildred D. Taylor, illustrated by Max Ginsburg, Dial
Nonfiction: *Anthony Burns: The Defeat and Triumph of a Fugitive Slave* by Virginia Hamilton, Knopf
Illustration: *The Boy of the Three-Year Nap* by Diane Snyder, Houghton Mifflin

1989   Fiction: *The Village by the Sea* by Paula Fox, Franklin Watts
Nonfiction: *The Way Things Work* by David Macaulay, Houghton Mifflin
Illustration: *Shy Charles* by Rosemary Wells, Dial

1990   Fiction: *Maniac Magee* by Jerry Spinelli, Little, Brown
Nonfiction: *The Great Little Madison* by Jean Fritz, Putnam
Illustration: *Lon Po Po: A Red-Riding Hood Story from China* retold and illustrated by Ed Young, Philomel

1991   Fiction: *The True Confessions of Charlotte Doyle* by Avi, Orchard
Nonfiction: *Appalachia: The Voices of Sleeping Birds* by Cynthia Rylant, illustrated by Barry Moser, Harcourt
Illustration: *The Tale of the Mandarin Ducks* retold by Katherine Paterson, illustrated by Leo and Diane Dillon,
Lodestar

1992   Fiction: *Missing May* by Cynthia Rylant, Orchard
Nonfiction: *Talking with Artists* by Pat Cummings, Bradbury
Illustration: *Seven Blind Mice* by Ed Young, Philomel

1993   Fiction: *Ajeemah and His Son* by James Berry, Harper
Nonfiction: *Sojourner Truth: Ain't I a Woman?* by Patricia C. and Fredrick McKissack, Scholastic
Illustration: *The Fortune-Tellers* by Lloyd Alexander, illustrated by Trina Schart Hyman, Dutton

1994   Fiction: *Scooter* by Vera B. Williams, Greenwillow
Nonfiction: *Eleanor Roosevelt: A Life of Discovery* by Russell Freedman, Clarion
Illustration: *Grandfather's Journey* by Allen Say, Houghton Mifflin

1995   Fiction: *Some of the Kinder Planets* by Tim Wynne-Jones, Kroupa/Orchard
Nonfiction: *Abigail Adams: Witness to a Revolution* by Natalie S. Bober, Atheneum
Illustration: *John Henry* retold by Julius Lester, illustrated by Jerry Pinkney, Dial

1996   Fiction and Poetry: *Poppy* by Avi, illustrated by Brian Floca, Orchard
Nonfiction: *Orphan Train Rider: One Boy's True Story* by Andrea Warren, Houghton
Picture Book: *In the Rain with Baby Duck* by Amy Hest, illustrated by Jill Barton, Candlewick

1997   Fiction and Poetry: *The Friends* by Kazumi Yumoto, Farrar
Nonfiction: *A Drop of Water: A Book of Science and Wonder* by Walter Wick, Scholastic
Picture Book: *The Adventures of Sparrowboy* by Brian Pinkney, Simon & Schuster

1998   Fiction and Poetry: *The Circuit: Stories from the Life of a Migrant Child* by Francisco Jiménez, University of New
Mexico Press
Nonfiction: *Leon's Story* by Leon Walter Tijllage, illustrated by Susan L. Roth, Farrar, Straus & Giroux
Picture Book: *And If the Moon Could Talk* by Kate Banks, illustrated by Georg Hallensleben, Farrar, Straus & Giroux

1999   Fiction and Poetry: *Holes* by Louis Sachar, Farrar
        Nonfiction: *The Top of the World: Climbing Mount Everest* by Steve Jenkins, Houghton Mifflin
        Picture Book: *Red-Eyed Tree Frog* by Joy Cowley, illustrated by Nic Bishop, Scholastic

2000   Fiction and Poetry: *The Folk Keeper* by Franny Billingsley, Atheneum
        Nonfiction: *Sir Walter Raleigh and the Quest for El Dorado* by Marc Aronson, Clarion
        Picture Book: *Henry Hikes to Fitchburg* by D. B. Johnson, Houghton Mifflin

2001   Fiction and Poetry: *Carver: A Life in Poems* by Marilyn Nelson, Front Street
        Nonfiction: *The Longitude Prize* by Joan Dash, illustrated by Susan Petricic, Farrar
        Picture Book: *Cold Feet* by Cynthia De Felice, illustrated by Robert Andrew Parker, DK Ink

2002   Fiction and Poetry: *Lord of the Deep* by Graham Salisbury, Delacorte
        Nonfiction: *This Land Was Made for You and Me: The Life and Songs of Woody Guthrie* by Elizabeth Partridge, Viking
        Picture Book: *"Let's Get a Pup!" Said Kate* by Bob Graham, Candlewick

2003   Fiction and Poetry: *The Jamie and Angus Stories* by Anne Fine, Candlewick
        Nonfiction: *Fireboat: The Heroic Adventures of the John J. Harvey* by Maira Kalman, Putnam
        Picture Book: *Big Momma Make the World* by Phyllis Root, illustrated by Helen Oxenbury, Candlewick

2004   Fiction and Poetry: *The Fire-Eaters* by David Almond, Delacorte
        Nonfiction: *An American Plague: The True and Terrifying Story of the Yellow Fever Epidemic of 1793* by Jim Murphy, Clarion
        Picture Book: *The Man Who Walked between the Towers* by Mordicai Gerstein, Roaring Brook

2005   Fiction and Poetry: *The Schwa Was Here* by Neal Schusterman, Dutton
        Nonfiction: *The Race to Save the Lord God Bird* by Phillip Hoose, Farrar
        Picture Book: *Traction Man Is Here!* by Mini Grey, Knopf

2006   Fiction and Poetry: *The Miraculous Journey of Edward Tulane* by Kate Di Camillo, Candlewick
        Nonfiction: *If You Decide to Go to the Moon* by Faith McNulty, Scholastic
        Picture Book: *Leaf Man* by Lois Ehlert, Harcourt

2007   Fiction: *The Astonishing Life of Octavian Nothing, Traitor to the Nation, Volume I: The Pox Party* by M. T. Anderson, Candlewick
        Nonfiction: *The Strongest Man in the World: Louis Cyr* by Nicholas Debon
        Illustration: *Dog and Bear: Two Friends, Three Stories* by Laura Vaccaro Seeger, Porter/Roaring Brook

2008   Fiction: *The Absolutely True Diary of a Part-Time Indian* by Sherman Alexie, Little
        Nonfiction: *The Wall: Growing up Behind the Iron Curtain* by Peter Sis, Farrar
        Illustration: *At Night* by Jonathan Bean, Farrar

2009   Fiction: *Nation* by Terry Pratchett, HarperCollins
        Nonfiction: *The Lincolns: A Scrapbook Look at Abraham and Mary* by Candace Fleming, Schwartz & Wade/Random House
        Illustration: *Bubble Trouble* by Margaret Mahy, illustrated by Polly Dunbar (Clarion)

2010   Fiction and Poetry: *When You Reach Me* by Rebecca Stead, Lamb/Random House
        Nonfiction: *Marching for Freedom: Walk Together, Children, and Don't You Grow Weary* by Elizabeth Partridge (Viking)
        Picture Book: *I Know Here* by Laurel Croza, illustrated by Matt James (Groundwood)

The Mildred L. Batchelder Award

Presented annually by the American Library Association, this award recognizes the most outstanding children's book originally translated from a language other than English.

1968   *The Little Man* by Erich Kastner, translated by James Kirkup, illustrated by Rich Schreiter, Knopf, 1966

1969   *Don't Take Teddy* by Babbis Friis-Baastad, translated by Lise Somme McKinnon, Scribner, 1967

1970   *Wildcat under Glass* by Alki Zei, translated by Edward Fenton, Holt, Rinehart & Winston, 1968

1971   *In the Land of Ur: The Discovery of Ancient Mesopotamia* by Hans Baumann, translated by Stella Humphries, illustrated by Hans Peter Renner, Pantheon Books, 1969

1972   *Friedrich* by Hans Peter Richter, translated by Edite Kroll, Holt, Rinehart & Winston, 1970

1973   *Pulga* by Siny Rose Van Iterson, translated by Alexander and Alison Gode, Morrow, 1971

1974   *Petros' War* by Alki Zei, translated by Edward Fenton, Dutton, 1972

1975   *An Old Tale Carved Out of Stone* by Aleksandr M. Linevski, translated by Maria Polushkin, Crown, 1973

1976   *The Cat and Mouse Who Shared a House* by Ruth Hurlimann, translated by Anthea Bell, Walck, 1974

1977   *The Leopard* by Cecil Bodker, translated by Gunnar Poulsen, Atheneum, 1975

1978   No Award

1979   *Konrad* by Christine Nostlinger, translated by Anthea Bell, illustrated by Carol Nicklaus, Watts, 1977
        Rabbit Island by Jorg Steiner, translated by Ann Conrad Lammers, illustrated by Jorg Muller, Harcourt Brace Jovanovich, 1978

1980   *The Sound of Dragon's Feet* by Alki Zei, translated by Edward Fenton, Dutton, 1979

1981   *The Winter When Time Was Frozen* by Els Pelgrom, translated by Raphael and Maryka Rudnik, Morrow, 1980

1982   *The Battle Horse* by Harry Kullman, translated by George Blecher and Lone Thygesen-Blecher, Bradbury, 1981

1983   *Hiroshima No Pika* by Toshi Maruki, translated by the author, Lothrop, 1982

1984   *Ronia, the Robber's Daughter* by Astrid Lindgren, translated by Patricia Crampton, Viking, 1983

1985   *The Island on Bird Street* by Uri Orlev, translated by Hillel Halkin, Houghton Mifflin, 1984

1986   *Rose Blanche* by Christophe Gallaz and Roberto Innocenti, translated by Martha Coventry and Richard Graglia, illustrated by Roberto Innocenti, Creative Education, 1985

1987   *No Hero for the Kaiser* by Rudolf Frank, translated by Patricia Crampton, illustrated by Klaus Steffans, Lothrop, 1986

1988   *If You Didn't Have Me* by Ulf Nilsson, illustrated by Eva Ericksson, translated by Lone Thygesen-Blecher and George Blecher, McElderry, 1987

1989   *Crutches* by Peter Hartling, Lothrop, 1988

1990   *Buster's World* by Bjarne Reuter, translated by Anthea Bell, Dutton, 1989

1991   *A Handful of Stars* by Rafik Schami, translated by Rika Lesser, Dutton, 1990

1992   *The Man from the Other Side* by Uri Orlev, translated by Hillel Halkin, Houghton Mifflin, 1991

1993   No Award

1994   *The Apprentice* by Pilar Molina Llorente, translated by Robin Longshaw, illustrated by Juan Ramón Alonso, Farrar, Straus & Giroux, 1993

1995   *The Boys from St. Petri* by Bjarne Reuter, translated by Anthea Bell, Dutton, 1994

1996   *The Lady with the Hat* by Uri Orlev, translated by Hillel Halkin, Houghton Mifflin, 1995

1997   *The Friends* by Kazumi Yumoto, translated by Cathy Hirano, Farrar, Straus & Giroux, 1996

1998   *The Robber and Me* by Josef Holub, edited by Marc Aronson, translated by Elizabeth D. Crawford, Holt, 1997

1999   *Thanks to My Mother* by Schoschana Rabinovici, edited by Cindy Kane, translated by James Skofield, Dial, 1998

2000   *The Baboon King* by Anton Quintana, translated by John Nieuwenhuizer, Walker, 1999

2001   *Samir and Yonaton* by Daniella Carmi, translated by Yael Lotan, Scholastic, 2000

2002   *How I Became an American* by Karin Gündisch, translated by James Scofield, Cricket/Carus, 2001

2003   *The Thief Lord* by Cornelia Funke, translated by Oliver Latsch, Scholastic, 2002

2004   *Run, Boy, Run* by Uri Orlev, translated by Hillel Halkin, Houghton Mifflin, 2003

2005   *The Shadows of Ghadames* by Joëlle Stolz, translated by Catherine Temerson, Delacorte, 2004

2006   *An Innocent Soldier* by Josef Holub, translated by Michael Hofmann, Arthur Levine Books, 2005

2007   *The Pull of the Ocean* by Jean-Claude Mourlevat, translated by Y. Maudet, Delacorte, 2005

2008   *Brave Story* by Miyuki Miyabe, translated by Alexander O. Smith, VIZ Media, 2006

2009   *Moribito: Guardian of the Spirit* by NahokoUehashi, translated by Cathy Hirano, Scholastic, 2007

2010   *A Faraway Island* by Annika Thor, translated by Linda Schenc, Delacorte Press, 2008

The Laura Ingalls Wilder Award

Named in honor of the beloved author of the Little House books (who was also its first recipient), this award is presented by the Association of Library Service to Children of the American Library Association to the individual, either author or illustrator, whose work has over the years proved to be a significant contribution to children's literature. Originally awarded every five years, it was awarded every three years from 1980 to 2001. It is now awarded every two years.

1954	Laura Ingalls Wilder	1992	Marcia Brown
1960	Clara Ingram Judson	1995	Virginia Hamilton
1965	Ruth Sawyer	1998	Russell Freedman
1970	E. B. White	2001	Milton Meltzer
1975	Beverly Cleary	2003	Eric Carle
1980	Theodore Geisel (Dr. Seuss)	2005	Laurence Yep
1983	Maurice Sendak	2007	James Marshall
1986	Jean Fritz	2009	Ashley Bryan
1989	Elizabeth George Speare		

The Coretta Scott King Award

Presented annually by the Social Responsibilities Round Table of the American Library Association, this award recognizes an African American author and illustrator (since 1974) who made an outstanding contribution to literature for children in the preceding year. The award is named for the widow of civil rights leader and Nobel Peace Prize winner Dr. Martin Luther King Jr., and it acknowledges the humanitarian work of both Dr. and Mrs. King.

1970   *Martin Luther King, Jr., Man of Peace* by Lillie Patterson, Garrard

1971   *Black Troubadour: Langston Hughes* by Charlemae Rollins, Rand

1972   *17 Black* Artists by Elton C. Fax, Dodd

1973   *I Never Had It Made* by Jackie Robinson (as told to Alfred Duckett), Putnam

1974   Author: *Ray Charles* by Sharon Bell Mathis, Crowell
Illustrator: *Ray Charles* by Sharon Bell Mathis, illustrated by George Ford, Crowell

1975   Author: *The Legend of Africana* by Dorothy Robinson, Johnson
Illustrator: *The Legend of Africana* by Dorothy Robinson, illustrated by Herbert Temple, Johnson

1976   Author: *Duey's Tale* by Pearl Bailey, Harcourt
Illustrator: No Award

1977   Author: *The Story of Stevie Wonder* by James Haskins, Lothrop
Illustrator: No Award

1978   Author: *Africa Dream* by Eloise Greenfield, Day/Crowell
Illustrator: *Africa Dream* by Eloise Greenfield, illustrated by Carole Bayard, Day/Crowell

1979   Author: *Escape to Freedom* by Ossie Davis, Viking
Illustrator: *Something on My Mind* by Nikki Grimes, illustrated by Tom Feelings, Dial

1980   Author: *The Young Landlords* by Walter Dean Myers, Viking
Illustrator: *Cornrows* by Camille Yarbrough, illustrated by Carole Bayard, Coward

1981   Author: *This Life* by Sidney Poitier, Knopf
Illustrator: *Beat the Story-Drum, Pum-Pum* by Ashley Bryan, Atheneum

1982   Author: *Let the Circle Be Unbroken* by Mildred Taylor, Dial
Illustrator: *Mother Crocodile: An Uncle Amadou Tale from Senegal* adapted by Rosa Guy, illustrated by John Steptoe, Delacorte

1983   Author: *Sweet Whispers, Brother Rush* by Virginia Hamilton, Philomel
Illustrator: *Black Child* by Peter Mugabane, Knopf

1984   Author: *Everett Anderson's Good-Bye* by Lucile Clifton, Holt
         Illustrator: *My Mama Needs Me* by Mildred Pitts Walter, illustrated by Pat Cummings, Lothrop

1985   Author: *Motown and Didi* by Walter Dean Myers, Viking
         Illustrator: No Award

1986   Author: *The People Could Fly: American Black Folktales* by Virginia Hamilton, Knopf
         Illustrator: *Patchwork Quilt* by Valerie Flournoy, illustrated by Jerry Pinkney, Dial

1987   Author: *Justin and the Best Biscuits in the World* by Mildred Pitts Walter, Lothrop
         Illustrator: *Half Moon and One Whole Star* by Crescent Dragonwagon, illustrated by Jerry Pinkney, Macmillan

1988   Author: *The Friendship* by Mildred D. Taylor, Dial
         Illustrator: *Mufaro's Beautiful Daughters: An African Tale* retold and illustrated by John Steptoe, Lothrop

1989   Author: *Fallen Angels* by Walter Dean Myers, Scholastic
         Illustrator: *Mirandy and Brother Wind* by Patricia McKissack, illustrated by Jerry Pinkney, Knopf

1990   Author: *A Long Hard Journey* by Patricia and Fredrick McKissack, Walker
         Illustrator: *Nathaniel Talking Iby* Eloise Greenfield, illustrated by Jan Spivey Gilchrist, Black Butterfly Press

1991   Author: *Road to Memphis* by Mildred D. Taylor, Dial
         Illustrator: *Aida* retold by Leontyne Price, illustrated by Leo and Diane Dillon, Harcourt

1992   Author: *Now Is Your Time! The African-American Struggle for Freedom* by Walter Dean Myers, HarperCollins
         Illustrator: *Tar Beach* by Faith Ringgold, Crown

1993   Author: *The Dark-Thirty: Southern Tales of the Supernatural* by Patricia McKissack, Knopf
         Illustrator: *Origins of Life on Earth: An African Creation Myth* by David A. Anderson, illustrated by Kathleen Atkins Smith, Sight Productions

1994   Author: *Toning the Sweep* by Angela Johnson, Orchard
         Illustrator: *Soul Looks Back in Wonder* compiled and illustrated by Tom Feelings, Dial

1995   Author: *Christmas in the Big House, Christmas in the Quarters* by Patricia and Fredrick McKissack, illustrated by John Thompson, Scholastic
         Illustrator: *The Creation* by James Weldon Johnson, illustrated by James E. Ransom, Holiday

1996   Author: *Her Stories* by Virginia Hamilton, illustrated by Leo and Diane Dillon, Scholastic
         Illustrator: *The Middle Passage: White Ships, Black Cargo* by Tom Feelings, Dial

1997   Author: *SLAM!* by Walter Dean Myers, Scholastic
         Illustrator: *Minty: A Story of Young Harriet Tubman* by Alan Schroeder, illustrated by Jerry Pinkney, Dial

1998   Author: *Forged by Fire* by Sharon M. Draper, Atheneum
         Illustrator: *In Daddy's Arms I Am Tall: African Americans Celebrating Fathers* by Javaka Steptoe, Lee & Low

1999   Author: *Heaven* by Angela Johnson, Simon & Schuster
         Illustrator: *I See The Rhythm* by Michele Wood, Children's Book Press

2000   *Bud, Not Buddy* by Christopher Paul Curtis, Delacorte
         Illustrator: *In the Time of the Drums* by Kim L. Siegelson, illustrated by Brian Pinkney, Hyperion

2001   Author: *Miracle's Boys* by Jacqueline Woodson, Putnam
         Illustrator: *Uptown* by Brian Collier, Holt

2002   Author: *The Land* by Mildred D. Taylor, Penguin
         Illustrator: *Goin' Someplace Special* by Patricia McKissack, Illustrated by Jerry Pinkney, Atheneum

2003   Author: *Bronx Masquerade* by Nikki Grimes, Dial
         Illustrator: *Talkin about Bessie* by E. B. Lewis, Scholastic

2004   Author: *The First Last Part* by Angela Johnson, Simon & Schuster
         Illustrator: *Beautiful Blackbird* by Ashley Bryan, Atheneum

2005   Author: *Remember: The Journey to School Integration* by Toni Morrison, Houghton Mifflin
         Illustrator: *Ellington Was Not a Street* by Ntozake Shange, illustrated by Nadir Nelson, Simon & Schuster

2006   Author: *Day of Tears: A Novel in Dialogue* by Julius Lester, Hyperion
         Illustrator: *Rosa* by Bryan Collier, Holt

2007   Author: *Copper Sun* by Sharon Draper, Simon & Schuster
        Illustrator: *Moses: When Harriet Tubman Led Her People to Freedom* by Kadir Nelson, Hyperion

2008   Author: *Elijah of Buxton* by Christopher Paul Curtis, Scholastic
        Illustrator: *Let It Shine* by Ashley Bryan, Atheneum

2009   Author: *We Are the Ship: The Story of Negro League Baseball* by Kadir Nelson, Disney
        Illustrator: *The Blacker the Berry* illustrated by Floyd Cooper, HarperCollins

2010   Author: *Bad News for Outlaws: The Remarkable Life of Bass Reeves, Deputy U.S. Marshal* by VaundaMicheaux
        Nelson, Carolrhoda
        Illustrator: *My People* by Langston Hughes, illustrated by Charles R. Smith Jr., Atheneum

The Scott O'Dell Award for Historical Fiction

Established by the noted children's novelist Scott O'Dell and administered by the Advisory Committee of the Bulletin of the Center for Children's Books, this award is presented to the most distinguished work of historical fiction set in the New World and written by a citizen of the United States.

1984   *The Sign of the Beaver* by Elizabeth George Speare, Houghton Mifflin

1985   *The Fighting Ground* by Avi, Harper

1986   *Sarah, Plain and Tall* by Patricia MacLachlan, Harper

1987   *Streams to the River, River to the Sea: A Novel of Sacagawea* by Scott O'Dell, Houghton Mifflin

1988   *Charlie Skedaddle* by Patricia Beatty, Morrow

1989   *The Honorable Prison* by Lyll Becerra de Jenkins, Lodestar

1990   *Shades of Gray* by Carolyn Reeder, Macmillan

1991   *A Time of Troubles* by Pieter van Raven, Scribner's

1992   *Stepping on the Cracks* by Mary Downing Hahn, Clarion

1993   *Morning Girl* by Michael Dorris, Hyperion

1994   *Bull Run* by Paul Fleischman, Harper

1995   *Under the Blood-Red Sun* by Graham Salisbury, Delacorte

1996   *The Bomb* by Theodore Taylor, Flare

1997   *Jip: His Story* by Katherine Paterson, Lodestar

1998   *Forty Acres and Maybe a Mule* by Harriet Gillem Robinet, Atheneum

1999   *Out of the Dust* by Karen Hesse, Scholastic

2000   *Two Suns in the Sky* by Miriam Bat-Ami, Front Street

2001   *The Art of Keeping Cool* by Janet Taylor Lisle, Atheneum

2002   *The Land* by Mildred Taylor, Dial

2003   *Trouble Don't Last* by Shelley Pearsall, Knopf

2004   *River Between Us* by Richard Peck, Dial

2005   *Worth* by A. LaFaye, Simon & Schuster

2006   *The Game of Silence* by Louise Erdrich, HarperCollins

2007   *The Green Glass Sea* by Ellen Klages, Viking

2008   *Elijah of Buxton* by Christopher Paul Curtis, Scholastic

2009   *Chains* by Laurie Halse Anderson, Simon & Schuster

2010   *The Storm in the Barn* by Matt Phelan, Candlewick

National Council of Teachers of English Award for Excellence in Poetry for Children

This award is presented every three years (from 1977 through 1982 it was awarded annually) by the National Council of Teachers of English and was established to recognize a living poet's lifetime contribution to poetry for children.

1977	David McCord	1991	Valerie Worth
1978	Aileen Fisher	1994	Barbara Juster Esbensen
1979	Karia Kuskin	1997	Eloise Greenfield
1980	Myra Cohn Livingston	2000	X. J. Kennedy
1981	Eve Merriam	2003	Mary Ann Hoberman
1982	John Ciardi	2006	Nikki Grimes
1985	Lilian Moore	2009	Lee Bennett Hopkins
1988	Arnold Adoff		

The Phoenix Award

The Phoenix Award, first presented in 1985, is given annually by the International Children's Literature Association for a book published exactly 20 years earlier that did not, at the time, win a major award but has stood the test of time and merited recognition for its contribution to children's literature.

1985   *The Mark of the Horse Lord* by Rosemary Sutcliff, Oxford, 1965

1986   *Queenie Peavy* by Robert Burch, Viking, 1966

1987   *Smith* by Leon Garfield, Constable, 1967

1988   *The Rider and His Horse* by Erik Christian Haugaard, Houghton Mifflin, 1968

1989   *The Night Watchmen* by Helen Cresswell, Faber, 1969

1990   *Enchantress from the Stars* by Sylvia Louise Engdahl, Atheneum, 1970

1991   *A Long Way from Home* by Jane Gardam, Hamish Hamilton, 1971

1992   *A Sound of Chariots* by Mollie Hunter, Hamish Hamilton, 1972

1993   *Carrie's War* by Nina Bawden, Gollancz, 1973

1994   *Of Nightingales That Weep* by Katherine Paterson, Harper, 1974

1995   *Dragonwings* by Laurence Yep, Harper, 1975

1996   *The Stone Book* by Alan Garner, Collins, 1976

1997   *I Am the Cheese* by Robert Cormier, Pantheon, 1977

1998   *A Chance Child* by Jill Paton Walsh, Macmillan, 1978

1999   *Throwing Shadows* by E. I. Konigsburg, Atheneum, 1979

2000   *The Keeper of the Isis Light* by Monica Hughes, Atheneum, 1980

2001   *The Seventh Raven* by Peter Dickinson, Gollancz, 1981

2002   *A Formal Feeling* by Zibby Oneal, Viking, 1982

2003   *The Long Night Watch* by Ivan Southall, Methuen, 1983/1984

2004   *White Peak Farm* by Berlie Doherty, Methuen, 1984

2005   *The Catalogue of the Universe* by Margaret Mahy, Dent, 1985

2006   *Howl's Moving Castle* by Diana Wynne Jones, Greenwillow, 1986

2007   *Memory* by Margaret Mahy, Dent 1987

2008   *Eva* by Peter Dickinson, Delacorte, 1988

2009   *Weetzie Bat* by Francesca Lia Block, HarperCollins, 1989

2010   *The Shining Company* by Rosemary Sutcliff, Farrar/Straus/Giroux and Bodley Head, 1990

Robert F. Sibert Informational Book Award

This annual award was established by the American Library Association in 2001 to honor the most distinguished information book published in English in the preceding year. It is named for the one-time president of Bound to Stay Bound Books, Inc., of Jacksonville, IL, which sponsors the award.

2001   *Sir Walter Raleigh and the Quest for El Dorado* by Marc Aronson, Clarion

2002   *Black Potatoes: The Story of the Great Irish Famine, 1845–1850* by Susan Campbell Bartoletti, Houghton Mifflin

2003   *The Life and Death of Adolf Hitler* by James Cross Giblin, Clarion

2004   *An American Plague: The True and Terrifying Story of the Yellow Fever Epidemic of 1793* by Jim Murphy, Clarion

2005   *The Voice that Challenged a Nation: Marian Anderson and the Struggle for Equal Rights* by Russell Freedman, Clarion

2006   *Secrets of a Civil War Submarine: Solving the Mysteries of the H. L. Hunley* by Sally M. Walker, Carolrhoda Books

2007   *Team Moon: How 400,000 People Landed Apollo 11 on the Moon* by Catherine Thimmesh, Houghton

2008   *The Wall: Growing up Behind the Iron Curtain* by Peter Sis, Farrar

2009   *We Are the Ship: The Story of Negro League Baseball* by Kadir Nelson, Disney

2010   *Almost Astronauts: 13 Women Who Dared to Dream* by Tanya Lee Stone, Candlewick Press

International Awards

The Astrid Lindgren Memorial Award

Named in honor of the beloved author of *Pippi Longstocking*, this international award from the Swedish government carries a prize of five million Swedish crowns, second only to the Nobel Prize among literature prizes in the world. The award (one or two a year) may be given to an individual or organization whose work has promoted children's and youth literature.

2003   Christine Nöstlinger (Austria) and Maurice Sendak (United States)

2004   Lygia Bojunga (Brazil)

2005   Ryoji Arai (Japan) and Philip Pullman (United Kingdom)

2006   Katherine Paterson (United States)

2007   Banco del Libro (Venezuela)

2008   Sonya Harnett (Australia)

2009   The Hamer Institute for Community Education (Palestine)

2010   Kitty Crowther (Belgium)

The Hans Christian Andersen Award

This medal, named for the great Danish storyteller, is presented every two years by the International Board on Books for Young People to a living author and (since 1966) living illustrator whose works have made a significant, international contribution to children's literature.

1956   Eleanor Farjeon (Great Britain)

1958   Astrid Lindgren (Sweden)

1960   Erich Kastner (Germany)

1962   Meindert DeJong (United States)

1964   Rene Guillot (France)

1966   Author: Tove Jansson (Finland)
        Illustrator: Alois Carigiet (Switzerland)

1968   Authors: James Kruss (Germany) and Jose Maria Sanchez-Silva (Spain)
        Illustrator: Jiri Trnka (Czechoslovakia)

1970   Author: Gianni Rodari (Italy)
        Illustrator: Maurice Sendak (United States)

1972   Author: Scott O'Dell (United States)
        Illustrator: Ib Spang Olsen (Denmark)

1974   Author: Maria Gripe (Sweden)
        Illustrator: Farsid Mesghali (Iran)

1976   Author: Cecil Bodker (Denmark)
        Illustrator: Tatjana Mawrine (U.S.S.R.)

1978   Author: Paula Fox (United States)
        Illustrator: Otto S. Svend (Denmark)

1980   Author: Bohumil Riha (Czechoslovakia)
        Illustrator: Suekichi Akaba (Japan)

1982   Author: Lygia Gojunga Nunes (Brazil)
        Illustrator: Zbigniew Rychlicki (Poland)

1984   Author: Christine Nostlinger (Austria)
        Illustrator: Mitsumasa Anno (Japan)

1986   Author: Patricia Wrightson (Australia)
        Illustrator: Robert Ingpen (Australia)

1988   Author: Annie M. G. Schmidt (Netherlands)
        Illustrator: Dusan Kallay (Yugoslavia)

1990   Author: Tormod Haugen (Norway)
        Illustrator: Lisbeth Zwerger (Austria)

1992   Author: Virginia Hamilton (United States)
        Illustrator: Keveta Pacovská (Czechoslovakia)

1994   Author: Michio Mado (Japan)
        Illustrator: Jörg Müller (Switzerland)

1996   Author: Uri Orlev (Israel)
        Illustrator: Klaus Ensikat (Germany)

1998   Author: Katherine Paterson (United States)
        Illustrator: Tomi Ungerer (United States)

2000   Author: Ana Maria Machado (Brazil)
        Illustrator: Anthony Browne (Great Britain)

2002   Author: Aidan Chambers (Great Britain)
        Illustrator: Quentin Blake (Great Britain)

2004   Author: Martin Waddell (Ireland)
        Illustrator: Max Velthuijs (The Netherlands)

2006   Author: Margaret Mahy (New Zealand)
        Illustrator: Wolf Erlbruch (Germany)

2008   Author: Jürg Schubiger (Switzerland)
        Illustrator: Roberto Innocenti (Italy)

2010   Author: David Almond (Great Britain)
        Illustrator: Jutta Bauer (Germany)

The Carnegie Medal

Awarded by the British Library Association to an outstanding book first published in the United Kingdom, this medal has been awarded annually since it was established in 1937 (the first award being presented to a book published in the preceding year). The date given is the date of publication.

1936   *Pigeon Post* by Arthur Ransome, Cape

1937   *The Family from One End Street* by Eve Garnett, Muller

1938   *The Circus Is Coming* by Noel Streatfield, Dent

1939   *Radium Woman* by Eleanor Doorly, Heinemann

1940   *Visitors from London* by Kitty Barne, Dent

1941   *We Couldn't Leave Dinah* by Mary Treadgold, Penguin

1942   *The Little Grey Men* by B. B., Eyre & Spottiswoode

1943   No Award

1944   *The Wind on the Moon* by Eric Linklater, Macmillan

1945   No Award

1946   *The Little White Horse* by Elizabeth Goudge, Brockhampton Press

1947   *Collected Stories for Children* by Walter de la Mare, Faber

1948   *Sea Change* by Richard Armstrong, Dent

1949   *The Story of Your Home* by Agnes Allen, Transatlantic

1950   *The Lark on the Wind* by Elfrida Vipont Foulds, Oxford

1951   *The Wool-Pack* by Cynthia Harnett, Methuen

1952   *The Borrowers* by Mary Norton, Dent

1953   *A Valley Grows Up* by Edward Osmond, Oxford

1954   *Knight Crusader* by Ronald Welch, Oxford

1955   *The Little Bookroom* by Eleanor Farjeon, Oxford

1956   *The Last Battle* by C. S. Lewis, Bodley Head

1957   *A Grass Rope* by William Mayne, Oxford

1958   *Tom's Midnight Garden* by Philippa Pearce, Oxford

1959   *The Lantern Bearers* by Rosemary Sutcliff, Oxford

1960   *The Making of Man* by I. W. Cornwall, Phoenix

1961   *A Stranger at Green Knowe* by Lucy Boston, Faber

1962   *The Twelve and the Genii* by Pauline Clarke, Faber

1963   *Time of Trial* by Hester Burton, Oxford

1964   *Nordy Banks* by Sheena Porter, Oxford

1965   *The Grange at High Force* by Philip Turner, Oxford

1966   No Award

1967	*The Owl Service* by Alan Garner, Collins
1968	*The Moon in the Cloud* by Rosemary Harris, Faber
1969	*The Edge of the Cloud* by K. M. Peyton, Oxford
1970	*The God Beneath the Sea* by Leon Garfield and Edward Blishen, Kestrel
1971	*Josh* by Ivan Southall, Angus & Robertson
1972	*Watership Down* by Richard Adams, Rex Collings
1973	*The Ghost of Thomas Kempe* by Penelope Lively, Heinemann
1974	*The Stronghold* by Mollie Hunter, Hamilton
1975	*The Machine-Gunners* by Robert Westall, Macmillan
1976	*Thunder and Lightnings* by Jan Mark, Kestrel
1977	*The Turbulent Term of Tyke Tiler* by Gene Kemp, Faber
1978	*The Exeter Blitz* by David Rees, Hamish Hamilton
1979	*Tulku* by Peter Dickinson, Dutton
1980	*City of Gold* by Peter Dickinson, Gollancz
1981	*The Scarecrows* by Robert Westall, Chatto & Windus
1982	*The Haunting* by Margaret Mahy, Dent
1983	*Handles* by Jan Mark, Kestrel
1984	*The Changeover* by Margaret Mahy, Dent
1985	*Storm* by Kevin Crossley-Holland, Heinemann
1986	*Granny Was a Buffer Girl* by Berlie Doherty, Methuen
1987	*The Ghost Drum* by Susan Price, Faber
1988	*Pack of Lies* by Geraldine McCaughrean, Oxford
1989	*My War with Goggle-Eyes* by Anne Fine, Joy Street
1990	*Wolf* by Gillian Cross, Oxford
1991	*Dear Nobody* by Berlie Doherty, Hamish Hamilton
1992	*Flour Babies* by Anne Fine, Hamish Hamilton
1993	*Stone Cold* by Robert Swindells, Hamish Hamilton
1994	*Whispers in the Graveyard* by Theresa Breslin, Methuen
1995	*Northern Lights* by Philip Pullman, Doubleday (U.S. title: *The Golden Compass*)
1996	*Junk* by Melvin Burgess, Andersen/Penguin
1997	*River Boy* by Tim Bowler, Oxford
1998	*Skellig* by David Almond, Hodder
1999	*Postcards from No Man's Land* by Aidan Chambers, Bodley Head
2000	*The Other Side of Truth* by Beverley Naidoo, Puffin
2001	*The Amazing Maurice and His Educated Rodents* by Terry Pratchett, Doubleday
2002	*Ruby Holler* by Sharon Creech, Bloomsbury
2003	*A Gathering of Light* by Jennifer Donnelly, Bloomsbury
2004	*Millions* by Frank Cottrell Boyce, Macmillan
2005	*Tamar* by Mal Peet, Walker
2007	*Just in Case* by Meg Rosoff, Penguin
2008	*Here Lies Arthur* by Philip Reeve, Scholastic
2009	*Bog Child* by Siobhan Dowd, David Fickling
2010	*The Graveyard Book* by Neil Gaiman, Bloomsbury

The Kate Greenaway Medal

Named for the celebrated nineteenth-century children's illustrator, this medal is awarded annually by the British Library Association to the most distinguished illustrated work for children first published in the United Kingdom during the preceding year. (Unless otherwise noted, the author is also the illustrator. The date given is the year of publication.)

1956   *Tim All Alone* by Edward Ardizzone, Oxford

1957   *Mrs. Easter and the Storks* by V. H. Drummond, Faber

1958   No Award

1959   *Kashtanka and a Bundle of Ballads* by William Stobbs, Oxford

1960   *Old Winkle and the Seagulls* by Elizabeth Rose, illustrated by Gerald Rose, Faber

1961   *Mrs. Cockle's Cat* by Philippa Pearce, illustrated by Anthony Maitland, Kestrel

1962   *Brian Wildsmith's ABC* by Brian Wildsmith, Oxford

1963   *Borka* by John Burningham, Jonathan Cape

1964   *Shakespeare's Theatre* by C. W. Hodges, Oxford

1965   *Three Poor Tailors* by Victor Ambrus, Hamilton

1966   *Mother Goose Treasury* by Raymond Briggs, Hamilton

1967   *Charlie, Charlotte & the Golden Canary* by Charles Keeping, Oxford

1968   *Dictionary of Chivalry* by Grant Uden, illustrated by Pauline Baynes, Kestrel

1969   *The Quangle-Wangle's Hat* by Edward Lear, illustrated by Helen Oxenbury, Heinemann; *Dragon of an Ordinary Family* by Margaret May, illustrated by Helen Oxenbury, Heinemann

1970   *Mr. Gumpy's Outing* by John Burningham, Jonathan Cape

1971   *The Kingdom under the Sea* by Jan Pienkowski, Jonathan Cape

1972   *The Woodcutter's Duck* by Krystyna Turska, Hamilton

1973   *Father Christmas* by Raymond Briggs, Hamilton

1974   *The Wind Blew* by Pat Hutchins, Bodley Head

1975   *Horses in Battle* by Victor Ambrus, Oxford; *Mishka* by Victor Ambrus, Oxford

1976   *The Post Office Cat* by Gail E. Haley, Bodley Head

1977   *Dogger* by Shirley Hughes, Bodley Head

1978   *Each Peach Pear Plum* by Janet and Allan Ahlberg, Kestrel

1979   *Haunted House* by Jan Pienkowski, Dutton

1980   *Mr. Magnolia* by Quentin Blake, Jonathan Cape

1981   *The Highwayman* by Alfred Noyes, illustrated by Charles Keeping, Oxford

1982   *Long Neck and Thunder Foot* by Michael Foreman, Kestrel; *Sleeping Beauty and Other Favorite Fairy Tales* by Michael Foreman, Gollancz

1983   *Gorilla* by Anthony Browne, Julia McRae Books

1984   *Hiawatha's Childhood* by Errol LeCain, Faber

1985   *Sir Gawain and the Loathly Lady* by Selina Hastings, illustrated by Juan Wijngaard, Walker

1986   *Snow White in New York* by Fiona French, Oxford

1987   *Crafty Chameleon* by Adrienne Kennsway, Hodder & Stoughton

1988   *Can't You Sleep, Little Bear?* by Martin Waddell, illustrated by Adrienne Kennaway, Hodder & Stoughton

1989   *War Boy: A Country Childhood* by Michael Foreman, Arcade

1990   *The Whale's Song* by Dyan Sheldon, illustrated by Gary Blythe, Dial

1991   *The Jolly Christmas Postman* by Janet and Allan Ahlberg, Heinemann

1992   *Zoo* by Anthony Browne, Julie MacRae Books

1993   *Black Ships Before Troy* retold by Rosemary Sutcliff, illustrated by Alan Lee, Frances Lincoln

1994   *Way Home* by Libby Hawthorne, Anderson

1995   *The Christmas Miracle of Jonathan Toomey* by Susan Wojciechowski, illustrated by P. J. Lynch, Candlewick

1996   *The Baby Who Wouldn't Go to Bed* by Helen Cooper, Doubleday

1997   *When Jessie Came Across the Sea* by Amy Hest, illustrated by P. J. Lynch, Doubleday

1998   *Pumpkin Soup* by Helen Cooper, Doubleday

1999   *Alice's Adventures in Wonderland* by Lewis Carroll, illustrated by Helen Oxenbury, Walker

2000   *I Will Not Ever Eat a Tomato* by Lauren Child, Orchard

2001   *Pirate Diary* by Chris Riddell, Walker

2002   *Jethro Byrde-Fairy Childa* by Bob Graham, Walker

2003   *Ella's Big Chance* by Shirley Hughes, Bodley Head

2004   *Jonathan Swift's "Gulliver"* by Marti Jenkins, illustrated by Chris Riddell

2005   *Wolves* by Emily Gravett, Macmillan

2007   *The Adventures of the Dish and the Spoon* by Mini Grey, Jonathan Cape

2008   *Little Mouse's Big Book of Fears* by Emily Gravett, Macmillan

2009   *Harris Finds His Feet* by Catherine Rayner, Little Tiger Press

Glossary

Alliteration The repetition of similar sounds at the beginning of words in close proximity—as in, "Billy Button bought a buttered biscuit."

Anachronism In a historical novel, a feature that is out of place for the time period—such a telephone in the Civil War—often the result of an author's carelessness

Anapest A poetic metrical foot consisting of two unstressed syllables followed by a stressed syllable, as in the phrase "in the still of the night"

Antagonist The character who is opposed to or works against the principal character in a literary work—often, not always, the villain

Anthropomorphism Giving human qualities (such as speech or emotions) to something nonhuman—such as an animal, plant, or machine

Artistic Medium The material an artist uses to produce an illustration—oil paints, watercolors, pencil, ink, and so on

Art Nouveau An artistic style developed in the late nineteenth century, characterized by fluid, sinuous lines and florid designs

Assonance The repetition of similar vowel sounds within words of close proximity—as the long "a" sounds in "slate" and "grey" and "lake" in this line: "The surface of a slate-grey lake is lit" (Seamus Heaney)

Autobiography The life story of an individual written by the individual himself or herself

Ballad A narrative poem—typically of folk origin, in four-line stanzas, and intended to be sung (see "Narrative Poem")

Bibliotherapy The treatment of psychological or emotional problems through the use of selected reading materials

Biography The life story of an individual written by another person

Border In book illustration, the framing element for a picture, usually consisting of white space, but sometimes decorated

Cartoon Art An artistic style characterized by simple, grossly exaggerated figures, usually for humorous effect

Censorship The act of restricting the public's access—through speech or the written word—to what certain authorities deem to be objectionable ideas

Cinquain A poem consisting of five lines, usually containing two, four, six, eight, and two syllables, respectively, with the first and last lines often bearing some relationship

Climax The high point of a dramatic plot when all the threads come together—it is usually the turning point

Collage An artistic composition made up of a variety of materials, usually nonpainterly, such as fabric, paper, wood, metal

Coming-of-Age Story A story in which the protagonist, through a variety of experiences, undergoes personal growth and development

Concrete Poem A poem in which the text is designed to resemble a shape on the page, usually illustrative of the poem's subject—a poem about a butterfly shaped like a butterfly, for example

Consonance The repetition of similar consonant sounds within words of close proximity—as in the "l" sounds in "Afternoon light falling beautifully into the room" (Richard Jones)

Cubism An artistic movement of the early twentieth century characterized by abstract drawings emphasizing the geometric shape and structure of an object rather than pictorial representation

Cumulative Plot A story consisting of an accumulation of events, which, in its telling, repeats the entire sequence with each addition—used most commonly in folktales such as *The Gingerbread Man* and usually for comic effect

Dactyl A poetic metrical foot consisting of one stressed syllable followed by two unstressed syllables, as in the word "beautiful"

Dénouement Literally, the "unraveling" or "untying," applied to the final outcome of a dramatic plot

Dialogue The words spoken by two or more characters in a story or play

Didacticism Instruction or teaching—when applied to literature it refers to stories whose purpose is to deliver a moral or ethical lesson

Digital Art   Art generated by computer programs

Dramatic Plot   A story consisting of a single major conflict, chronologically organized and leading up to a climax and a concluding dénouement

Dynamic Character   A fictional character—always a round one—who undergoes a significant change or emotional growth in the course of the action

Episodic Plot   A story, usually told in chapters describing a series of adventures, tied together by characters, setting, or theme

Exposition   The information provided in a literary work to supply needed background information to the audience

Expressionism   In picture book art, a style that evokes the artist's emotional response to the subject rather than a realistic portrayal, characterized by unusual distortions (elongated figures, for example), unrealistic use of colors, shapes that only suggest objects, and so on

First-Person Narrator   A storyteller who is a character in the story and who refers to himself or herself as "I"

Flashback   In a narrative, a shift backward in time to reveal events that happened earlier, chiefly used as a means of explaining character motivation

Flat Character   A two-dimensional fictional character without depth or complexity, common among minor characters and always a static character

Foil Character   A fictional character whose personality traits sharply contrast with those of another character in the work

Folk Art   In picture book art, a style that is associated with a specific folk culture, usually identified by uncomplicated drawings and the use of cultural symbols and culturally specific colors, patterns, or designs

Foreshadowing   In a narrative, hints of what is to come; a device used to create suspense and to avoid what might otherwise seem incredulous

Free Verse   Poetry that observes no strict rules about rhythm or rhyme or stanza length—but most free verse still uses such devices as simile, metaphor, personification, and so on

Functionary Character   A minor character whose role is to perform specific necessary functions—as a servant, for example, or an official

Graphic Novel   A book-length work that uses both text and art, usually in comic-book format, to tell the story (*Manga* refers specifically to Japanese graphic novels)

Graphic Technique   A method by which a graphic artist creates images through the use of block, plates, or type, including woodblocks, linocuts, and so on

Gutter   In a book, the crease caused by the binding—an important consideration in picture books that use double-page spreads

Haiku   A Japanese poetic form usually consisting of 17 syllables in three lines and reflecting on nature

Iamb   A poetic metrical foot consisting of one unstressed syllable followed by one stressed syllable, as in the word "arise"

Illustrated Book   A book using illustrations to highlight or support specific points in the text—as opposed to a picture book in which the pictures share equally with the text

Irony   Literary incongruity—when there is a difference between what is said and what is meant, or between what happens and what we would normally expect to happen

Limerick   A humorous five-line poem, with an a-a-b-b-a rhyme scheme and regular rhythm

Limited Narrator   A third-person storyteller who is not a character in the story, but tells the story from just one character's point of view

Lyric Poem   A poem expressing the poet's personal feelings or thoughts about a subject (rather than telling a story), often following a verse pattern, sometimes intended to be sung—sonnets, odes, cinquains, and so on, are examples

Metaphor   An implied comparison, giving the attributes of one thing to another—"All the world's a stage" (Shakespeare)

Meter   A pattern of stressed and unstressed syllables (called metrical feet) in a line of poetry (see also "Anapest," "Dactyl," "Iamb," and "Trochee")

Montage   An artistic composition created by combining a number of separate pictures, in contrast with the collage, which uses a variety of materials

Motif   A recurring thematic or plot element in literature, especially the recurring plot devices found throughout folktales

Motivation In a fictional story, the reason(s) behind a character's actions, that which causes a character to behave in a certain way or to do certain things

Naïve Art An artistic style deliberately resembling childlike drawings, usually appearing two-dimensional and disproportioned

Narrative Poem A story, complete with characters, setting, and plot, told in verse

New Realism A type of fiction begun in the 1960s characterized by more realistic portrayal of social and personal issues confronting teenagers, including sexuality, drugs, gangs, and similar matters

Nonsense Verse Comical verse featuring outlandish characters, absurd actions, and, often, made-up words and rollicking rhyme and rhythm

Omniscient Narrator A third-person storyteller who is not a character in the story, usually both all-seeing and all-knowing

Painterly Technique A method by which an artist creates images by applying a medium (paint, ink, gouache, tempera, and so on) to a surface (usually paper), in contrast with digital art, or woodblocks, for example

Panel In a picture book, a framed illustration, usually used in combinations of two or more, that permit the simultaneous depiction of varying perspectives or passing time

Parallel Plot A story consisting of two or more dramatic plots, often interwoven, operating simultaneously

Parody A literary work (e. g., a story or a poem) that imitates another in order to poke fun

Personification Giving inanimate objects human qualities—"around us the trees full of night lean hushed in their dreams" (W. S. Merwin)

Picture Book A book in which the illustrations share equally with the text in conveying the story or information

Plot The interrelated sequence of events making up a story; see cumulative, dramatic, episodic, and parallel plot

Problem Novel A type of realistic fiction, developed in the 1960s, that focuses on a specific psychological or social issue confronting the protagonist

Protagonist The principal sympathetic character in a literary work, the main character

Reader-Response Theory A reading theory (sometimes called "Transactional Analysis") proposing that each reader derives something personal from reading a text based on past experiences and knowledge, and that rereading a text will result in a still different response

Realism In picture book art, representational drawing or painting that attempts give lifelike detail to objects

Renaissance In European history, the time period from about 1400 to1650 that experienced a flowering of art and culture based on a revived interest in the civilizations of ancient Greece and Rome

Round Character A fictional character with a fully developed personality with numerous facets

Satire A literary work that pokes fun, often through the use of irony, at some human folly or vice

Scanimation Originally a term used to describe analog computer animation (which gave way to digital animation), now applied to a technique, developed by Rufus Seder Butler, by which scrambled images are passed behind a transparent film marked with thin stripes, giving the images the illusion of motion

Sentimentalism A literary tone that expresses excessive emotion—overly sweet, overly mournful, overly passionate; feeling dispropor-tionate to the circumstances

Setting The time and place in which the action of a story occurs

Simile An explicit comparison using the words "like" or "as"—"His breath hung in the air like a white balloon" (Baron Wormser)

Static Character A fictional character—either flat or round—who does not undergo any significant change throughout the work

Stylized Intensification In folk narratives, the exaggeration of a repeated plot element for dramatic purposes—each of the three little pigs builds a slightly sturdier house, for example

Stock Character A fictional character—always a flat one—who represents a type rather than an individual: the boor, the buffoon, the ingénue, the penny-pincher, the prude, and so on

Surrealism In picture book art, a style that is drawn with realistic detail, but with unrealistic, even unsettling subject matter, often with a nightmarish quality

Tabula Rasa Latin for "blank slate," a term used by the philosopher John Locke to describe his notion of a child's intellectual capacity at birth; the idea helped to spur a multitude of didactic children's books in the eighteenth century

Theme The controlling idea of a literary work, the fundamental concept the author is attempting to convey

Tone The author's attitude—comical, satirical, cynical, and so on—toward the subject of a literary work

Transactional Analysis See "Reader-Response Theory"

Trochee A poetic metrical foot consisting of one stressed followed by one unstressed syllable, as in the word "happy"

Typography The way in which letters are designed (including size and shape) and their arrangement on a page

Vignette In a picture book, a small picture integrated into a larger illustration to supply additional information or perhaps to add humor

Visual Poem See "Concrete Poem"

Zone of Proximal Development (ZPD) A term created by the psychologist Vygotsky to refer to the difference between what a person can learn on his or her own and what can be learned with the assistance of others

Children's Literature Resources

General Reference Works

These are ongoing publications that help keep children's literature scholarship up to date. They can be found in all academic and most large public libraries.

Something about the Author, v.1 (1971–). Detroit: Gale.

A multivolume series including biographical entries on children's authors and illustrators. A good place to find an introductory overview of an individual's life and work.

Dictionary of Literary Biography, v. 1 (1978–). Detroit: Gale.

A multivolume series including extensive scholarly essays on literary figures; each volume focuses on a specific type of writing, with several volumes dealing with children's writers and illustrators. A good place to find biographical material as well as some in-depth critical commentary on an individual's work.

Children's Literature Review, v. 1 (1976–). Detroit: Gale.

A series devoted to assembling critical commentary on children's authors, with each volume focusing on approximately 10 individuals; excerpts are taken from scholarly journals, book reviews, and similar sources. A good place to find out what critics are saying about a specific work.

Periodicals

Among the many periodicals that publish articles on children's literature are the following. Notice that some publications are devoted largely to book reviews, and others are scholarly publications, featuring essays on topics in children's literature.

ALAN Review (A publication of the Assembly on Literature for Adolescents of the National Council of Teachers of English—features articles on adolescent literature)

Bookbird (A quarterly publication of International Board on Books for Young People—IBBY—devoted to international children's literature)

Booklist (The review journal of the American Library Association; includes recommended books for both children and adults and reviews some 7,500 books a year)

Bulletin of the Center for Children's Books (A monthly publication featuring reviews of the latest books for children)

Children's Literature (An annual publication of the Children's Literature Association with scholarly articles on the entire range of children's literature)

Children's Literature Association Quarterly (A quarterly publication of the Children's Literature Association with scholarly articles on the entire range of children's literature)

Children's Literature in Education (A quarterly publication featuring scholarly articles of special interest to educators)

The Horn Book Magazine (A bimonthly publication with both articles on a wide range of subjects and reviews of the most recently published children's books)

School Library Journal (A monthly publication of book reviews, intended, as the name implies, for libraries, but very helpful for educators as well)

Professional Organizations

Many professional organizations related to the field of children's literature exist, each with a slightly different focus. The following are only some of the most prominent. (Notice that professional associations are fond of acronyms.)

Children's Literature Association (ChLA)—for those interested in the scholarly pursuit of children's literature, especially educators and scholars

International Board on Books for Young People (IBBY)—for those interested in international children's literature

International Reading Association (IRA)—for those interested primarily in the instruction and scholarship of reading skills

Modern Language Association (MLA)—for those interested in the scholarly pursuit of literature in general; MLA includes a Children's Literature section

National Council of Teachers of English (NCTE)—for those interested in the profession of English education, especially, but not exclusively, at the middle and high school levels

Popular Cultural Association—for those interested in the broader issues of popular culture, including music, art, media

Index